Ownership Paradigms in American Civil Law Jurisdictions

Legal History Library

VOLUME 21

Studies in the History of Private Law

VOLUME 11

The titles published in this series are listed at *brill.com/shpl*

Ownership Paradigms in American Civil Law Jurisdictions

Manifestations of the Shifts in the Legislation of Louisiana, Chile, and Argentina (16th–20th Centuries)

By

Agustín Parise

BRILL
NIJHOFF

LEIDEN | BOSTON

Cover illustration: M.C. Escher's "Drawing Hands" (1948), © 2016 The M.C. Escher Company B.V. – The Netherlands. All rights reserved. www.mcescher.com.

Library of Congress Cataloging-in-Publication Data

Names: Parise, Agustin, author.
Title: Ownership paradigms in American civil law jurisdictions : manifestations of the shifts in the legislation of Louisiana, Chile, and Argentina (16th-20th centuries) / by Agustin Parise.
Description: Leiden ; Boston : Brill Nijhoff, 2017. | Based on author's thesis (doctoral - Maastricht University, 2015). | Includes bibliographical references and index.
Identifiers: LCCN 2016055773 (print) | LCCN 2016056164 (ebook) | ISBN 9789004338197 (hardback : alk. paper) | ISBN 9789004338203 (E-book)
Subjects: LCSH: Right of property--Argentina. | Right of property--Chile. | Right of property--Louisiana. | Civil law systems--America.
Classification: LCC KDZ171 .P37 2017 (print) | LCC KDZ171 (ebook) | DDC 346.04/32--dc23
LC record available at https://lccn.loc.gov/2016055773

Typeface for the Latin, Greek, and Cyrillic scripts: "Brill". See and download: brill.com/brill-typeface.

ISSN 1874-1793
ISBN 978-90-04-33819-7 (hardback)
ISBN 978-90-04-33820-3 (e-book)

This book is printed on acid-free paper and produced in a sustainable manner.

This book is dedicated to my parents María Cristina and Roberto Enrique; to my grandmother Lotte Mathilde; and to the memory of my grandparents María Esther, Alberto Mario, and Roberto Enrique.

El Derecho contemporáneo es original como el que corresponde a cada época nueva, pero no se comprende sin la indagación de su historia y la comparación con las instituciones pretéritas.

RICARDO LEVENE (1885–1959)[1]

•••

Such is the unity of all history that any one who endeavours to tell a piece of it must feel that his first sentence tears a seamless web.

FREDERIC WILLIAM MAITLAND (1850–1906)[2]

•••

Ist es denn möglich, die Gegenwart eines organischen Zustandes anders zu begreifen, als in Verbindung mit seiner Vergangenheit, d. h. anders, als auf genetische Weise?

FRIEDRICH CARL VON SAVIGNY (1779–1861)[3]

•••

Folk building growing in response to actual needs, fitted into environment by people who knew no better than to fit them with native feeling.

FRANK LLOYD WRIGHT (1867–1959)[4]

•••

The old form receives a new content, and in time even the form modifies itself to fit the meaning which it has received.

OLIVER WENDELL HOLMES, Jr. (1841–1935)[5]

∴

1 Levene 1962, p. 18.
2 Maitland 1898, p. 13.
3 Savigny (von) 1840, p. 169.
4 Oliver 2003, p. 9.
5 Holmes 1881, p. 5.

Contents

Acknowledgments

The research and writing process for this book was conducted at the Faculty of Law of Maastricht University. The environment was optimal and the result of this project is a combination of the work and generosity of many people. Professors, fellow researchers, librarians, and support staff, together with family and friends, provided a unique background for the development of the ideas encapsulated in this book.

Friends and colleagues from Maastricht University and beyond offered useful comments and feedback. Remco van Rhee and Sjef van Erp provided constant support and guidance, and were always willing to present new ideas and challenging perspectives. Their intervention in the project resulted in an exquisite amalgam of legal history and private law expertise, embedded in a comparative law perspective. Their generosity is deeply appreciated. Abelardo Levaggi made comments that undoubtedly improved the quality of the manuscript: his expertise in legal history and property law, on both sides of the Atlantic, was extremely beneficial. Lars van Vliet was always ready to share his friendship, his knowledge on property law, and his collection of books.

Members of several academic circles generously shared their time and knowledge. The content of this book, at different stages of development, was presented at a number of conferences and ultimately submitted to the members of the PhD Assessment Committee. The author is indebted to all the members of that Committee, namely, Louis Berkvens, René de Groot, Dirk Heirbaut, Abelardo Levaggi, and Jan Smits. He is also indebted to the participants at those conferences for the feedback they generously offered. Special mention must be made of Pablo Bravo Hurtado, Thomas Duve, Matthew Dyson, María del Refugio González, Aniceto Masferrer, Michael Milo, Olivier Moréteau, Osvaldo Rodolfo Moutin, Heikki Pihlajamäki, Peter Reich, Víctor Tau Anzoátegui, and Eduardo Zimmermann. The universe of knowledge was further expanded with research stays and visits at a number of universities and institutes across the globe. Accordingly, the author was affiliated with the *École normale supérieure* (Paris), the Institute of European and Comparative Law at University of Oxford (Oxford), and the University of Technology (Sydney); and he is indebted to his hosts: Shaunnagh Dorsett, Jean-Louis Halpérin, and Stefan Vogenauer. Members of M-EPLI provided timely feedback and the Property-Law Group at Maastricht University offered a forum to exchange ideas. Finally, Sascha Hardt and Serban Vacarelu also shared their knowledge in their areas of expertise.

The author benefited from the collections of numerous personal and public libraries. He is indebted to the owners of and to the staff at those temples of knowledge. In the period 2011–2015, the author worked with the collections of the Library of Maastricht University, and he is grateful to Paula Hermans and Ine Verbeet for their excellent reference work and assistance with interlibrary loans. In the same time period, the author visited the Louisiana Law Library (New Orleans); the library of the University of Technology (Sydney); the library of the *École normale supérieure* (Paris), the Bodleian Library at University of Oxford (Oxford); the library of Marval, O'Farrell & Mairal (Buenos Aires); the law library of the *Universidad de Buenos Aires* (Buenos Aires); the library of the *Max-Planck-Institut für europäische Rechtsgeschichte* (Frankfurt am Main); the Brand van Zyl Law Library of University of Cape Town (Cape Town); the law library of the *Universidad Autónoma de Madrid* (Madrid); and the Hill Memorial Library, Middleton Library, and Law Library at Louisiana State University (Baton Rouge). He is indebted to many librarians at those libraries, and he especially thanks Georgia D. Chadwick, Nora Gómez, Phillip Gragg, Susan Gualtier, Gonzalo Lopez Martinez, and Melanie Sims. The research was indeed made possible by the work of all those professional librarians. Furthermore, materials used in this book were made accessible by the following people: Bram Akkermans, Louis V. de la Vergne, Alexis Nicole Fetzer, Elisabetta Fiocchi, Gonzalo Garfias von Fürstenberg, Jess Gilbert, Jennifer Lane, Osvaldo Rodolfo Moutin, Alexandru-Daniel On, María Rosario Polotto, Rachael Walsh, and Spencer D. Wood. Javier E. Rodriguez Diez deserves special mention due to his generosity with Chilean materials.

The author thanks the anonymous reviewers of the Studies in the History of Private Law series, which with their insights and feedback helped improve this book. The editorial team at Brill made possible the conversion of the manuscript of the PhD dissertation of the author into this book. The author is especially indebted to Ms. Jennifer Obdam for her active role in the editorial process.

The unique background for the development of the ideas encapsulated in this book benefited from a fundamental group of contributors and friends. Hildegard Schneider offered constant support and motivation that nurtured an optimal environment for the academic and personal development of the author. Paul Adriaans, Lydie Coenegrachts, Ine Corstjens, José Crijnen, Suzanne Jongste, Roger Snijders, Noëlle Tillie, Henk Verkoeijen, and Peggy van Wersch made sure that every administrative and technical aspect was smoothly taken care of. Licette Poll, always enthusiastic and efficient, accompanied the author throughout the entire PhD process. Francesca Guadagno, Charlotte Guillard, Tianxiang He, Simone Sasso, and Jie Wang kindly shared their working space with the author and always expressed a positive attitude. Mariano Parise, Roberto E. Parise, and María Cristina Sáenz de Parise were never too busy or too tired to help the author bridge the difficulties of undertaking a transatlantic project. Julieta made it all possible and meaningful.

List of Illustrations

Figures

Tables

CHAPTER 1

Introduction

1.1 Motivation

A look into history demonstrates that ownership is remote from consideration as being a dormant institution in American Civil Law Jurisdictions. The interplay of actors and things, together with the different concurring interests of the former, motivates paradigm shifts of ownership. Furthermore, history is above all the science of change, as Marc Bloch correctly indicated;[1] while law is not static and changes incessantly.[2] Accordingly, new social conditions indeed affect local cultures and those impacts trigger changes in property-law institutions, such as ownership.[3] A comparative legal historical approach assists in identifying the transformations of property-law institutions, hence making manifest that current understandings are not uncontested dogmas.[4]

This book examines the paradigm shifts of ownership in American Civil Law Jurisdictions, starting in the sixteenth century and extending until the final decades of the twentieth century. The book focusses on events that took place in the US state of Louisiana, in the Republic of Chile, and in the Republic of Argentina. Those three jurisdictions serve in this book as case studies for the analysis of, amongst other things, paradigm shifts. This book aims to provide an inventory of some of the main motivations that accompanied and help explain the changes in the history of ownership in American Civil Law Jurisdictions.[5] That exercise should expose the dual character of property law: homogeneity and heterogeneity.[6] If seeking for integration of property law across jurisdictions—in Europe, the Americas, or beyond—comparative and interdisciplinary analyses are required.[7]

1 Bloch 1952, p. x.
2 Sacco 1991b, p. 390.
3 Beaglehole 1935, p. 316.
4 Azcárate (de) 1879–1883, I, p. xviii; and Azcárate (de) 1879–1883, III, p. 352.
5 The idea of an "inventory" was borrowed from Paolo Grossi, who used it in 1976 when presenting a seminal collection of articles dealing with property law during the nineteenth and twentieth centuries. See Grossi 1976–1977, p. 3.
6 Jean-Louis Bergel alerted on that duality. See Bergel 1994, p. 2.
7 The claim by J.H.M. van Erp is focused on European property law, yet it can be extended to studies in other jurisdictions. See van Erp 2008b, p. 107.

 | DOI 10.1163/9789004338203_002

Readers should be mindful that studies in both property law[8] and legal history[9] traditionally have had a local or vernacular character. That trend is being reversed, yet at a slow pace. Already in 2000, C.H. van Rhee and J.H.M. van Erp highlighted that comparative legal historical studies on property law can result in illuminating exercises.[10] This book, accordingly, intends to provide new light on the property law of the Americas and its relations with Europe. This book aims to benefit from looking at the traits of the different jurisdictions, since differences and similarities must be traced by looking into the background provided by, amongst other things, law, history, politics, culture, and economy.[11] It has been claimed that "one can hardly find a more significant and fascinating field of comparative study than the law of property;"[12] nevertheless, comparative property law studies are still relatively neglected.[13] In Europe, property law is no longer taught with a purely local or vernacular approach,[14] yet if compared with other areas of the law, such as contract law, the literature of comparative property law is indeed scarce.[15] As this book will show, that type of literature is likewise scarce in American Civil Law Jurisdictions.

This chapter addresses a multiplicity of points, setting the methodological framework for the entire book. It first problematizes ownership, followed by the posing of the main research question and sub-questions. The chapter then provides two needed conceptualizations. Accordingly, the understanding given in this book to American Civil Law Jurisdictions and to Ownership Paradigms is provided. The methodology implemented, together with a description of the use of sources and the presentation of the structure of the book, are finally addressed.

1.2 Problematization

Problematizing property law requires the reconstruction of events and institutions, such as ownership, across time and space.[16] Ownership is mainly a

8 van Erp 2008a, p. 1044.

9 See generally 2.3 of this book.

10 van Rhee & van Erp 2003, pp. 279, 281. In the Americas, for example, Ezequiel Abásolo suggested the comparative legal historical study of ownership. See Abásolo 2009, at § 23.

11 van Erp 2003, p. 396.

12 Merryman 1974, p. 916.

13 van Erp 2008a, p. 1048.

14 van Erp 2013a, p. 159.

15 van Erp 2002, p. 69.

16 Levaggi 2009, p. 160.

matter of mentality,[17] and understanding the mentality of a certain time and place helps in grasping the full extent of a right. It is possible to trace historically all problems in society,[18] and in order to do so Paolo Grossi encourages scholars to change their spectacles before looking back in time, and to try to answer their questions through a historical perspective.[19] If they do not do so, the outcome of their view could be deformed or out of focus, with the current perspective. In this book, readers should remove the spectacles they use for the twenty-first century, and do their best to put on the ones that would help them see through the different centuries in different jurisdictions. Grossi described this activity as "consigning the archetype to the history books."[20] The best way for comparative legal historians to change spectacles is to work with a diversity of sources from different times and places. In this process many *ghosts* may appear, but those ghosts will help comparative legal historians in their process of discovery.[21]

Boundaries between the interests of different actors (*i.a.*, state, individual owners) are troublesome.[22] Property-law institutions provide fertile ground for problems when boundaries overlap.[23] Those problems attract the attention of scholars beyond the law, welcoming studies by economists, sociologists, political scientists, and even theologians.[24] Hence, problematizing ownership often results in raising questions that deal with the role of the different actors. As this book aims to show, ownership indeed evolves around the interplay of the different actors. A comparative legal historical study of ownership helps integrate aspects that are often analyzed individually or as watertight compartments. As previously mentioned, studies on ownership should examine legal aspects, yet also, amongst others, social, economic, political, cultural, and ideological aspects,[25] all of them across time and space, and all resulting in a broader understanding of the emerging background.

---

17 The expression was shared by Abelardo Levaggi while dictating a course on the history of property law at the University of Buenos Aires in August 2001.

18 Barraclough 1973, p. 3.

19 Grossi 1992c, p. 611. See also Parise 2008c, p. 115.

20 Grossi 1992c, p. 611.

21 The term "ghosts" was borrowed from Paul R. Baier who, while communicating with his students at Louisiana State University, several times reached into his archives and brought to life some ghosts by means of pictures, video and audio recordings, or even theatrical representations.

22 Reich 1964, p. 733.

23 Castán Tobeñas 1963, p. 7.

24 Castán Tobeñas 1963, p. 7.

25 Congost 2007a, p. 22.

It is impossible to speak of a single paradigm of ownership that crosses through time and space. American Civil Law Jurisdictions, at different times, experienced different Ownership Paradigms. Much can be learned by looking at *how* solutions to problems were developed in different places at different times.[26] Ownership entails a historical evolution that cannot be overlooked;[27] and, together with other property-law institutions, they are key elements of culture and civilizations: architectural pillars for society.[28] Ownership is linked to the role of different actors within society and to the evolution of social organization, hence exceeding the exclusive realm of legal studies, and ultimately making manifest the existing structure at a certain time and place.[29]

1.3 Research Questions

This book encompasses a comparative legal historical study of American and European law and culture. Its main objective is to determine the extent to which American Civil Law Jurisdictions shared the evolution of the prevailing Ownership Paradigms, while tracing in American and European law the reasons for the shaping of those paradigms. The book, therefore, addresses the shifts in the Ownership Paradigms that took place in the studied jurisdictions. The book intends to provide new knowledge on the interplay between American Civil Law Jurisdictions and European jurisdictions: an interplay that resulted in shifts in Ownership Paradigms. Transplantation and circulation of ideas and paradigms are fundamental aspects of this book, helping to identify foreign and vernacular creations. Accordingly, some sections in the book will assist in tracing the "genetic" history of the resulting paradigm shifts.[30]

The book provides answers to one main research question and five sub-questions. The main research question is:

- How did American Civil Law Jurisdictions share the evolution of the prevailing Ownership Paradigms?

26 Gordley 2007, p. 3.
27 Salvat 1962, p. 6.
28 Cordero Quinzacara 2008, p. 494.
29 Delgado de Miguel 2002, p. 57.
30 See the reference to "genetics" in Eidenmüller *et al.* 2012, p. 307. On that occasion, and in a different context, the authors advocated for "a genetic comparison in order to trace and evaluate the development of each individual text."

The following sub-questions must be addressed in order to answer the main research question:

- To what extent can the prevailing Ownership Paradigms in the US state of Louisiana and in the republics of Chile and Argentina during the sixteenth to the twentieth centuries be defined as allocation-oriented (Allocation), Liberal, and Social Function?
- To what extent did the shift in Ownership Paradigms reflect the circulation of ideas and the flow of paradigms?
- To what extent did American Civil Law Jurisdictions share the evolution of the prevailing Ownership Paradigms, both across time and space?
- To what extent did the transplantation of European private law legal sources affect the shaping of the prevailing Ownership Paradigms in American Civil Law Jurisdictions?
- To what extent did the transplantation of vernacular private law legal sources affect the shaping of the prevailing Ownership Paradigms in American Civil Law Jurisdictions?

The main elements of each sub-question contribute to answering the main research question. Accordingly, the three Ownership Paradigms are identified within the three case studies. The tracing of paradigms therefore assists in showing the circulation of ideas and the flow of paradigms across the Americas, while bridging the divide between jurisdictions from both sides of the Atlantic. The results of the analyses of the case studies may be projected to all American Civil Law Jurisdictions. Finally, the transplantation of European and American private law legal sources assists in better understanding the paradigm shifts.

1.4 Conceptualizations

Two original conceptualizations are fundamental for a comprehensive understanding of the contents of this book. On the one hand, the conceptualization of "American Civil Law Jurisdictions" sets the limits to the extent of the book, identifying what the subject of study is. On the other hand, the conceptualization of "Ownership Paradigms" sets the limits to the scope of the book, identifying what the object of study is.

1.4.1 *American Civil Law Jurisdictions*

The conceptualization of American Civil Law Jurisdictions is a product of both social and legal history. In this book American Civil Law Jurisdictions consist of former Spanish territories that currently comprise jurisdictions from the Americas where the Continental European system of law[31] prevails in private law.[32] These also consist of mixed jurisdictions[33] (*v.gr.,* Louisiana), which are excellent objects for the study of transplantation and circulation of ideas and paradigms.[34] Pure common law jurisdictions are not American Civil Law Jurisdictions. The latter likewise exclude American territories that are traditionally assimilated as having been dependents of European jurisdictions beyond Spain. Examples of these exclusions are found in former territories linked with Denmark,[35] the Duchy of Courland,[36] France,[37] the

---

31 The terms "Civil Law," "Romano-Germanic," and "Continental European" are used interchangeably throughout this book.

32 It should be noted that several meanings have been given to the term *jurisdiction*. For example, the term *jurisdiction* has been defined as "the indication of the territorial limits in which a state exerts sovereignty" (Arazi 1995, p. 13). In similar lines, *Black's Law Dictionary* indicates that jurisdiction is "a geographic area within which political or judicial authority may be exercised" (Black's Law Dictionary 2014). Furthermore, *The Oxford English Dictionary* states that *jurisdiction* is "the extent or range of judicial or administrative power; the territory over which such power extends" (Oxford English Dictionary 2015a). In this book, *jurisdiction* is understood as the geographical space—the limits of which may mutate across different time periods—in which an authority exerts judicial control. According to this definition, multiple jurisdictions can co-exist within the limits of, for example, a single nation. Comparative legal historians must therefore consider paramount to first identify and isolate the specific geographical spaces to be studied. Comparative legal historians must then undertake a comparative study of those specific geographical spaces. Accordingly, *jurisdiction* must be understood in this book as flexible or subject to mutation, aiming to give complete freedom to researchers when analyzing the characteristics of a specific geographical space.

33 See generally Palmer 2006.

34 See Zimmermann 2012, p. 1181.

35 *v.gr.*, Danish West Indies, and Greenland (which was previously Norwegian).

36 *v.gr.*, Tobago.

37 Quebec deserves special attention due to its mixed-jurisdiction nature within continental North America. That jurisdiction adopted the *Civil Code of Lower Canada* on August 1, 1866 (Brierley & Macdonald 1993, p. 24). Codification was expected as a natural and logical development in Quebec because of its antecedents and the success codification had had in France (Brierley 1994, p. 116). The civil code of Louisiana of 1825, which will be addressed in Chapters 4 and 5 of this book, was a source for codifiers in Quebec. The Louisiana text occupied for Quebec a prominent role as a formal and linguistic source, rather than as a substantive model (Richert & Richert 1973, p. 518).

Netherlands,[38] Portugal,[39] Russia,[40] Scotland,[41] Sweden,[42] and the United Kingdom.[43]

American Civil Law Jurisdictions share common roots. This book highlights some of the resulting "branches" that share their origins in the same "Spanish tree." Nevertheless, generalizations should not overshadow particularities of each jurisdiction. Despite substantial differences, these jurisdictions share basic legal structures that derive from common sources,[44] mainly that of being subjects of the Spanish Crown from the sixteenth century on until the ignition of independence movements across the continent during the nineteenth century. Those common roots necessarily demand the exclusion of Brazil from the conceptualization of American Civil Law Jurisdictions. Brazil is indeed a key player in the current world economy,[45] and a comparative legal historical study of ownership in that jurisdiction could be certainly of interest. However, Brazil was not a Spanish royal holding, and even where similarities may be found amongst the Iberian (both Spanish and Portuguese) experiences in the Americas, the legal order and the subsequent developments were different.[46] The claims put forward in this book and the answers to the research questions can therefore not be necessarily extended to Brazil.

Readers should be mindful that in this book Latin American jurisdictions are not equivalent to American Civil Law Jurisdictions. The former include "the countries of South America and North America (including Central America

38 *v.gr.*, Suriname.

39 *v.gr.*, Brazil.

40 *v.gr.*, Alaska.

41 *v.gr.*, Nova Scotia.

42 *v.gr.*, New Sweden.

43 *v.gr.*, Saint Lucia.

44 Rosenn 1971, p. 692.

45 The following passage clearly illustrates the place of Brazil within the world economy: "In 2009, Brazil became the world's eighth largest economy with a nominal Gross Domestic Product (GDP) of USD $1.574 trillion. It is the largest economy in Latin America and the second largest in the western hemisphere. As a result of its recent advances in economic development, financial analysts classify Brazil as a BRIC country. In addition, Brazil is an active member of several economic organizations, including the World Trade Organization (WTO) and the Common Market of the South (Mercosur). In 2009, Brazil exported approximately USD $153 billion and imported USD $127.6 billion, totaling USD $281 billion in foreign trade flow. It has been predicted that this volume is likely to grow because Brazil is one of the fastest-growing economies in the world. Brazil's main trading partners include the United States, China, Argentina, Netherlands, Germany, and Japan." (Slomp Aguiar 2011, pp. 489–490)

46 See generally 3.4 of this book.

and the islands of the Caribbean) whose inhabitants speak a Romance language."[47] Multiple jurisdictions (*v.gr.*, Argentina, Chile), therefore, fall within both conceptualizations, being at the same time American Civil Law Jurisdictions and Latin American jurisdictions. Both types of jurisdictions should not be confused, because the claims and the answers to research questions do not apply necessarily to all Latin American jurisdictions. This book will focus on three jurisdictions that fall within the conceptualization of American Civil Law Jurisdictions. The US state of Louisiana and the republics of Chile and Argentina, as previously mentioned, serve in this book as case studies that will assist in answering the research questions. The three selected jurisdictions may be deemed as the most influential and representative amongst American Civil Law Jurisdictions, because they developed a vast scholarly production on the topic from an early period on and their legal developments served as models to other jurisdictions in the region. The references indicated throughout this book confirm that scholarly production. Furthermore, this book will confirm that the selected jurisdictions shared common elements within the different Ownership Paradigms. When looking specifically at codification, Louisiana enacted a civil code (1825) inspired by European provisions to preserve its civil law heritage. Throughout the world, especially in American Civil Law Jurisdictions, codifiers looked at Louisiana when drafting local civil codes. Louisiana is also valued in current recodification projects in the Americas, and could be of interest for the current debates on European private law harmonization, being one of the few jurisdictions where civil law is drafted in English. Historical records are well preserved in that jurisdiction. Argentina has been, and still is, one of the most representative and influential jurisdictions in the Americas. For example, the civil code of Argentina (1871) was a blueprint for other codes in the region (*v.gr.*, Paraguay, 1877). Other jurisdictions looked again to Argentina as a result of the twentieth-century recodification processes. Historical records are well preserved in Argentina. Chile led the way for codification in the region. The civil code of Chile (1857) spread throughout the American continent when sections were adopted—and are still to be found—in the codes of, amongst other jurisdictions, El Salvador (1860), Panama (1860), Ecuador (1861), Venezuela (1862), and Honduras (1880). Historical records are likewise well preserved in Chile.

1.4.2 *Ownership Paradigms*

The conceptualization of Ownership Paradigms used in this book derives from the more generic understandings of scientific paradigms used by philosophers

47 See Encyclopædia Britannica 2007, p. 180; and Moréteau & Parise 2009, p. 1121.

of science and of legal paradigms used by jurists. A paradigm, as defined by *The Oxford English Dictionary*, is "a conceptual or methodological model underlying the theories and practices of a science or discipline at a particular time; (hence) a generally accepted world view."[48]

Thomas Samuel Kuhn offered groundbreaking, and currently seminal, ideas on scientific paradigms in his work *The Structure of Scientific Revolutions* (1962).[49] According to Kuhn, a scientific paradigm—referred to by part of the literature as model, *Leitbild*, or archetype[50]—is an achievement that is "sufficiently unprecedented to attract an enduring group of adherents away from competing modes of scientific activity"[51] and "sufficiently open-ended to leave all sorts of problems for the redefined group of practitioners to resolve."[52] A scientific revolution results in the generation of a consensual model that modifies the historical perspective of a certain scientific community;[53] and acquiring scientific paradigm status reflects indeed maturity in the development of a scientific field.[54] The American philosopher of science understood that scientific paradigms are "universally recognized scientific achievements that for a time provide model problems and solutions to a community of practitioners."[55]

---

48 Oxford English Dictionary 2015b.

49 Kuhn 1970.

Thomas Samuel Kuhn introduced several modifications and clarifications to his 1962 work, mainly in his *Postscript-1969*. See Haba 1996, p. 122; and Ramos Núñez 1996, p. 23.

See the recent approach to the work of Kuhn in Mirow 2016, pp. 183–186. That work by Matthew Mirow came to the attention of the author of this book after the submission of his PhD manuscript in 2015, yet it could be included in this book.

50 Ramos Núñez 1996, p. 23.

51 Kuhn 1970, p. 10.

52 Kuhn 1970, p. 10.

53 Ramos Núñez 1996, p. 23.

54 Kuhn 1970, p. 11.

55 Kuhn 1970, p. viii.

Kuhn referred to a broad and narrow meaning for paradigm: "On the one hand, it stands for the entire constellation of beliefs, values, techniques, and so on shared by the members of a given community. On the other, it denotes one sort of element in that constellation, the concrete puzzle-solutions which, employed as models or examples, can replace explicit rules as a basis for the solution of the remaining puzzles of normal science." (Kuhn 1970, p. 175)

In 1969, for example, Kuhn elaborated on what he referred to as "disciplinary matrix." He proposed the value of a "disciplinary matrix" to deal with different aspects of paradigms in a broad sense. He stated that it was: "'disciplinary' because it refers to the common possession of the practitioners of a particular discipline; 'matrix' because it is composed of ordered elements of various sorts, each requiring further specification.

A scientific paradigm invites consensus on a certain assumption that enables the devising of a problem and of arguments and solutions to deal with that problem.[56] These scientific paradigms provide tools for the observation of a body of knowledge,[57] being informative of the type of research questions that must be posed and on how answers should be interpreted.[58]

Legal paradigms are welcomed by the legal narrative. Some scholars used the work of Kuhn as a means to understand legal disciplines,[59] while others claimed that the Kuhnian model did not apply to social sciences, such as law.[60] Looking at paradigms within the realm of law, however, welcomes the study of *how*, at a certain time and place, legal orderings are affected by social interaction.[61] Paradigms, in the legal realm, can deal with an overarching legal doctrine or dogma, as combined with the prevailing ideologies in a certain society.[62] In a narrower sense, legal paradigms can consist of, amongst other things, laws, customs, court decisions, and doctrinal writings that provide solutions to specific problems (*v.gr.*, ownership) at specific times and places, and that have gained recognition amongst jurists.[63] Accordingly, a legal paradigm can be defined as a value or concept that is shared by a legal community at a certain time and place.[64] Jean Louise Cohen further stated that legal paradigms are "an integrated set of cognitive and normative background assumptions about the relationship the law should establish between the state and society, and the form legal regulation must take."[65] Other literature highlighted that legal paradigms are useful tools to assess the conditions of certain matters that are subject to regulation.[66] Legal paradigms, indeed, can refer to the implicit images that actors might have of their own societies and that guide

All or most of the objects of group commitment that my original text makes paradigms, parts of paradigms, or paradigmatic are constituents of the disciplinary matrix, and as such they form a whole and function together." (Kuhn 1970, p. 182)

See also Haba 1996, p. 122.

56 de Vries 2013, p. 8.

57 de Vries 2013, p. 9.

58 de Vries 2013, p. 9.

59 Schultz 2014, p. 64.

60 See the examples mentioned in de Vries 2013, p. 11.

61 de Vries 2013, p. 12.

62 Haba 1996, p. 122.

63 Haba 1996, p. 123.

64 Boulot 2012, p. 10.

65 Cohen 2002, p. 143.

66 de Vries 2013, p. 7.

the law-making and application processes.[67] Finally, recent comparative law literature recurred to legal paradigms, defining them as "the manner in which legal systems address problems in specific (cultural) ways to attain (functionally equivalent) solutions."[68]

The legal literature previously referred to paradigms of ownership,[69] yet no leading definition seems to have been proposed. In this book, Ownership Paradigms consist of the abstract understanding of what constitutes the right of ownership and what this right comprises. That abstract understanding finds consensus amongst jurists, provides model problems and solutions, and changes according to time and space. Ownership Paradigms should be considered tools to assess the conditions of the right of ownership, and the way actors perceive societies and trigger law change and application.

Ownership Paradigms are affected by the prevailing ideologies in a certain society, and are shaped after the interplay of things (movable or immovable) with individual actors (*v.gr.*, settlers, Native Americans, Crown, State, Church) and society at large. When these three elements interact, one of them tends to prevail while the other two do not fully disappear, shaping an Ownership Paradigm, and resulting in the abovementioned abstract understanding. Figure 1.1 provides an illustration of the three elements and their interaction:

This book will show that three Ownership Paradigms developed in American Civil Law Jurisdictions during the period subject to study. All three resulted from the interplay of the three-abovementioned elements, followed a chronological order, and offered an abstract understanding of what constitutes the right of ownership and what this right comprises. Firstly, the Allocation paradigm (Chapter 3 *infra*) was shaped when individual actors and society at large offered a place of prominence to things. In this paradigm, both individual and communal allocation of things was experienced, and being that

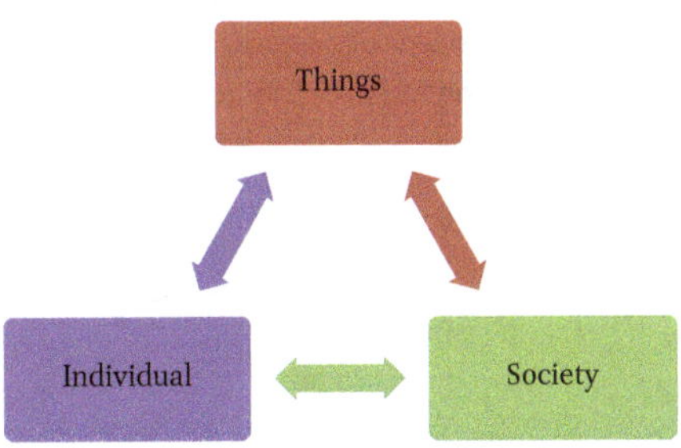

FIGURE 1.1
Interaction of elements in Ownership Paradigms

67 Habermas 1996, p. 771.

68 Michaels 2012, p. 298.

69 See, amongst the copious literature, the references in Gambaro 2011.

allocation paramount, it exceeded the interests of individual actors and of society at large. Secondly, the Liberal paradigm (Chapter 4 *infra*) was shaped when things and society at large offered a place of prominence to individual actors. The Modern Period welcomed the development of a new paradigm that was present mainly in the nineteenth-century civil codes that embraced the ideal of an absolute and perpetual right for individual actors. Finally, the Social Function paradigm (Chapter 5 *infra*) was shaped when things and individual actors offered a place of prominence to society at large. Private law experienced a socialization process at the turn of the nineteenth century that resulted in a less "egoistic" understanding of ownership, where society at large occupied the paramount position.

This book expects to identify *what* motivated shifts[70] in Ownership Paradigms across American Civil Law Jurisdictions. Comparative legal historians must abstract the different conceptions (*v.gr.*, ownership) across their evolution, focusing on essential features that turn conceptions immutable and non-essential features that explain their shifts.[71] Legal institutions are subject to mutation[72]—and being creations of humanity—are transformed together with societies, with political structures, and with mentalities.[73] Legal institutions, including those of property law, such as ownership, are in constant evolution and transformation, either at a slow or at a fast pace.[74] Resilience is a characteristic of property law institutions,[75] since these tend to change according to time and space: they are far from being eternal.[76]

Paradigms never fade overnight, yet the main points of inflection can be spotted.[77] A shift or scientific revolution will break with a previous paradigm and place a new one that will be likewise accepted.[78] Therefore, an established

---

70 A paradigm shift, as defined by *The Oxford English Dictionary*, is "a conceptual or methodological change in the theory or practice of a particular science or discipline; (in extended sense) a major change in technology, outlook, etc." Oxford English Dictionary 2015b.

71 Lesaffer 2011, p. 141.

72 Levaggi 1996b, p. 6; and Congost 2007b, p. 40.

73 Halpérin 2008, p. 2.

74 Levaggi 1996b, p. 3.

75 Moccia 2011, p. 36.

76 Halpérin 2008, p. 2.

77 See, for example, the reference to the paradigm shift in Germany from codification to constitution in Nörr 1992, especially p. 149.

78 Ramos Núñez 1996, p. 23. Kuhn claimed that "scientific revolutions, and the successive transition from one paradigm to another via revolution is the usual developmental pattern of mature science." Kuhn 1970, p. 12.

assumption will be replaced when a paradigm shift occurs.[79] These revolutions and shifts evolve around the idea of reaching equilibrium. The normativity and social condition of legal institutions may attain equilibrium, yet if they dissociate due to the emergence of anomalies, mutation will take place and society will interpret or apply the legal institution (*v.gr.*, ownership) in a different way. Ultimately, if the dissociation continues, a reform will take place, and the legal institution will need to be reformed.[80] As societies and mentalities evolve, anomalies evolve. These anomalies sometimes may not be explained by prevailing paradigms, showing weaknesses that will ultimately demand new paradigms to emerge.[81] Anomalies are deemed to resist problematization within the limits offered by existing paradigms.[82]

1.5 Methodology

Comparative legal history across American Civil Law Jurisdictions must start with jurisdictions with a rich legal historiography,[83] such as Louisiana, Chile, and Argentina. Readers should note *ab initio* that the value and role of comparative legal history as an autonomous discipline is addressed in-depth in Chapter 2 of this book. This book relies on qualitative methodologies used by social sciences—mainly history and law—that can assist in the further exploration and development of comparative legal history. This book mainly intends to understand the phenomenon of shifts in Ownership Paradigms. In order to understand this phenomenon, this comparative legal historical exercise uses comparative case study and process-tracing techniques, while also benefiting from traditional historical techniques to analyze sources and from the functionalist approach to the comparative study of law.

Case studies are not foreign to the law curricula, where they are used in the process of helping students bridge the divide that exists between practice and foundational studies.[84] This method—not free from criticism—is extensively followed across different disciplines,[85] and comparative legal history may likewise find benefits in its application. Case studies, differently from other

79 de Vries 2013, p. 7.
80 Levaggi 1996b, p. 3.
81 Schultz 2014, pp. 63–64.
82 de Vries 2013, p. 10.
83 Tau Anzoátegui 2010, p. 49.
84 Berg 2010, p. 318.
85 Berg 2010, p. 317.

methods, provide detailed perspectives into existing mechanisms, interests of actors, and limitations they face at specific moments.[86] Case studies must evolve around objects of research that are limited in both time and space, while they should also welcome meaningful abstractions.[87] A case study could be defined as a means to systematically look into an institution (*v.gr.*, ownership) aiming to its description, exploration, and explanation.[88]

This book offers the results of a comparative case study of three jurisdictions, aiming to offer a more comprehensive understanding.[89] That same comparative case study is exploratory, and as such, the assemblage of sources was undertaken before defining clearly all research questions.[90] Accordingly, the study undertaken in this book departed from an overarching research idea that was translated into a set of research questions as the exploration developed. The comparative case study used in this book mainly follows an exploratory approach, in which the phenomenon of shifts of Ownership Paradigms is studied, exploring which are the elements that are of importance to motivate this phenomenon.

Case studies can be used to understand the interaction of relevant facts that are characteristic of an institution (*v.gr.*, ownership).[91] Consisting of studies of institutions in single instances, case studies can then shed light on broader arguments.[92] They ultimately may assist in the development of theory, such as one explaining shifts in Ownership Paradigms.[93] Generalizations are difficult when working with case studies, since the resulting research has to demonstrate that the selected cases (*i.e.*, Louisiana, Chile, and Argentina) are representative of other cases where similar occurrences may take place.[94] However, case study methodologists claim that a hypothesis may be generalized if it explains a hard case or a case that seemed unlikely to be explained.[95] That demanding case, in this book, is found in the US state of Louisiana, which at first glance seems not to follow the events of other American Civil Law Jurisdictions.

86 Hancké 2009, p. 61.
87 Hancké 2009, p. 62.
88 Berg 2010, p. 317.
89 Berg 2010, p. 326.
90 Berg 2010, p. 327.
91 Berg 2010, p. 318.
92 Hancké 2009, p. 62.
93 Berg 2010, p. 321.
94 Hancké 2009, p. 61.
95 Bennett & Checkel 2015, p. 13.

Process-tracing techniques are used—within the comparative case study—to link conditions with outcomes.[96] Alexander L. George stated that process tracing was the identification of evidence that was available in case studies and that could be used to elaborate inferences about historical explanations.[97] Process tracing, therefore, offers intermediate steps in processes, enabling the elaboration of inferences about hypotheses on *how* processes occur and to determine *if* and *how* processes generate the outcome of interest.[98] The snapshots provided by process tracing may result in avoiding a full narrative when moving from cause to outcome, however.[99] Process tracing is closely linked to historical explanations, and Clayton Roberts used it to define important steps that lead to the causation of an outcome.[100] Process-tracing case studies build on the observation that most social science arguments and theories are condensed representations of causal links (if A, then B follows).[101] For example, in this book, the changes introduced in second-generation civil codes could be deemed important steps that lead to a shift in paradigm.[102] Furthermore, as implemented in this book, process tracing assists in identifying the causes of shift in Ownership Paradigms across American Civil Law Jurisdictions. That technique may assist in the elaboration of a generalizable theoretical explanation to be extracted from the evidence found in the causal mechanisms that are identified in the specific cases and that can be ultimately generalized.[103] Process tracing can result in generalizations, and the solution in a specific case can be used to explain or understand similar situations, in this book, across American Civil Law Jurisdictions.[104]

This book further benefits from the application of traditional historical techniques to the analysis of sources. Sources deal both with internal and with external comparative legal history elements, since law should be regarded *in totum*.[105] An approach from causes to effects should help in identifying the

96 Schimmelfennig 2015, p. 101.

97 Bennett & Checkel 2015, pp. 4–5.

98 Bennett & Checkel 2015, p. 6.

99 Schimmelfennig 2015, p. 125.

100 Bennett & Checkel 2015, p. 8.

101 Hancké 2009, p. 66.

102 See generally 5.4 of this book.

103 Beach & Pedersen 2013, pp. 3, 11.

A causal mechanism is "a complex system which produces that behavior by of [sic] the interaction of a number of parts according to direct causal laws." Glennan 1996, p. 52. See also Beach & Pedersen 2013, p. 1; and Bennett & Checkel 2015, p. 9.

104 Hancké 2009, pp. 67–68.

105 Bunge 1912–1913, I, p. xxxii.

"genetic" history of the institution and of the shifts in Ownership Paradigms.[106] Moving in a regressive way, from the present to the past, may lead researchers to lose their path,[107] leading to mistakes.[108] The historical flow of events suggests a progressive and chronological approach to the study. The progressive method, within process tracing, is therefore followed in this book, being more suitable since it better addresses, amongst other things, the historicity and the changes in the meaning of terms and words.[109]

This research follows mainly a functionalist approach to understand shifts in Ownership Paradigms, since different jurisdictions may refer to the same phenomena in different ways.[110] This type of approach, promoted by Konrad Zweigert and Hein Kötz,[111] understands that law reacts to social problems that are faced and shared by all societies alike:[112] a systemic totality.[113] That shared function enables the comparison across legal institutions (*v.gr.*, ownership) even if facing divergent doctrinal structures.[114] It deals with what legal institutions *do* instead of what they *claim* to do.[115] The functionalist approach has been applied successfully to property law institutions.[116] Those who advocate for a functionalist approach deem it the only fruitful means to understand reality, while those who advocate against its use deem it the epitome of negative elements in comparative studies.[117] When looking into the realm of comparative property law, van Erp stated that

> The functional [approach] works both ways: it focuses on convergences and divergences at the same time. The latter aspect is sometimes forgotten and it is particularly this aspect which is highly important for property law. From a functional perspective the various layers of property law in the EU [yet also in American Civil Law Jurisdictions] can

106 See the reference to the interaction of genetic method and cause-effect in Bunge 1912–1913, I, p. xxxii.
107 Levaggi 1996b, p. 9.
108 Levaggi 1996b, p. 9.
109 Levaggi 1996b, p. 9.
110 See, amongst the copious literature, the study in Michaels, 2008.
111 Zweigert & Kötz 1984.
112 Michaels 2012, p. 297; and Örücü 2006, p. 444.
113 Husa 2013, p. 6.
114 Michaels 2012, pp. 297–298.
115 Brand 2007, p. 409.
116 Akkermans 2013, p. 110.
117 Michaels 2008, p. 340; and Husa 2013, p. 21.

> be examined on the basis of how they solve comparable problems in a comparable way.[118]

Functionalist studies are interested in the transplantation of institutions.[119] Those approaches deal with the circulation of ideas and the flow of paradigms, identifying differences and similarities, and providing channels amongst jurisdictions. Accordingly, the research for this book is based on a comparative case study analyzing a selection of legal sources according to the functionalist approach, assisting in comparing the law in different jurisdictions, at different time periods, and providing a better understanding of the past and existing law.

Two final remarks are needed with regards to methodological aspects of this book. First, that the research analyzes events that took place in the Americas from the 1490s to the 1970s. In the three studied jurisdictions, however, events took place beginning in the sixteenth century, when legislation took care of needs beyond the islands. The division between contemporary law and legal history is not settled by dates, but mainly by intellectual interests and perceptions.[120] It is indeed a challenge to assess when a study shifts from being legal to being legal historical: researchers should not lose their historical perspective, and a close cut in time could force that lack of perspective.[121] This book, therefore, allows approximately for a 40-year distance with the topics it addresses. That distance aims to avoid the study of contemporary events that might have triggered ongoing changes, such as the departure from the studied Ownership Paradigms that may have occurred due to the development of a new shift in paradigm (*v.gr.*, Ecological Function paradigm) or due to reversals to previous stages. This cut will, furthermore, reaffirm the comparative legal historical character of the book. Second, that the book deals mainly with events that affect one of the sources of law (*i.e.*, legislative enactments). Legislative enactments—within the understanding of process tracing—could be regarded as elements to establish causal mechanisms. Furthermore, the functional approach is appropriate when looking at legislative enactments since those rules are meant to solve human problems.[122] Time and space constraints make impossible a comprehensive study of all sources of law (*i.a.*, customs, doctrine,

118 van Erp 2013b, p. 93.

119 Brand 2007, p. 410.

120 Tau Anzoátegui 2010, pp. 50–51.

121 Tau Anzoátegui 2010, pp. 50, 53.

122 Örücü 2006, p. 444.

jurisprudence) dealing with ownership in this book.[123] Accordingly, legislative enactments have been mainly selected as the topic of study, though the book includes needed references to socio-historical events and practices and to other sources of law, such as seminal court decisions and groundbreaking scholarly writings. Further studies should look at other sources of law autonomously or collectively, and use this book as a first building block: this book claims to be an initial step in this area of comparative legal history. Readers should be mindful that comparative legal historical studies should likewise consider the normative framework, the application of law, and the doctrinal assessment.[124] Therefore, a comprehensive approach requires attention to the three aspects,[125] because other human acts may indeed show potential problems.[126] This book therefore deals mainly the manifestations of the shifts in Ownership Paradigms within the legislation of Louisiana, Chile, and Argentina; while the gestation of those shifts, which many times find fundamental grounding on doctrinal elaborations and court decisions, requires further study.

1.5.1 *Louisiana as a Hard Case for American Civil Law Jurisdictions*[127]

The geographical location, historical background, and resulting legal culture of Louisiana tend to attract comparative-law scholars. René David, when referring to Louisiana, indicated that it is "ruled by mixed laws, borrowing certain elements from the common law but, to a certain extent, retaining [its] membership in the Romano-Germanic family."[128] Louisiana is the only US state that is considered to be a member of that family, and is the only state with a civil code that originally followed the tenets of nineteenth-century continental European codes. As a consequence of many of the events that will be developed in this book (and other events that exceed its scope), a number of scholars now consider Louisiana a traditional mixed jurisdiction, where the predominant legal system is no longer pure, and the influence of the common law is sensed.[129]

The state of Louisiana was no exception to the nineteenth-century codification movement that spread throughout the Western hemisphere. The legal

123 Other works advocated for a study of only a selection of problems or matters dealing with ownership, avoiding an *in totum* approach. Cordero Quinzacara 2008, p. 495.

124 See generally Coing 1976. See also Levaggi 1990a, p. 160.

125 Levaggi 1990a, p. 160.

126 Martiré 1977, p. 20; Altamira y Crevea 1890, p. 27; Bunge 1912–1913, I, p. xxxiii; Levaggi 2009, pp. 154–155; and Levaggi 1996b, pp. 12, 15.

127 See generally Parise 2012a; Parise 2012b; and Parise 2013b.

128 David & Brierley 1968, pp. 59–60.

129 Palmer 1999, p. 4.

culture of Louisiana was an isolated "civil law island" partially surrounded by a "sea of common law," a status that had to be safeguarded to survive.[130] A look into the early American period in Louisiana (c. 1803–1830) provides an illustration of a clash of legal systems between continental European and common law principles.[131]

In Louisiana, during the early 1800s, the first decisions on the adoption of provisions from different systems were taken in criminal law and procedure, and in civil procedure. A group of inhabitants advocated for the implementation of the American law courts and another group advocated for the continuity of the continental European court system (*n.b.,* excluding criminal law).[132] In criminal law and criminal procedure the common law achieved a first bastion, and its principles prevailed. In civil procedure, at least during the first years, the bastion was shared between continental European and common law principles, although there was a pre-eminence of principles from the former.[133]

In the area of civil law, paramount for this book, the bastion was controlled by continental European ideas. Early, the inhabitants opted for those principles, perhaps due to cultural and economic interests,[134] and to protect the property rights they had received during the French and Spanish periods.[135] Some local inhabitants wanted to codify following continental European principles and in that way preserve the law and rights they previously had. Those continental European ideas, however, were not adopted blindly in Louisiana.[136] Civil law codification endeavors in Louisiana had an early projection on other US states and territories. For example, David Dudley Field, who advocated for codification in the US during the nineteenth century,[137] presented a Project of a Civil Code for the State of New York before the legislature in 1865.[138] Many sections of the project had notes indicating references to, among others, the *Code Napoléon,* and paramount for this book, the civil code of Louisiana of 1825.

Even when a commercial code was drafted in the 1820s, following to some extent continental European principles, the last bastion was won by general commercial practices also effective in other US states. In commercial law, local inhabitants seemed to prefer the flexibility that those practices provided.

130 Parise 2006b.
131 See generally Dargo 2009b.
132 Dargo 2009b, p. 222.
133 Parise 2012a.
134 Trahan 2003, p. 1024.
135 Kilbourne 1987, p. 41.
136 Parise 2012a.
137 See generally Batiza 1986.
138 Civil Code New York 1865, p. ix.

That flexibility would also grant the ability of locating local traders in a similar standing with the ones from other nations and US states.[139]

Louisiana and its legal system, however, kept evolving in the twentieth and twenty-first centuries. In 1935, the Louisiana State University Law School (LSU) appointed Gordon Ireland to teach law.[140] After two years of teaching in Louisiana, Ireland claimed that it should be admitted that Louisiana had become a common-law state.[141] Ireland understood that France and its legal texts had been left aside, that the civil code of Louisiana was nothing other than a compilation that was applied whenever a local decision was not rendered in that area, and that the legal system of Louisiana resembled that of other states of the Union that at some point had been Spanish or French colonies.[142] A reaction to this statement was quick to come. In 1937, Paul M. Hébert, together with three other law professors, challenged Ireland's position,[143] and concluded that Louisiana continued to be a civil law jurisdiction.[144] This scholarly discussion, known as the Great Debate,[145] is considered positive for the civil law in Louisiana. It generated a movement towards the enhancement of the civil law; the creation of the *Louisiana Law Review*, which aimed to develop the civil and comparative law in Louisiana; the appointment of foreign civil law professors, mainly at the Tulane Law School and at LSU; and the creation of the Louisiana State Law Institute (LSLI), which was envisioned to be a tool for law reform in the state.[146] The Great Debate also resulted in further revisions in the text of the Louisiana Civil Code, which started in the 1970s and extended into the twenty-first century. There is an on-going revision process of the Louisiana Civil Code, and it was estimated, already by 2003, that 72% of the nineteenth-century text had been revised.[147]

As mentioned before, case study methodologists claim that a hypothesis may be generalized if it explains a hard case or a case that seemed unlikely to be explained.[148] Louisiana offers such case, since at first glance, as this book will further show, seems not to follow the events of other American Civil Law Jurisdictions.

139 Parise 2012a.
140 Murchison 1988, p. 3.
141 Ireland 1937, p. 596. See also Murchison 1988, p. 4.
142 Ireland 1937, pp. 595–597.
143 Daggett *et al.* 1937, p. 12.
144 Daggett *et al.* 1937, p. 41.
145 See generally Brosman 1938, p. 239; and Figueroa-Torres 2008, pp. 155–156.
146 Murchison 1988, p. 4.
147 Palmer 2003a, p. 1112.
148 Bennett & Checkel 2015, p. 13.

1.6 Sources

American Civil Law Jurisdictions share to a great extent common roots and language uniformity.[149] These are indeed advantages when working with historical sources. Yet there are still challenges when undertaking research in the sources needed for a comparative legal historical study. For example, even the most well-stocked university libraries present gaps in their holdings, and researchers have to be familiar with different legal systems in order to circumvent potential misrepresentation of sources.[150] Archives naturally still present mobility restrictions when working with manuscript sources.

Vernacular legal histories developed steadily during the past centuries,[151] and it is now time to explore the legal history of different jurisdictions at different time periods. Yet there may be no overreaching study of history when local or vernacular histories are absent.[152] Comparative legal historical studies require elaborations and specializations that cannot be assembled at once in a single study.[153] The more detailed a comparative legal historical study is, the more need there is to undertake collaborative work.[154] There is indeed a need to reach for a broad collaboration,[155] and existing local or vernacular studies can serve as a means to achieve that outreach, since legal historical studies have reached a degree of satisfaction at the local or vernacular level.[156] The reconstruction of a common image of the legal past for American Civil Law Jurisdictions will necessarily build on the gathering of prior studies.[157] Thomas Duve, from the Max Planck Institute for European Legal History (*Max-Planck-Institut für europäische Rechtgeschichte*), correctly stated that a:

> global perspective will rely heavily on research carried out in area studies, like those on 'Latin America', 'Africa', or 'Asia'. These Area Studies and the regional specialization of disciplines like 'European Legal History' are indispensable for studying a region worthwhile to be studied as such, for example as the result of a historical process of regional integration, like in

149 See generally 2.3.2.1 of this book.

150 Ibbetson 2013, p. 1.

151 See generally Chapter 2 of this book; and Ibbetson 2013, p. 2.

152 Duve 2014, pp. 60–61.

153 García-Gallo 1987a, p. 1077.

154 David Ibbetson invited the participation of multiple scholars in collaborative work. Ibbetson 2013, p. 3.

155 García-Gallo 1987a, p. 1077.

156 García-Gallo 1987a, p. 1078.

157 Abásolo 2009, at § 14.

> the case of Europe. Regional expertise is also necessary as an institutional framework for producing the essential historical, philological or other expertise and providing it to those who do comparative or global research. Regional expertise thus creates the preconditions for a fruitful disciplinary, but also for transnational, transregional or even 'global' research.[158]

Comparative legal historical studies are bound to build upon primary and secondary sources alike. The more ambitious a project might be (*i.a.*, crossing continents, languages, religions, or time periods), the more need for researchers to rely on secondary sources. These sources—if authoritative—will assist in making a project feasible, eliminating some of the geographical boundaries and time constraints that exclusive archival work may encompass. Yet not every secondary source is of value for a comparative legal historical project. Similar to nineteenth-century codifiers, comparative legal historians must embark in treasure trove activities, seeking for the most authoritative and useful sources that might help them answer their research questions.[159]

This book relies on, as illustrated in its references, the work of renowned legal historians from both Europe and the Americas. The book benefits mainly from the rich legal historiography that developed in American Civil Law Jurisdictions. The US state of Louisiana and the republics of Chile and Argentina have produced significant legal-historical output, which built on rich primary sources and authoritative secondary sources.[160] For example, as suggested by several authors,[161] this book builds on the excellent existing studies on *Indiano* law.[162] Many of those erudite studies, sometimes extending into the post-independence periods, are a source of pride for the Americas.[163] *Standing on the shoulders of giants* assists in the development of comparative legal historical exercises such as the one presented in this book. The research undertaken for this book builds to a certain degree on the results of source research undertaken by previous scholars from a multiplicity of jurisdictions, and therefore benefits from those past and rich exercises. Those previous studies, even when vernacular or segmented, are indeed fundamental building blocks for an exercise of comparative legal history. New research questions may now deal with existing sources. The research questions that are addressed in this

158 Duve 2014, pp. 56–57.

159 See generally 4.2.1 and 4.4.2 of this book.

160 See generally 2.3.1.2.1 of this book.

161 Tau Anzoátegui 2010, p. 49.

162 *Indiano* law is dealt with in-depth in 3.3 and 3.4 of this book.

163 Abásolo 2009, at § 6.

book can be answered by looking at those previous exercises, indeed. An active interrogation of sources is required, and research questions, such as the ones posed in this book, should trigger meaningful comparisons across time and space.[164]

The evolution of Ownership Paradigms in the Americas has been—understandably—a somewhat neglected topic by European scholars. Previous segmented works have studied different aspects of the evolution of ownership on both sides of the Atlantic. No previous work, however, has attempted a comprehensive approach for American Civil Law Jurisdictions: stretching across time and space. The gathering and consultation process of primary and secondary sources that resulted in this book took place on both sides of the Atlantic. The book benefited from archival research undertaken in the Americas and from consultation of holdings in libraries and research institutes in Africa, the Americas, Australia, and Europe. In addition, the chapters draw on—occasionally *verbatim*—and benefit from published works of the author.[165] Sources, as indicated in the references of this book, are mainly in English and Spanish, though copious references are made to texts in, amongst other languages, French, German, and Italian. Passages of texts in their original languages were transcribed in footnotes whenever this would be of special relevance or would provide for better illustration. The book tried to benefit from the digitalization of sources, which, as will be further explained,[166] is a fundamental tool for comparative legal historical studies. Therefore, when possible, references were made to sources available on the Internet. The book, naturally, makes manifest the overabundant Spanish literature that deals with property law institutions in American Civil Law Jurisdictions. That literature, as already mentioned and as will be further explained,[167] mainly took a vernacular approach, was mainly originated in the Americas, and rarely developed across different time periods. Whenever possible, footnotes in the book include references to English language sources, offering non-Spanish readers additional venues for consultation, while also aiming to facilitate further studies in the area. Readers should be mindful that English-language literature dealing with legal historical aspects of property law institutions in individual

164 Ibbetson 2013, p. 2.

165 Those works are: Parise 2002a; Parise 2002b; Parise 2004; Parise 2006a; Parise 2008b; Parise 2008c; Parise 2009b; Moréteau & Parise 2009; Parise 2010a; Parise 2010b; Parise 2011b; Parise 2012a; Parise 2012b; Parise 2013a; Marotta & Parise 2014; Parise 2014a; and Parise 2014b.

166 See generally 2.3.2.1 of this book.

167 See generally Chapter 2 of this book.

American Civil Law Jurisdictions is scarce,[168] and that English language literature dealing with the same institutions in a comparative legal historical way is almost inexistent.[169]

1.7 Structure

This book addresses the study of Ownership Paradigms in three time periods and in three jurisdictions. This novel approach distinguishes the book from previous studies. Periodization is a useful tool to structure the study of a legal institution across time. Yet, readers should note that history is an amorphous and indivisible *continuum* that never fully adapts to artificial periodization.[170] Changes and shifts (such as those experienced in Ownership Paradigms) do not take place overnight; and, hence, periodization in this book, as in others, aims only to distinguish main brakes in law and society, even when changes might require additional time to be sensed.[171]

This book is divided into six chapters. All chapters aim to provide answers to the main research question and five sub-questions. Chapter 1 sets the methodological framework for the entire book, while Chapter 2 highlights the added value that comparative legal historical studies may bring to American Civil Law Jurisdictions. Chapters 3 to 5 address, in chronological order, the three Ownership Paradigms (*i.e.*, Allocation, Liberal, and Social Function). Chapter 6, finally, provides the general and specific conclusions and invites the exploration of areas of future research.

168 Louisiana is naturally an exception.

169 The works by, amongst others, Mirow and by Kenneth Karst and Keith Rosenn offer exceptions to that lack of literature. There seems to be a lack of literature when seeking teaching materials in the English language for courses on Latin American legal history. See Mirow 2014, p. 237; and Abásolo 2009, at § 14.

170 Tomás y Valiente 1997c, p. 944.

171 Tomás y Valiente 1997c, p. 944.

CHAPTER 2

The Value of Comparative Legal History for American Civil Law Jurisdictions

2.1 Introduction

Comparative legal history receives attention in American Civil Law Jurisdictions; yet, in Europe, it is currently in vogue. In Europe, the discipline gained momentum when reconsidering teaching guidelines, and finds a precedent in, amongst others, the celebrated work of Paul Koschaker.[1] Furthermore, comparative legal history gained a place within the curriculum of European law schools, longing for the study of legal history with a comparative approach. Accordingly, a comparative approach to legal history in Europe is reflected in the classrooms,[2] in the literature,[3] and in academic circles.[4] However, comparative legal history is not something new. This chapter will show that comparative legal history in the Americas also gained strength recently in the literature and in academia, where its importance was highlighted. American Civil Law Jurisdictions should—nevertheless—welcome more studies and activities that undertake a comparative legal historical approach to law. In the Americas, collaborative and overreaching efforts already occur, since several decades, in the field of *Indiano* law, encompassing the period from 1492 until the independence of the different jurisdictions. In the period following the independence movements, however, few attempts to achieve collaborative and overreaching efforts at national and multi-jurisdictional levels were undertaken.

Studies in Europe and the US display an interest in the legal history of American Civil Law Jurisdictions. In Europe, there is interest in these jurisdictions. For example, valuable contributions have been made by the Association of European Historians that Study Latin America (*Asociación de Historiadores Latinoamericanistas Europeos*), linking—already for several decades—scholars

1 Koschaker 1947. A recent appraisal of that early work was included in Duve 2014, pp. 38–39.

2 Van Rhee and van der Meer explain the teaching of legal history within the European Law School bachelor program at Maastricht University, where the study of legal history evolves beyond the borders of the Netherlands. See van Rhee & van der Meer 2011.

3 The literature has indeed developed. See, for example, Lesaffer 2009; Sunde and Skodvin 2010; Wesel 2014; and Robinson *et al.* 2000.

4 Modéer & Nilsén 2011, p. 9.

 | DOI 10.1163/9789004338203_003

from both sides of the Atlantic.[5] Comparative legal historical Ph.D. projects—such as the one that motivated this book—also provide (and have provided) a bridge between America and Europe. Furthermore, an International Research School of Legal History was created, being a joint effort of the Research Institute for Legal History (*Instituto de Investigaciones de Historia del Derecho*) from Buenos Aires, of the Brazilian Institute of Legal History (*Instituto Brasileiro de História do Direito*), and of the Max Planck Institute for European Legal History. There is similar interest in American Civil Law Jurisdictions in the US. Matthew Mirow, for example, observed a decade ago that "recent scholarly activity attests to the growing importance of Latin American legal history as a field of academic pursuit, and researchers are increasingly turning to the field."[6] That claim can naturally be applied to American Civil Law Jurisdictions. Furthermore, in 2013, the annual meeting of the American Society for Legal History specifically aimed to attract scholars from other parts of the Americas.[7]

The chapter deals with the role of comparative legal history as a tool for the study of American Civil Law Jurisdictions. It will demonstrate that scholars on both sides of the Atlantic should undertake and eventually benefit from these types of comparative and historical studies. The chapter is divided into three main parts. Firstly, the chapter presents comparative legal history as an autonomous discipline. The building blocks of that discipline are addressed, and ultimately a definition is proposed. Secondly, the chapter reports on the development of comparative legal historical studies in Europe and in American Civil Law Jurisdictions. In that part, the chapter explores favorable and unfavorable conditions for the development of these studies in American Civil Law Jurisdictions. Thirdly, a short part highlights the interplay of comparative legal history and legal borrowings or transplantation. That interplay, as the subsequent chapters in this book show, is fundamental for the understanding of the circulation of ideas and the flow of paradigms. It should be noted that the existence of common roots across American Civil Law Jurisdictions does not imply a lack of profound differences; though differences should not be considered impeding factors for the dialogue between jurisdictions.[8] The chapter, above all, aims to show that American Civil Law Jurisdictions would benefit from an increase in the number of comparative legal historical studies.

---

5 See AHILA 2015.

6 Mirow 2000–2001, p. 43.

7 See ASLH 2013.

8 Troiano 2004, p. ix.

2.2 Construction

Legal history and comparative law offer a fruitful combination for the development of legal science. As early as 1903, Édouard Lambert[9]—who later established the Institute of Comparative Law (*Institut de droit comparé*) of Lyon (France)—mentioned that "the comparatist is obliged to constantly work as an historian."[10] Nevertheless, legal history and comparative law emerged as different disciplines, and triggered autonomous studies of law in time and space, neglecting a uniform approach.[11] That autonomous evolution of the two disciplines resulted also in the emergence of comparative legal history as an autonomous discipline.

2.2.1 *Building Blocks*

Comparative law and legal history are indeed fundamental blocks when dealing with the value of the resulting autonomous discipline. This section only aims to highlight a selection of aspects of the two building blocks that encompass comparative legal history.

There is an imminent need, due amongst other reasons to the impact of globalization, to include comparative elements in legal research. Zweigert and Kötz observed that it is often the dissatisfaction with a local solution that triggers the comparatist to look for better solutions in other systems.[12] A number of scholars, across jurisdictions, have addressed the value and purpose of comparative law already for decades. For example, Mario Rotondi, who directed the Angelo Sraffa Institute of Comparative Law (*Instituto di Diritto Comparato Angelo Sraffa*) of Milan (Italy), characterized the objective of comparative law as the confrontation of the legal orders of different jurisdictions.[13] Rodolfo Sacco, also from Italy, correctly pointed out that comparative law aims to provide knowledge on the rules and institutions that are subject to comparison, and that multiple comparative studies can result in further knowledge of a legal system.[14] The Italian *maestro* further highlighted that comparative law can assist in identifying the connection, diversification, and transplantation of legal

9 For additional information on Édouard Lambert, see Moréteau 2007; and Petit 1995.

10 The text in French read: "le comparatiste est obligé de faire constamment œuvre d'historien." Lambert 1903, p. 3.

11 Gordley 2008, p. 772.

12 Zweigert & Kötz 1984, p. 34.

13 Fleitas Ortiz de Rozas 1967, p. 197. Some of the dogmas of Mario Rotondi are available in Rotondi 1968.

14 Sacco 1991a, p. 6.

institutions across jurisdictions.[15] That claim can be applied to the analysis of paradigms, indeed, such as the one that is undertaken starting in Chapter 3 of this book.

One of the purposes of legal history is to understand a legal system at a certain place and at a past time.[16] Therefore, legal history examines the development of law across time.[17] Legal history should not be limited, however, to the reconstruction of the law of a certain period; it should also aim to show how law evolved through successive periods, unveiling its persistent elements and variations.[18] These studies—differently to those of other disciplines—provide an empirical approach to law when dealing with the evolution and shift in concepts, methods, ideas,[19] and paradigms. Legal history serves as a means to show the relativity that law experiences because of its evolution and of the shifts regarding, amongst other things, concepts and interpretations.[20] These statements will be illustrated in this book, when looking at the evolution of Ownership Paradigms across American Civil Law Jurisdictions. The book will aim to unveil variations, to demonstrate the empirical approach of historical studies, and to demonstrate the abovementioned relativity.

The scientific study of law becomes incomprehensible when lacking a historical perspective.[21] History is indeed one of the three pillars for the scientific study of law, the other two being the dogmatic study of current law and the philosophical study of what law ought to be (*de lege ferenda*).[22] History is intrinsic to law, and hence it is impossible to fully understand the law when neglecting history.[23] Neglecting history would result in a fragmentary and incomplete knowledge of law that attains only a superficial and external understanding.[24]

There is proximity and natural cooperation between both building blocks.[25] The inclusion of comparative and historical studies in the analysis of law helps to turn potential lawyers into jurists.[26] Jurists do not limit their studies to the

15 Sacco 1991b, p. 388.
16 Lesaffer 2011, p. 136.
17 Levaggi 1996b, p. 11; and Martiré 1977, p. 18.
18 Levaggi 1996b, p. 11.
19 Levaggi 1996b, p. 7.
20 Tau Anzoátegui 2010, pp. 86–87.
21 Tau Anzoátegui 2010, p. 86.
22 Tau Anzoátegui 2010, p. 86.
23 Levaggi 1996b, p. 4.
24 Levaggi 1996b, p. 4.
25 Liebrecht 2012, p. 1066.
26 Abelardo Levaggi referred exclusively to legal history, yet it could be extended to comparative law. Levaggi 1996b, p. 4.

current law as it is, and, naked of a scientific and social context. Jurists, on the contrary, seek amongst other qualities the origins and the reception of legal institutions in different geographical points and time periods.[27] Jurists who benefit from comparative and historical studies will therefore know the *raison d'être*, the meaning, and the value of the existing law.[28] Accordingly, the scientific requirement of knowing the causes, explanations, and precedents of the law will be reached by means of revealing the historical and comparative evolution.[29]

2.2.2 *Autonomous Discipline*

Comparative legal history can be deemed an autonomous discipline, even when its two building blocks are indeed interrelated. For example, already in the nineteenth century, Lambert acted both as a legal historian and as a comparatist in France;[30] while in Spain Rafael Altamira y Crevea, from his chair of legal history at the University of Oviedo (*Universidad de Oviedo*), advocated for the teaching of foreign history and comparative legislation, already in the period 1897 to 1910.[31] Altamira y Crevea further defended that comparative studies enlightened legal history.[32] In Italy, since the second half of the twentieth century, Sacco has averred that "the comparative perspective is historical *par excellence*."[33] Law actually experiences an ever-present historical dimension that should appear in every comparative study.[34] It is, therefore, natural to deem legal history "comparative law across time."[35]

Comparatists and legal historians travel in time and space, respectively;[36] yet comparative legal historians necessarily undertake endeavors in both dimensions. These bi-dimensional studies no longer belong exclusively to the domain of comparative law or legal history. Researchers who follow the

27 See Parise 2002a, p. 37.

28 Levaggi 1996b, p. 4.

29 Levaggi 1996b, p. 5.

30 Petit 2001, p. 61.

Édouard Lambert taught legal history, while he also followed the comparative approaches of his master Raymond Saleilles. Petit 2001, p. 55.

31 Altamira y Crevea 1914, pp. 9–10.

32 He further claimed that comparative studies were unavoidable in order to fully understand and reconstruct local historical institutions when more sources were available in other jurisdictions. Altamira y Crevea 1914, p. 14.

33 Sacco 1991a, p. 24.

34 Brand 2007, p. 421.

35 Tau Anzoátegui 2010, p. 86.

36 Donlan & Masferrer 2013, p. iii.

comparative legal historical path can claim independence from the two building blocks mentioned above. Comparative legal history can be deemed a very young discipline;[37] scholars in Europe started during the past decades to search for paths towards the study of legal history beyond jurisdictional boundaries, breaking with vernacular limitations.[38] Accordingly, legal historical studies are no longer circumscribed or reduced exclusively to vernacular or local law,[39] and a way has been paved for the development of comparative legal history. Comparative legal history may examine the migration, flow, or circulation of legal ideas, looking at the product of that movement as a means to better characterize a specific legal culture.[40] David Ibbetson correctly stated recently that "legal history can only benefit from a transcending of national or systemic boundaries."[41]

Comparative legal history appeals for the use of different perspectives to approach a similar issue, hence enriching the understanding of what motivates the law.[42] James Gordley already observed that what has happened elsewhere or at different times should not be ignored.[43] Comparative legal historians do not assume that law consists of watertight compartments wherein each jurisdiction experienced its own events, while they do acknowledge that current systems result from a blend of previous solutions.[44] The law in a specific time and space should not be regarded as an independent object of study.[45] A watertight study would result in an obstacle to the development of comparative legal history and to a complete understanding of the law.

Different definitions have been offered for comparative legal history. For example, Heikki Pihlajamäki has presented a broad definition that understands comparative legal history "simply [as] the opposite of purely national legal history."[46] The Finnish jurist more recently provided a more elaborated explanation that understands that the discipline:

37 Löhnig 2014, p. 116.
38 Tau Anzoátegui 2010, p. 47.
39 Abásolo 2014, p. 16.
40 Abásolo 2014, p. 16.
41 Ibbetson 2013, pp. 1–2.
42 Oosterhuis 2011, pp. 3–4.
43 Gordley 2008, p. 763.
44 These are amongst the most common mistakes that James Gordley identified for comparative lawyers and legal historians. See Gordley 2008, p. 763.
45 Gordley 2008, p. 757.
46 Pihlajamäki 2011, p. 40.

> can use a systematic method of comparison in much the same way comparative law can. The comparative legal historian can thus [...] choose a certain number of essential features that the objects of comparison have in common and then analyze their functioning [...]. But comparative legal history can also be less systematic. The comparative legal historian can take a national or regional legal institution as his [/her] concern, exactly as a traditional legal historian working within the boundaries of a national legal system would. However, and this is a major difference to the traditional method, the comparative legal historian would always position the research object in an international context.[47]

Other European scholars recently referred to comparative legal history as "the comparison of individuals, ideas and institutions—independent or entangled—from two or more legal traditions."[48] The US legal discourse also participated of the disciplinary discussions, and proposed a very challenging characterization for comparative legal history that:

> involves laying two legal systems side by side in all of their aspects. One must understand the top-level generalizations that lie behind the statements of rules and doctrines, one must understand the history in which these statements are embedded, one must understand how the society and institutions operate in order to understand how the rules and doctrines operate within the society. Only when one understands all of these things can one safely make comparisons.[49]

Finally, it should be mentioned that Ibbetson advocated for an understanding that defines the discipline as the "study of related or parallel phenomena in two or more different places or at different times."[50]

A hereby-proposed definition for comparative legal history understands the discipline as the study of external and/or internal aspects of law necessarily undertaken across different time periods and jurisdictions. A comparative legal historical study needs to comply with both requirements: a study of an aspect of the law in at least two different time periods and at least in two different jurisdictions. Comparative legal historical studies require research across the vertical and horizontal axes, accordingly. It should be noticed that

47 Pihlajamäki 2014, pp. 129–130.

48 Donlan & Masferrer 2013, p. iii.

49 Donahue 1997, p. 11.

50 Ibbetson 2013, p. 3.

the circulation of ideas or the flow of paradigms can only be fully grasped by using a comparative legal historical approach. Esin Örücü already observed that vertical and horizontal comparisons are needed when tracing normative transfers.[51] Table 2.1 provides an illustration of a comparative legal historical study that—similarly to this book—addresses three jurisdictions across three different time periods:

A study that compares an aspect of the law at a given time, yet in different jurisdictions would be a comparative law study that may benefit from the use of the legal historical method to better understand that specific aspect of the law at that specific time period. Table 2.2 provides an illustration of a comparative law study that addresses three jurisdictions across a single time period:

Finally, a study that compares an aspect of the law at a given jurisdiction, yet at different time periods would be a legal historical study that may benefit from the use of the comparative method to contrast that specific aspect of the law in that specific jurisdiction. Table 2.3 provides an illustration of a legal historical study that addresses one jurisdiction across three time periods:

Comparative legal historians do not undertake pure legal history or pure comparative law. The product of their research experience—that benefits from the techniques and approaches used in both disciplines—is more than the mere

TABLE 2.1 *Comparative legal history matrix*

	Jurisdiction 1	**Jurisdiction 2**	**Jurisdiction 3**
Time 1	x	x	x
Time 2	x	x	x
Time 3	x	x	x

TABLE 2.2 *Comparative law matrix*

	Jurisdiction 1	**Jurisdiction 2**	**Jurisdiction 3**
Time 1			
Time 2	x	x	x
Time 3			

51 Örücü 2006, p. 451.

TABLE 2.3 *Legal history matrix*

	Jurisdiction 1	Jurisdiction 2	Jurisdiction 3
Time 1	x		
Time 2	x		
Time 3	x		

addition of the two building blocks: it provides a means to understand the evolution of legal science across time and space in a collegiate way. A division into external and internal comparative legal history may facilitate the study of the discipline.[52] External comparative legal history deals with the sources of law (*i.a.*, legislative enactments, customs, doctrine, jurisprudence) and of socio-political events that explain the law at different times and in different jurisdictions. Internal comparative legal history, building on the external component, deals with the transformations of aspects of the law (*i.a.*, contract law, torts, adoption) across time and space. Comparisons in time and space can help unveil *why* events took place and not only *what* events took place,[53] and also help to identify a precedent (where an aspect of law may *originate*), a subsequent (where an aspect of law may *lead*), and a concordance or difference (degrees of *parallelism*).[54] Comparative legal historical studies, for example across American Civil Law Jurisdictions, should articulate the product of their efforts with that of other contemporary expressions, aiming to identify similarities or differences, while overcoming the limitations that emerge from experiences circumscribed to the national or local sphere.[55]

Comparative legal historical studies may likewise assist in better understanding, characterizing, and differentiating local law.[56] These studies help to understand the law at a specific time and place, while locating that same law within a broader context, assisting in better understanding its traits. Law can be understood as a blend of solutions to situations faced in the past,[57] not necessarily within a single jurisdiction. Those problems could have triggered

52 Parise 2002b, p. 201.

53 Ibbetson 2013, p. 2.

54 See Parise 2002a, where the scope is limited to comparative law.

55 Abásolo 2009, at § 4.

56 García-Gallo 1987a, p. 1078.

57 Gordley 2008, p. 762.

new ideas—in Sacco's word, 'formants'–that may find their origins beyond the borders of a particular jurisdiction and at another time.[58]

The autonomous discipline under study may assist in understanding that law is a social science that must contemplate at least three aspects when applied to a specific society.[59] First, that application of the law not always finds geographical boundaries. Second, that application not always finds language barriers. Third, that application not always finds time limitations. Law aims to present the experiences and the *ethos* of a society, and to achieve that goal it may benefit from texts drafted in other latitudes, in other languages, and in other time periods.[60] The *ethos* of a specific society, *mutatis mutandis*, may also be replicated in other societies, and the researcher may face a local *ethos* that encapsulates global elements.[61] For example, Reinhard Zimmermann highlighted the value of historical studies to elaborate a blueprint of the common ground across European national legal systems that shared common traditions.[62] He stated that these studies provide tools to understand intellectual stimulation and migration of legal rules,[63] ideas, or paradigms. Accordingly, Michael Stolleis naturally pointed to the usefulness of comparative legal history when referring to the development of European legal history.[64] Again, as this book will show, comparative legal history may fulfill a similar purpose in the study of Ownership Paradigms across American Civil Law Jurisdictions.

2.3 Development

Comparative legal history is an important discipline for the development of legal science in American Civil Law Jurisdictions. Even when Europe seems to be taking the lead in the development of the discipline, the ideas are not foreign to American Civil Law Jurisdictions. The development of the discipline in that part of the Americas presents some advantageous and some challenging conditions when compared with Europe. Comparative legal history will likewise bring some benefits to both sides of the Atlantic, and will ultimately assist in

58 Gordley 2008, p. 762.

59 This claim can be made also for legal history and comparative law as autonomous disciplines, however.

60 Parise 2013a, p. 376.

61 See generally Parise 2002a.

62 Zimmermann 2008, p. 575.

63 Zimmermann 2008, p. 575.

64 Stolleis 2009, p. 29.

the better understanding and development of legal provisions and ideas in the different jurisdictions.

2.3.1 *Emergence*

Comparative legal history evolves differently in different parts of the world. Scenarios and output, naturally, differ if studies focus on Africa, Asia, Australia, Europe, or the Americas, or a combination of jurisdictions from these continents. That divergence depends on—amongst other things—the interests of scholars, on the availability of primary and secondary sources, on language use, on potential traces of colonialism, and on the multi-jurisdictional interaction that prevails or is lacking in the studied territories. This chapter, hereby, displays the evolution of the discipline briefly in Europe and more extensively in American Civil Law Jurisdictions.

2.3.1.1 Europe

The discipline became a European necessity after the adoption of the *Magna Charta Universitatum europaeum* of Bologna (1988), which generated new academic exchanges and new courses.[65] In academic circles, the discipline recently gained momentum with the creation of the European Society for Comparative Legal History, which serves as a platform for the interaction of scholars interested in the development of the discipline.[66] Furthermore, the idea of European integration affected the study of legal history at universities and a European perspective prevails.[67]

Pihlajamäki explained that in Europe there are peripheral and central jurisdictions.[68] In peripheral jurisdictions it is necessary to look beyond the borders of each jurisdiction, and hence reach a full understanding of local legal history. On the one hand, the Finnish jurist stressed that the discipline has greater acceptance in peripheral or small jurisdictions (*v.gr.*, Belgium, the Netherlands).[69] On the other hand, he stressed that vernacular approaches are welcomed by central or large jurisdictions (*v.gr.*, Germany, Spain).[70] Pihlajamäki mentioned that, according to his teaching experiences, peripheral jurisdictions rely on the use of comparative approaches.[71] Likewise, experiences at

65 Modéer 2011, pp. 13–14.
66 That society was established in 2009. Donlan & Masferrer 2013, p. iii.
67 Lesaffer 2009, p. viii.
68 See generally Pihlajamäki 2011.
69 Pihlajamäki 2011, pp. 39–40.
70 Pihlajamäki 2011, pp. 39–40.
71 Pihlajamäki 2011, p. 40.

the University of Ghent (*Universiteit Gent*) indicated that Belgian legal history requires to some extent the study of French legal history.[72] While in Holland, another peripheral jurisdiction, professors explore legal history and aspects of European history at large while delivering education at some law schools, including Maastricht University.[73]

What temporal and spatial limitations should studies on European legal history encounter? Aspects of ancient law (*v.gr.*, Babylonian, Egyptian) should not be neglected, since they provide important precedents for the existing law.[74] These studies also assist in broadening the context—and ultimately—the understanding of medieval and modern concepts, for example. Similar reasons seem to indicate that other events should not be discarded. Accordingly, attention should be devoted to the division between the Western Roman Empire and the Roman Catholic Church, on the one hand; and the Byzantine Empire and the Orthodox Catholic Church, on the other hand.[75] Further attention should be devoted to Eastern European jurisdictions, a number of which have been neglected for some years amongst the main participants of the discourse.[76] Finally, the European curricula should incorporate aspects of Islamic law, because of the early influence they had, even before the medieval incursion into the Iberian Peninsula.[77]

2.3.1.2 American Civil Law Jurisdictions

Law studies attract many students across American Civil Law Jurisdictions, and constantly rank amongst the most popular in higher education.[78] In 2008, for example in Argentina, 78 institutions taught law, with an enrolment of 200,511 students.[79] That number is significant, in a total population of 40 million inhabitants,[80] if compared, for example, with the 152,033 students[81] enrolled in the 200 institutions that teach law in the US,[82] out of a total population of

72 See generally Heirbaut 2011.

73 See generally van Rhee & van der Meer 2011.

74 See generally Osipova 2011.

75 See generally Osipova 2011.

76 Stolleis 2009, p. 30.

77 See generally Osipova 2011.

78 Parise 2010b, pp. 126–127.

79 Parise 2010b, p. 127; and Secretaría de Políticas Universitarias 2009, p. 37.

80 The 2010 Argentine Census indicated that the total Argentine population was 40,117,096. See Censo 2010.

81 ABA & LSAC 2009, p. 870.

82 ABA & LSAC 2009, p. i.

308 million inhabitants.[83] A similar scenario takes place in other parts of the Americas, with 188,422 law students enrolled in Mexico and 44,000 in Venezuela.[84] Enrolment numbers must have changed by now. The numbers, however, most probably do not show a drastic reeducation; on the contrary, they accompany population growth.[85]

Comparative legal history—differently from the European scenario—seems not yet to be a necessity for the significant number of students enrolled and for the researchers who are active in American Civil Law Jurisdictions. Nevertheless, legal historical studies have a long and rich tradition in that part of the Americas. The first chair of legal history was created in Peru in 1875 at the University of San Marcos (*Universidad de San Marcos*).[86] In American Civil Law Jurisdictions, the discipline grew significantly only during the second half of the twentieth century, however. For example, in 1952 the International Congress of Jurists (*Congreso Internacional de Juristas*) met in Peru, and advocated for the need to teach legal history.[87] The following decade, in 1961, during the Second Conference of Latin American Law Schools (*II Conferencia de Facultades Latinoamericanas de Derecho*), the teaching of legal history was again deemed a core element in the curriculum.[88] Abelardo Levaggi mentioned in his seminal *Manual* that Argentina, Chile, Mexico, and Peru were amongst the leaders in legal-historical output.[89] In the Americas, yet beyond American Civil Law Jurisdictions, significant legal-historical output is being developed by Brazilian, Canadian, and US scholars.

Alfonso García-Gallo, from his legal history chair in Spain, stated that legal-historical studies should always be done within the framework provided by a definite community or nation.[90] This should not deter, nevertheless, scholars from undertaking comparisons with the legal developments in other communities or nations, to better characterize, differentiate, and understand the given

83 The 2010 US Census indicated that the total US population was 308,745,538. See Census 2010. Law studies in the US are initiated after completion of undergraduate studies. Accordingly, juris doctor studies at law schools should be considered postgraduate studies in other American jurisdictions, and that might explain the difference in enrolment numbers between Argentina and the US.

84 Pérez-Perdomo 2006, p. 105.

85 See generally Centro de Estudios de la Educación Argentina 2015.

86 Levaggi 1996b, p. 18.

87 Tau Anzoátegui 2010, p. 91.

88 Conferencia de Facultades 1961, p. 95.

89 Levaggi 1996b, p. 23.

90 García-Gallo 1987a, p. 1078.

legal history.[91] The framework could now be extended to all American Civil Law Jurisdictions, such as this study aims to do. In addition, Enrique Aftalión argued in 1963 that all history is universal history.[92] That notwithstanding, in practice, legal history continued to be approached from a national or vernacular vision across American Civil Law Jurisdictions. For example, the leading texts and the curricula in law schools were always linked to the different jurisdictions, by means of the corresponding national adjectives (*v.gr.*, *Historia del Derecho Argentino*, *Historia del Derecho Chileno*).[93]

It is time to extend the study of legal history to a multi-jurisdictional level (*i.e.*, American Civil Law Jurisdictions), having already deepened, to some extent, at the local level.[94] Some comparative legal-historical studies have been made at the multi-jurisdictional level and within the post-independence periods, however. For example, Víctor Tau Anzoátegui[95] correctly highlighted that Bernardino Bravo Lira efficiently explored the area of constitutional law[96] and that Alejandro Guzmán Brito exhaustively explored the area of civil law codification, both with a comparative approach.[97] Furthermore, Ismael Sánchez Bella said, for example, that the work of Jorge Basadre in Peru complied perfectly with the attempt to unveil the common roots and to expand the limits of national legal history, beyond the limits of Peru.[98] An English-language study—sambitious, overarching, and inspirational for other studies such as the one that resulted in this book—was produced by Mirow, when he was able to provide a comparative approach to private law in Latin America across time, while dealing with comprehensively multiple vernacular events.[99]

Comparative interests are rare across American Civil Law Jurisdictions, although they had an early start. In the 1930s, Ricardo Levene had already recognized that the national scope did not suffice when aiming to fully and comprehensively study the Argentine past, and hence, he advocated for expanding the scope towards a greater geographical area: the American world that was linked

91 García-Gallo 1987a, p. 1078.

92 Díaz Couselo 2006, p. 40.

93 Tau Anzoátegui 2010, pp. 46–47. See, for example, the Argentine publication of Levene 1962 and earlier editions.

94 See the claim by Víctor Tau Anzoátegui to extend the study to Ibero-America, and hence include Brazil. Tau Anzoátegui 2010, pp. 48–49.

95 Tau Anzoátegui 2010, p. 49.

96 Bravo Lira 1993.

97 Guzmán Brito 2000.

98 Sánchez Bella 1958, p. 401.

99 Mirow 2004.

with the Iberian Peninsula.[100] Studies on *Indiano* law therefore emerged, since different branches of the same tree had to be looked upon. Accordingly, the American activities of the Spanish and Portuguese crowns have been studied from different perspectives. These studies gained importance with the creation in 1966 of the International Institute of *Indiano* Legal History (*Instituto Internacional de Historia del Derecho Indiano*).[101] The institute promotes the interaction of specialists in the field and has welcomed studies by European and American scholars. An important step was recently taken with the creation of the Latin American Institute of Legal History (*Instituto Latino Americano de Historia del Derecho*) in 2007.[102] The scope of that institute exceeds the *Indiano* period, and offers fertile ground in which American Civil Law Jurisdictions could be further studied. In addition, the activities of the institute may help avoid the isolation of the region from the rest of the academic world, developing a multi-jurisdictional context. It is time to move on and compare jurisdictions in the Americas, this time including the national period. Indeed, José María Díaz Couselo already advocated correctly for a broad study, claiming that "[...] supranational studies may be undertaken, not aiming to be universal, [yet] reduced to a spatial ambit that shares the same influences [...] or undertaken in regards to specific institutions."[103] That is indeed the aim of this book: to focus on a selection of jurisdictions (*i.e.*, Louisiana, Chile, and Argentina) that share similar influences, while focusing on a specific institution (*i.e.*, Ownership Paradigms). Scholars may undertake a multi-jurisdictional approach to study those areas that indeed shared a common core.

A comparative legal historical approach in American Civil Law Jurisdictions should not neglect studies on Native American groups and their legal culture. As this book will show in the chapters that follow, Native American groups are fundamental actors in the shaping of the law, and in the case of property law, they participated in the shaping of the different Ownership Paradigms. A pan-indigenous common discourse has emerged, and aims to reconstruct and enhance the Native American identities within societies that are multicultural and multi-ethnic.[104] Such studies analyze the role and place of the

100 Tau Anzoátegui 1987, pp. 114–115. See also Dagrossa 2010, p. 496; and Pihlajamäki 2014, pp. 124–125.

101 Tanzi 1976, p. 210.

102 See ILAHD 2015. However, Ezequiel Abásolo indicated that the institute was established in 2008. See Abásolo 2009, at § 12.

103 Díaz Couselo 2010, p. 268.

104 Rojas 2002, p. 480.

different Native American groups during the different time periods.[105] A comparative legal historical approach could ultimately assist in further developing Native American studies.

2.3.1.2.1 *Legal Historiography in Louisiana, Chile, and Argentina*

Legal historiography has a long tradition in American Civil Law Jurisdictions. The US state of Louisiana and the republics of Chile and Argentina produced significant legal-historical output, which has built on rich primary sources and authoritative secondary sources.[106] As the references included in the different chapters of this book will show, a multiplicity of scholars has examined the legal history of the three jurisdictions. This section does not aim to be exhaustive, it only aims to present readers with an overview of the status of legal history (*i.e.*, a selection of scholars and forums) in the three jurisdictions.

Louisiana contributed to the development of legal historiography. Elements of legal history—similarly to other American Civil Law Jurisdictions—were taught early in Louisiana within the courses of introduction to law. For example, already in the 1850s, elements of Spanish legal history were taught by the German immigrant Christian Roselius at the University of Louisiana.[107] No institutes in Louisiana address exclusively legal history, yet there are a number of historical institutions that offer a forum for legal historians (*v.gr.*, Louisiana Historical Society, 1835;[108] Louisiana Historical Association, 1889[109]). At the national level, Louisiana legal historians may engage in the activities of the American Society for Legal History, which was established in 1956.[110] Around that same time, legal historians in Louisiana were mainly judges and law professors.[111] Louisiana legal history was considered as inwards looking, since for decades it had been deemed to be distant from the US legal history or Southern history narrative.[112] In the 1960s, US universities started to include legal history within the curriculum of history departments.[113] Legal history continued to be taught in law schools. In Louisiana, due to the coexistence of the civil law and the common law, some professors put special emphasis on the historical

105 Rojas 2002, p. 480.

106 See, for example, the work by Warren M. Billings highlighting the rich sources of Louisiana and areas of potential research. Billings 1983.

107 Parise 2009b, pp. 224–225; and Reich 2007, pp. 80–81.

108 See LHS 2015.

109 See LHA 2015.

110 See ASLH 2015.

111 Fernandez 2001, p. 9.

112 Fernandez 2001, p. 1.

113 Fernandez 2001, pp. 2–3.

background of substantive areas of law, including property.[114] A group of scholars, referred to as "New Louisiana Legal Historians," took the stage and aim to place Louisiana within the broader US narrative.[115] Their main representatives are Warren M. Billings and Mark F. Fernandez, both professional historians rather than trained lawyers.[116] Yet trained lawyers keep developing abundant literature, in the state (*v.gr.*, Vernon V. Palmer, Alain A. Levasseur, Richard H. Kilbourne, Jr.) and abroad (*v.gr.*, John W. Cairns), showing there is likewise an exogenous interest.[117] In addition, Rodolfo Batiza and Robert A. Pascal lead a scholarly debate that will be dealt in depth *infra*;[118] while George Dargo, trained in law and history, provided a unique understanding of the legal and socio-historical events of nineteenth-century Louisiana.[119] The main periodicals that include literature on legal history in Louisiana are the *Louisiana Historical Quarterly* (1917) and *Louisiana History* (1960); while at the national level, the two main forums are the *American Journal of Legal History* (1957)[120] and the *Law & History Review* (1983).

Chile has actively contributed to the development of legal historiography in American Civil Law Jurisdictions.[121] Legal history was taught at Chilean universities already at the turn of the twentieth century.[122] For example, in 1902, legal history was already required in Chile as a mandatory course to obtain a degree in law.[123] The Chilean Institute of Legal History and Roman Law (*Instituto Chileno de Historia del Derecho y Derecho Romano*) was established in 1975, mainly due to the support of the Catholic University of Valparaíso (*Universidad Católica de Valparaíso*).[124] That institute started, therefore, to offer a forum for many scholars participating in the activities of the deemed "School of Chilean Legal History" (*Escuela Chilena de Historia del Derecho*).[125] The main exponents of that "School" are Alamiro de Ávila Martel, Javier Barrientos Grandón, Antonio Dougnac Rodríguez, and the already mentioned Guzmán

114 Reimann & Levasseur 1998, p. 4.
115 Fernandez 2001, p. 14; and Dargo 2009a, pp. xxiii–xxiv.
116 Donlan 2012, p. 70.
117 Dargo 2009a, p. xxvii.
118 See generally 4.5.1.2 of this book.
119 Parise 2011a, p. 631.
120 See AJLH 2015.
121 See generally Dougnac Rodríguez & Vicencio Eyzaguirre 1999–2000.
122 Palma González 2009b, at § 9.
123 Palma González 2009a, p. 45.
124 Palma González 2009b, at f. 17.
125 Palma González 2009b, at f. 17.

Brito.[126] The "School" is interested in a series of themes, amongst others, Roman law and its role in shaping Western legal traditions; and *Indiano* law, as a common element across the Americas.[127] In Chile, legal historical studies were almost exclusively undertaken by scholars who had acquired training in law.[128] The main legal history periodicals in Chile are the *Revista Chilena de Historia del Derecho* (1959) and the *Revista de Estudios Histórico-Jurídicos* (1976).[129] In addition to the scholars mentioned *supra*, and as the sources cited in this book will show, Chile has provided an array of legal historians, amongst many others, Bravo Lira, and Fernando Campos Harriet.[130] Special mention is due Mario Góngora, who was actively engaged with scholars and institutes beyond the borders of Chile.[131] Chilean scholars indeed study legal history beyond their national borders, building a broader context for the understanding both of local and of foreign legal histories. For example, Bravo Lira—as was already mentioned—approached the legal historical aspects of constitutional law in a comparative way, while Guzmán Brito provided perhaps the most authoritative work on the legal history of civil law codification across the Americas.[132]

Argentina has a long and rich legal history tradition. Legal history was taught at Argentine universities towards the end of the nineteenth century. For example, in 1895, legal history was taught at the University of Córdoba (*Universidad de Córdoba*),[133] undeniably one of the cultural cradles of the country. Legal history institutes have been established in Argentina, linking scholars that share similar interest for the discipline. The Legal History Institute (*Instituto de Historia del Derecho*) was established in Buenos Aires in 1936, within the scope of the University of Buenos Aires (*Universidad de Buenos Aires*), following the initiative of Ricardo Levene.[134] The already mentioned Research Institute for Legal History[135] was established in 1973 likewise in Buenos Aires—yet not within the university—and led by Ricardo Zorraquín Becú,[136] offering a forum after the political intervention of the first institute.[137] In Córdoba, the

126 Palma González 2009b, at f. 17.

127 Palma González 2009b, at § 29.

128 Palma González 2009b, at § 9.

129 Palma González 2009b, at § 25 and fn. 17; Levaggi 2013b, p. 7; and RChHD 2015.

130 See generally Levaggi 2013b.

131 Bravo Lira 2000, p. 622.

132 Martinez-Fraga 2008, p. 527.

133 Aspell 2010, p. 16.

134 Tanzi 1992, p. 165; and Levene 1953, p. 108.

135 See generally 2.1 of this book.

136 Tanzi 1992, p. 165.

137 Tanzi 1992, p. 165.

Institute of Legal History and Political Ideas (*Instituto de Historia del Derecho y de las Ideas Políticas*) was established in 1986 within the scope of the National Academy of Law and Social Sciences of Córdoba (*Academia Nacional de Derecho y Ciencias Sociales de Córdoba*), under the leadership of Roberto I. Peña.[138] Recent decades showed new developments in legal-historical studies in Argentina, when a National Association of Legal History Professors and Researchers (*Asociación Argentina de Profesores e Investigadores de Historia del Derecho*) was established in 2005.[139] In Argentina, legal-historical studies were traditionally undertaken by scholars trained mainly in law, though some of these scholars also had history degrees. More recently, historians have gained more access to the discipline, developing new lines of research and occasionally even outnumbering the scholars trained exclusively in law. The main legal history periodicals in Argentina are the *Revista de Historia del Derecho* (1973), *Cuadernos de Historia* (1990), and *Iushistoria* (2005).[140] In addition, early scholarship was published beginning in 1949 in the now interrupted *Revista del Instituto de Historia del Derecho*,[141] a forerunner amongst American Civil Law Jurisdictions.[142] In addition to the previously mentioned scholars, and as the references in this book will show, Argentina provided renowned legal historians, amongst many others, Levaggi, José María Mariluz Urquijo, and Tau Anzoátegui. Argentine scholars show interest for the study of legal history beyond their national borders. For example, Tau Anzoátegui suggested expanding the study of legal history in two directions: Ibero-American legal history and contemporary law.[143] And Levaggi included several years ago references to Member States of Mercosur in his emblematic university textbook.[144] In addition, the proceedings of a 2007 meeting of the National Association of Legal History Professors and Researchers highlighted that legal history should examine the Hispanic-American context.[145]

---

138 See IHDIP 2015.

139 Asociación Argentina de Historia del Derecho 2006.

140 Levaggi 2013b, p. 7.

141 Tanzi 1992, p. 166.

That journal changed names on two occasions: *Revista de Historia del Derecho "Ricardo Levene," Revista del Instituto de Historia del Derecho "Ricardo Levene."* Instituto Gioja 2015.

142 Levaggi 1996b, p. 23.

143 Tau Anzoátegui 2010, p. 78.

144 See, for example, the references to codification in other jurisdictions in Levaggi 1996b, pp. 239–242.

145 Aspell 2010, p. 19.

2.3.2 *Conditions*

American Civil Law Jurisdictions, as other jurisdictions across the globe, share favorable and unfavorable conditions for the development of comparative legal history. Already in 1953, Juan Beneyto Pérez stated in the *Tijdschrift voor Rechtsgeschiedenis* that the Americas at large provided fertile ground for the study of comparative legal history. He suggested first to study clear similarities, and then to study intrinsic and extrinsic differences, looking both at the national and international spheres.[146] The following sections, therefore, aim to increase attention on the most salient conditions for the development of comparative legal history in American Civil Law Jurisdictions.

2.3.2.1 Favorable

American Civil Law Jurisdictions undeniably have favorable conditions for the development of comparative legal historical studies. These jurisdictions provide fertile ground for the implementation of the discipline, and—as will be mentioned again in Chapter 4 of this book—have even been defined by experts as *a comparativist's dream*.[147] There are at least three favorable conditions in these jurisdictions when compared with those in Europe.

A first condition relates to the common roots and the preponderance of a legal system. The common roots go back to the early expansionist movements of the Castilian Crown. Ricardo D. Rabinovich-Berkman clearly explained that "the permanent and important elaboration of common provisions, the exchange of officials amongst the various regions, and the mobility of neighbors, always preserved the reality and the common consciousness of a legal identity."[148] For example, several present-day jurisdictions were part of the same viceroyalties and shared specific elements of the *Indiano* legal order. Common roots should be studied now by scholars, yet during the national periods, hence beyond the *Indiano* period. Those efforts would assist in, amongst other things, the tracing of similarities and differences, and in the identification of issues that survived and others that were eradicated. The circulation of ideas and the flow of paradigms could result from these exercises. The Continental European system of law crosses all American Civil Law Jurisdictions, having been inherited from Spain. There is a common trunk shared by these jurisdictions, and different branches grow from that same tree, mainly starting at the end of the *Indiano* period. The fruits of each branch, during the national period, are to be collected by comparative legal historians. This common root

146 Beneyto Pérez 1953, p. 57.

147 Rosenn 1971, p. 692.

148 Rabinovich-Berkman 2006, p. 241.

or trunk is a clear advantage for American Civil Law Jurisdictions if compared to the situation in Europe, where the common law divide eradicated the idea of a fully shared trunk. It should be noted, however, that this does not imply that comparative legal history is an impossible task across the civil law and common law divide.

A second favorable condition is provided by the existence of a linguistic uniformity. Spanish crosses through all jurisdictions, with the exception of Haiti, where French prevails, and Louisiana where English has prevailed for at least the last 200 years.[149] Linguistic uniformity in American Civil Law Jurisdictions favors daily life and commerce, and facilitates research activities, by simplifying cooperative work and access to output by scholars in other jurisdictions that share the same language. Scholars in these jurisdictions should aim to broaden the horizons of their output, and hence draft their monographic work likewise in the English language, thus inviting feedback from external academic circles, and assisting in showcasing and broadening the output across the globe, especially in the US academic discourse, in jurisdictions that were former Castilian possessions in North America. Other languages should be welcomed by scholars, to further expose and enrich the output in American Civil Law Jurisdictions. Accordingly, scholars should contemplate the Portuguese language as a means to share and enrich their output with Brazilian and Portuguese colleagues. Transatlantic approaches—as will be demonstrated mainly starting in Chapter 4 of this book—will require knowledge of the French language, mainly to assess the impact of codification and of the Exegetical School; and of the German language, mainly to assess the impact of the German Historical School, of Scientific Positivism, and ultimately of Conceptual Jurisprudence.

The potential for cooperation provides a third favorable condition for the development of comparative legal historical studies in American Civil Law Jurisdictions. The potential for cooperation, it should be noticed, also exists in other jurisdictions. The cooperation includes two aspects: the migration of human resources and the promotion of research tools and output.

In 1972, García-Gallo called attention to the need to develop further cooperation for the development of legal history courses.[150] He also called for grants and scholarships to enable studies in other jurisdictions, fostering the acquisition of new skills and knowledge, and the ultimate importation or transfer of that new value into the home jurisdictions.[151] This would naturally achieve

---

149 It should be noted, nevertheless, that archival work in Louisiana, especially for the *Indiano* period, may be undertaken in the abundant Spanish sources.

150 García-Gallo 1987a, p. 1090.

151 García-Gallo 1987a, p. 1090.

an increase in student, faculty, and research mobility, which are already being sensed amongst various American Civil Law Jurisdictions. The migration of students is currently sensed at the graduate level, where students already acquire instruction in the legal history of their home jurisdictions, hence resulting in a more enriching comparative approach to be experienced at the host jurisdiction. Temporary migration at the faculty level—which already exists—should be even further developed by means of additional mobility agreements amongst different universities and research institutes.

The promotion of academic communication is necessary for the further development of comparative legal history. In the words of Michael Hoeflich and Steve Sheppard[152]—who wrote from a US perspective—the "application of digital and internet technology to the publication of legal historical material has given [legal history] an unprecedented boost."[153] Several steps can be taken to further develop academic communication and increase the output of comparative legal historical studies in American Civil Law Jurisdictions. For example, university textbooks should include a comparative approach, placing local legal histories within broader contexts. Course materials similarly could benefit from the advantages in American Civil Law Jurisdictions: a common root or trunk, and linguistic harmony. Expanding horizons should be welcomed, something not foreign to these jurisdictions, where, as already mentioned, Levaggi included references in his university textbook to the legal history of Brazil, Paraguay, and Uruguay. The digitization of archives provides another tool.[154] Digital databases tend to eliminate research boundaries. Furthermore, primary sources may be "transferred" across jurisdictions, at high initial cost, but eventually reaching a very low cost. Finally, the creation of virtual courses may turn into an additional tool to further develop academic communication and increase the output of comparative legal historical studies in American Civil Law Jurisdictions. These courses help develop areas of study without mobility costs. The OZCAN project provides an example of such a course,[155] linking universities in Australia and Canada and aiming to compare the legal evolution of two jurisdictions that were former British territories.[156] The following passage illustrates the value of the endeavor:

152 The claim by Michael Hoeflich and Steve Sheppard was circumscribed to legal history. Hoeflich & Sheppard 2006, p. 24.

153 Hoeflich & Sheppard 2006, p. 24.

154 See, for example, Rocca Mones-Ruiz 2009.

155 See Australian-Canadian Legal History 2015; and Ozcan 2000.

156 McLaren 2003, p. 202.

> In discussions leading to the program its architects saw a firm pedagogical and scholarly basis for the link between Australian and Canadian legal history. Comparing the experience and cultures of two British "settler" colonies allows exploration of similarity and difference along several historical and socio-legal trajectories. If one mission of historical study is to "render the past familiar and the present strange," then the task of comparative legal history-particularly between similarly situated colonies of the same Imperial and legal metropolis-is doubly worthwhile. Notwithstanding the inheritance of English legal tradition, continued fealty to its case authority, subordination to the Privy Council, and other mechanisms of metropolitan "policing" of law in empire, the legal cultures of the colonies were refracted, rather than reflected, through the prism of local needs and conditions. Settlers may have sought to emulate the practices at "home," but the law and its institutions were challenged by situations and contexts that had no parallel in British experiences, and on which British authority was either lacking or inappropriate.[157]

The OZCAN experience could be replicated across American Civil Law Jurisdictions, where the British presence could be replaced by that of Spain.

2.3.2.2 Challenges

American Civil Law Jurisdictions encounter challenging conditions for the development of comparative legal history. These American jurisdictions, when compared with most European jurisdictions, have at least three distinct disadvantages or challenges. These last evolve around aspects of geography, economy, and innovation.

A first challenge relates exclusively to a geographical fact. The size of the American continent, together with the location of main cities in a vertical (North–south) distribution, makes distances significantly large. This fact presents indeed a challenge, if compared with Europe, because mobility requires more resources in American Civil Law Jurisdictions. Great distances not only require more time to bridge, they also demand the allocation of more financial resources. Regrettably, the opportunity cost of a choice does not allow reallocation of those scarce financial resources, such as the needed promotion of academic communication.

A second challenge deals with the economic instability that affects several American Civil Law Jurisdictions. The aforementioned instability burdens academic-mobility opportunities and hampers the scarce research resources.

157 Ozcan 2000, pp. 447–448.

This disadvantage is occasionally visualized clearly in the output, when, for example, digitization projects are delayed or publication of results are postponed. Furthermore, the scarcity of financial resources, combined with economic instability, likewise present an obstacle to teamwork or cooperative work across jurisdictions. Some long- or medium-term projects turn out to be difficult, since it is hard to assess what resources will be available in the near future.

A third challenge relates to an alleged lack of innovation within the curricula of law schools across American Civil Law Jurisdictions. Legal education is traditional in these jurisdictions, consisting mainly of lectures,[158] and hence not fully welcoming the use of the Socratic method or of problem-based learning.[159] Even when changes are being implemented, some authors claim that more innovation should be welcomed. For example, an article recently published in the *Journal of Legal Education* stated that innovative schools in those American jurisdictions continue offering relatively little to foster in students a better understanding of the broader historical and philosophical legal context.[160] Comparative legal history could help in broadening the legal contexts, bringing more interdisciplinary approaches to the teaching and learning of law. The inclusion of historical and comparative law courses in the curriculum will necessarily expand the scope of learning, both in time and space.

2.3.3 *Benefits*

The development of comparative legal history in the Americas could be beneficial on both sides of the Atlantic.[161] From a European perspective, these studies could help to better understand legal developments in American Civil Law Jurisdictions. They could further help explain differences and similarities in the new continent. Scholars occasionally tend to take an overly simplistic approach to the understanding of law in American Civil Law Jurisdictions, and generalizations tend to overshadow completely particularities. A comparative legal historical approach may help reverse that tendency. For example, it is not rare to read that American Civil Law Jurisdictions adopted the *Code Napoléon* during the nineteenth-century codification period. That overly simplistic

158 Montoya 2010, pp. 546–547.

159 A clear example is Louisiana law schools, where the Socratic method prevails, similarly as in other US law schools.

160 Montoya 2010, p. 562.

161 See, for a broader scope of the benefits of comparative legal history, beyond American Civil Law Jurisdictions, the approximation by US scholars. Reimann & Levasseur 1998, p. 15.

statement is currently embedded also in non-legal literature.[162] A detailed study—such as the one previously mentioned on civil law codification by Guzmán Brito—clearly shows that there were local elaborations and pollination from a diversity of texts, especially from Chile and Argentina.

There is a second aspect by which scholars could benefit from the development of comparative legal history across American Civil Law Jurisdictions. A comparative legal historical approach would show that legal problems or occurrences are not unique to a particular jurisdiction or group of jurisdictions. Societies may indeed experience at the same or different time periods similar events: circulation, migration, and flows in society also transfer needs and occurrences. This second aspect could indeed be linked to the idea of a *Recurrence of Legal Cycles*, as expressed by John Henry Wigmore already in 1912. On that occasion, the American jurist noted that "similar problems, methods, abuses, remedies, seem to recur, amidst diverse surroundings."[163] As this book will show in the subsequent chapters, many European legal institutions were reproduced in the Americas, with different results. America could therefore provide more case studies with which to assess the operation of European institutions. American Civil Law Jurisdictions could serve as an open laboratory for study. Manlio Bellomo correctly stated that European legal historians should look into the writings of pre-Independence American jurists; and there they would find a mirror that would help them "better understand the physiognomic traits of European Medieval law."[164] For example, this book will show in Chapter 3 that the royal land grant system in the Americas had its origins in the Iberian Peninsula during the *Reconquista* period, being transplanted to the new continent at the time of the establishment of the first settlements. Outcomes were different on both sides of the Atlantic, and looking at the American experience with royal land grants may provide European scholars with new means to better assess the Peninsular experience.

A third aspect relates to the previously mentioned distinction between central and peripheral jurisdictions. American Civil Law Jurisdictions could be seen—for study purposes—by scholars as peripheral jurisdictions. As this book will show in the subsequent chapters, common elements tie these peripheral jurisdictions together, while other common elements tie them to a central jurisdiction (*i.e.*, Spain). For example, American Civil Law Jurisdictions

162 See the example found in popular culture as represented by Stanley Kowalski in Williams 1947, where that New Orleans citizen incorrectly referred to the *Code Napoléon* in Louisiana.

163 Wigmore 1912, p. xlii.

164 Bellomo 2003, p. 16.

shared a common legal grounding during the entire pre-independence period, and experienced a common perception of their legal identity.[165] The interplay of central and peripheral jurisdictions could be tested in the American context, and new perspectives may result for scholars on both sides of the Atlantic. Furthermore, scholars could look at the American experiences and assess European peripheral jurisdictions in light of the events that took place in the new continent.

Yet the benefits of comparative legal history go beyond the three above-mentioned aspects. Applying the discipline to American Civil Law Jurisdictions could assist in better understanding internal and external local legal histories, while broadening the comprehension of the current local and multi-jurisdictional contexts. Furthermore, more interest in the discipline could enable an increase in the multi-jurisdictional interaction of students, professors, and researchers, while resulting in more clear multi-jurisdictional identities. Collaborative scholarship across jurisdictions could also increase with the reception of the discipline in the different American Civil Law Jurisdictions. It is undeniable that team efforts generate more visibility for the output of projects, finding additional forums for their results. The use of comparative legal history across jurisdictions may help in achieving an increase in team efforts for American or American-related studies. However, as Andrés Botero Bernal stated, preservation of time and space are key when undertaking legal history,[166] and that applies especially when addressing comparative studies, both in American Civil Law Jurisdictions and in Europe. As a corollary, comparison should not imply a lack of attention towards local identities. On the contrary, it should imply a more inclusive perspective that would help reach a needed multi-jurisdictional context.

2.3.4 *Corollary*

Comparative legal history is developing on both sides of the Atlantic. Louisiana, Chile, and Argentina have a long and rich legal history tradition, and some local studies have indeed extended their scopes to other jurisdictions, placing local events within broader contexts. Comparative legal history finds favorable conditions for its development in American Civil Law Jurisdictions. For example, these jurisdictions share language uniformity, common historical roots, and potential for cooperation. Yet these jurisdictions also face challenges, such as those posed by geography, economics, and an alleged lack of innovation. Implementing the discipline across jurisdictions would bring benefits on both

165 Rabinovich-Berkman 2006, p. 241.

166 Botero Bernal 2010, p. 58.

sides of the Atlantic. For example, these studies could help explain differences and similarities in the Americas, could demonstrate that legal problems or occurrences are not unique to particular jurisdictions, and could provide fertile ground to test the distinction into central and peripheral jurisdictions. Comparisons both in time and in space could assist in improving local provisions already existing or those to be created in the future, and could assist in better understanding the circulation of ideas and the flow of paradigms.

2.4 Impact on Transplantation

The implementation of comparative legal history across American Civil Law Jurisdictions can have an impact on legal transplantation or on normative transfers. One of the objectives of comparative legal history is to expand the perspective and the study of legal provisions and ideas, and hence, by comparison both in time and in space, improve local products already existing or those to be created in the future. While analyzing foreign or past legal provisions and ideas, the intent to borrow the provisions and ideas may be triggered. Drafters of local legal products may look at foreign or past legal products and find in the latter a source for their elaborations. If the provisions and ideas seem to be suitable, the drafters may adopt them to their legal framework. That borrowing may develop into what Alan Watson calls "legal transplantation," that is to say, "the moving of a rule or a system of law from one country to another, or from one people to another."[167] It may also develop into a "normative transfer," that is to say, the reception of foreign or past legislative acts, customs, doctrine, and jurisprudence by a borrowing jurisdiction.[168] The borrowing of legal provisions and ideas has experienced in the past decades an exponential growth that results from economic development, democratization, and globalization.[169] The flow of elements has ultimately distorted the theoretical and artificial classification of jurisdictions into legal families.[170] It should be noted that the diffusion of law across jurisdictions, indeed, encounters a number of hurdles that ought to be considered.[171]

The adoption of a foreign or past legal provision and idea makes the recipient its new owner. In turn, the recipient makes the borrowed product new,

167 Watson 1974, p. 21.

168 Parise 2014b, p. 317.

169 Miller 2003, p. 839.

170 Fedtke 2006, p. 434.

171 Niglia 2010, p. 135.

because when the original product interacts with the *ethos* of the recipient society, the interaction results in a body of its own.[172] The borrowing of legal provisions and ideas may be experienced, in addition, both in an active and in a passive way. Active borrowing takes place when one seeks a foreign or past legal provision and idea, and introduces them into a local legal framework. Passive borrowing takes place when a local legal provision and idea are sought after and are introduced into a foreign and legal framework.[173]

The legal borrowing can be either of entire systems or of individual provisions and ideas, and has been around for thousands of years.[174] More than 2,000 years ago, Plato explained that in order to make a new colony successful, legal borrowing could be implemented. The Greek philosopher wrote, in his work *The Laws*, within the conversation of Clin, Athen, and Megil, that the first of his actors claimed that:

> For the greatest part of Crete is attempting at present to establish a certain colony, and orders the Cnossians to take the care of the matter; but the city of the Cnossians (imposes it) upon me and nine others; and at the same time orders us to lay down laws (taken) from this place, if any are pleasing to us, and, if there are any, from elsewhere, making no account of their foreign character, should they appear to be better. Let us then grant this favour to myself and you. After making a selection out of what has been said, let us in our discourse form a state, and colonize it, as if from its commencement; and there will be to us at the same time an inquiry into what we are in search of, and at the same time I may perhaps make use of this formation for the city that is to be.[175]

Ideas tend to spread quickly when they are successfully implemented. Legal ideas are no exception, and jurists have been, and are, familiar with the concept of borrowing ideas.[176] Borrowings, to succeed, must be suitable for the general and legal culture of the borrowing society.[177] In addition, each borrowing experience has its own history that requires examination;[178] and, as defended by Watson in his seminal book, "to a truly astounding degree law is

172 Parise 2012b, p. 71.

173 Parise 2014b, p. 317.

174 Parise 2012b, p. 72.

175 Plato 1852, pp. 119–120. See also Parise 2012b, p. 72.

176 Parise 2012b, p. 71.

177 Del Duca & Levasseur 2010, p. 1.

178 Nelken 2003, p. 459.

rooted in the past."[179] Comparative legal history shows that the borrowing of legal provisions, both passively and actively, occurred with no geographical or temporal limitation. Ibbetson correctly pointed out that normative transfers can represent a break with the past, and the comparative legal historian must first recognize the borrowing and then acknowledge the potential for breaking with the past, hence fully understanding the impact of the transfer.[180]

The study of the circulation of ideas and the flow of paradigms benefits from the understanding of legal borrowings or transplants, these being fundamental elements for the circulation or flow. Legal transplantation may be used as a tool to assess the relation amongst legal systems and the interplay of the influences they exert.[181] It can also assist in tracing the genetic history of legal products.[182] Scholars should note that there are vernacular creations that go beyond legal borrowings, however. For example, Chapters 3 to 5 of this book aim to demonstrate by looking at three jurisdictions the interplay of borrowings and vernacular elaborations. Comparative legal history, therefore, should acknowledge that jurisdictions do not limit themselves to undertaking legal borrowings, they likewise welcome intellectual challenges regarding creation and adaptation.[183] Borrowed products may be subject to criticism in the adopting jurisdiction and consequently applied after further reflection.[184] Original vernacular innovation and borrowings coexist, and ultimately produce distinctive legal products.[185] Identifying examples of that coexistence is one of the main purposes of this book.

2.5 Closing Remarks

Comparative legal history is a valuable discipline for the study of American Civil Law Jurisdictions. This autonomous discipline should ideally evolve initially amongst jurisdictions that have achieved solid studies on their own jurisdictional (*i.a.*, national, state) law. Having achieved a study of local and vernacular identities in those jurisdictions would enable a movement towards

179 Watson 1974, p. 95.
180 Ibbetson 2013, p. 10.
181 Sánchez Echevarría 2014, p. 60.
182 See, again, the reference to "genetics" in Eidenmüller *et al.* 2012, p. 307.
183 Parise 2014b, p. 354.
184 See the Mexican example provided in Keiser 2012, p. 271.
185 Graziadei 2008, p. 474.

a multi-jurisdictional level.[186] For example, comparative legal historical studies could build on the excellent existing studies on *Indiano* law[187] and in the studies that have been undertaken at the jurisdictional level. This book aims to provide an example of such an approach. The US state of Louisiana and the republics of Chile and Argentina have indeed developed a significant legal historiography that can provide fertile ground for the development of comparative legal historical studies.

The chapter first presented comparative legal history as an autonomous discipline. Accordingly, legal history and comparative law were identified as two fundamental building blocks for the autonomous discipline. That same part, furthermore, defined comparative legal history as the study of external and/or internal aspects of law necessarily undertaken across different time periods and jurisdictions. That definition aims to assist in differentiating the disciplinary studies from the studies undertaken exclusively by legal historians and comparatists. The definition, likewise, should be valuable because it requires a movement across the horizontal and vertical axes that are provided by time and space, hence reaching the framework needed to understand fully the circulation of ideas and the flow of paradigms.

The chapter further traced the development of comparative legal historical studies in both European and American Civil Law Jurisdictions. That second part also devoted special attention to the three jurisdictions subject to study, making manifest therefore that Louisiana, Chile, and Argentina have a long and rich legal historiographical tradition. The second part of the chapter presented a set of favorable and challenging conditions. Accordingly, the language uniformity, common historical roots, and potential for cooperation were mentioned as favorable conditions; while geography, economics, and an alleged lack of innovation were pointed out as challenges. Finally, that part addressed some of the main benefits that the study of comparative legal history would have for American Civil law Jurisdictions and beyond.

The chapter, finally, highlighted the interplay of comparative legal history and legal borrowings or transplantation. A study of the circulation of ideas and the flow of paradigms requires understanding of that interplay. Comparative legal history, due to its design across both the horizontal and vertical axes, may necessarily encounter at some point legal borrowings. Neglecting or ignoring those borrowings may be detrimental for the output of comparative legal historians. Law, as previously stated, does not consist of watertight compartments where each jurisdiction experiences its own events unrelated to previous

186 Tau Anzoátegui 2010, p. 49.

187 Tau Anzoátegui 2010, p. 49.

occurrences. Law in a specific time and space should not be regarded as an independent object of study, and watertight studies would provide incomplete understandings of the law. Legal borrowings, transfers, and transplants are therefore of critical importance for the disciplinary value of comparative legal history.

The chapter, above all, aimed to show that an increase in the number of comparative legal historical studies would be beneficial for American Civil Law Jurisdictions. The benefit could also be extended to scholars beyond those jurisdictions. Scholars could gain new perspectives to explain differences and similarities with and within the Americas; while they could grasp—again—that law does not consist of watertight compartments, and that legal occurrences can appear amongst different jurisdictions in an advertently or inadvertently manner.

CHAPTER 3

The Allocation Paradigm of Ownership in American Civil Law Jurisdictions

3.1 Introduction

The interaction of Spanish and Native American cultures within American Civil Law Jurisdictions developed into a unique Ownership Paradigm. An Allocation paradigm of ownership was shaped during the pre-independence period, and started with the arrival of Europeans to the Americas in 1492. That paradigm extended for more than 300 years, until the different new American republics and states dictated their own legislation that dealt with ownership of property, mainly during the nineteenth century. Property was allocated to different actors within that early period, reacting to their different interests at different times. These jurisdictions shared a common legal grounding during the entire period, however.[1] That common ground grew from the constant enactment of common norms, from the exchange of officers amongst regions, and from the internal migration of actors, ultimately resulting in a common perception of legal identity.[2] Understanding the Allocation paradigm of ownership helps better explain many of the existing elements of ownership throughout American Civil Law Jurisdictions.

An uninterrupted chain of Ownership Paradigms developed in American Civil Law Jurisdictions. The Allocation paradigm, being central to this chapter, was the first link in that uninterrupted chain of Ownership Paradigms in American Civil Law Jurisdictions. That link extends mainly during the time period commonly referred to as the Early Modern Period. The second link comprised the Liberal paradigm, which developed mainly during the nineteenth century, together with the legislation that emanated from the new republics and states. The third link comprised the Social Function paradigm, which started to develop at the turn of the century, and took force during the first decades of the twentieth century. A new paradigm, which exceeds the scope of this book, is developing in American Civil Law Jurisdictions, having as the central element the environment. This new link in the uninterrupted chain may be referred to

1 Rabinovich-Berkman 2006, p. 241.

2 Rabinovich-Berkman 2006, p. 241.

 | DOI 10.1163/9789004338203_004

as the Ecological Function paradigm, where there is a duty to conserve and cultivate the land.[3]

The interaction of law and culture shaped the different links in that chain of Ownership Paradigms. The Allocation paradigm was shaped by the interaction of individual actors and society at large with things. A group's social customs and rules dealing with property tended to change when interacting with new social conditions.[4] This chapter deals with the Allocation paradigm of ownership, the first link of the referred chain of Ownership Paradigms. The chapter is divided into six parts. Firstly, the chapter addresses the land relations of Native Americans prior to the arrival of the Spanish explorers and settlers. The communal character that ownership had in those groups is mainly analyzed. Secondly, the chapter addresses the access by Spaniards to the new territories. The main grounds for the Castilian holding of those territories is therefore explained. Thirdly, the chapter deals with the *Indiano* legal order. It therefore identifies the main components of that legal system, and the place of ownership within that order. Fourthly, the chapter focuses on the different interests that different actors had in ownership in American Civil Law Jurisdictions. The interests of the Castilian Crown, the Catholic Church, Native Americans, and settlers are accordingly addressed. Fifthly, the chapter explains how the individual allocation of ownership was undertaken in the Americas. The system of royal land grants is fundamental in that part of the chapter. Sixthly, the chapter explains how the communal allocation of ownership was instrumented during the same time period. The understanding of communal holdings by settlements and Native Americans is central to this part of the chapter. All parts of the chapter devote special attention to the events in the current, that is to say, present-day territories of the US state of Louisiana and the republics of Chile and Argentina. The chapter, above all, aims to show that American Civil Law Jurisdictions shared the Allocation paradigm. It should be noted that abundant contextual information is provided for readers who are not familiar with the Spanish regime in the Americas: that information is needed to fully grasp the place of the Ownership Paradigm in the New World.

3.2 Native American Land Relations

The American continent was inhabited before the arrival of explorers and settlers in 1492. Native American groups—also referred to by part of the legal

3 See generally Bryner 2012; Barnes 2013; and Boulot 2012.

4 Beaglehole 1935, p. 316.

literature as *Indians* or *American Indians*[5]—had shaped their own cultures through centuries,[6] and at the time of encountering the Spaniards they comprised a population of 53 million.[7] These groups had no homogenous culture or legal precepts, and generalizations should therefore be avoided.[8] They considered their living space a holy land, being the central point of, amongst other things, their lives, religion, and culture.[9] Native Americans had a metaphysical vision that was in clear contrast with the predominantly economic and utilitarian vision of the Spaniards.[10]

The original inhabitants lived in a multiplicity of groups, with different governmental and family organizations.[11] The most advanced groups were those of the Aztec, Inca, and Maya, and the least advanced were those inhabiting the Antilles;[12] while groups in the meridional cone of South America presented less centralized societies.[13] Furthermore, most groups occupied reduced geographical spaces, with the exception of advanced groups, such as that of the Inca, which spread across several parts of the Americas.[14] Living environment (*i.a.*, geographical location, language, and economic structure) had an impact on the way those groups understood and developed legal precepts.[15] For example, Nahuatl, which could be considered at some point a *lingua franca* across Mesoamerica, had developed words that had legal effects, such as rights to land and to water.[16]

3.2.1 *America as a Mosaic of Different Legal Systems*

Native American groups had, in the words of García-Gallo, a "mosaic of different legal systems [*derechos*]."[17] Those legal systems had reached different degrees of development, depending on the different groups.[18] The knowledge

5 A recent report by the American Law Institute indicated that Native Americans in North America preferred to be identified by their tribal name, rather than by a generic term such as Indian. ALI 2014, p. 26.
6 Alterini *et al.* 2005, p. 14.
7 Merryman *et al.* 1994. p. 351.
8 See, for example, Alterini *et al.* 2005, p. 11.
9 Riley 2013, p. 369.
10 Levaggi 2004, p. 107.
11 Hermes 2008, p. 32.
12 Levaggi 1994, p. 334.
13 Hidalgo 1997, p. 91.
14 Levaggi 1994, p. 334.
15 Hermes 2008, p. 32.
16 Hermes 2008, p. 38.
17 García-Gallo 1987b, p. 300. See also Levaggi 1994, p. 334.
18 Hermes 2008, p. 38.

of the different components of that mosaic is limited and incomplete, in part because there is a significant lack of written sources for the period that preceded the arrival of the Spaniards.[19] Moreover, early accounts by explorers and official Spanish documents tended to be accompanied by some superstitions and exaggerations, yet describing important aspects of the life and culture of some of the groups.[20] The Western understanding of Native American life therefore tended to simplify reality, by depicting a singular and unified vision, often identified in a romantic manner.[21] It should be noted that the lack of written sources did not imply that Native American groups lacked laws and were ruled only by customs, because the fact of having oral or written legal precepts was indeed indifferent.[22] Even when no written techniques were implemented to record legal precepts, laws were preserved by means of accounts and memory.[23] Examples are found in the unwritten *inkapsimi* (*i.e.*, 'word of the Inca'), which were legal precepts that emanated from the ruler.[24]

Land relations of Native American groups were marked by communal and individual control over property. Native American groups had property rights that aimed to fulfill their needs,[25] while not sharing the European understanding of ownership.[26] Native American land relations included the union with nature and the connection of the community with the territory.[27] Early accounts by Spaniards attested to the existence of communitarian holdings of land amongst members of a determined Native American group, mainly when dealing with crops and pastures.[28] The trend towards holdings in common was related to the conception that those groups had regarding land, marked with spiritual connotations that derived from their religious beliefs.[29] Territorial boundaries were recognized by different groups,[30] and their land was the setting for spiritual and ancestral relations that went beyond the geographical extension,[31] therefore showing that there was indeed a weak idea of individual

19 Levaggi 1994, p. 334. See also Mirow 2004, p. 1.
20 Bunge 1912–1913, I, pp. 18, 21.
21 Bryan 2000, p. 17.
22 Levaggi 1994, p. 336. See also Hermes 2008, p. 38, regarding the existence of law for Native American groups in North America.
23 Rabinovich-Berkman 2006, p. 219.
24 Rabinovich-Berkman 2006, p. 221.
25 Bobroff 2001, p. 1573.
26 Bryan 2000, p. 17.
27 Bryan 2000, p. 26.
28 Altamira y Crevea 1890, p. 301.
29 Alterini *et al.* 2005, p. 41.
30 Hermes 2008, p. 43.
31 Alterini *et al.* 2005, p. 41.

private property.[32] Yet not all land was held in common, because some groups recognized some rights in land, enabling, *inter alia*, transfers of land and inheritance.[33] In some American regions (*v.gr.*, Mesoamerican, Andean), land use and production indicated the coexistence of communal and individual holdings.[34] It should be noticed that most advanced groups granted control over land to the dominant elites, enabling the drawing of parallels with feudalism in Europe.[35] Furthermore, Native American groups that focused on agricultural subsistence acknowledged exclusive rights on land, while hunting and gathering groups required less acknowledgment of such rights.[36] Agricultural groups acknowledged possession of dwellings, weapons, and tools; while a hunting ground was defended by the entire group,[37] where even nomad groups would claim domain over those grounds.[38]

The most advanced Native American groups had elaborated governmental and legal structures, while in the case of the Aztec and the Inca, the leaders tried to respect the private law practices of the groups they conquered.[39] Furthermore, advanced groups had developed agricultural and irrigation techniques that enabled them to supply large armies and urban settlements.[40] In the Aztec Empire, land relations were marked by communal and individual control over property.[41] The male Aztec population of a certain social and political status had a right to possess land,[42] and communitarian holdings were assigned to families subject to their needs.[43] The *calpulli* were community lands that coexisted with tenures of individual possession.[44] The *calpulli* consisted of extended families (from 50 to 500), where land was distributed amongst families that could benefit from the use of the tracts.[45] The Inca Empire also had elaborated structures. In that Empire, land was under the rule of the Inca,[46]

32 Alterini *et al.* 2005, p. 42.
33 Bobroff 2001, p. 1571.
34 Brito Figueroa 1982, pp. 16–17.
35 Ankersent & Ruppert 2006, pp. 76–77.
36 Bobroff 2001, p. 1573.
37 Bunge 1912–1913, I, p. 54.
38 Levaggi 1987, p. 211.
39 Levaggi 1994, p. 336.
40 Barraclough 1973, p. 3.
41 Mirow 2004, p. 3.
42 Ankersent & Ruppert 2006, p. 77.
43 Ankersent & Ruppert 2006, p. 77.
44 Brito Figueroa 1982, p. 17.
45 Merryman *et al.* 1994, p. 360.
46 Levaggi 1987, p. 210.

though some land would be held commonly in an *ayllu*.[47] This pre-Incan structure enabled Native American groups to benefit from the use of the land, while the property would be in the hands of the Inca.[48] In the *ayllu*, tracts were divided into three areas: one for the state, one for religious ceremonies, and one for the community.[49] Nevertheless, within the *ayllu* the private property of dwellings, fruit trees, and domestic animals was respected.[50] Individual holdings of land were likewise possible in this Empire, when the Inca granted tracts of land to those subject to favors.[51] A final note should clarify that the Inca Empire was far from being what today is known as a socialist society. The Inca never aimed to distribute benefits and duties equally amongst Native Americans: the aim was always to benefit an oligarchic group through the work of all members of society.[52]

3.2.2 *Louisiana, Chile, and Argentina within the Mosaic*

The present-day territories of Louisiana, Chile, and Argentina were inhabited by a diversity of Native American groups. Generalizations in these jurisdictions should be also avoided, yet some information may be provided as an illustration. Native American groups in Louisiana[53] were divided mainly into six families or language communities: Atakapan, Caddoan, Chitimachan, Muskhogean, Natchezan, and Tunican.[54] Groups lived in different geographical areas and used their own languages, though most members of all groups understood that of the Muskhogean.[55] Interaction amongst groups was generally peaceful,[56] and their structures were divided into smaller clusters.[57] In Louisiana, Native American groups tended to settle on the riversides, to access fertile grounds and facilitate communication.[58] The area occupied by each of the six Native American groups was not clearly demarcated, yet there was a common

47 Ankersent & Ruppert 2006, p. 78.
48 Ankersent & Ruppert 2006, p. 78.
49 Ankersent & Ruppert 2006, p. 78; and Levaggi 2004, pp. 109–110.
50 Ruíz-Giménez 1961, p. 84.
51 Mirow 2004, p. 6.
52 Rabinovich-Berkman 1990, p. 22.
53 For general information on the Native American groups of Louisiana, see Kunkel 1951 and Smith 1996. See also the study in Weber 1992, which is not limited to Louisiana.
54 Davis 1978, p. 4.
55 Davis 1978, p. 4.
56 Davis 1978, p. 7.
57 Davis 1978, p. 4.
58 Kunkel 1951, p. 178.

understanding that groups would not hunt or fish in the areas of the other groups.[59]

Several Native American groups lived in Chile (*i.a.*, Aymara, Mapuche) at the time the Spaniards arrived in the Americas.[60] The Mapuche, for example, lived in the southern Andes, extending from the valley of the Aconcagua to the island of Chiloe.[61] Some of the Mapuche groups practiced shifting agriculture that deterred them from settling and increasing population density, and that practice even developed in occasional warfare amongst groups.[62] The term *mapu* represented the dwelling and agricultural domain of a community over a tract of land, which was distinguished from the vacant tract, referred to as *tue*.[63] There was a link between the residents and the communal lands,[64] and therefore property of the *mapu* presented parallels with the *calpulli* of the Aztec and the *ayllu* of the Inca.[65]

There were at least 58 Native American groups that lived in the present-day territory of Argentina (*i.a.*, Matacos, Quilmes).[66] The family and property structure of each group depended on their production techniques and development.[67] There were three types of land relations for these Native American groups of present-day Argentina: (i) in the North-Western part, some groups were under the control of the Inca, and therefore had the *ayllu* tracts, with one of the three areas reserved for the community;[68] (ii) in the North-Eastern part, some tracts were divided for the use of families individually and other tracts were divided for the use of the community at large;[69] and (iii) in the Central-South part, inhabited by a number of nomad groups, with the ability to benefit from hunting, fishing, and gathering.[70] In the period prior to the arrival of the Spaniards, the groups in the present-day Argentine territory had a tendency towards holding land in common, while individual property was mainly reserved

59 Davis 1978, p. 7.

60 See generally the clear overview, with links to the current scenario in Chile, in Instituto de Estudios Indígenas 2003.

61 Hidalgo 1997, p. 92.

62 Hidalgo 1997, p. 107.

63 Inostroza Córdova 2011, p. 101.

64 Inostroza Córdova 2011, p. 113.

65 Inostroza Córdova 2011, p. 107.

66 Bunge 1912–1913, I, pp. 31–33. For information on the different groups that inhabited the territory of present-day Argentina, see, amongst others, Alterini *et al.* 2005, pp. 14–39.

67 Bunge 1912–1913, I, p. 53.

68 Rosti 2004, p. 78.

69 Rosti 2004, p. 78.

70 Rosti 2004, p. 78.

to movables.[71] It should be noted that several Native American groups inhabited areas that spread between the present-day territories of both Chile and Argentina (*v.gr.*, Selk'nam, Mapuche).[72]

3.2.3 *Corollary*

Land relations of Native American groups were indeed marked by communal and individual holdings. The arrival of Spanish explorers and settlers did not bring to an end the communal and individual control over property. Some Native American laws and customs prevailed, as long as they would not contradict the Catholic faith, Natural Law, and the Crown's jurisdiction.[73] Accordingly, the communal holdings prevailed, together with other Native American institutions, such as the *cacicazgo*, which allowed the rule by a chief over a group.[74] This coexistence of Native American and Peninsular legal precepts, as mentioned by Jan Kleinheisterkamp, provided the first challenge for comparative studies in American Civil Law Jurisdictions.[75] Later, in the period of the new republics and states during the nineteenth century, the emergence of a Liberal paradigm of ownership motivated the elimination of many of the holdings in common, aiming to enhance the individualistic character of ownership.[76]

3.3 Spanish Access to Lands in the Americas

Indiano is the term to be used when referring to the period of time that elapsed between the first Spanish possessions in America that accompanied the fifteenth-century European arrival until the independence by the different republics and states during the early nineteenth century. Colonialism took the main stage only starting in the seventeenth century. Accordingly, the early expansionist movements of the Castilian and Portuguese crowns may be defined as foundational,[77] or within the scope of this chapter, may be defined

71 Alterini *et al.* 2005, p. 40.

72 For information on the Native Americans of Chile and Argentina, see Hidalgo 1997, pp. 91–117.

73 Levaggi 1996b, p. 170.

74 Law 3, Title 7, Book 6 of the *Recopilación de Leyes de Indias* of 1680 instructed the preservation of the way in which the chief of a group (*cacique*) was to be succeeded. The text in Spanish read: "que ſe guarde la coſtumbre en la ſuceſsion de los Cacicazgos." Recopilación de Indias 1680, II, at f. 219v. See also Levaggi 1996b, p. 170.

75 Kleinheisterkamp 2008, p. 264.

76 Levaggi 1990b, p. 260.

77 Bravo Lira 1989, p. 193.

as a means to allocate the recently discovered territories. Bravo Lira depicted clearly that scenario, highlighting that the early movements aimed to the settlement and creation of new societies, with their own cultures, being different from that of European and Native American groups, yet building on the preexisting conditions on both sides of the Atlantic.[78] This explains why the term used to refer to the events at that time in the Americas is *Indiano* and not colonial.[79] *Indiano* aimed to explain the events that took place in the Indies, the name given by Europeans to the Americas.[80] *Indiano* also aimed to distinguish the events that took place solely in Spanish America from the events that took place in Europe.[81] This term likewise distinguished the pre- and post-discovery events in America.[82] The *Indiano* period therefore extends from 1492 until the independence of the different American republics and states during the nineteenth century,[83] falling mainly within the Early Modern Period. Accordingly, the term "Colonial" should be avoided when possible, and replaced by the more suitable *Indiano*.[84] This chapter will show that the term *Indiano* was used by the different actors during the period under study, and that this chapter does not suggest an anachronistic use of the term. For example, legislation and the writings of scholars referred to *Indiano*, especially since the seventeenth century.[85]

3.3.1 *Territories as Royal Holdings of Castile*

All discovered territories were a royal holding (*regalía*) of the Crown of Castile. The monarchs did not own those territories, only having dominium and jurisdiction over them, something similar to the eminent domain of which Hugo Grotius would later speak in the early seventeenth century.[86] Monarchs therefore had a primordial ownership, being at a merging point between the Medieval—more absolute—"*señorío*" and the Modern "sovereignty."[87] The *Recopilación de Leyes de Indias* of 1680—the authoritative compilation of *Indiano* laws that will be further explained *infra*—stated in law 1, Title 1, Book 3 that the "Occidental Indies shall always be united to the Crown of Castile and may not

78 Bravo Lira 1989, p. 193.
79 Bravo Lira 1989, p. 194.
80 Bravo Lira 1989, p. 193.
81 Bravo Lira 1989, p. 193.
82 Bravo Lira 1989, p. 193.
83 Bravo Lira 1989, p. 193.
84 Bravo Lira 1989, p. 193.
85 Bravo Lira 1989, pp. 193–194.
86 Dougnac Rodríguez 1994, p. 400.
87 Dougnac Rodríguez 1994, p. 400.

be alienated."[88] Furthermore, law 14, Title 12, Book 4 of the same 1680 text stated that monarchs held all territories,[89] while that royal holding extended to the surface and underground.[90] These were part of the Crown of Castile, and were not owned individually by the monarchs, hence explaining the royal interest in exploiting the land.[91] Accordingly, any possible rights of others on the land had to be granted by the monarch, by means of a grace (*gracia*).[92] This understanding was ratified in the seventeenth century by the renowned scholar Juan de Solórzano Pereira in his *Política Indiana*. Title 12 of Book 6, on the rights of the Royal Treasury on lands—while drawing parallels with the situation in the Iberian Peninsula—stated that monarchs had a *regalía* on the American territories, and accordingly, lands were and should be held by the Crown.[93] It should be highlighted that recognizing the Crown as the holder and allocator of land may be seen as an early emergence of the idea of a nation-state.[94]

The royal holding by the Castilian Crown found grounding at least on three points. The previously mentioned law 1, Title 1, Book 3 of the 1680 *Recopilación* aimed to showcase the grounds for the royal holding, and it stated that: "by Donation of the Sacred Apostolic See, and other just and legitimate titles, we are Lords of the Occidental Indies."[95] The royal holding by the Castilian Crown

---

88 The text in Spanish read: "Que las Indias Occidentales eſtèn siempre unidas à la Corona de Caſtilla, y no ſe puedan enagenar." Recopilación de Indias 1680, II, at f. 1.

89 The text in Spanish read: "Por haver Nos ſucedido enteramente en el Señorio de las Indias, y pertenecer á nueſtro Patrimonio y Corona Real los valdios, ſuelos y tierras, que no eſtuvieren concedidos por los ſeñores Reyes nueſtros predeceſſores, ó por Nos, ó en nueſtro nombre[...]." Recopilación de Indias 1680, II, at f. 103v.

It should be noted that the law was interpreted by some scholars as not meaning necessarily the nationalization of all land. See Mariluz Urquijo 1970, p. 155; and Mariluz Urquijo 1978, p. 22.

90 Daract 2005–2007, p. 25.

91 Cueto 1999, p. 85.

92 Ots Capdequí 1946, p. 41.

93 The text in Spanish read: "[...] las tierras, prados, paſtos, montes, y aguas, que por particular gracia, y merced ſuya, ſe hallaren concedidas à las ciudades, villas, ò lugares de las meſmas Indias, ò à otras comunidades, ò perſonas particulares dellas, todo lo demas de aſte genero, y eſpecialmente lo que eſtuviere por romper, y cultivar, es y debe ſer de ſu Real Corona, y dominio [...]." (Solórzano Pereira (de) 1703, p. 511)

See also Ots Capdequí 1946, p. 88.

94 Cueto 1999, p. 84.

95 The text in Spanish read: "Por Donacion de la Santa Sede Apoſtolica, y otros juſtos y legitimos titulos, ſomos Señor de las Indias Occidentales, Islas y Tierra firme del mar Occeano, deſcubiertas, y por deſcubrir, y eſtán incorporadas en nueſtra Real Corona de Caſtilla." Recopilación de Indias 1680, II, at f. 1.

found grounding, firstly, in the Capitulations (*Capitulaciones*) of Santa Fe, by which Christopher Columbus agreed with the monarchs on April 17, 1492, the extent of his expeditionary rights.[96] These capitulations were not a contract, because they were only a grace by which the monarchs gave to Columbus the petitions he had made, as long as he would comply with his project of sailing west towards India.[97] Columbus aimed with his petitions to gain, amongst other things, nobility status, privileges, honor, and dignity.[98]

The royal holding found grounding, secondly, in a series of papal bulls.[99] These official papal communications—with lead seals (*bullas*) affixed to them—allocated different geographical areas for the commercial and evangelization activities of the Castilian and Portuguese crowns.[100] These bulls were the donations referred to by the abovementioned law of the 1680 text. Three bulls were dated May 3 and 4, 1493,[101] and aimed to bring to similar standing the pretensions of the Castilian Crown with those of the Portuguese Crown.[102] The *Inter caetera*[103] of May 3 established sovereignty in lands not previously occupied by other Christian monarchs;[104] while the *Eximiae*

96 See the text of the Capitulations in the version preserved in the Archives of the Crown of Aragon, available at Santa Fe Capitulations 1492. See also the text in Morales Padrón 1979, pp. 54–55.

97 Morales Padrón 1979, p. 50.

The relevant part of the text in Spanish read: "Las cosas suplicadas e que Vuestras Altezas dan e otorgan a don Christoval de Colon, en alguna satisfacion de los que ha descubierto en los Mares Oceanas y del viage de agora, con el ayuda de Dios, ha de fazer por ellas en servicio de Vuestras Altezas [...]." Morales Padrón 1979, p. 54.

98 Morales Padrón 1979, p. 49.

99 This chapter addresses only three bulls (*i.e.*, first and second *Inter caetera* and the *Eximiae devotionis*). There were, however, other bulls that preceded them (mainly referring to Portugal), and other bulls that aimed to further explain the three previously mentioned. Amongst those other bulls, it is possible to mention *Dudum siquidem* (September 26, 1493), *Piis fidelium* (June 25, 1493), *Mius falciti* (June 8, 1505), and *Universalis ecclesiae* (1508). See Cruz Barney 2012, p. 71; and Sánchez Bella *et al.* 1992, p. 119.

For a comprehensive study of the Bulls of Pope Alexander VI, see García-Gallo 1987c.

100 Seckinger 1984, p. 56; and Levaggi 1994, p. 337.

101 There is debate on the date of the different bulls. See Sánchez Bella *et al.* 1992, p. 117.

102 On the parallels between the three Castilian bulls and the three Portuguese bulls, see García-Gallo 1977, at § 1191.

103 The texts in Latin and Spanish of the bulls *Inter caetera* of May 3 and 4 are available at García-Gallo 1987c, pp. 623–633.

104 The relevant part of the text in Latin read: "[...] omnes et singulas terras et insulas praedictas, sic incognitas et hactenus per nuntios vestros repertas et reperiendas imposterum,

devotionis[105] stated that evangelization was the reason for permitting that sovereignty,[106] and it granted no lesser rights than those previously established for the Portuguese Crown.[107] Finally, the second *Inter caetera* of May 4, set out the geographical scope of the rights and duties of the Castilian Crown.[108] That bull placed a north–south line 100 leagues west of the Azores and Cape Verde islands, and all territories west of that line, not occupied by a Christian monarch by the Christmas of 1492, would since then belong to the Castilian Crown.[109]

---

quae sub dominio actuali temporali aliquorum dominorum christianorum constitutae non sint [...]." García-Gallo 1987c, p. 627.

See also Cruz Barney 2012, p. 70.

105 The text in Latin and Spanish of the bull *Eximiae devotionis* is available at García-Gallo 1987c, pp. 633–636.

106 The relevant part of the text in Latin read: "Eximiae devotionis sinceritas et integra fides, quibus Nos et Romanam reveremini Ecclesiam, non indigne merentur, ut ilia vobis favorabiliter concedamus, per quae sanctum et laudabile propositum vestrum et opus inceptum in quaerendis terris et insulis remotis ac incognitis Indies melius et facilius ad honorem omnipotentis Dei, et imperii christiani propagationem, ac fidei catholicae exaltationem prosequi valeatis [...]." (García-Gallo 1987c, p. 633)

See Sánchez Bella *et al.* 1992, p. 117.

107 Cruz Barney 2012, p. 70.

The relevant part of the text in Latin read: "vobis ac heredibus et successoribus vestris praedictis, ut in insulis et terris per vos seu nomine vestro hactenus repertis huisusmodi et reperiendis in posterum, omnibus et singulis gratis, privilegiis, exemptionibus, libertatibus, facultatibus, immunitatibus, litteris et indultis Regibus Portugalliae concessis huismodi, quorum omnium tenores ac si de verbo ad verbum praesentibus insererentur haberi volumus pro sufficienter expressis et insertis, uti potiri et gaudere libere et licite possitis et debeatis in omnibus et per omnia perinde ac si omnia illa vobis ac heredibus et successoribus vestris praefatis specialiter concessa fuissent, auctoritate apostolica tenore presentium, de specialis dono gratiae indulgemus, illaque in omnibus et per omnia ad vos heredesque ac successores vestros praedictos extendimus pariter et ampliamus, ac eisdem modo et forma perpetuo concedimus, non obstantibus constitutionibus et ordinationibus apostolicis, necnon omnibus illis quae in litteris Portugalliae Regibus concessis huiusmodi concessa sunt non obstare, ceterisque contrariis quibuscumque." (García-Gallo 1987c, p. 634)

108 García-Gallo 1987c, p. 627; and Sánchez Bella *et al.* 1992, p. 117.

109 Cruz Barney 2012, p. 70.

The relevant part of the text in Latin read: "[...] omnes insulas et terras firmas inventas et inveniendas, detectas et detegendas versus occidentem et meridiem fabricando et constituendo unam lineam a polo arctico, scilicet septentrione, ad polum antarcticum, scilicet meridiem, sive terrae firmae et insulae inventae et inveniendae sint versus Indiam aut versus aliam quancunque partem, quae linea distet a qualibet insularum quae vulgariter nuncupantur de los Azores et Cabo Verde centum leucis versus occidentem et meridiem.

The papal donations resulted from a request of the Catholic Monarchs (*Reyes Católicos*) to Pope Alexander VI.[110] The papal bulls instructed that the Catholic Monarchs, Ferdinand II (Fernando II) of Aragon and Isabella I (Isabel I) of Castile, held the discovered territories as conjugal property, yet upon the death of either of them, the lands would be held solely by the ruler of the Castilian Crown.[111] The Catholic Monarchs aimed to reach a similar standing to that of the Portuguese Crown, and to prevent control by John II (João II) of Portugal of the new territories.[112] The bulls further served as titles of sovereignty and evangelization for the Castilian Crown; they also served to place Castilian monarchs as vicars of the Catholic Church in the Americas; and they were important components of the political interplay that took place between Rome, Spain, and Portugal after the discovery of the new territories.[113] The extension of the discovered territories motivated negotiations between the Castilian and Portuguese crowns to settle their exclusive zones of discovery and navigation.[114] Accordingly, the Treaty of Tordesillas was subscribed on June 7, 1494, later ratified by Pope Julius II with the papal bull *Ea quae pro bono* of January 24, 1506.[115] That treaty, amongst other points, moved the imaginary north–south line to 370 leagues west of the Azores and Cape Verde islands,[116] and—as very visually

---

Ita quod omnes insulae et terrae firmae repertae et reperiendae, detectae et detegendae a prefata linea versus occidentem et meridiem per alium Regem aut Principem christianum non fuerint actualiter possessae usque ad diem Nativitatis domini nostri Ihesu Christi proxime praeteritum, a quo incipit annus presens millesimus quadringentesimus nonagesimus tertius, quando fuerunt per nuntios et capitaneos vestros inventae aliquae predictarum insularum [...]." (García-Gallo 1987c, pp. 627–628)

110 Bravo Lira 1989, p. 194.

111 Cairns 2015, pp. 46–47.

112 Cruz Barney 2012, p. 69.

113 Sánchez Bella *et al.* 1992, p. 117.

114 Cruz Barney 2012, p. 71.

115 Cruz Barney 2012, p. 71.

The text in Latin and Spanish of the bull *Ea quae pro bono* is available at García-Gallo 1987c, pp. 654–656.

The Spanish Crown tried to document its rights. On November 4, 1605, a notarial act drafted in Valladolid stated that the King of Spain had bought from the descendants of Moctezuma, represented by Don Juan de Toledo, all the pretentions they had and could have over the Empire of (present-day) Mexico. The King granted a pension in consideration, and that amount was paid until the year 1820. Zavala 1935, p. 20.

116 Cruz Barney 2012, p. 71.

The relevant part of the text in Spanish read: "[...] Sus Altezas plaze, é los dichos sus procuradores en su nombre, é por virtud de los dichos sus poderes, otorgaron é consintieron,

described by Ron Seckinger—it "cut off the eastern 'hump' of [present-day] Brazil from the rest of South America."[117] That would remain for centuries the boundary between Spanish and Portuguese claims in the Americas.[118]

3.3.1.1 Spanish Scholasticism and the Right to Conquest and Just War

The royal holding found grounding, thirdly, in the right to conquest and just war.[119] Accordingly, the prolonged process of conquest and settlement also provided further grounding to justify the royal holding.[120] The prevailing *Ius commune* in Europe stated that conquering monarchs should have *potestas* over the discovered territories and inhabitants.[121] Scholars (amongst others, Francisco de Vitoria, Alberico Gentili, Grotius) advocated for that understanding, providing support to the claims of sovereignty and taking by the different monarchs.[122]

The Spanish Scholasticism of the sixteenth century, also called Neo-Scholasticism, was important in defending the right to conquest and just war.[123] Spanish Scholasticism was a unique production of minds, something

que se haga é señale por el dicho mar Océano una raya, ó línea derecha de polo á polo, convien á saber, del polo ártico al polo antartico, que es de Norte á Sul, la qual raya ó línea se aya de dar, é dé derecha, como dicho es, á trecientas é setenta leguas de las islas del Cabo Verde, hacia la parte del Poniente, por grados ó por otra manera como mejor y mas presto se pueda dar, de manera que no sean mas, é que todo lo que hasta aquí se ha fallado é descobierto, é de aquí adelante se hallare, é descobriere por el dicho señor de Portugal, é por sus navíos, asy islas como tierra firme, desde la dicha raya, é línea dada en la forma susodicha, yendo por la dicha parte del Levante dentro de la dicha raya á la parte del Levante, ó del Norte, ó del Sul della, tanto que no sea atravesando la dicha raya, que esto sea, é finque, é pertenezca al dicho señor rey de Portugal é á sus subcesores, para siempre jamas, é que todo lo otro, asy islas, como tierra firme, halladas y por hallar, descobiertas y por descobrir, que son ó fueren halladas por los dichos señores rey é reyna de Castilla, é de Aragón, etc., é por sus navios desde la dicha raya dada en la forma susodicha, yendo por la dicha parte del Poniente, después de pasada la dicha raya hacia el Poniente, ó el Norte, ó el Sul della, que todo sea, é finque, é pertenezca á los dichos señores rey é reyna de Castilla, de León, etc., é á sus subcesores para siempre jamas [...]." (Aranda 1890, p. 11)

117 Seckinger 1984, p. 57.

118 The boundary experienced minor shifts that were eventually accepted and found grounding in the theory of effective occupation (*uti possidetis de facto*). Seckinger 1984, pp. 57–58.

119 Daract 2005–2007, p. 25; Sánchez Bella *et al.* 1992, p. 345; and Levaggi 1994, p. 337.

120 Cueto 1999, p. 85.

121 Cueto 1999, p. 109; and Bravo Lira 1989, p. 195.

122 Burger & Frymer 2013, p. 11.

123 Dougnac Rodríguez 1994, pp. 34–53.

not seen before in legal history.[124] The Neo-Scholastics advocated a close connection between law and theology. Acts were judged exclusively by their moral significance; while issues were appraised not solely from a social or political perspective, but as cases of conscience.[125] These scholars then pursued the identification of a superior law that would conduit cohabitation of different societies, such as that of Europeans with non-Christian Native Americans, where the *Ius commune* could not be solely invoked.[126] Amongst the main exponents of the Spanish school of thought were: Alfonso de Castro, Bartolomé de las Casas, Juan de Mariana, Luis de Molina, Domingo de Soto, Juan Ginés de Sepúlveda, Francisco Suárez, and Gabriel Vázquez.[127]

De Vitoria,[128] called by many the founder of international law,[129] was one of the main exponents of Spanish Scholasticism. He was an authority in legal affairs in his time, and very popular throughout Europe.[130] De Vitoria was a Dominican priest who occupied, starting in 1526,[131] a chair of theology[132] at the University of Salamanca (*Universidad de Salamanca*),[133] and who had never been in America.[134] While delivering his lectures (*lecciones*) in Salamanca, his students and disciples[135] drafted class notes that turned out to be valuable documents called *relecciones*.[136] The first and the last *relecciones* are missing, but

---

124 They were studied, amongst many others, by Ángel Losada, James Brown Scott (who translated *Las Partidas* into English), and Lewis Hanke. See Marks 1990, p. 14; and Hanke 1986.

125 Castro y Bravo (de) 1955, p. 173.

126 Guzmán Brito 2000, p. 78.

On the understanding of property by members of the Spanish Scholasticism (with special focus on de Vitoria), see López 2008; Renoux-Zagamé 1987, pp. 94–97; and de los Mozos 1993, pp. 30–41. See also the approximation to the topic in Grossi 1992d.

127 Levaggi 1996b, p. 113.

128 Pagden & Lawrance 1991, p. xxix-xxx. For further readings on de Vitoria, see Phillipson 1915, p. 176.

129 See, for example, Phillipson 1915, p. 197; and Scott 1928, p. 139.

130 Even Henry VIII of England referred to de Vitoria about his divorce. Phillipson 1915, p. 177.

131 Hernández 1992, p. 1031.

132 De Vitoria occupied the chair of theology at Salamanca from 1526 to 1546. Phillipson 1915, p. 176.

133 The University of Salamanca had been created in 1212 by Alphonse IX (Alfonso IX), who was the grandfather of Alphonse X the Wise (Alfonso X el Sabio). By the mid-sixteenth century, 5,000 students attended courses there, and 70 professors occupied chairs. Phillipson 1915, p. 176.

134 Watson 2006, p. 504.

135 By the year of his death, at least 24 renowned professors had been his disciples. Hernández 1992, p. 1041.

136 Phillipson 1915, p. 177.

13 have survived.[137] The best known *relecciones* are entitled *On the American Indians* (*De indis*) and *On the Law of War* (*De indis relectio posterior, sive de iure belli*), dictated in 1539.[138] De Vitoria spoke of a reciprocal *jus inter gentes*[139] or law of nations: a law of nations that not only forced a pact or agreement among men, but also created the force of law for the World as a whole.[140] He claimed that transgressions to that law of nations by Native Americans could serve to justify the Spanish conquest and hegemony in the Americas.[141] According to the *jus inter gentes*, some basic duties were imposed (universally binding) on the Native American societies.[142] Among them were: (i) to respect natural society and fellowship, by which Spaniards should be allowed to travel, if they did no harm, within the American territories; (ii) to permit a free and open commerce within the Americas and with the European immigrants (*i.e.* if a Native American could dig for gold, the Spanish should likewise be allowed, as long as they did no harm); and (iii) to propagate Christianity, by allowing the preaching of the gospel.[143] After an analysis of the situation, de Vitoria concluded that if Native Americans did not obey the basic duties, Spaniards had the right to declare a just war on them.[144] The writings of de Vitoria, and those of other members of the Spanish Scholasticism, were alternatively used as means to provide support or opposition to different claims of sovereignty.

3.3.2 *Louisiana, Chile, and Argentina as Royal Holdings of Castile*

The present-day territories of Louisiana, Chile, and Argentina were also Castilian holdings. Louisiana was, at alternate periods, under Spanish and French control.[145] Spaniards were the first to explore the region, starting in the sixteenth century.[146] Later, during the following century, France expanded its presence in the Americas,[147] when René Robert Cavelier took possession

---

137 Hernández 1992, p. 1039.

138 Pagden & Lawrance 1991, p. 231, 293.

139 It is said that de Vitoria was the first to use the technical term *jus inter gentes*. Scott 1928, p. 139.

140 Williams 1983, p. 77.

141 Williams 1983, p. 70.

142 Williams 1983, p. 79.

143 Williams 1983, pp. 79–80, 82.

144 Williams 1983, p. 83.

145 For a brief overview of the oscillations in Louisiana, see Parise 2014c, pp. 314–315. For a more exhaustive study of the oscillations, see Parise 2013a, pp. 29–55.

146 de la Harpe 1851, pp. 9–10. See also Fortier 1966–1985, I, pp. 3–10.

147 See generally Gayarré 1903, I–II.

of the lower region of the Mississippi River, naming it *Louisiane*.[148] In 1762, France ceded the territory to Spain.[149] Seven year later, Spain implemented the *Indiano* system of government and replaced the French laws.[150] Hence, Peninsular laws were since then the law in Louisiana.[151] That province was subordinate to the Captaincy General of Cuba for military and political matters, and received financial subsidy for support from the Viceroyalty of New Spain.[152] In 1800, Napoleon I (Napoléon I) secured the return of Louisiana to France.[153] The territory would live briefly under French domain, because during the first days of May 1803,[154] the Treaty of Paris was settled, resulting in the Louisiana Purchase.[155] In December of that same year,[156] the French flag was replaced by the flag of the US in Louisiana.[157] The first proclamation of William C.C. Claiborne, then Commissioner, was to preserve the laws that applied at the time of the Louisiana Purchase[158] (*i.e. Indiano* laws and the French *Code noir*).

The present-day territory of Chile was formerly a possession of the Castilian Crown. In 1536, Diego de Almagro led the first European expedition to the valley of Quillota, also called Chile.[159] Starting in 1541, the territory would comprise the Captaincy General of Chile,[160] which would then be a dependent of the Viceroyalty of Peru.[161] In September 1810, inhabitants in the region held an open meeting aiming to bring local certainty on the scenario faced in Spain by Ferdinand VII (Fernando VII), and that resulted in one of the first steps

148 Davis 1978, p. 19. See also Lobingier 1932, p. 174.

149 See Hoffman 1992, pp. 60–64. See generally Andreu Ocariz 1975.

150 See the analysis in Batiza 1962.

151 Levasseur 1994, p. 382. There is some debate on the abrogation of French law. The memoirs of Pierre C. Laussat (Papeles de Cuba, Legajo, 220. 5 Luisiana), however, include a document that seems to put an end to the debate. Levasseur 1996, pp. 8–12, 34–35.

152 Beers 1989, p. 26. See also the clear flowcharts illustrating the administration and court system for Louisiana in Din & Harkins 1996, pp. 100–101.

It was noted that, by 1781, the territories of Louisiana, Mobile, Pensacola, and West Florida were part of a new Captaincy General. McGinty 1951, p. 87.

153 Martin 1975, p. 286.

154 Marshall 1914, pp. 7–8.

155 Text available in English in Louisiana Purchase Treaty 1803.

156 Davis 1978, p. 122.

157 Gruning 2004, p. 442; Groner 1947, p. 357; and Marshall 1914, p. 19 (actual French possession was on November 30, 1803).

158 Martin 1975, p. 319.

159 Bravo Lira 1993, pp. 80–81.

160 Bravo Lira 1993, pp. 80–81.

161 Villalobos R. 2002, p. 14.

towards emancipation.[162] Independence in Chile would be finally declared on February 12, 1818.[163]

The present-day territory of Argentina, likewise, was formerly a possession of the Castilian Crown.[164] Historically, it has been referred to as Río de la Plata, due to the name of the main fluvial artery that crosses through the territory. In 1516, Juan Díaz de Solís led the first European expedition that arrived in the region.[165] In 1776, the territory mainly comprised the newly created Viceroyalty of Río de la Plata.[166] During the following century, inhabitants joined other movements towards independence that arose in South America.[167] In May 1810, a short but intense revolution overthrew the local Viceroy, who was then replaced by members of a first *junta*.[168] Independence would be finally declared on July 9, 1816.[169]

3.3.3 *Corollary*

All American Civil Law Jurisdictions were a royal holding of the Crown of Castile. The royal holding by the Castilian Crown found grounding at least on three points (*i.e.*, capitulations, papal bulls, and the right to conquest and just war). American Civil Law Jurisdictions were all, at some point in time, Spanish possessions in the Americas. They therefore experienced a common period that is referred to as *Indiano*, a period that shared a common legal order, and that helps explain many of the aspects of their current legal systems. Common legal products were implemented and developed during that period. An Allocation paradigm of ownership likewise developed during the period, being part of that common legal order, and spreading throughout the continent.

3.4 *Indiano* Legal Order

Indiano should be, in addition, used to refer to the legal order that applied in all the Indies.[170] *Indiano* legislation comprised Canon, Castilian, Native American, and Roman provisions, together with a set of provisions created especially

162 Villalobos R. 2004, pp. 345–349.

163 Villalobos R. 2004, p. 396.

164 See the brief overview in Parise 2014b, p. 324.

165 Rock 1987, p. 8.

166 Lewis 2003, p. 31.

167 Sweet 1929, pp. 140–146.

168 Amongst the copious bibliography on the periods covering the Argentine revolution and independence, see the early and widely circulated—though contested—account in Domínguez 1861, pp. 201–238.

169 Domínguez 1861, pp. 398–411.

170 Guzmán Brito 2000, p. 158.

for the Indies, known as strictly (*propiamente*) *Indiano*.[171] Property law was an area where abundant "strictly *Indiano*" provisions developed due to the diverse interests of the different actors.[172] Customs developed by American inhabitants, both Creole and Native, also fell within the broad definition of *Indiano* legal order.[173] It has been claimed that property law matters were occasionally governed by local practices or customs that preceded the arrival of legislative enactments.[174] Furthermore, court decisions and doctrinal writings formed part of the *Indiano* legal order.[175] Court rulings, however, had some limitations as sources of law, because they were indeed decisions without reasons for judgment, a practice that existed in Castile.[176] Furthermore, courts could depart from the legislation when ruling, if they found that legislative enactments would clearly lead them towards an unfair ruling in a particular case.[177] Doctrinal writings dealing with the evolving American legal precepts, as will be mentioned *infra*, were developed on both sides of the Atlantic.[178] As a corollary, all these elements eventually evolved into what some scholars called *Corpus iuris indiarum*.[179]

Legal borrowing can take place within different territories that are subject to the same monarch or administration. Legal borrowing is, therefore, noticeable when looking at the Americas.[180] The American continent has been subject to many legal transplants or normative transfers. As will be addressed immediately in this chapter, the first borrowing was the transplantation of Castilian law to the Hispanic possessions beginning in the early sixteenth century. García-Gallo, in his seminal textbook on the history of Spanish law, indeed stated that there was a transplantation of Castilian law to the Indies, and that Castilian law was initially transplanted *in totum* and only with time did it start to differentiate from the *Indiano* law.[181] It is known, for example, that

171 Guzmán Brito 1982, p. 39; and García-Gallo 1977, at § 216.
172 Mariluz Urquijo 1970, p. 154.
173 Tomás y Valiente 1997c, p. 1255. On the role of customs in Spanish America, see Guzmán Brito 1982, p. 64; and Dougnac Rodríguez 1994, p. 13.
174 Cueto 1999, p. 84.
175 Dougnac Rodríguez 1994, p. 11.
176 Dougnac Rodríguez 1994, p. 262.
177 Dougnac Rodríguez 1994, p. 14.
178 Dougnac Rodríguez 1994, pp. 263–276.
179 Levaggi 1996b, p. 153. See the diagram of the elements of the *Corpus* in Levaggi 1994, p. 362.
180 See generally Parise 2012b, pp. 72–73.
181 García-Gallo 1977, at § 214, 774.

in that period most Castilian general rules on the requirements of real estate transactions were incorporated into the *Indiano* legal order.[182]

In that same region—as will be shown later in this work when looking at the Liberal paradigm of ownership—many drafters used legal borrowings when elaborating their first national civil codes during the early nineteenth century.[183] For example, the civil codes of Andrés Bello for Chile and of Dalmacio Vélez Sarsfield for Argentina were two important exponents of legal borrowing. Furthermore, their works served as models for many other American Civil Law Jurisdictions, while they were also elaborated in part with borrowed provisions. In Louisiana, legal borrowing occurred at that same time,[184] when the Digest of 1808 was applied in the region to comprise the *Indiano* legal precepts that were still in effect. Legal borrowing was not limited to Hispanic possessions in America, naturally. In present-day Brazil, for example, Portuguese legal provisions applied since the time of the early settlements, coexisting with local legal elaborations.[185] The 13 Colonies, likewise, experienced an early reception of—in their case—English common law within their territory;[186] while in Quebec the 1866 civil code did not neglect borrowings, and many of its compounding elements (*i.a.,* Canon, English, French, and Roman laws) could be traced back to Europe, where they were originally envisioned as a reaction to local needs.[187]

3.4.1 *Castilian Precepts as Models for the Americas*

It has been deemed impossible to understand the legal developments in the Americas without being aware of the influence that Peninsular ideas and dispositions exerted on the new territories.[188] Castilian precepts served as models for the Americas,[189] where *Indiano* dispositions found precedents in medieval institutions. That medieval projection into the Americas was expected,

182 Baade 1978, p. 676.

183 See generally 4.4.2 and 4.4.3 of this book; and Parise 2012b, pp. 72–73.

184 An early paper by Thomas J. Semmes demonstrated in its title that some scholars had already looked at the civil law in Louisiana as a transplant. See generally Semmes 1883.

185 Levaggi 1996b, pp. 180–181.

186 About the early American period, see, for example, Reinsch 1907; Schwartz 1974, pp. 8–18; and Hall *et al.* 1991, pp. 24–25.

187 Parise 2014b, p. 315.

188 Mariluz Urquijo 1978, p. 123.

189 It should be acknowledged that, vice versa, some *Indiano* precepts served as models for Castile. Tomás y Valiente 1997c, pp. 1268–1269.

because the American settlement took place towards the emergence of the Modern Period, being in contact with the last stages of the Middle Ages, acting as a bridge between two periods: between medieval and modern.[190] Overlapping of time periods is unavoidable, because as Levaggi highlighted, historiography undertakes periodization, and the start and end of a period in reality is never absolute.[191]

The Catholic Monarchs shifted the Peninsular institutional and political structure towards a proto nation-state understanding. However, they recurred to some medieval institutions and instruments when administering the Indies. Accordingly, they introduced town halls (*cabildos*) and the office of *Adelantados* with broad powers, resembling those of medieval lords.[192] In addition, the capitulations were implemented in the Americas as a means to distribute newly acceded lands, and found their origin in the Iberian Peninsula.[193] Claudio Sánchez Albornoz[194] mentioned that many Castilian medieval modes survived and were reproduced across the Atlantic.[195] He enumerated examples of that survival, amongst others, the *encomienda*, which had a significant impact on ownership.[196] There was indeed an assimilation tendency, in which the American reality would be discovered while aiming to organize that reality according to the legal instruments available in the Peninsula.[197] Mariluz Urquijo pointed out that the assimilation prevailed even when facing the unknown. He stated, for example, that as early as 1510 a *Real Cédula* indicated that forests of pineapple should be a common good, for the benefit of all members, even when similar trees did not exist in the Peninsula.[198]

The conquest of America was interpreted as a continuation of the Peninsular *Reconquista*;[199] and the experience of land allocation that followed the retreat of Muslims from the Iberian Peninsula served as the model for the Americas.[200] The *Reconquista* provided to the monarchs many vacant tracts

190 Levaggi 1996a, p. 199.
191 Levaggi 1996a, p. 199.
192 Cueto 1999, p. 75.
193 Cueto 1999, p. 75.
194 Several scholars shared that understanding, amongst others, Charles Verlinden, Richard Konetzke, Mario Góngora, Luis Weckmann, and Horst Pietschmann. Abelardo Levaggi indicated that those scholars supported the claim. See Levaggi 1996a, p. 200.
195 Sánchez Albornoz 1983, p. 128. See also Levaggi 1996a, p. 200.
196 See generally 3.6 of this book. See also Sánchez Albornoz 1983, p. 128; and Levaggi 1996a, p. 200.
197 Mariluz Urquijo 1978, p. 99.
198 Mariluz Urquijo 1978, p. 99.
199 Levaggi 1996a, p. 199.
200 Daract 2005–2007, p. 25.

of land, while others were occupied precariously by members of the lower segments of society, who looked for the assistance from a powerful *señor* by means of subjection (*encomendación*). In that context, resettlement had to secure: (i) the effective occupation of lands previously occupied by Muslims, (ii) the reward for those that contributed to the *Reconquista* efforts, (iii) the supply of goods to new urban centers, (iv) the defense of lands against potential reactions of enemies, and (v) the promotion of the Catholic faith in lands previously in the hands of those regarded as infidels.[201] The objectives were therefore economic, political, military, and religious, and required a common plan for the entire Peninsula.[202] A similar scenario took place in the Americas, where similar settlement needs were encountered by monarchs, who were inclined to recur to solutions that had proved successful in the resettlement of the Iberian Peninsula.[203] It is worth mentioning that the *señorío* regime—which had some similarities with the feudal regime of other European jurisdictions, though being different and not to be confused—was not transplanted to the Americas, however.[204] There was, accordingly, no rural population subject to a *señor* or noble lord in the Americas, and the latter did not implement government control over the former.[205] Legal borrowing, in time and space, was therefore applied in the Americas yet not in a blind or *in totum* manner.

Castilian law had a broad application scope in the Americas, being applicable to all areas not specifically addressed by the provisions created especially for the Indies.[206] The *Recopilación de Leyes de Indias* of 1680 found an important precedent in the previous Castilian law. The *Recopilación* expressly provided that whenever a relevant legal area was not contained within it or within another royal decree, the law in force was that of Castile according to the *Leyes de Toro* of 1505.[207] These later laws, following the *Ordenamiento de Alcalá* of 1348,[208]

201 Mariluz Urquijo 1978, p. 17.

202 Mariluz Urquijo 1978, p. 17.

203 Mariluz Urquijo 1978, p. 18.

204 García-Gallo 1977, at § 1371. On general aspects of the *señorío* regime, see, amongst many others, García-Gallo 1977, at § 1058–1085. On the end of the *señorío* regime in the Peninsula, see Hernández Montalbán 1999.

205 There were indeed very few *señoríos* established in the Americas (*v.gr.*, the Ducado of Vergara for the descendants of Christopher Columbus). García-Gallo 1977, at § 1073.

206 Bravo Lira 1989, p. 91.

207 The *Leyes de Toro* were a total of 83 laws, enacted in the year 1505, in the Spanish city of Toro. The main drafter was Juan López de Palacios Rubios. See Levaggi 1996b, p. 145.

208 Law 1, Title 28 of the *Ordenamiento de Alcalá* read: "Como todos los pleytos se deben librar primeramente por las Leys deste Libro; et lo que por ellas non se pudiere librar, que se libre por los Fueros; et lo que por los Fueros non se pudiere librar, que se libre por las Partidas." Códigos Españoles 1847–1851, I, p. 462.

stated the order of application of Castilian legislation: first, were to be applied the royal enactments; second, the municipal *fueros*; and third, the *Siete Partidas*.[209] In the event of lacunae in the legislation, therefore, the ultimate source was the *Siete Partidas*. Accordingly, the text of law 2, Title 1, Book 2 of the *Recopilación de Leyes de Indias* of 1680 stated:

> That the laws of Castile are applied when the laws of the Indies are silent. We order and demand that the laws of Castile, according to the Laws of Toro, should be applied to all cases, businesses and claims that are not decided nor regulated in the laws of this Compilation, Legal Documents, Provisions or Collections of Laws, that are not eliminated in the Indies and were emanated under our orders. The laws of Castile will be applied not only regarding the substance, resolution and decision of the cases, businesses and claims [...].[210]

That same title of the *Recopilación* provided further important provisions. Law 39 of the same title and book indicated that local authorities should acknowledge, yet not enforce (*obedezcan y no cumplan*), resolutions of the royal councils, only if passed by the Council (*Consejo*) of the Indies.[211] Furthermore, the

---

209 Law 1 of the *Leyes de Toro* read: "[...] Por las quales leyes de este nuestro libro mandamos que se libren primeramente todos los pleytos Civiles y Criminales, y los pleytos, y las contiendas que no se pudieren librar por las leyes de este nuestro libro, y por los dichos fueros, mandamos que se libren por las leyes de las siete partidas [...]." (Códigos Españoles 1847–1851, VI, p. 557)

See Ots Capdequí 1945, pp. 79–80. See also the English explanation about the order of application in Cairns 2015, p. 47.

210 That resolution had been taken by Charles V (Carlos V) in 1530. See the text on the margin of law 2; and Guzmán Brito 2000, p. 152.

Law 2, Title 1, Book 2 of the 1680 *Recopilación* in Spanish read: "Ordenamos Y mandamos, que en todos los caſos, negocios y pleytos en que no eſtuviere decidido, ni declarado lo que ſe deve proveer por las leyes de eſta Recopilacion, ó por Cedulas, Proviſiones, ó Ordenanças dadas, y no revocadas para las Indias, y las que por nueſtra orden ſe deſpacharen, ſe guarden las leyes de nueſtro Reyno de Caſtilla, conforme á la de Toro, aſsi en quanto á la ſubſtancia, reſolucion y deciſion de los caſos, negocios y pleytos [...]." (Recopilación de Indias 1680, I, at f. 126v)

211 The text in Spanish in part read: "Mandamos á los Virreyes, Preſidentes y Oidores, Governadores y Iuſticias de las Indias, que obedezcan y no cumplan las Cedulas, Proviſiones y otros qualeſquier deſpachos dados por nueſtros reales Conſejos, ſi no fueren paſſados por el de las Indias, y deſpachada por él nueſtra Real Cedula de cumplimiento [...]." (Recopilación de Indias 1680, I, at f. 131v) See also Cairns 2015, pp. 45–52; and García-Gallo 1977, at § 778.

succeeding law of that 1680 text required that royal enactments dealing with areas of general interest (*pragmáticas*)[212] also had to pass before the Council of the Indies.[213] It should be noted that Castilian legislation had been automatically valid in the Americas until 1614.[214] After that, the reenactment of Castilian legislation by the Council of the Indies was required.[215] Accordingly, *Indiano* legal precepts were first tinted by *Ius commune*, as had been the case for other jurisdictions throughout Continental Europe.[216] Natural law soon started to replace that early *Ius commune*, and its postulates, in harmony with the writings of Spanish Scholasticism, as it evolved on both sides of the Atlantic, hence having an impact on the *Indiano* legal order.[217]

3.4.2 Corpus Iuris Indiarum: *Legislative Enactments and Doctrine*

The *Siete Partidas* and the *Recopilación de Leyes de Indias* were seminal *corpus* for American Civil Law Jurisdictions, dealing mainly with private and public law, respectively. The *Siete Partidas* are traditionally attributed to the reign of Alphonse X (Alfonso X), being drafted during 1256–1265.[218] They were subject to several text alterations over time, and the most circulated edition is the one of 1555, containing glosses by Gregorio López.[219] The *Siete Partidas* are the legal *corpus* with the longest and widest application in American Civil Law Jurisdictions,[220] and can be deemed a law that was general and common for the Indies.[221] The name derives from their division into seven parts, and not into books, making them different from other legal bodies that predated their publication.[222] Furthermore, the *Siete Partidas*, different from other *corpus* of that time, were systematical and integral.[223] Each *partida*, or part, was divided into titles and laws, and dealt with an area of the law: (i) sources of law, Catholic faith, and Church; (ii) kings, royal officials, and war; (iii) administration of justice and rights on things; (iv) marriage and persons; (v) contracts and other

212 The English definition of *Pragmática* was extracted from Mirow 2000–2001, p. 75.
213 Recopilación de Indias 1680, I, at f. 131v. See also Cairns2015, pp. 45–52.
214 Cairns 2015, p. 47.
215 Cairns 2015, p. 47.
216 Bravo Lira 1989, p. 194.
217 Bravo Lira 1989, p. 194.
218 See generally Parise 2014c, pp. 318–319; and Levaggi 1996b, p. 89.
219 Levaggi 1996b, p. 89.
220 Bravo Lira 1989, p. 89.
221 Guzmán Brito 2000, p. 160.
222 Bravo Lira 1989, p. 90.
223 Levaggi 1996b, p. 90.

civil institutions; (vi) successions; and (vii) crimes and punishments.[224] *Partida* 3 dealt with the main aspects of ownership.

The number and diversity of legal dispositions throughout the Middle Ages and the Modern Period drove Iberian monarchs to pursue compilations. The result was a unique body that made access possible to all rules and included all dispositions in a chronological order. Although the compiled laws maintained their independence and substance within the compilation,[225] confusion resulted from the variety and disorder of the existing legislation.[226] For Castile, some of those compilations[227] were: the *Ordenamiento de Montalvo* (1484),[228] the *Libro de Bulas* (1503),[229] the *Nueva Recopilación* (1567),[230] and the *Novísima Recopilación* (1805).[231] In the Americas, the *Recopilación de Leyes de Indias* of 1680 had been long expected because of the dispersion and abundance of *Indiano* legal precepts.[232] That *corpus* indeed welcomed "strictly *Indiano*" provisions, and several editions followed that of 1680. No changes were incorporated into the editions published in 1744, 1756, 1774, and 1791; while an 1841 edition did include part of the legislation enacted since 1680,[233] though being irrelevant for several American Civil Law Jurisdictions that at that time

224 Enumeration translated from the work of Abelardo Levaggi. See Levaggi 1996b, p. 90.

225 García Valdecasas 1983, p. 41.

226 Altamira y Crevea 1912, p. 694. See also Parise 2014c, p. 328.

227 See generally Vance 1943.

228 Alonso Díaz de Montalvo was entrusted by the Castilian monarchs to elaborate the first general recompilation. It included all the court rules since the *Ordenamiento de Alcalá de Henares*, pragmatics, royal ordinances, and some chapters of the *Fuero Real*. See Levaggi 1996b, p. 142.

229 Under the supervision of Juan Ramírez, the *Libro de las Bulas* included for the first time all the laws without being abstracted or integrated with others. It also included all the royal provisions regarding good governance and administration of justice. See Levaggi 1996b, p. 143.

230 Philip II (Felipe II) enacted a work of Bartolomé de Atienza that completed a work by Alonso Díaz de Montalvo, which had been ordered by the text of the codicil of Isabella I (Isabel I) of Castile. It was divided into nine books and included approximately 4,000 laws. See Levaggi 1996b, p. 143. Between 1567 and 1777, the *Nueva Recopilación* was republished from time to time to include the new dispositions. See Puig Brutau 1987, p. 33.

231 The work in twelve books, by Juan de la Reguera y Valdelomar, had the objective of compiling the new dispositions together with the ones of the *Nueva Recopilación* in a methodological body of legislation. Nevertheless, the dispersion of legal norms subsisted because the derogation of previous laws was not procedurally effective. Levaggi 1996b, p. 144.

232 Bravo Lira 1989, pp. 22–23.

The text was published in 1681. Earlier attempts had been undertaken – see García-Gallo 1977, at § 781–788; Tomás y Valiente 1997c, pp. 1270–1271; and Dougnac Rodríguez 1994, pp. 241–247.

233 Ots Capdequí 1945, p. 338; and Bravo Lira 1989, p. 35.

were no longer subject to Spain. Antonio de León Pinelo worked on a draft that served as groundwork for the 1680 enactment,[234] and can therefore be considered one of its main authors. The 1680 *Recopilación* had nine books, divided into 218 titles and 6,377 laws.[235] Each law was accompanied by an indication of its origins and date.[236] Different books addressed different areas of law; while the main elements were distributed as follows: (i) Catholic faith and government; (ii) legislation and the Council of the Indies; (iii) just titles and war; (iv) discoveries, settlements, and mining; (v) Governors and procedure; (vi) Native Americans; (vii) criminal law and Blacks; (viii) Royal Treasury; and (ix) commerce and navigation.[237] Book 4 dealt with the main aspects of ownership and the Allocation paradigm that developed in American Civil Law Jurisdictions.

Scholarly writings helped in shaping the American *Ius commune*. A vast array of authors, on both sides of the Atlantic, developed doctrinal writings that helped to better understand and apply the *Ius commune* that existed in the Americas.[238] Authors elaborated on both civil and canon law, though there was more production in the former than in the latter.[239] It should also be noted that the majority of works was drafted in the vernacular (*i.e.*, Spanish), followed by a second majority that was drafted in Latin.[240] Amongst the scholars of this American *Ius commune* are the already mentioned de León Pinelo and de Solórzano Pereira, and the likewise important Juan de Hevia Bolaños, Juan de Matienzo, Pedro Murillo Velarde, and Antonio Xavier Pérez y López.[241]

---

234 Ots Capdequí 1945, p. 336.

235 Ots Capdequí 1945, p. 337.

236 Ots Capdequí 1945, p. 337.

For example, law 2, Title 12, Book 4 dealing with the manner of allocating lands in new settlements indicated that the provision was enacted by Emperor Don Carlos in Toledo on May 19, 1525. The text in Spanish read: "El Emperador D. Carlos en Toledo á 19. de Mayo de 1525." (Recopilación de Indias 1680, II, at f. 102)

237 See generally Recopilación de Indias 1680, I–IV. See Levaggi 1996b, p. 176; and Mirow 2004, pp. 47–48.

238 Bravo Lira 1989, p. 37.

The most complete catalogue included 1250 scholarly writings that shaped the American *Ius commune* (Luque Talaván 2003, pp. 255–638). That same work included valuable information on, amongst other things, the reception of the *Ius commune* in the Americas (Luque Talaván 2003, pp. 115–150) and on the circulation of ideas by means of the legal literature (Luque Talaván 2003, pp. 151–190).

239 Luque Talaván 2003, p. 643.

240 Luque Talaván 2003, p. 644.

241 See the information by Ots Capdequí 1945, pp. 345–350; Levaggi 1996b, pp. 177–180; and Sánchez Bella *et al.* 1992, pp. 102–104. English language information is provided by Mirow 2004, pp. 45–53.

De Solórzano Pereira and his *Política Indiana* deserve special attention, due to their impact on the development of the *Corpus iuris indiarum.* This important actor, similarly to de Vitoria, was a professor at the University of Salamanca, trained in both canon and civil law. Yet, differently from his predecessor, de Solórzano Pereira did live in America and did have practical experience on *Indiano* matters, having been involved with the activities of the *Audiencia* of Lima and counselor at the Council of the Indies.[242] De Solórzano Pereira participated in the works that led to the *Recopilación* of 1680,[243] and before that time he drafted a treatise on the law of the Indies (*De Indiarum iure,* 1629), which was then translated into Spanish and adapted to become his already mentioned *Política Indiana* of 1647, dealing with Indian policies.[244] The latter work was divided into six books, addressing the most important elements of the American *Ius commune*: (i) conquest and settlement of the new territories; (ii) liberty, status, and conditions of Native Americans; (iii) *encomiendas* of Native Americans; (iv) ecclesiastical matters; (v) secular government; and (vi) the Royal Treasury.[245] The content of Book 1 of the work of de Solórzano Pereira may be considered essential for the shaping of the Allocation paradigm of ownership.

3.4.3 *Louisiana, Chile, and Argentina within the* Indiano *Legal Order*

The present-day territories of Louisiana, Chile, and Argentina were subjected to the *Indiano* legal order, while in addition they experienced transplantation and normative transfer of institutions originated in the Iberian Peninsula. The Spanish judicial records confirm that *Indiano* legal precepts applied in Louisiana.[246] In 1769, Alejandro O'Reilly[247] implemented the *Indiano* system of government and replaced the French laws (*v.gr., Coutume de Paris*) in Louisiana.[248] In addition, the 1680 *Recopilación* was mentioned repeatedly in official correspondence in Louisiana.[249] Amongst the new provisions by O'Reilly were the *Ordinances and Instructions*[250] and the *Instructions as to the Manner of*

242 Ots Capdequí 1945, p. 348.

243 Ots Capdequí 1945, p. 348.

244 Ots Capdequí 1945, p. 347; Sánchez Bella *et al.* 1992, pp. 102–103; and Tomás y Valiente 1997c, p. 1273.

245 See generally Solórzano Pereira (de) 1703.

246 Cairns 2015, p. 52.
On the different special laws enacted for Louisiana, see Wallach 1960, pp. 209–212.

247 For additional readings on Alejandro O'Reilly, see generally Torres Ramírez 1969.

248 See the analysis in Batiza 1962.

249 Din & Harkins 1996, p. 102.

250 Text available in English in Schmidt 1841, pp. 1–27.

Instituting Suits,[251] of November 25, 1769, regulating procedure in the region.[252] Other important regulations were the property-law related *Ordinance on Land Grants* of February 18, 1770 by O'Reilly;[253] and the *Regulations on Land Grants* by Juan Ventura Morales of July 17, 1799.[254] Louisiana courts continued relying on Spanish sources even after the Louisiana Purchase, mainly during the period 1809 to 1828.[255]

The present-day territory of Chile, likewise, experienced the borrowing of Peninsular provisions. A multiplicity of examples can be mentioned in this respect. In 1795, a *Real Cédula* extended to Chile the application of the *Ordenanzas de Bilbao* of 1737, which were fundamental for the regulation of commerce.[256] Private law, mainly, was also affected by the application of the *Siete Partidas* in Chile for more than 300 years.[257] Amongst the new provisions enacted for Chile were the *Ordinances for the Royal Audiencia of Santiago* (*Ordenanzas para la Real Audiencia de Santiago*), adopted by *Real Cédula* of February 17, 1609, important for the administration of justice in the territory.[258]

The present-day territory of Argentina experienced transplantation and normative transfer. For example, the annuities secured by land (*censos consignativos*)[259] that had their origins in the Peninsula, were transplanted to the

251 Text available in English in Schmidt 1841, pp. 27–60.

252 Parise 2014c, p. 314.

For more information on these instructions, see Baade 1978, pp. 682–683.

253 Text available in English in Schmidt 1841, pp. 61–65.

254 Wallach 1960, p. 211.

255 The references to Spanish materials focused mainly in the *Siete Partidas*, the *Librería de Escribanos*, and the *Curia Filípica*. The *Curia Filípica*, by Juan de Hevia Bolaños, had a strong presence in Spain and Spanish America. The work of José Febrero, *Librería de Escribanos é instrucción jurídica teórica práctica de principiantes*, was also well circulated in America. See generally Rabalais 1982; Castán Vázquez 2000, p. 526; and Castán Vázquez 1984, p. 81.

That nineteenth-century interest for Spanish law demanded, for example, a translation of the *Siete Partidas* into the English language. In 1818, Louis Moreau-Lislet and Henry Carleton translated the titles of the *Siete Partidas* that dealt with promises and obligations (*Partida* v, Title 11), sale and purchase (*Partida* v, Title 5), and exchange (*Partida* v, Title 6). A second translation of other titles of the *Siete Partidas* was undertaken by the same jurists and dated 1820. See generally 4.5.1.2 of this book; generally Parise 2014c; and Tucker 1942, p. 29.

256 Guzmán Brito 1982, p. 50.

257 Bravo Lira 1989, p. 141.

258 Guzmán Brito 1982, p. 42.

259 See the short, though clear definition provided in Mirow 2000–2001, p. 53.

Americas.[260] Furthermore, in present-day Argentina, as in other regions, parts of the assets of Native American groups were allotted for annuities in funds (*cajas de censos indígenas*).[261] That system tended to disappear, even when the *Real Ordenanza de Intendentes* of 1782 for Río de la Plata subjected those funds to the scrutiny of the Royal Treasury and even when beginning in 1785 those funds were subject to the scrutiny of the *Audiencia* of Buenos Aires.[262] It is worth noting that the 1782 *Ordenanza* was extended to present-day Chile by means of a *Real Orden* of February 6, 1787.[263]

3.4.4 *Corollary*

The *Indiano* legal order applied across all American Civil Law Jurisdictions. *Indiano* legal precepts, comprised of Canon, Castilian, Native American, Roman, and "strictly *Indiano*" provisions applied, therefore, in the present-day territories of Louisiana, Chile, and Argentina. Furthermore, customs, court decisions, and doctrinal writings likewise formed part of that *Corpus iuris indiarum.* Legal borrowing—achieved by means of transplantation or normative transfer—helped develop that *corpus*, and to establish the resulting *Indiano* legal order. It was necessary to borrow Peninsular provisions in the Americas, yet also to create new special provisions that adapted to the new territories whenever facing lacunae.[264] It should be noted, furthermore, that there was a lack of absolute uniformity of the *Indiano* legal precepts, varying according to the demographic and economic divergences of each region.[265] *Indiano* legal precepts were casuistic, meaning that when a new situation arose and had no precedence in the Peninsula, a solution would be created for that new territory of the Crown in the Americas.[266] The *Indiano* legal order was indeed instrumental in the development of the Allocation paradigm of ownership, avoiding a vacuum and providing a context in which it could emerge.

3.5 Allocating Multiple Interests

Multiple actors had, and defended, multiple interests in the new territories, while some of those interests overlapped and were concurrent. Many interests

---

260 Levaggi 1982, pp. 117–124.
261 Levaggi 1982, pp. 122–123.
262 Levaggi 1982, p. 124.
263 Guzmán Brito 1982, pp. 42–43.
264 Sánchez Bella *et al.* 1992, p. 161; and García-Gallo 1977, at § 215.
265 Baade 1978, p. 743; and García-Gallo 1977, at § 215.
266 Ots Capdequí 1940, p. 414.

aimed to the allocation of ownership, hence shaping a unique and new paradigm. The Pope had universal ownership,[267] the Crown had primordial ownership, and Native Americans and European settlers could have private ownership on the different territories.[268] That private ownership, however, was limited if compared with the one that prevailed during the period in which the Liberal paradigm of ownership prevailed (*i.e.*, nineteenth century). This Allocation paradigm, accordingly, motivated the existence of private ownership, though more limited than in the Liberal understanding. When property was allocated, it aimed to the common good, being therefore subject to termination if the requirements made at the time of granting the right were not fulfilled.[269]

Provisions on ownership were found in code-like texts during the pre-independence period in the Americas. Authority, indeed, was found by the different actors mainly in the already mentioned *Siete Partidas* and the 1680 *Recopilación*. The latter legal *corpus* addressed different aspects of ownership mainly in Titles 1 and 12 of Book 4. For example, law 1, Title 1 repeated the interests of the Crown, while all of Title 12 dealt with the emission of royal land grants (*mercedes reales de tierras*). In the Peninsula, provisions were primarily found in Title 28 of *Partida* 3. Pérez y López, in his *Teatro de la Legislación Universal de España e Indias* (1791–1798), excelled in assisting the legal community in the interpretation of legal precepts, while providing the legal community with a *small library* of the multiple volumes of existing legislation.[270] In his encyclopedic work, Pérez y López summarized law 1, Title 28, *Partida* 3 indicating that there were three types of *señorío*:

> First, that of the Kings to punish wrongdoers and to deliver and do justice to everyone. Second, that of men on movable or immovable things during their lifetime, and after their death, it is given to their heirs or to those to whom they transferred them. Third, that being held in usufruct.[271]

267 It should be noted that, amongst others, de Vitoria refuted the claim that the Pope had universal ownership. Accordingly, the Pope lacked temporal authority, and thus, the Pope could not give something he had no control, possession, or dominium over. See Parise 2008c, p. 123; and Williams 1983, p. 75. See generally 3.3.1.1 of this book.

268 Dougnac Rodríguez 1994, p. 402.

269 Dougnac Rodríguez 1994, p. 402.

270 Parise 2014c, p. 331.

271 The text in Spanish read, following closely the *Siete Partidas*: "primero, el supremo que tienen los Reyes para castigar los malhechores, y dar ó hacer justicia á cada uno: segundo, el que los hombres tienen en su vida en las cosas muebles ó raices, y despues de su muerte pasa á los herederos, ó á aquellos á quienes las enagenasen mientras viviesen: tercero el que tienen en el usufructo." (Pérez y López 1791–1798, II, pp. 363–364)

Even at the turn of the nineteenthcentury, Juan Sala Bañuls, author of the *Ilustración del Derecho Real de España* (1803), which was very well circulated on both sides of the Atlantic,[272] explained the different kind of things according to the *Siete Partidas*,[273] preserving the understanding of ownership.[274] Sala Bañuls explained that things, according to law 2, Title 28, *Partida* 3 were divided into five categories, those that belonged: (i) to every living creature, including humans; (ii) only to humans; (iii) exclusively to a village; (iv) *privately*[275] to each individual man or woman, enabling them to gain or lose *señorío* of them; and (v) to the *señorío* of no man or woman.[276] The *Siete Partidas*, therefore, explained that things could be allocated to different actors and could be held in common by everybody (*v.gr.*, air and rain water);[277] in common only by the inhabitants of a village (*v.gr.*, water fountains, surrounding crop lands);[278] exclusively by the monarchs (*v.gr.*, harbor and tollgate taxes);[279] and as guardians by the Church, due to their sacred value (*v.gr.*, chalices, crosses).[280] Accordingly, different interests would play a role in respect of the different things.

Indiano legal precepts—following the Castilian understanding—referred to *señorío*, *dominio*, and *propiedad*. These were concepts with similar content, where one individual had a particular right on a corporeal thing.[281] They, therefore, excluded things considered sacred, public, or to be held in common;[282] while they also excluded incorporeal things.[283] Ownership was divided into perfect (*plena*), where the owner could dispose of the thing and preserved the utility of the thing; and imperfect (*menos plena*), where the owner preserved disposition yet delegated to another the benefits and utility of the thing.[284] The authoritative work of José Febrero, *Librería de Escribanos é instrucción jurídica teórica práctica de principiantes* (1769), which was well circulated in

272 Barrientos Grandón 2009, p. 354.

273 Sala 1803, pp. 95–100.

274 Blasco 2000, p. 15.

275 It should be noted that "privadas ó de particulares" was the Spanish wording used in Sala 1803, p. 98.

276 Sala 1803, p. 95. See also law 2, Title 28, *Partida* 3 in Las Partidas, tomo 3, p. 155vta; and Ots Capdequí 1945, pp. 102–103.

277 See, for example, law 3, Title 28, *Partida* 3 in Siete Partidas 1587, III, pp. 156–156v.

278 See, for example, law 9, Title 28, *Partida* 3 in Siete Partidas 1587, III, pp. 156v–157.

279 See, for example, law 11, Title 28, *Partida* 3 in Siete Partidas 1587, III, p. 157v.

280 See, for example, laws 12–13, Title 28, *Partida* 3 in Siete Partidas 1587, III, pp. 157v–158.

281 Sánchez Bella *et al.* 1992, p. 343.

282 See generally 3.7 of this book.

283 Sánchez Bella *et al.* 1992, p. 343.

284 Sánchez Bella *et al.* 1992, p. 343.

America—from Louisiana to Río de la Plata—and played an important role in the practice before courts,[285] explained that ownership:

> is called perfect because he alone [*i.e.*, the owner], and nobody else has that right on the thing, and being absolute owner he does not recognize others, and he can transfer the thing during his lifetime, to whom he pleases, and if he does not alienate the thing, it passes to his heirs upon his death.[286]

Settlement in the Americas was undertaken both by private and by Crown intervention.[287] In the early period, the private endeavors prevailed, though with time the Crown started to take on paramount intervention.[288] There was a concurrence of interests between the Crown and the settlers, where the Crown tried to assure that land grants were adequately offered and used.[289] One of the main aims of the monarchs, as will be further developed *infra*, was to occupy and inhabit the territories. Not achieving that aim many times resulted from the use and abuse of the different actors and not from the wording of the existing legislation.[290] It was likewise argued that land holding soon became a means to indicate wealth and social status.[291] Furthermore, *Indiano* legal precepts considered the different personal circumstances of actors, and these were diverse, due to the ethnic and cultural diversity of the different coexisting groups.[292] Ultimately, in the Americas a corporative approach was experienced, where each group was an active member of society.[293]

285 Parise 2014c, p. 318.

286 The text in Spanish read: "Se llama perfecto porque él solo, y nadie mas lo tiene en ellos, y como que por ser dueño absoluto no reconoce á otro, puede transferirlos en vida, á quien le parezca, y si no los enagena, pasan por su muerte á sus herederos." (Febrero 1783, p. 470)

287 See, for example, the reference to the private character of some discovery expeditions, as mentioned in law 17, Title 1, Book 4: "Ley xvii. Que ningun deſcubrimiento, ni poblacion ſe haga à coſta del Rey. Mandamos, Que ningun deſcubrimiento, nueva navegacion, ni poblacion ſe haga á coſta de nueſtra hazienda, ni los que governaren puedan gaſtar en eſto ninguna coſa della, aunque tengan nueſtros poderes, é inſtrucciones para hazer deſcubrimientos, y navegaciones, ſi no tuvieren poder eſpecial para que ſea á nueſtra coſta." (Recopilación de Indias 1680, II, at f. 82)

288 Cueto 1999, p. 69.

289 Ots Capdequí 1946, p. 15, 107.

290 Cueto 1999, p. 83.

291 Sánchez Bella *et al.* 1992, p. 361.

292 Dougnac Rodríguez 1994, p. 21.

293 Dougnac Rodríguez 1994, p. 21.

3.5.1 *Crown of Castile*

The Crown was an important actor, and had multiple interests in the allocation of ownership. The central three aims of the Crown, when dealing with ownership, dealt with the effective settlement of population (political interest), the transformation of land into a means of economic production (economic interest), and the inclusion of local populations as subjects of taxation (tax interests).[294] Two other interests of the Crown were related to the allocation of ownership, at least tangentially: monarchs were interested in protecting Native Americans, as was indicated by the inclusion of a specific reference by Isabella I in her testament; and they were likewise interested in the propagation of the Catholic faith, as was indicated by the inclusion of representatives of the Church in discovery expeditions.[295] Accordingly, monarchs kept under their holding some territories that were initially not financially profitable (*i.a.*, Chile, Buenos Aires), indicating that spiritual interests prevailed over material interests.[296] That hierarchy of interests was encapsulated in the 1680 *Recopilación*, where law 1, Title 1, Book 4 read that: "[…] the main objective, which encourages us to undertake new discoveries is the preaching and expansion of the Holy Catholic Faith and that Indians are taught and that they live in peace […]."[297] The Crown was truly interested in having lands effectively cultivated, and this interest moved some scholars to claim that there was a social function of ownership, yet that anachronistic claim should be challenged, because even when the Crown intervened, its objectives were tainted by the protection of economic and tax interests.[298]

The intervention of the Crown was made by means of settlement policies, aiming to secure its interests, while incorporating Native Americans and the

294 Levaggi 1987, p. 210.

295 Dougnac Rodríguez 1994, pp. 18–19; and Ots Capdequí 1946, p. 14.

296 Dougnac Rodríguez 1994, p. 18.

297 The entire law in Spanish read: "Que antes de conceder nuevos deſcubrimientos, ſe pueble lo deſcubierto. Porque El fin principal, que nos mueve á hazer nuevos deſcubrimiéntos es la predicacion, y dilatacion de la Santa Fé Catolica, y que los Indios ſean enſeñados, y vivan en paz, y policia. Ordenamos y mandamos, que antes de conceder nuevos deſcubrimientos y poblaciones, ſe dé orden de que lo deſcubierto, pacifico y obediente á nueſtra Santa Madre Igleſia Catolica, ſe pueble, aſsiente y perpetúe, para paz y concordia de ambas Republicas, como ſe diſpone en las leyes, que tratan de las poblaciones, y haviendoſe poblado, y dado aſſiento en lo que aſtá deſcubierto, pacifico, y debaxo de la obediencia eſpiritual de la Santa Sede Apoſtolica, y de la nueſtra, ſe trate de deſcubrir y poblar lo que con ello confina, y de nuevo ſe fuere deſcubriendo." (Recopilación de Indias 1680, II, at f. 80)

298 Ots Capdequí 1946, p. 28, 53.

establishment of a nucleus of population.[299] The policies changed together with time, and they have been subject to periodization, evolving around the idea of allocation of ownership.[300] For example, José María Ots Capdequí mentioned three periods of settlement policies.[301] The first period started with the initial discoveries, and was marked by regulatory attempts undertaken by the Crown, often corrected by trial-and-error experiences, and reaching its most organic representation in the *Ordenanzas* of Philip II (Felipe II) of 1573.[302] Those successful guidelines of 1573 called for a three-phase approach: first to discover, then to settle, and finally to pacify.[303] The guidelines could further be deemed early urban planning, leaving an impact on the current design of many cities.[304] The second period started with the *Real Cédula* of 1591,[305] which can be deemed a first land reform in the Americas.[306] The text of that *Cédula*, which was also included in the already mentioned law 14, Title 12, Book 4 of the 1680 *Recopilación*,[307] tried to avoid confusion, and the monarch therefore ordered the revision of all titles to land.[308] The third period started with the *Real Instrucción* of 1754[309] and ended with the independence movements.[310]

The last period corresponded with that of the eighteenth-century Bourbon Reforms. Those reforms found counterpart movements in Europe, in for

299 Ots Capdequí 1946, p. 42.

300 For example, Adolfo Omar Cueto indicated that the royal policies towards lands could be divided into four periods: (i) the territorial approximation and consolidation period; (ii) the organization period, triggered by the 1591 reform; (iii) the intermediate period; and (iv) the reorganization period, modified by the 1754 reforms. Cueto 1999, pp. 117–145.

301 See generally Ots Capdequí 1946.

302 The Spanish text is available at Morales Padrón 1979, pp. 489–518. See also Ots Capdequí 1946, p. 42. An English translation of part of the *Ordenanzas* is available at Nuttall 1921. For more information on the *Ordenanzas*, see Sánchez Bella 1989, pp. 541–548; and generally Vas Mingo (del) 1985.

303 Morales Padrón 1979, p. 487; and Ots Capdequí 1946, p. 48.

304 Nuttall 1921, p. 743.

305 The Spanish text is available at Real Cédula 1591.

306 Ots Capdequí 1946, p. 67.

307 See note 89 of this chapter, and accompanying text.

308 Ots Capdequí 1946, p. 70.

309 See the text of the *Real Instrucción* of 1754 as incorporated in Pérez y López 1791–1798, XXVIII, pp. 514–521. For information on the application of the 1754 text in different parts of the Americas, see the illustration for Córdoba del Tucumán (present-day Argentina), available at Luque Colombres 1985.

310 Ots Capdequí 1946, p. 79.

example Austria, France, Portugal, and Prussia.[311] In Spain, these reforms were led by, amongst others, Pedro Rodríguez de Campomanes y Pérez, Pedro Pablo Abarca de Bolea, Count of Aranda, and by Gaspar Melchor de Jovellanos.[312] Within the realm of property law, the reforms dealt with removals and restraints (*amortización*) and with "dead hands" (*manos muertas*). As explained by Levaggi, the first consisted of the transfer of ownership to a family or entity with the prohibition to alienate; while the second referred to the owners of restraints, who could not legally alienate the property.[313] De Jovellanos drafted his *Informe sobre la Ley Agraria* (1795)[314] in which he provided a report on the agrarian law claiming that Spain should "cut, once and for all, the ties that shamefully enchained its agriculture,"[315] and where he enrolled in the efforts of the Enlightened reforms that aimed to reduce secular and ecclesiastical[316] removals and restraints in the circulation of immovable property.[317] Yet, de Jovellanos advocated for *laissez-faire* and the move towards the new Liberal paradigm, while in the Americas, the reform of 1754 still advocated for the role of the state in allotting ownership.[318] At that time in the Americas there were several territories where land was held and not exploited or occupied, enabling large tracts of land to be individually held (*latifundios*), some of which persisted well into the nineteenth century and even beyond. Also, land was occasionally not correctly registered for tax purposes. This scenario triggered the need

311 Ots Capdequí 1946, p. 105. For more information on the land reforms of the Bourbons, see Tomás y Valiente 1997a, especially pp. 555–566.

312 Ots Capdequí 1946, p. 106.

313 Levaggi 1982, p. 107.

314 See generally Jovellanos (de) 1795.

315 The text in Spanish read: "Cortemos pues de una vez los lazos, que tan vergonzosamente encadenan nuestra agricultura." Jovellanos (de) 1795, p. 58, at § 169.

316 The reduction originally targeted secular removals and restraints. See Tomás y Valiente 1997b, p. 3382.

317 This would be finally accomplished in the following century. See Garriga 2012, p. 277.

For more information on reduction of ecclesiastical removals and restraints, see Levaggi 1992, pp. 139–142.

For a more comprehensive study, by the same author, on the secular and ecclesiastical removals, see generally Levaggi 1999.

For an early nineteenth-century approach to the Iberian history of removals and restraints, such as *mayorazgos*, see generally Sempere y Guarinos 1805.

In an 1851 text by Gustavus Schmidt, for Louisiana, *mayorazgos* were broadly, yet effectively defined as "the right to the enjoyment of certain aggregate property, left with the condition therein imposed, that they are to pass in their integrity perpetually, successively, to the eldest son." Schmidt 1851, p. 62.

318 Ots Capdequí 1946, p. 107.

for reforms during the eighteenth century.[319] Finally, it has been claimed that in Spain, for example, the attack on removals and restraints was an important element for a shift of Ownership Paradigm and for the development of codification efforts,[320] topics that are central to Chapter 4 of this book.

3.5.2 *Roman Catholic Church*

The Church was likewise an important actor, and its interests were present in the Americas. It should be preliminarily noted that some canonists, at the time of Pope Paul V, claimed unsuccessfully that the papal bulls had only granted the Crown a precarious holding, in which the supreme ownership was preserved by the papacy.[321] Monarchs had indeed the exclusive duty to evangelize the new territories, being a paramount interest that was naturally shared with the Church.[322] All other interests were subordinated to evangelization: *Salus animarum suprema lex esto*.[323] Accordingly, the first book of the 1680 *Recopilación* dealt with the Catholic faith throughout 24 titles.[324] Furthermore, as early as 1501, the Crown devoted efforts—that persisted during the sixteenth and seventeenth centuries—to avoid the settling of, amongst others, heretics, Jews, and Muslims in the Americas, welcoming Europeans who had received the sacrament of baptism.[325] In addition, universities and printing houses were established to bring the catechism to Native Americans.[326] Likewise, economic efforts—comparable to those of the Carolingian period—were undertaken to establish the Church across the Americas, appointing bishops, and building churches, convents, and missions.[327] For example, law 1, Title 2, Book 1 of the 1680 *Recopilación* asked Crown officers to provide information on the churches that should be established for the conversion of Native Americans.[328] Law 1, Title 23 of the same book, moreover, instructed on the creation of seminary

319 Ots Capdequí 1946, pp. 107–108.

320 Maluquer de Motes 1986, pp. 703–710.

321 García-Gallo 1977, at § 1368.

322 Bravo Lira 1989, p. 196; and Dougnac Rodríguez 1994, p. 277.

323 Bravo Lira 1989, p. 196.

324 See generally Recopilación de Indias 1680, I.

325 Sánchez Bella *et al.* 1992, p. 308.

326 Bravo Lira 1989, p. 197.

327 Bravo Lira 1989, p. 197.

328 The law in Spanish in part read: "[…] Ordenamos y mandamos á los Virreyes, Preſidentes y Governadores de nueſtras Indias, que nos informen y dén cuenta de las Igleſias que eſtán fundadas, y de las que pareciere conveniente fundar, para que los Indios que han recevido la Santa Fé Catolica, ſean enſeñados y doctrinados como conviene […]." (Recopilación de Indias 1680, I, at f. 7)

schools.[329] All those steps had an impact in the allocation of ownership, requiring the separation of land for the establishment of the Church's structure. Some religious orders (*v.gr.*, Jesuits) increased their land holdings over time, aiming to secure funds to maintain colleges. Those increments in land resulted from bequests from other landowners or from the default of landowners in complying with financial obligations with the Church, which had acted on occasion as creditor. Some of the holdings of the religious orders extended over the most attractive tracts of land, which many times were located at suitable distances from markets.[330] It should also be remembered that according to the *Siete Partidas*, sacred things, the temples and the tracts where they were built, belonged to the Church.[331]

The evangelization purpose of the American settlement motivated the creation of ecclesiastical enactments by the Crown, even with the approval of the Church. Those secular enactments aimed to facilitate the organization of the Church in the Americas, and occasionally could prevail over dispositions of canon law.[332] Secular enactments included, amongst others, matters dealing with the celebration of provincial or diocesan councils[333] or the applicability of papal bulls.[334] The Holy See needed to accept secular intervention because even when it had the missionaries to settle in America, it lacked the infrastructure (*v.gr.*, churches, hospitals, monasteries, schools) with which to develop the evangelization.[335] Ownership had to be allocated for all those spaces that assisted in the propagation of the Catholic faith. The Crown assisted in the propagation, yet required control and direction of those efforts.[336] That secular intervention was known as right of patronage (*derecho de patronato*), and had its origins, as did many other transplants, in the Peninsula.

329 The law in Spanish in part read: "[…] que funden, ſuſtenten, y conſerven los Colegios Seminarios, que diſpone el Santo Concilio de Trento […]." Recopilación de Indias 1680, I, at f. 121.

330 Mörner 1997, p. 194.

331 Bunge 1912–1913, II, p. 318.

332 García-Gallo 1977, at § 216.

333 The need to assure the evangelization of the Native Americans introduced the need to undertake the Provincial councils (*i.a.*, Lima, 1552, 1567, 1586, 1591, 1601, 1722; and Mexico, 1555, 1565, 1585, 1771). See Dougnac Rodríguez 1994, p. 284, 311; and Sánchez Bella *et al.* 1992, p. 277.

The 1680 *Recopilación* included provisions on councils in Title 8, Book 1. See Recopilación de Indias 1680, I, at f. 42–43v.

334 Sánchez Bella *et al.* 1992, p. 258.

335 Sánchez Bella *et al.* 1992, p. 259.

336 Sánchez Bella *et al.* 1992, p. 259.

During the *Reconquista*, *señores* were granted that right while settling new territories, securing the construction and financial support of churches, in exchange for the right to appoint officials in those churches.[337] Pope Julius II granted the right of patronage to the Crown by means of the papal bull *Universalis ecclesiae* of July 28, 1508,[338] offering an early start for that inherence of the Crown in Church affairs. The right of patronage was included in the 51 laws of Title 6, Book 1 of the 1680 *Recopilación*. For example, law 2 of that title stated that no church or pious place should be built without authorization by the Crown.[339]

3.5.3 *Native American Groups*

Native Americans were actors that likewise had an interest in the allocation of ownership. Native Americans, as they had done before the arrival of European settlers, generally held and exploited lands in common.[340] With time, settlers started to seek some lands held by Native Americans, due to the good location and quality of the lands.[341] Peninsular and creole settlers found it difficult to accept the idea of hunting grounds being held by nomadic groups, and this motivated the belief that ownership was acknowledged only in cases of sedentary groups.[342] Even when Native Americans had some privileges at the time of disposing of property[343] and had an officer that acted as their protector (*protector de naturales*), they were subject to many abuses and usurpations due to their lack of knowledge of the law and the lack of supervision.[344] The abuses ranged from illegal occupation to the sale of lands at extremely low prices.[345]

The Crown demonstrated interest in protecting Native Americans and the lands they were allocated by means of enacting legal precepts for the new territories.[346] Important provisions were placed in Book 4 of the 1680 *Recopilación*. For example, law 1, Title 7 of that book stated that new settlements should be made in vacant tracts and should not be made to the detriment of Native

337 Sánchez Bella *et al.* 1992, p. 273.

338 Sánchez Bella *et al.* 1992, p. 274.

339 The law in Spanish in part read: "[…] Mandamos, que no ſe erija, inſtituya, funde ni conſtituya Igleſia Catedral ni Parroquial, Monaſterio, Hoſpital, Igleſia votiva, ni otro lugar pio ni religioſo ſin licencia expreſſa nuestra […]." Recopilación de Indias 1680, I, at f. 21v.

340 Levaggi 1987, p. 210.

341 Levaggi 1987, p. 210.

342 Levaggi 1987, p. 211; and Sánchez Bella *et al.* 1992, p. 347.

343 Native Americans had, for example, the right to retract (*retracto*) and sales had to be publicly announced (*pregones*). Dougnac Rodríguez 1994, p. 324.

344 Levaggi 1987, p. 211.

345 Levaggi 1987, p. 211.

346 Sánchez Bella *et al.* 1992, p. 347.

Americans, or without their consent.[347] The detriment to Native Americans had to be avoided, and several laws of Title 12 of the same book referred to that detriment in different ways (*v.gr.*, grievance,[348] damage[349]); while law 18 indicated that sales should not affect lands that Native Americans held in common nor the waters they used for irrigation.[350] All of Book 6 of the 1680 text dealt exclusively with Native Americans.[351] For example, Title 10 of that book dealt in 23 laws with the good treatment that Native Americans should receive and—as indicated in law 3—Crown officers should be informed of mistreatment and abuses inflicted on Native Americans.[352] That same book devoted all 76 laws of Title 16 to the Native Americans that inhabited the present-day territory of Chile,[353] while all 14 laws of Title 17 were devoted to the Native Americans who inhabited parts of present-day Argentina.[354] Finally, a law from Title 17 of Book 4, for example, indicated that settlers should not allow their livestock to trespass onto Native American lands.[355]

3.5.4 *Corollary*

Provisions on ownership were found in code-like texts (*i.e.*, *Siete Partidas*, 1680 *Recopilación*) during the pre-independence period in the Americas. Furthermore, settlement in the Americas was undertaken both by private and by Crown intervention. All actors had concurrent interests in the allocation of ownership. Crown, Church, and Native Americans were part of that allocation scheme, and they defended their own interests. Allocation also included

---

347 The law in Spanish in part read: "[…] elijan el ſitio de los que eſtuvieren vacantes, y por diſpoſicion nueſtra ſe pueda ocupar, ſin perjuizio de los Indios, y naturales, ó con ſu libre conſentimiento […]." (Recopilación de Indias 1680, II, at f. 90v)

348 Law 7 included the Spanish term "agravio." Recopilación de Indias 1680, II, at f. 103.

349 Law 9 included the Spanish term "perjuizio." Recopilación de Indias 1680, II, at f. 103.

350 The law in Spanish in part read: "[…] ſe haga con tal atencion, que á los Indios ſe les dexen con ſobra todas las que les pertenecieren, aſsi en particular, como por Comunidades, y las aguas, y riegos […]." (Recopilación de Indias 1680, II, at f. 104v)

351 Recopilación de Indias 1680, II, at f. 188–274v.

352 The law in Spanish in part read: "[…] Mandamos [..] que tengan ſiempre mucho cuidado, y ſe informen de los exceſſos, y malos tratamientos, que ſe huvieren hecho, ó hizieren á los Indios incorporados en nueſtra Real Corona […]." (Recopilación de Indias 1680, II, at f. 234v)

353 Recopilación de Indias 1680, II, at f. 259–268v.

354 Recopilación de Indias 1680, II, at f. 269–271.

355 Law 10 in Spanish read: "Nvuestras Iuſticias no conſientan, que en las tierras de labor de los Indios ſe metan ganados, y hagan ſacar de ellas los que huviere, imponiendo, y executando graves penas contra los que contravinieren." (Recopilación de Indias 1680, II, at f. 113)

European settlers, who certainly played a most important role when receiving the grants of land from the Crown, and who aimed to benefit from the Allocation paradigm, exploiting the land they received. The allocation, as will be described *infra*, was individual or communal, and aimed to fulfill the different interests of the actors.

3.6 Individual Allocation

The Crown allotted individual ownership to settlers starting with the first expeditions. That allocation responded to the main interests of the Crown, both secular and spiritual. The Crown found in the settlers a partner to comply with the allocation of the new territories. Several efforts were devoted to allot ownership, and they were instrumented by different means, starting with the previously mentioned capitulations. For example, allotment of individual ownership could be effectively achieved through public auction of tracts of land since 1591,[356] or it could be pursued by means of the *encomienda*.[357] The primary means to allot individual ownership, however, was the emission of royal land grants, *i.e.*, the already mentioned *mercedes*.

The *encomienda* system, by which the activities of some Native Americans were regulated, was implemented in 1503 in the Americas.[358] The system was very important to the pursuit of Crown interests in the Americas, and was addressed mainly in Titles 8 to 11 of Book 6 of the 1680 *Recopilación*.[359] The transplantation of the *encomienda* from the Peninsula[360] was indeed part of the settlement process in the Americas.[361] The system—which exceeds the scope of this book—consisted in the division (*repartimiento*) of Native Americans into groups, and by assigning each group to a settler/landlord (*encomendero*) for work.[362] The Native Americans were kept in "deposit" by the *encomendero*, and by 1513, it was determined that that deposit would last for two lifetimes (*i.e.*, the life of the Native American and that of his son or daughter).[363] The *encomenderos* were obligated to pay the Native Americans a wage for their day

356 Cueto 1999, pp. 91–93, 229–238; and Ots Capdequí 1946, pp. 55–58.

357 Barraclough 1973, p. 4.

358 See generally Zavala 1992.

359 Recopilación de Indias 1680, II, at f. 221–240v.

360 Góngora 1951, p. 104.

361 For the implementation in Chile, see, for example, Góngora 1970.

362 See García-Gallo 1977, at § 1281 *et seq.*; and Margadant 1980, p. 967.

363 García-Gallo 1977, at § 1282.

of work and for their maintenance, and starting in 1509, they were obligated to instruct them in the Catholic faith, and to teach them how to read and write. Finally, the *encomenderos* had to pay as taxation one *peso* in gold for every Native American who belonged to the *encomienda*.[364] It should be noted that the *encomienda* did not provide a right on the land, yet it did provide a factual link with the land, and several *encomenderos* ultimately claimed the right of ownership on the land they had occupied.[365]

3.6.1 *Transplantation of the Royal Land Grants System*

The *mercedes* system—being the dominant means to allot individual ownership—was likewise transplanted from the Peninsula, and was introduced in the Americas during the sixteenth and seventeenth centuries. Royal land grants can be conceptualized—following the words of Levaggi—as the way by which the Crown disposed of vacant tracts of lands, which were not considered the property of Native Americans. The Crown granted land, onerously or gratuitously, to the vassals of every kind (including Native Americans[366]), who had established cities, had rendered a service, or had simply requested it.[367] Royal confirmation (*confirmación*), furthermore, was needed when land was granted by an official (*i.a.*, viceroy) on behalf of the monarch.[368] This confirmation by the monarch was important for different aspects of the American settlement, assisting in the control by the Peninsular authority. The confirmation was addressed by the already mentioned de León Pinelo, who drafted his *Tratado de confirmaciones reales de Encomiendas, Oficios i Caſos, en que ſe requieren para las Indias Occidentales* (1630), an influential *opus* dedicated exclusively to the topic. In Chapter 23 of Part 2 of that work, he mentioned that *mercedes* required royal confirmation within the first year and a half of their granting.[369]

The *mercedes* system—as already mentioned—had its origins in the Iberian Peninsula, during the *Reconquista* period, and was transplanted to the Americas. Mariluz Urquijo pointed out that the *Reconquista* provided significant amounts of vacant tracts of lands in the Peninsula, and that resettlement

364 García-Gallo 1977, at § 1282.

365 Borde & Góngora 1956, p. 3; Barraclough 1973, p. 4; and Levaggi 1987, pp. 210–211.

366 Miller Astrada 1985, pp. 389–390. Native American groups, in practice, encountered more difficulties to own land. Sato 1976, p. 17.

367 Levaggi 1987, p. 211.

368 See law 2, Title 19, Book 6 in Recopilación de Indias 1680, II, at f. 273v. See also Levaggi 1987, p. 211.

369 The text in Spanish in part read: "gracia i merced, en remuneracion de ſervicios [...] llevaſſe confirmacion del Rey, dentro de año i medio." (León Pinelo (de) 1630, at f. 170v) See also Ots Capdequí 1945, p. 282.

had to secure economic, political, military, and religious objectives.[370] In Castile, some *mercedes* were granted on the condition of building castles or fortifications to secure territories. Others required farming and the constructions of dwellings, on occasion even restricting ownership to the completion of conditions that aimed at the well-being of the Crown and of society at large.[371] Furthermore, during the *Reconquista*, the requirement of the *aprisio* emerged, being a title required for the acquisition of ownership and being granted by the monarch to nobles who had accompanied him in military campaigns during the *Reconquista*. Nobles could occupy tracts of land once they received the *aprisio*, and ownership (*i.e.*, *señorío*, *dominio*, *propiedad*) occurred only with the effective occupation and settlement of the land.[372] The granting of lands also implied a service to the monarch. That required service was prescribed in the 1464 *Ordenanzas Reales de Castilla* of Henry IV (Enrique IV). According to law 2, Title 9, Book 5 of the *Ordenanzas*, those who had been granted *mercedes* had to support the monarch in times of war and peace, demonstrating that there was a clear duty to render services.[373] *Mercedes* could indeed be terminated if the service was not rendered, as was made clear in the already mentioned encyclopedic *Teatro* of Pérez y López, where it was specified that a *merced* would be terminated—even with an additional pecuniary sanction—if the beneficiary did not react to the request of the monarch to serve during war.[374] Accordingly, it may be concluded that in the Peninsula monarchs opted to grant *mercedes* to those who had contributed in the reconquering of lands from the Muslims, offering therefore rewards or prizes.

The land-grant system that was applied in the Peninsula to resettle lands taken from the Muslims was a handy tool when searching for ways to settle the American territories.[375] The transplantation of the system had positive results in the Americas, and it helped in ordering the distribution of land recently acquired. Levene stated that the settlement of America was a joint endeavor between the monarch and the settler, and it was not solely a despotic decision of the monarch. The individual initiative of settlers and the rewards and

370 Mariluz Urquijo 1978, p. 17.

371 Mariluz Urquijo 1978, p. 17.

372 Ots Capdequí 1946, p. 43.

373 The text in Spanish in part read: "[...] que aquellos á quien fuesen fechas las tales donaciones, y mercedes, sean tenidos de facer guerra, y paz por mandato del rey à su señorio real, y no la puedan del apartar [...]." (Códigos Españoles 1847–1851, VI, p. 412)

374 Pérez y López 1791–1798, XX, p. 124.

375 Miller Astrada 1985, p. 373. See also Godreau & Giusti 1993, pp. 397–400; and Lira Montt 1998, pp. 236–237.

guarantees by the monarch proved to be a successful partnership.[376] It was with the rewards that settlers received, by means of the *mercedes*, that the American settlement took strength.[377] For example, in the present-day territory of Argentina, an overwhelming majority of *mercedes* were granted to conquerors, members of the military, or other privileged members of society, all having indicated in their petition of land grant the services they had rendered to the monarch during the pacification of the territory.[378] It was henceforth reaffirmed that all territories were royal holdings of the Crown of Castile, and that any individual right was subject to the grace of the monarch, instrumented by means of a *merced*.[379]

The rewards implemented by the *mercedes* operated within a legal framework, and may be seen as the antecedents for the *latifundios* that persisted over the centuries in American Civil Law Jurisdictions.[380] The 1680 *Recopilación* encapsulated the reward system of *mercedes* mainly in Title 12 of Book 4.[381] Two provisions made the aims of the monarch especially visible. On the one hand, law 1, which stated that "[…] new settlers [should] receive lands […]," hence making the allocation of ownership of paramount importance for the American endeavor.[382] On the other hand, law 10, which instructed that "lands should be divided amongst discoverers and settlers, not being able to sell them to the Church […] subject to losing the land and that the land is granted to another petitioner […],"[383] hence demonstrating that monarchs indeed expected the allocation to follow their settlement policies.

3.6.2 *Implementation of Royal Land Grants* (*Argentine Illustration*)

Mercedes were implemented in a ritualistic manner, and documents that were issued mainly for the present-day territory of Argentina help illustrate the

376 Levene 1934, p. 84.

377 Vitar 1995, p. 35.

378 García 1953, p. 23.

379 Ots Capdequí 1946, p. 41.

380 Stavenhagen 1970, p. 6.

381 Recopilación de Indias 1680, II, at f. 102–105v.

382 The heading of the law in Spanish read: "Que à los nuevos pobladores ſe les den tierras, y ſolares […]." (Recopilación de Indias 1680, II, at f. 102)

383 The law in Spanish read: "Repártanse Las tierras ſin exceſſo entre deſcubridores, y pobladores antiguos, y ſus deſcendientes, que hayan de permanecer en la tierra, y ſea preferidos los mas calificados, y no las puedan vender á Igleſia, ni Monaſterio, ni á otra perſona Ecleſiaſtica, pena de que las hayan perdido, y pierdan, y puedan repartirſe á otros." (Recopilación de Indias 1680, II, at f. 103)

modus operandi.[384] The documents that were studied showed that *mercedes* were generally granted after an individual petition of land grant.[385] Those initial petitions were followed by a survey of the land and the drafting of a title of *merced*. Beneficiaries, ultimately, had to enter into possession of lands, a ritual that was registered in a notarial act.[386] It should be initially noted that *mercedes* were granted on territories that were vacated at the time of request. For example, a document in San Salvador de Jujuy dated on December 3, 1593, issued by the Lieutenant Governor Don Francisco de Argañaras in favor of the Jesuit order, clearly read that the *merced* was granted on a tract of land that was at that time vacated.[387] *Mercedes* were likewise granted on tracts of land that had been granted previously, though previous owners had not occupied them according to the dispositions of Title 12 of Book 4 of the 1680 *Recopilación*. For example, the *cabildo*[388] of Lima (in present-day Peru) stated in a document dated January 17, 1539, that a tract of land should be given to a new beneficiary (*i.e.*, Hernand Goncales) because the previous beneficiary (*i.e.*, Diego Ruiz) had not settled and fenced the land as it was required by law.[389] Another important preliminary aspect is that individual allocation could also be achieved by a *merced* that affected several individual and distinct beneficiaries in a single document. Accordingly, multiple individual allocations could be included in a single document of *merced*. This type of individual allocation was present in, for example, a *merced* granted by Jerónimo Luis de Cabrera to, amongst other beneficiaries, Nunflo de Aguilar and Mexia Mirabal in 1573 in the city of Córdoba.[390]

---

384 See the complete study by José María Mariluz Urquijo, providing valuable information on different aspects of the *mercedes*. Mariluz Urquijo 1978, pp. 33–57. See also, in general, the complete study that deals with the present-day Argentine territory of Salta, in Miller Astrada 1985.

385 Greve 1941, p. x.

386 Greve 1941, p. xvi.

387 The document in Spanish in part read: "[...] esta chacra viene a caer en la 28 suerte. Ya las 12 suertes ya no ay cosa. Con que esta despoblada [...]." (Archivo General)

388 *Cabildos* were originally allowed to issue *mercedes*. However, starting in 1589, those grants required the confirmation of the monarch. See law 20, Title 12, Book 4 of the 1680 *Recopilación*. Recopilación de Indias 1680, II, at f. 104v. See also Dougnac Rodríguez 1994, pp. 177–178.

389 The text in Spanish read: "en xvij de henero de Udxxxjx años [...] este dia hernand goncales Regidor pidio a sus mercedes le den un solar para hernand goncales su sobrino que era de Diego Ruiz por no le aver poblado e cercado como era obligado [...]." (Lee 1935, p. 294)

390 The text in Spanish read: "[...] Iten, dixo que señalava y señalo otro pedazo, como el de arriba, a Nunflo de Aguilar: alinde con Mexia Mirabal [...]." (Grenón 1930, p. 18)

The petition or request—being the first step towards the allocation of individual ownership—was made before the officials that were authorized to grant *mercedes* (*v.gr.*, viceroy, lieutenant governor) and with time it required royal confirmation.[391] One document, for example, indicated that Diego de Tapia requested a *merced* on June 11, 1583, before the Captain Antonio de Alfaro, Lieutenant Governor and Justice of the city of Salta.[392] Another document, this time from Lima and dated February 7, 1539, showed that the local *cabildo* dealt with petitions.[393]

All petitions indicated the name of petitioners and the reasons for their requests. For example, in 1612, in the present-day Argentine province of Tucumán, the petition of Don Francisco de Salcedo read: "that being treasurer of this holy Cathedral Church and Commissioner of the Inquisition and of the Holy Crusade, I hereby state that I am in need of a tract of land for the raising of livestock."[394] There was likewise need to clearly circumscribe the extension of the *merced*, either in a unit of length or by describing geographical landmarks that would help in locating the tract of land. For example, a 1579 *merced* granted by Gaspar de Medina to Juan Bautista Muñoz in the city of San Miguel de Tucumán read:

> that [the tract of land] extends from the water source of Belicha, that runs across the intersection of the two roads that direct to the area of Natives of Turibio Gonzalez and the other to the area of Natives of Luis Caldera; and that extends for three miles, running from the Seco river until the Guaucombo river.[395]

---

391 Levaggi 1987, p. 211; and Mariluz Urquijo 1978, pp. 33–37.

392 The text in Spanish read: "[…] ante el ilustre senor capitán Antonio de Alfaro teniente de gobierno y justicia mayor ensta dha zudad por su magestad […]." (Cornejo & Vergara 1938, p. 16)

393 The text in Spanish read: "siete de hebrero de I Udxxxjx años […] este dia se Juntaron en su cabildo e ayuntamiento segund que lo an de uso e de costumbre los magnificos señores Justicia e regidores desta dicha cibdad es a saber francisco de chaves tenyente de governador e domingo de la presa e francisco de herera alcaldes ordinarios e el veedor garcia de salzedo e el licenciado benito de carabajal e hernand goncales e Juan de leon Regidores para entender e proueer en las cosas del seruicio de dios nuestro señor e de su magestad e bien e proComun en presencia de mi pedro de salinas escriuano de su magestad e de Cabildo […]." (Lee 1935, p. 300)

394 The text in Spanish read: "[…] tesorero de esta santa Iglesia Catedral y Comisario del Santo Oficio y de la Santa Cruzada, digo que yo tengo necesidad de un pedazo de tierra para chácaras y estancias de ganados […]." (Lizondo Borda 1936, III, p. 46)

395 The text in Spanish read: "[…] que corra desde la ramada o aguada de la punta de Belicha, que se entiende desde la junta de los dos caminos que van a los indios de Turibio

Titles of *merced* followed petitions, being documents that stated the granting of the tract of land. These documents included references to time and place, name of grantors, reasons for granting, restrictions, and the order to enter into possession.[396] Firstly, all consulted titles included references to the time and place where they were subscribed. Those references were made visible in the header of titles, as mentioned, for example, in a title by de Cabrera that stated "in the city of Córdoba on the thirtieth day of the month of December of the year one thousand, five hundred and seventy three; beginning of the year one thousand, five hundred and seventy-four."[397] References were made also in the footer of titles, as indicated in a text signed by Alfonso de Vera y Aragón "in the city of Vera [present-day city of Corrientes] on the twenty-third day of the month of August of one thousand, five hundred and ninety-one."[398] Secondly, titles included the name of the person who granted the *merced* on behalf of the monarch. For example, a 1570 title indicated that Juan García received a tract of land on behalf of the monarch from "Diego de Saldaña, Captain and Lieutenant Governor of this city of San Miguel de Tucumán."[399] Thirdly, titles indicated the reasons why *merceds* were granted: either due to a petition or due to the self-motivated will of the monarch. In the former cases, references were made to the motivating petitions, as indicated in a title of 1631 in Tucumán, which stated that "the granting was made [...] according to and in the place and part

Gonzalez y el otro a los indios de Luis Caldera; que tenga de cabezada una legua, que corra el río Seco abajo e lo demás hasta el río de Guaucombo [...]." (Lizondo Borda 1936, I, p. 68)

396 Language-use provides valuable information on the law at different time periods. Analyses on language-use are external tools for legal historians in their work. On the language used in the documents dealing with *mercedes* in Córdoba, see the interesting study in Prevedello 1992.

397 The text in Spanish read: "En la dha. Ciudad de Córdova en treinta dias del mes de diciembre de mill e quinos. setenta e tres años principio del año mill quinos. setenta e quatro el Dho. Govor. Don Gmo. Luis de Cabrera [...]." (Grenón 1930, p. 27)

398 The text in Spanish read: "[...] que es fecho en la ciudad de Vera en veinti y tres dias del mes de Agosto de mil y quinientos y noventa y uno. [Sgd.] Alfonso de Vera y Aragón." (Corrientes (Provincia de) 1877, p. 7)

399 The text in Spanish read: "[...] Diego de Saldaña, capitan y teniente de gobernador en esta ciudad de San Miguel de Tucumán, sus terminos y jurisdission, por el muy ilustre señor Francisco de Aguirre, gobernador y capitan general e justicia mayor de estas provincias de Tucumán, Juries y Diaguitas y todo lo de mas de esta parte de la Cordillera, por su Magestad [...]." (Lizondo Borda 1936, I, p. 37)

indicated in the petition"[400] In the latter cases, monarchs could aim to comply with their allocation interests (*i.e.*, political, economic, tax), rewarding settlers for their services. For example, an early document, dated in 1592, read "[you receive this grant] because you, Captain Melián de Leguisamo, neighbor of the city of San Miguel de Tucumán, [were] conqueror and settler of these provinces."[401] Another title, likewise, mentioned that the *merced* was granted

> since you, Francisco Ortis de Leguisamo, are a meritorious person and served the King for more than twelve years in this part of the Provinces of Río de la Plata, on every possible occasion, with your weapons and horses (at your own cost), and you are one of the first settlers and conquerors of this city, [...] where you have worked and undergone excessive endeavors and suffered hunger [...].[402]

Fourthly, titles of *merced* included references to the prohibition to grant if being to the detriment of third parties or Native Americans. This restriction was mentioned in most consulted titles. For example, a 1592 title from Tucumán read "[granted] with no detriment to naturals [*i.e.*, Native Americans] or any other person;"[403] while a 1583 title, from Salta, read "with no detriment to a third person."[404] Finally, titles concluded with a statement ordering the effective entering into possession by the beneficiary. For example, a 1596 title read:

---

400 The text in Spanish read: "[...] le hacia e hizo merced [...] según y como y en la parte y lugar que contiene el pedimento [...]." (Lizondo Borda 1936, III, p. 192)

401 The text in Spanish read: "[...] por cuanto vos el capitan Melian de Leguisamo, vecino de la ciudad de San Miguel de Tucumán, conquistador y poblador destas provincias [...]." (Lizondo Borda 1936, I, p. 104)

402 A more extensive part of the excerpt in Spanish read: "[...] atento a que vos Francisco Ortis de Leguisamo, soys persona benemerita habeys servido a S.M. de mas de doce años a esta parte en estas Provincias del Rio de la Plata en todas las ocasiones que se han ofrecido con vuestra, armas y caballos a vuestra costa y mi...sion y soys uno de los primeros descubridores, pobladores y conquistadores desta ciudad y os hallasteys a la fundacion de ella en compañia del adelantado Jn. de Torres de Vera y Aragón Gobernador, Capitan General y Justicia Mayor de todas estas Provincias del Rio de la Plata por S.M., donde habeis trabajado y padecido mucho eccesibos trabajos y hambre en esta conquista de los naturales de ella, todo a vuestra costa minsion y armas y caballos [...]." (Lizondo Borda 1936, I, p. 104)

403 The text in Spanish read: "[...] sin perjuicio de naturales ni de otra persona [...]." (Mariluz Urquijo 1978, p. 80)

404 The text in Spanish read: "[...] syn perjuyzio de tercera persona [...]." (Cornejo & Vergara 1938, p. 55)

> I hereby request justices of this city to give actual possession of the abovementioned lands, and to protect the holder from evictions without being head or defeated by means of law or *fuero*, subject to a penalty of five hundred *pesos* to be paid to the treasury of the King.[405]

Titles of *merced* were followed by the entering into possession of the lands, and hence, the individual allocation of ownership was completed. The entering into possession was mandatory, and if it did not occur, *mercedes* were not valid. The 1680 *Recopilación* instructed in law 11, Title 12, Book 4 that the actual possession had to be taken within three months of the drafting of the title of *merced*.[406] Beneficiaries had to be present *in situ*, as exemplified in a document that read "I came to the lands mentioned in the *merced* by the Governor."[407] Beneficiaries were generally accompanied by witnesses and by a local authority. In addition, a notary would join the group to provide full proof of the acts that took place, and to draft a notarial act. For example, a notarial act drafted during the entering into possession of a *merced* granted in 1599 in Lules (Tucumán), read that a notary, witnesses, the beneficiary, and the mayor (being the local authority) were present at the time of entering into possession.[408] Once parties were present at the locations, the titles of *merced* were read aloud. The parties assured that geographical descriptions were accurate, and followed the beneficiaries into the tracts of land. Local authorities guided the beneficiaries by the hand, and explored the tracts of land. Finally, beneficiaries would try to show full rights to dispose of the property. Several documents clearly illustrated the efforts to achieve full enjoyment of rights. For example, one document read that "to show possession [a beneficiary] cut weeds and drew his sword

405 The text in Spanish read: "[…] mando a las justicias mayores y ordinarias de esta ciudad le den la posesion de las dichas tierras y en ella le amparen y defiendan y no consientan sea desposeido sin primero ser oido y vencido por fuero y derecho, so pena de quinientos pesos de oro, para la camara de su Magestad […]." (Lizondo Borda 1936, I, p. 108)

406 The text in Spanish read: "Todos Los vezinos y moradores á quien ſe hiziere repartimiento de tierras, ſean obligados dentro de tres meſes, que les fueren ſeñalados, á tomar la poſſeſsion de ellas […] pena de que paſſado el termino […] dar á otro qualquiera poblador […]." (Recopilación de Indias 1680, II, at f. 103–103v)
See also Mariluz Urquijo 1978, p. 55.

407 The text in Spanish read: "[…] vine a las tierras que en la merced del Señor Gobernador se contienen […]." (Lizondo Borda 1936, I, p. 145)

408 The text in Spanish read: "[…] parecio presente ante el susodicho y por ante mi el presente escribano y de los testigos […]." (Mariluz Urquijo 1978, p. 82)

and cut down branches [from a tree];"[409] and likewise that a beneficiary "cut some weeds from the field."[410] Furthermore, another document indicated that a beneficiary "requested that everybody would leave his lands."[411] Finally, titles indicated that no third parties opposed the entering into possession. Several documents accordingly specified that lack of opposition, for example, by stating that the beneficiary "took possession with nobody opposing, on a clear day, and before witnesses."[412]

3.6.3 *Royal Land Grants in Louisiana and Chile*

The *mercedes* system was the main means by which individual allocation of ownership was instrumented. Even when geographically close to Río de la Plata, *mercedes* in the present-day territory of Chile showed particularities, and—naturally—similarities with the application in other parts of the Americas. *Mercedes* were granted in Chile, as early as in other territories, to advance the settlement, being indeed one of the main interests of the Crown.[413] For example, it is known that Pedro de Valdivia alloted *mercedes* when he established Santiago.[414] In addition, in present-day Chile, until 1575, the *cabildos* granted *mercedes*, and that afterwards that duty fell on the representatives of the Crown, such as viceroys and governors.[415] Likewise, royal confirmation was not fully enforced in the territory.[416] In Chile, both the *cabildos* and the representatives of the monarch tended to grant *mercedes* in a broad and liberal manner.[417] Furthermore, there were no effective means to protect the land of Native Americans when granting *mercedes* in Chile.[418] For example, Tomás Pastene received a tract of land in Curacaví in 1583, and he then relocated the Native Americans who had been under his *encomienda* to Pomaire, a territory about 50 kilometers south.[419] Some *mercedes* naturally followed from previous

---

409 The text in Spanish read: "[…] en señal de posesion arranco yerbas y saco su espada y destronco ramas […]." (Lizondo Borda 1936, III, p. 197)

410 The text in Spanish read: "[…] arranco algunas yerbas del campo […]." (Mariluz Urquijo 1978, p. 83)

411 The text in Spanish read: "[…] y a todos mando se fuesen de sus tierras […]." (Lizondo Borda 1936, III, p. 122)

412 The text in Spanish read: "[…] tomo la dicha posesión sin contradicción de persona alguna, de día claro y en presencia de testigos […]." (Lizondo Borda 1936, III, p. 131)

413 Góngora 1951, p. 151.

414 Campos Harriet 1956, p. 70.

415 Borde & Góngora 1956, p. 30.

416 Borde & Góngora 1956, p. 33.

417 Borde & Góngora 1956, p. 31.

418 Borde & Góngora 1956, p. 32.

419 Borde & Góngora 1956, p. 32.

encomiendas.[420] A 1547 document showed that tracts of land, some even neighboring those of *encomiendas*, would be given preferably to *encomenderos*.[421] The need to clearly circumscribe the extension of a *merced,* either in a unit of length or by describing geographical landmarks, was required in Chilean documents. For example, a 1604 document subscribed by Captain Ginés de Lillo y Gil, dealing with lands in Curacaví, described the extension of the *merced* by referring to landmarks that enclosed the tract, landmarks such as the "Curacaví valley," the "Poangue river," and the "two mountain ranges."[422] The entering into possession also presented similarities with the *mercedes* granted in the present-day territory of Argentina. For example, in Chile, a notarial act by Alonso del Castillo, dated June 9, 1567, read

> he held him by the hand and walked through [the land], and gave him actual corporal possession. Juan Perez Gabilán strolled around the tract to show the possession and acquisition of his right. He also shot his harquebus and asked for testimony of how he peacefully and quietly took possession; and he indeed took possession and the Alcalde order he would have [possession].[423]

Boundaries between tracts of lands (*i.e.*, between *mercedes*), were sometimes vague, motivating disputes before courts or *cabildos*, not only in Santiago.[424] Accordingly, as early as 1586, the *cabildo* of Santiago instructed beneficiaries of grants to produce their titles for inspection.[425] Finally, it should be noted that in Santiago and Buenos Aires, distribution of tracts by *cabildos* tended to favor some neighbors, generally neglecting extensive tracts to new settlers.[426]

---

420 Góngora 1951, p. 161.

421 Góngora 1951, pp. 162–163.

422 The text in Spanish read: "[…] desde la punta del dicho valle de curacavi que cae sobre el rio de poangue en aquella deresera a los propios cerros del dicho curacavi y de largo río arriba de la una y otra parte dél linderos las dos cordilleras en el cual dicho valle se incluyen ciento y cinco cuadras del dicho título." (Greve 1941, p. l)

423 The text in Spanish read: "[…] le tomó por la mano y paseó por ella y le dió la dicha posesion actual corporal vel cuasi y el dicho Juan Perez Gabilán en señal de posesion y adquisicion de su derecho se paseo por la dicha chacara y dió ciertos arcabuzazos y lo pidió por testimonio como quieta y pacificamente tomaba e tomó la dicha posesion y el dicho señor alcalde se la mandó dar […]." (Greve 1941, p. liii)

424 See, for example, the reference to the boundary problems in Córdoba in Tagle 2003, p. 184.

425 Sato 1976, p. 7.

426 Sato 1976, p. 7.

Mercedes were granted in the present-day territory of Louisiana.[427] A number of these were issued during the French[428] and Spanish[429] periods,[430] by the Superior Council or the New Orleans *Cabildo*[431] and by officers representing the monarchs.[432] In that part of the Americas, large tracts of land were likewise given as *merced* to those settlers who had rendered services to the Crown.[433] The already mentioned *Ordinance on Land Grants*[434] of 1770 by O'Reilly described the way in which concessions of land were to be made in "the name of the King."[435] Furthermore, the previously mentioned *Regulations*

---

427 See, for example, information on the *mercedes* implemented in the region of the Ouachita river in Chambers 1925, pp. 382–385. See also Farnan 1972, pp. 1–9; and Arnold 1996, pp. 133–137.

428 Even when it exceeds the scope of this book, it can be stated that the French Superior Council dealt with the petitions of land grants during the French period in Louisiana. This is illustrated in a February 8, 1724 land grant petition by D'Artiguiéres and de Bénét for a site on behalf of Count d'Artagnan (Chambers 1925, p. 127). It has been claimed that the French and Spanish crowns' interests in the Americas had similar aims and similar land-tenure systems, hence facilitating the assimilation of the former French territory as part of the Spanish Crown. See Arena 1974, pp. 52–54.

429 The Spanish Crown recognized previous French land grants. For example, in upper Louisiana, French land grants were confirmed in 1770 by Captain Pedro Piernes, who was appointed Lieutenant Governor by Alejandro O'Reilly. See Chambers 1925, p. 297.

430 Bailey 1942, p. 28.

431 On the role of the *cabildo* in granting *mercedes*, see Din & Harkins 1996, pp. 259–268.

432 *Mercedes* were granted by the Spanish monarchs in Louisiana even during the period 1800–1803, after Napoleon I (Napoléon I) had secured the return of Louisiana to France. The US government committed to recognize and honor the grants that had been given during the French and Spanish periods. See Bailey 1942, p. 28, 41.

See, for example, the petition of *merced*, in Spanish, by Josef Denese, dated September 2, 1803, available at Favrot Papers 1801–1803, pp. 161–162.

433 Farnan 1972, p. 4; and Arena 1974, p. 60.

434 The Spanish title was *Ordenanza relativa a Mercedes de Tierras y Solares*. For more information on the Spanish land-laws in Louisiana, see generally Burns 1928.

435 Article 12 of the *Ordinance* read: "All grants shall be made in the name of the King, by the governor general of the province, who will, at the same time appoint a surveyor to fix the bounds thereof, both in front and depth, in presence of the ordinary judge of the district, and of two adjoining settlers, who shall be present at the survey. The above mentioned four persons shall sign the process verbal which shall be made thereof, and the surveyor shall make three copies of the same; one of which shall be deposited in the office of the escribano of the Government and cabildo, another shall be delivered to the governor general, and the third to the proprietor, to be annexed to the titles of his grant." (Schmidt 1841, p. 64)

For more information on the changes implemented by Alejandro O'Reilly dealing with land grants, see Ker Texada 1968, pp. 162–164.

on Land Grants of 1799 by Ventura Morales were amongst the most comprehensive land laws in Spanish Louisiana.[436] Through 38 articles,[437] made available additionally in French,[438] the text of the regulations aimed to provide the basic tenets for dealing with land grants. Louisiana, differently from other American Civil Law Jurisdictions, presented a melting pot of languages, and article 33 of the regulations stated nevertheless that "as far as it shall be practicable the inhabitants shall endeavor that the petitions presented to ask for lands be written in the Spanish language [...]."[439] A document dated February 12, 1799—months before the enactment of the *Regulations on Land Grants*—showed that petitions and corresponding reactions from officers were indeed multilingual, surely presenting additional challenges for the administration of land grants.[440] Similarly to *mercedes* in other territories of the Americas, Ventura Morales set down in article 15 of his Regulations that

> all concessions shall be given in the name of the King, by the general intendant of this province, who shall order the surveyor general or one particularly named by him to make the survey, and mark the land by fixing bounds, not only in front but also in the read; this [survey] ought to be done in the presence of the commandant or syndic of the district, and of two of the neighbors, and these four shall sing the *proces verbal*, which shall be drawn up by the surveyor.[441]

Article 16, furthermore, stated that "The said *proces verbal* [giving an account of events], with a certified copy of the same, shall be sent by the surveyor to the intendant, to the end that on the original there be delivered, by the consent of the King's attorney, the necessary title paper [...]."[442] *Mercedes* were instrumented in Louisiana according to the *Indiano* legal order, including the

436 Burns 1928, p. 569.

437 See Regulations of Ventura Morales 1799. There is an abbreviated version in Burns 1928, pp. 570–574.

438 The Regulations indicated in the footer that the text should be translated into French by Pierre Derbigny, who acted as interpreter of the king (Regulations of Ventura Morales 1799, p. 734). Derbigny later played a significant role in the drafting of the 1825 Louisiana Civil Code. See generally 4.3.1 of this book.

439 Regulations of Ventura Morales 1799, p. 734.

440 That document dealt with the petition in French by Adam Boyd to Governor Manuel Gayoso de Lemos and the reaction of the latter officer in Spanish. Favrot Papers 1796–1799, pp. 134–135.

441 Regulations of Ventura Morales 1799, p. 733.

442 Regulations of Ventura Morales 1799, p. 733.

abovementioned regulations and ordinances.[443] For example, documents showed that Narcisse Carriere petitioned a grant of a tract of land of 3.2 square kilometers on the Vermilion river on November 24, 1777. That petition, resulted in fixing "the boundaries of the said land in presence of the said Narcisse Carriere and the neighbors,"[444] and resulted in a title dated in New Orleans on June 23, 1781, being subscribed by Governor Bernardo de Gálvez y Madrid, in favor of the petitioner.[445] Finally, it should be highlighted again that in Louisiana the Crown was interested—as in other parts of the Americas—in having lands settled,[446] and documents stated that land had to be surveyed and that grants required royal confirmation.[447]

3.6.4 *Corollary*

The individual allocation of ownership responded to the different concurring interests of the different actors. The allocation through royal land grants was applied in the Americas, being the dominant means to allot individual ownership, and finding its origins in the Iberian Peninsula. *Mercedes* were indeed implemented in a ritualistic manner (*i.e.*, petition, survey, drafting of title, entering into possession, registration in notarial act). The present-day territories of Louisiana, Chile, and Argentina were no exceptions to the implementation of the *mercedes* system. That system indeed enabled settlers to become partners of the Crown in the American efforts. The *Indiano* legal order provided the common framework within which the allocation had to be implemented, yet each territory had its own particularities at the time of implementing those rules. The implementation of *mercedes* showed that there was a joint effort between the monarchs who granted those documents and the different settlers who aimed to secure the different tracts of land. The Allocation paradigm, which is central to this chapter, was likewise sensed by means of the communal allocation of ownership. The communal allocation, as will be illustrated *infra*, also responded to the interests of the different actors, and together with the individual allocation secured the feasibility of a monumental endeavor throughout a vast territory.

---

443 Joseph M. White provided a rich repository of land law provisions. See generally White 1839.

444 Land Claims in Louisiana 1859, p. 506.

445 Land Claims in Louisiana 1859, p. 506. See also Burns 1928, p. 575.

446 Kniffen & Hilliard 1988, p. 129.

447 Bailey 1942, p. 28.

3.7 Communal Allocation

The Allocation paradigm was shaped both by the individual and by communal control over property. The Crown allotted communal ownership, again, starting already with the first expeditions[448] and responding to its main interests, both secular and spiritual. Communitarian holding continuously influenced the settlement endeavors of the Crown.[449] Communal allocation, therefore, coexisted with individual allocation, and found its origins, as other legal transplants, in the Iberian Peninsula.[450] For more than 300 years, and on both sides of the Atlantic, the Crown allotted communal ownership through different means and to different actors. Communal allocation responded, beyond the American experience, to the early needs to secure life and offer protection.[451] In America, for example, water sources and pastures were of paramount importance for the raising of livestock, while woodlands were fundamental sources for timber.[452] Accordingly, at that time some property could be held in common (*comunales*) by all neighbors[453] of a settlement (*v.gr.*, city, village) and by all members of a Native American group. Property held in common belonged to and was exploited jointly by all those actors, and it extended over woodlands (*montes*), pastures (*pastos*), and water sources (*aguadas*).[454] Those actors comprised a universality of holders. Only members of that universality could benefit from the ownership, and as clearly advocated by José Berní y Catalá, in his *Instituta Civil y Real* (1745), "those foreign to the neighborhood could not use [the property] unless they had a permit from the universality."[455] Furthermore, property could be held commonly directly by settlements (*propios*), when local administrations secured on behalf of all settlers the exploitation of property, aiming to generate income for the settlement.[456] Allotting communal holdings, both in *comunales* and in *propios*, aimed to achieve one

448 Ots Capdequí 1940, p. 80.

449 Ots Capdequí 1945, p. 451.

450 For more information on the evolution of communal holdings in the Iberian Peninsula (together with some primary documents), see Nieto 1964, pp. 101–132.

451 Camps y Arboix (de) 1953, p. 95.

452 Storni 1997, p. 20.

453 The term "neighbor" was given a broad interpretation during the first decades. Accordingly, neighbors were all who had an inhabited dwelling within the city. See Sánchez Bella *et al.* 1992, p. 175.

454 Levaggi 1987, p. 212.

455 The text in Spanish read: "[…] los de agena vecindad no pueden uſar à menos que con licencia de la Univerſidad […]." Berní y Catalá 1760, pp. 55–56.

456 Clemente Campos 1994–1995, p. 441.

of the paramount interests of the Crown, *i.e.*, secure the effective settlement of population, establishing a nucleus of population.[457] Communal allocation could indeed assist in achieving that objective.

3.7.1 Comunales *and* Propios: *Origins and Implementation*

Comunales and *propios* found their origins in the Iberian Peninsula, and were implanted in the new continent.[458] Other European territories were familiar with somehow similar forms of communal holdings—as indicated by references to *commons* or *commune*[459]—that developed in, amongst others, France, Italy, and Portugal, and in areas occupied by Celtic and Germanic groups.[460] The general doctrine that advocated for a common holding of woodlands, pastures, and water sources applied both in the Peninsula and in the Americas.[461] It naturally found its origins in similar juridical principles and was applied by a bureaucracy that emerged from the same cast or mold.[462] The *comunales* and *propios* were characteristic of Castile, and were generally plotted by the first settlers of villages or cities.[463] Communal holding was used as a means to secure the resettlement of territories reconquered from the Muslims during the *Reconquista*.[464] In the Americas, however, some *cabildos* confused the administration of *comunales* and *propios*. For example, a document from the *cabildo* of Montevideo (Uruguay) indicated that officers leased a tract of land belonging to the *comunales*—instead of to the *propios*—for a five-year period.[465]

Comunales included several elements. For example, they comprised the *ejido*, which was located close to dwelling areas, and was used for grazing livestock and crop cultivation; and the *dehesa*, which was located farther away from dwelling areas, and was used also in common.[466] *Ejidos* took their name from the Latin word *exitus* and were intended for the benefit of all neighbors, rich and poor.[467] In the Peninsula, these *ejidos* were the most enduring forms of communal ownership.[468] Official documents in the Americas occasionally

457 Ots Capdequí 1946, p. 27.
458 Storni 2000, p. 628.
459 Godreau & Giusti 1993, p. 431.
460 Page 2004, p. 636.
461 Ots Capdequí 1946, p. 95.
462 Demélas 2003, p. 219.
463 Sato 1976, p. 9.
464 Ots Capdequí 1945, p. 451.
465 Mariluz Urquijo 1978, p. 66. See also Sato 1976, p. 9.
466 Sato 1976, p. 9.
467 Godreau & Giusti 1993, p. 431.
468 Godreau & Giusti 1993, p. 431.

referred without distinction to *ejidos*, *dehesas*, or even *propios*; yet the predominant term was indeed *ejido*.[469] The use of *ejidos* spread across all three Ownership Paradigms in the Americas, as is shown *infra* in the chapter dealing with the Social Function paradigm, when, for example, the 1934 Agrarian Code for Mexico advocated for the creation of such communal holdings.[470]

Propios, likewise, had their origins in the Peninsula during the *Reconquista*.[471] At that time, some settlements held more land than what their settlers could exploit in common. Therefore, the surplus of land was yielded, generally, by the *cabildos* for exploitation to third parties, generating revenue that could be used to cope with the administration costs of a settlement.[472] *Propios* consisted, amongst other things, of urban and rural dwellings, tracts of land, factories, and harbors.[473] In the Americas, on occasion, motivated by the lack of financial resources of a settlement, even the service of Native Americans could be deemed as *propios*.[474]

Altamira y Crevea depicted clearly the importance and role of communal lands in the Peninsula during the Middle Ages[475] and the Early Modern Period.[476] Even when monarchs would take tracts of land and municipalities would undertake imprudent sales, during the Modern Period the existence of communal ownership subsisted.[477] Henceforth, when Europeans arrived in the Americas in 1492, in the Peninsula the elements of communal holding were clearly defined and scholars embraced the Latin expression *potest quis facere in alieno fundo quod ei prodest et domino fundi non nocet*.[478] For example, de Solórzano Pereira in his *Política Indiana* referred to communal holdings. He highlighted in Chapter 12 of Book 6 that monarchs had dominium over all American territories other than those "[...] lands, prairies, pastures, woodlands, and water sources that—due to a specific grace or *merced* of the Monarch—have been granted to cities, villages, or places of the same Indies or to other communities or persons in particular [...]."[479]

---

469 Luque Colombres 1958, p. 98.

470 See generally 5.5.1.2 of this book.

471 Some authors traced the origins of the *propios* to pre-Roman Spain. Clemente Campos 1994–1995, p. 442.

472 Clemente Campos 1994–1995, pp. 441–442; and Page 2004, p. 637.

473 Levaggi 2010b, p. 943.

474 Ots Capdequí 1945, p. 383.

475 Altamira y Crevea 1890, pp. 151–155.

476 Altamira y Crevea 1890, pp. 231–237.

477 Altamira y Crevea 1890, p. 234.

478 Mariluz Urquijo 1978, pp. 97–98.

479 As previously mentioned, the text in Spanish read: "[...] las tierras, prados, paſtos, montes, y aguas, que por particular gracia, y merced ſuya, ſe hallaren concedidas à las ciudades,

Provisions on *comunales* and *propios* from the medieval *Siete Partidas* had been assimilated into the legal order of the Modern Period.[480] Accordingly, the prevailing doctrine welcomed the understanding of the *Siete Partidas,* in which things could be allocated to different actors and in which some things could be held in common by the inhabitants of a settlement (*v.gr.*, water fountains, surrounding crop lands).[481] Two laws of the *Siete Partidas* clearly referred to *comunales* and *propios,* and that Castilian model was actually followed with fidelity in the Americas.[482] On the one hand, law 9, Title 28, *Partida* 3, openly advocated for *comunales* and stated that

> The things which belong separately to the commons of cities or towns, are the water fountains, the places where fairs and markets are held, or where the city councils meet the sandy places on the banks of rivers; the thrashing (*e*[j]*idos*) and race grounds; the forests and pastures, and all other similar places which have been appropriated and granted for the common use of each city, town, castle, or other place. For every person living there, may use these things, they being common alike to every man, to the poor as well as to the rich. But they who reside in other places, can not use them, against the consent or prohibition of those who live there.[483]

On the other hand, law 10, Title, 28, *Partida* 3, advocated for *propios*—even when not referring explicitly to that word[484]—and stated that

villas, ò lugares de las meſmas Indias, ò à otras comunidades, ò perſonas particulares [...]." (Solórzano Pereira (de) 1703, p. 511)

See also Miller Astrada 2003, p. 308.

480 Miller Astrada 2003, p. 308.

481 See, for example, law 9, Title 28, *Partida* 3 in Siete Partidas 1587, III, pp. 156v–157.

482 See Levaggi 2010b, p. 942.

483 English translation extracted from Moreau Lislet & Carleton 1820a, pp. 338–339. The original text in Spanish read: "Apartadamenteſon del comú de cada vna cibdad o villa, las fuentes elas plaças o fazé las ferias elos mercados elos lugares o ſe ayuntan acócejo elos arenales q ſon en las riberas delos rios, elos otros exidos elas carreras o corren los cauallos, elos montes elas deheſas, etodos los otros lugares ſemejátes deſtosque ſon eſtablecidos eotorgados para pro comunal de cada cibdad o villa o caſtillo o otro lugar. Ca todo ome q fuere y morador puede vſar de todas eſtas coſas ſobredichas e ſon comunales a todos tábien a los pobres comoa los ricos. Mas los qfueſſen moradores en otrolugar, non pueden vſar dellas contra voluntad o defendimiento de los que moraſſen y." (Siete Partidas 1587, III, pp. 156v–157)

484 Clemente Campos 1994–1995, p. 446.

> Cities and towns may possess vineyards, gardens, olive fields and other estates; or cattle, or slaves, or other things which produce fruits or revenue. And though they belong in common to all the inhabitants, nevertheless, each one cannot make a particular use of them. But the fruits and revenues they produce, ought to be applied to the common good of the city, or town to which they belong: as for the repairs of the walls, bridges, fortifications, or the maintenance of cattle; or to pay the judges who preside at the gates (*aportellados*); or for other like purposes which appertain to the common good of the whole city or town.[485]

These two subsequent laws—which were transplanted to the Americas—encapsulated the scope of communal lands in the Peninsula.

3.7.2 *Communal Property in European Settlements*

Communal property could be held by settlements in the Americas. The use of *comunales* and *propios* during the *Reconquista* had highlighted the need for implementing a similar system in the new American territories.[486] Communal holdings were first introduced in American settlements in New Spain, during the first half of the sixteenth century.[487] They also found a place in the *Ordenanzas* of Philip II of 1573, which instructed, for example, that *ejidos* should be developed foreseeing population growth and always assure that neighbors could recreate and livestock graze without causing damage.[488] The seminal

485 English translation extracted from Moreau Lislet & Carleton 1820a, p. 339. The original text in Spanish read: "Campos, e viñas, e huertas, e oliuares e otras heredades e ganados e ſieruos e otrascoſas ſemejantes q dan fruto de ſi orenta, pueden auer las cibdades o las villas como qer q ſeá comunalméte detodos los moradores de la ciudad o de lavilla cuyosfueré, có todo eſſo nó puede cada vno por ſi apartadamente vſar de tales coſas como eſtas: mas los frutos elas rétas que ſalieren dellas: deuéſser metidasen pro comunal detoda la cibdad, o villa, cuyas fueren las coſas onde ſalen aſsi como en lauor de los muros, e de las puentes, o de las fortalezas, o en tenencia de los caſtillos, o en pagar los aportellados en las otras coſas ſemejantes deſtas que pertenecieſſen al pro comunal de toda la cibdad o villa." (Siete Partidas 1587, III, pp. 157–157v)

486 Ots Capdequí 1945, p. 451.

487 Levaggi 1987, p. 212.

488 Chapter 129 of the *Ordenanzas* in Spanish read: "Señalese a la poblaçion exido en tan competente cantidad que aunque la poblaçion vaya en mucho crecimiento siempre quede bastante espacio adonde la gente se pueda salir a recrear y salir los ganados sin que hagan daño." (Morales Padrón 1979, p. 513) See also Nuttall 1921, p. 748; Ots Capdequí 1945, p. 451; and Mariluz Urquijo 1978, p. 64.

1680 *Recopilación* naturally dealt with *comunales*, and the main dispositions were placed in laws 5 to 9, Title 17, Book 4.[489] For example, law 5—which originated from the merging of *real cédulas* and *real provisiones* of 1541 and 1550[490]—stated that

> We [the monarch] order that the use of all pastures, woodlands, and water sources of the Provinces of the Indies are to be common to all neighbors therein, those who are [neighbors] now and those who will be. They may enjoy them freely and build their cabins near to any shack, introduce their livestock, together or separately, as they please, regardless of any [conflicting] ordinances, that if necessary, are hereby overruled and ignored, and [turn to be] of no value and effect.[491]

Other important laws, this time referring mainly to *propios*, were included in Title 7, Book 4 of the 1680 text. For example, law 7 of that title stated that settlements resulting from capitulations had to preserve tracts of lands for *comunales* and also for *propios*.[492] Furthermore, law 14 indicated that a "good amount" of land should be used for *propios* of a settlement.[493] The encyclopedic *Teatro*

The provision of Chapter 129 was then included as law 13, Title 7, Book 4 of the 1680 *Recopilación*. The latter law in Spanish read: "Los Exidos ſean en tan competente diſtancia, que ſi creciere la poblacion, ſiempre quede baſtante eſpacio para que la gente ſe pueda recrear, y ſalir los ganados, ſin hazan daño." (Recopilación de Indias 1680, II, at f. 92) See also Levaggi 2010b, p. 943.

489 Recopilación de Indias 1680, II, at f. 112v–113. See also Ots Capdequí 1940, p. 80; and Martínez de Codes 2003, p. 230.

490 Greve 1941, p. xxiv; and Mariluz Urquijo 1978, p. 122.

491 The text in Spanish read: "[...] Mandamos, que el vſo de todos los paſtos, montes, y aguas de las Provincias de las Indias ſea comun á todos los vezinos de ellas, que aora ſon, y deſpues fueren, para que los puedan gozar libremente, y hazer junto á qualquier buhio ſus cabañas, traer alli los ganados, juntos, ó apartados, como quiſieren, ſin embargo de qualeſquier ordenanças, que ſi neceſſario es, para en quanto á eſto las revocamos, y damos por ningunas, y de ningun valor y efecto [...]." (Recopilación de Indias 1680, II, at f. 112v)

492 The text in Spanish read: "[...] territorio, que ſe diere á poblador por capitulacion, ſe reparta en la forma ſiguiente. [...] y mas otro tanto para los propios del lugar [...]." (Recopilación de Indias 1680, II, at f. 91v)

493 The text in Spanish read: "Haviendo Señalado competente cantidad de tierra para exido de la poblacion, y ſu crecimiento, en conformidad de lo proveido, ſeñalen los que tuvieren facultad para hazer el deſcubrimiento y nueva poblacion [...] alguna buena cantidad mas, q ſea propios del Consejo [...]." (Recopilación de Indias 1680, II, at f. 92)

See also Levaggi 2010b, p. 943.

of Pérez y López correctly mentioned that Title 13, Book 4 of the 1680 *Recopilación* dealt extensively with *propios*.[494] Through its 11 laws, that title tackled the main elements of *propios*, and its first law indicated that viceroys and governors should provide to each new settlement the tracts of lands that would serve as *propios*, with no detriment to third parties.[495]

The interests of advocates for livestock production and crop cultivation were different in the Americas,[496] and the Crown initially debated which sector to favor.[497] The Castilian monarchs indeed attempted to introduce in the Americas provisions on livestock production.[498] Even when the severe rules of the Castilian *mesta* (*i.e.*, association of sheep ranchers) did not succeed in the Americas, other Castilian provisions did guarantee that livestock production would benefit from communal landholdings.[499] Livestock production initially prevailed over crop cultivation in the Peninsula, though that tendency slowly shifted, and by the time of the Bourbon Reforms, the paramount position was occupied by crop cultivation.[500] Law 13, Title 12, Book 4 of the 1680 *Recopilación* presented—as mentioned by Ots Capdequí—an example of the clash of interests in the Americas. That law indicated that viceroys should order livestock to be removed from lands used for irrigation and to grow wheat.[501]

3.7.3 *Communal Property in Native American Towns*

Communal property could be held by Native American groups living in towns of Native Americans (*pueblos*). These types of communal holding, together with that of settlements, were the two more notable in the Americas.[502] Towns of Native Americans held lands in common, for communal exploitation and for

494 Pérez y López 1791–1798, XXIV, pp. 447–451.

495 The text in Spanish read: "Los Virreyes, y Governadores que tuvieré facultad, ſeñalen á cada Villa, y Lugar, que de nuevo ſe fundare, y poblare, las tierras, y ſolares, que huviere meneſter, y ſe le podrán dar, ſin perjuizio de tercero, para propios [...]." (Recopilación de Indias 1680, II, at f. 105v) See also Ots Capdequí 1945, p. 383.

496 For information on the struggle during the sixteenth and seventeenth centuries, see Mariluz Urquijo 1978, pp. 100–115.

497 Dougnac Rodríguez 1994, p. 405.

498 Greve 1941, p. xxiv.

499 Greve 1941, p. xxiv.

500 Storni 1997, p. 19.

501 Ots Capdequí 1946, p. 96.

The complete text in Spanish read: "Ordenamos A los Virreyes, que ſe informen de las tierras, que huviere de regadio, y ordenen, que ſe ſaqué dellas los ganados, y ſiembren de trigo, ſi no tuvieren los dueños titulos para tener eſtancias deſta calidad." (Recopilación de Indias 1680, II, at f. 103v)

502 Levaggi 2010b, p. 941.

the benefit of the universality of their members.[503] Communal activities were not limited to the exploitation of lands, however, and they further extended to the fulfillment of needs dealing with clothing, housing, and trade.[504] That means of communitarian holding ultimately helped in the development of a communitarian *ethos* amongst Native Americans.[505] Towns, likewise, aimed to the promotion of the Catholic faith, terminating the isolation and dispersion of some groups; while they also secured an acculturation.[506] Therefore, towns aimed to introduce Native American groups into Western customs and beliefs.[507] It should not be ignored that the Crown additionally defended one of its main aims, *i.e.*, to secure that Native Americans would be subject to taxation.[508] One of the most successful organizations into towns was undertaken by the Jesuit order in the present-day territory of Paraguay.[509] Throughout America, towns of Natives received several names, which followed different criteria, these being demographical (*reducción*), geographical (*pueblo*), or religious (*misión* and *doctrina*).[510] The diversity of names is likewise found in the *Indiano* legal order, when, for example, law 1, Title 3, Book 6 of the 1680 *Recopilación* referred to *pueblos, reducción,* and *doctrina.*[511] That same law encapsulated the motivations for the establishment of towns, and it stated that:

> With significant care and special attention it has been always tried to interpose the most convenient means to instruct Indians in the Holy Catholic Faith and in the Evangelical Law [...]. In order to implement this with better results, on several occasions the members of our Council of Indies and other people have met [...]. They resolved that Indians should be confined into Towns and stop living divided and separated by mountain ranges and mounts, [and stop] being deprived of every spiritual and temporal benefit, [having] no help of our Ministers, nor [being deprived of the benefit] that derives from the human needs that humans owe to each other.[512]

503 Cañedo-Argüelles 1999, p. 201.

504 Cañedo-Argüelles 1999, p. 203.

505 Cañedo-Argüelles 1999, p. 196.

506 Dougnac Rodríguez 1994, p. 326.

507 Cañedo-Argüelles 1999, p. 201.

508 Ots Capdequí 1946, p. 100; and Demélas 2003, p. 220.

509 Dougnac Rodríguez 1994, p. 331.

510 Cañedo-Argüelles 1999, p. 201.

511 Recopilación de Indias 1680, II, at f. 198–198v.

512 The text in Spanish read: "Con Mucho cuidado, y particular atencion ſe ha procurado ſiempre interponer los medios mas convenientes, para que los Indios ſean inſtruidos en

Not all pre-discovery communal holdings disappeared with the arrival of European settlers. The Crown aimed, from an early start, to preserve the individual and communal holdings that Native American groups had had before the arrival of European settlers.[513] For example, the *Ordenanzas* of Philip II of 1573 instructed that "settlers should establish villages without taking what was particularly of Indians, and without causing more damage than that necessary for the defense of settlers."[514] Accordingly, Native American groups retained ownership of the lands they had held before the arrival of European settlers. This was reaffirmed in the 1680 *Recopilación,* as indicated in law 9, Title 3, Book 6 which stated that "with more will and promptness will Natives [Americans] be confined to towns if they are not deprived of lands [...] they have in the places they yield. We instruct that nothing is changed and that [lands] are preserved as before, for [Native Americans] to cultivate and to attempt to exploit them."[515] Furthermore, when sent to live in towns, Native American groups

la Santa Fé Catolica, y la Ley Evangelica [...] y para que eſto ſe executaſſe con mejor acierto ſe juntaron diverſas vezes los de nueſtro Conſejo de Indias, y otras perſonas [...] reſolvieron, que los Indios fueſſen reducidos á Pueblos, y no vivieſſen divididos, y ſeparados por las Sierras, y Montes, privandoſe de todo beneficio eſpiritual, y temporal, ſin ſocorro de nueſtros Miniſtros, y del que obligan las neceſsidades humanas, que deven dar vnos hombres á otros [...]." (Recopilación de Indias 1680, II, at f. 198)

513 Ots Capdequí 1946, p. 99.

514 Chapter 136 of the *Ordenanzas* in Spanish read: "Si los naturales se quisieren poner en defender la poblaçion se les de a entender como se quiere poblar alli no para hazerles algun mal ni tomarles sus haziendas sino para tomar amystad con ellos y enseñarlos a biuir politicamente y mostrarles a conocer a dios y enseñarles su ley por lo qual se salbaran dandoseles a entender por medio de los religiossos y clerigos y personas que para ello diputare el gouernador y por buenas lenguas y procurando por todos los buenos medios posibles que la poblaçion se haga con su paz y consentimiento y si todavia no lo consintieren hauiendoles requerido por los dichos medios diuersas vezes los pobladores hagan su poblaçion sin tomar de lo que fuere particular de los indios y sin hazerles mas daño del que fuere menester para defensa de los pobladores y para que la poblaçion no se estorue." (Morales Padrón 1979, p. 515)

See also Nuttall 1921, p. 749; and Ots Capdequí 1946, p. 99.

515 The text in Spanish read: "Con Mas voluntad, y promptitud ſe reducirán á poblaciones los Indios, ſi no ſe les quitan las tierras, y grangerias, que tuvieren en los ſitios, que dexaren. Mandamos, que en eſto no ſe haga novedad, y ſe les conſerven como las huvieren tenido antes, para que las cultiven, y traten de ſu aprovechamiento." (Recopilación de Indias 1680, II, at f. 199)

See also Levaggi 2010b, p. 942.

were not deemed to lose the lands they had previously held.[516] Accordingly, Native Americans had full capacity to possess land and several dispositions of the *Indiano* legal order indicated that when allotting land to settlers, Native American lands should be respected.[517] Finally, Native Americans should also be allotted land whenever they had any.[518]

The organization of towns of Native Americans was regulated throughout the 29 laws included in Title 3 of Book 6 of the 1680 *Recopilación*.[519] *Cacicazgo* preserved an important role in the daily activities of the town, while the government of the town was undertaken by the *cabildo*.[520] Furthermore, the communal holdings were under the control of the protectors and the administrators.[521] Native Americans, it should be nevertheless mentioned, were subject to abuses, regardless of the existing legal framework, because many European settlers aimed to acquire the lands they held.[522] Other laws of the 1680 text dealt with the communal holdings of Native American groups. For example, laws 5,[523] 7,[524] 9,[525] 12,[526] 16–19,[527] Title 12, Book 4 and

---

516 Ots Capdequí 1945, p. 459.

517 Ots Capdequí 1940, p. 112.

518 Ots Capdequí 1940, p. 114.

519 Recopilación de Indias 1680, II, at f. 198–201v. See also Dougnac Rodríguez 1994, p. 328.

520 Miller Astrada 2003, p. 318.

521 Góngora 1970, p. 173.

522 Ots Capdequí 1945, p. 462.

523 The text in Spanish read: "[…] y á los Indios ſe les dexen ſus tierras, heredades, y paſtos, de forma, que no les falte lo neceſſario, y tengan todo el alivio y deſcanſo poſsible para el ſuſtento de ſus caſas, y familias." (Recopilación de Indias 1680, II, at f. 102v)

524 The text in Spanish read: "Mandamos, Que los repartimientos de tierras, […] ſe hagan con toda juſtificacion, ſin admitir ſingularidad, accepcion de perſonas, ni agravio de los Indios." (Recopilación de Indias 1680, II, at f. 103)

525 The text in Spanish read: "Mandamos, Que las eſtancias, y tierras, que ſe dieren á los Eſpañoles, ſean ſin perjuizio de los Indios, y que las dadas en ſu perjuizio y agravio, ſe buelvan á quié de derecho pertenezcan." (Recopilación de Indias 1680, II, at f. 103)

526 The text in Spanish read: "[…] Mandamos, que no ſe dén eſtancias ningunas en partes y lugares de donde puedan reſultar daños, y no pudiédoſe eſcuſar, ſean lexos de los Pueblos de Indios […]." (Recopilación de Indias 1680, II, at f. 103v)

527 Law 16 in Spanish read: "[…] mirando ſiempre por el bien de los Indios […]." (Recopilación de Indias 1680, II, at f. 104)
Law 17 in Spanish read: "Para Mas favorecer y amparar á los Indios, y que no recivan perjuizio […]." (Recopilación de Indias 1680, II, at f. 104v)
See the text of law 18 that in Spanish read: "Ordenamos, Que la venta, beneficio y compoſicion de tierras, ſe haga con tal atencion, que á los Indios ſe les dexen con ſobra todas las que les pertenecieren, aſsi en particular, como por Comunidades, y las aguas, y riegos: y las tierras en que huvieren hecho azequias, ó otro qualquier beneficio, con

laws 8[528] and 20,[529] Title 3, Book 6 all aimed to legitimize the protection of the right of Native American groups to hold communal property, both by securing that allotments would not be to the detriment of Native Americans and by assuring that livestock would be distant from the lands of the towns.[530] Furthermore, law 10, Title 17, Book 4 also aimed to deter livestock from entering into the lands that Native Americans used for crop cultivation.[531]

Towns of Native Americans could hold *comunales* and *propios*. Communal lands in a town were held by the Native American groups, though ownership persisted to be held by the Crown.[532] It should be noted that Native Americans could dispose of their property, with the prior consent of the Crown.[533] They could, eventually, gain ownership, as effectively happened in several cases, by means of, amongst others, a *merced*, by donation, or by sale.[534] Native Americans had a usufructuary right on the lands held in common, while ownership persisted to be held by the Crown.[535] Accordingly, *dominium directum* was held by the Crown and the *dominium utile* by Native Americans.[536]

---

que por induſtria perſonal ſuya ſe hayan fertilizado, ſe reſerven en primer lugar, y por ningun caſo no ſe les pueden vender, ni enagenar, y los Iuezes, que á eſto fueren enviados, expecifiquen los Indios, que hallaren en las tierras, y las que dexaren á cada vno de los tributarios, viejos, reſervados, Caciques, Governadores, auſentes, y Comunidades." (Recopilación de Indias 1680, II, at f. 104v)

See also Ots Capdequí 1946, p. 99.

Law 19 in Spanish read: "[...] y las Comunidades de Indios ſean admitidas á compoſicion, con prelacion á las demás perſonas particulares, haziendoles toda conveniencia." (Recopilación de Indias 1680, II, at f. 104v)

528 The law in Spanish read: "Los Sitios en que ſe han de formar Pueblos, y Reducciones, tengan comodidad de aguas, tierras y montes, entradas, y ſalidas, y labranças, y vn exido de vna legua de largo, donde los Indios puedan tener ſus ganados, ſin que ſerebuelvan con otros de Eſpañoles." (Recopilación de Indias 1680, II, at f. 199)

See also Dougnac Rodríguez 1994, p. 328.

529 Law 20 in Spanish read: "[...] y los Indios puedan matar el ganado, que entrare en ſu tierra ſin pena alguna [...]." (Recopilación de Indias 1680, II, at f. 200v)

530 Martini & Mayorga García 2004, p. 36.

531 The complete text in Spanish read: "Nvestras Iuſticias no conſientan, que en las tierras de labor de los Indios ſe metan ganados, y hagan ſacar de ellas los que huviere, imponiendo, y executando graves penas contra los que contravinieren." (Recopilación de Indias 1680, II, at f. 113)

532 Sánchez Bella *et al.* 1992, p. 347.

533 Díaz Rementería 1990, p. 137.

534 Sánchez Bella *et al.* 1992, p. 347.

535 Levaggi 2010b, p. 942.

536 Zorraquín Becú 1966, p. 195.

Towns indeed had *comunales*, and even when they were subject to abuses, the legislation aimed to guarantee such holdings.[537] *Comunales* could fall on land and on livestock.[538] For example, an *Instrucción* dated August 12, 1593, for Captain Gonzalo Martín, when distributing the lands of the Native Americans of Capinota (a part of present-day Bolivia), stated that Native American groups should have "[…] lands that serve as pasture and *dehesas* for everyone […]."[539] The *Ordenanzas* of Francisco de Alfaro of 1611 and 1612—for parts of the present-day territory of Argentina—provided another example when referring to the need of *ejidos* for Native American groups.[540] The 1680 *Recopilación*, naturally, included references to communal holdings, as presented in law 8, Title 3, Book 6 that established the need of *ejidos* for Native Americans.[541]

Native American groups could have *propios*, and could therefore rent their lands, for example, for the operation of a general store (*pulpería*).[542] Title 4 of Book 6 addressed the *Cajas de Censos y Bienes de Comunidad* of Native Americans.[543] Throughout the 38 laws of that title, the Crown instructed how to administer the funds that resulted from, amongst other things, the exploitation of *propios*. The income that the renting of those communal holdings produced had to be used for the benefit of the entire town. Crown officials would administer the funds of those financial sources.[544] These funds played a fundamental social role, because the financial resources they administered were used to support widows, orphans, and elderly members of the community.[545] *Cajas* also had an important tax function, because the financial resources could be used to cover taxes that some members could not afford.[546] Law 2 of that same title stated that funds should encompass goods held by all town members, and should be used for the common good of everyone.[547]

537 Ots Capdequí 1940, p. 117.

538 Díaz Rementería 1990, p. 118.

539 The text in Spanish read: "[…] tierras que sirvan de pastos y dehesas comunes para todos […]." (Díaz Rementería 1990, p. 133)

540 Mariluz Urquijo 1978, p. 117.

541 See the text of law 8 in note 528 of this chapter. See also Dougnac Rodríguez 1994, p. 328.

542 Díaz Rementería 1990, p. 119.

543 Recopilación de Indias 1680, II, at f. 201v–207v. See also Ots Capdequí 1940, p. 117; and Ots Capdequí 1945, p. 461.

544 Ots Capdequí 1940, p. 117; and Ots Capdequí 1945, p. 461.

545 Ots Capdequí 1946, pp. 102–103; and Ots Capdequí 1945, p. 461.

546 Ots Capdequí 1946, p. 103.

547 The law in Spanish read: "En Las Caxas de Comunidad há de entrar todos los bienes, que el cuerpo, y coleccion de Indios de cada Pueblo tuviere, para que de alli ſe gaſte lo

3.7.4 *Communal Property in Louisiana, Chile, and Argentina*

Communal allocation spread across the continent, being present in American Civil Law Jurisdictions, such as Louisiana, Chile, and Argentina. This allocation aimed, together with agrarian policies and the existing *Indiano* legal order, to achieve the common good and to fulfill the basic needs of new settlements.[548]

Louisiana indeed welcomed communal allocation during the Spanish period. The use of community held lands, however, had already existed in Louisiana during the prior French period.[549] For example, it is known that Spanish Governor Antonio de Ulloa could not prevail in the construction of a fortification on a tract of land held in common because French settlers had claimed exclusive control over that land.[550] *Comunales* and *propios* were implemented in Spanish Louisiana. Accordingly, references to *ejidos*, *dehesas*, and *propios* were included in the applicable legal precepts.[551] Provisions dealing with *ejidos* were specific, indicating, for instance, the distance from the limits of settlements, and as previously indicated, they should foresee the growth of settlements.[552] For example, an *Instrucción* dated March 14, 1767, by de Ulloa, to establish a fort and a settlement in upper Louisiana,[553] read in rule 71 that

> corn plantations or fields large enough to be of great relief shall be made immediately, and that will provide against famine. Later when the settlement has some stability fields of wheat shall be planted as well as of other grains, for the common welfare, all the people sharing in them in common.[554]

---

preciſo en beneficio comú de todos, y ſe atienda á ſu cóſervacion, y aumento, y todo lo demás, que convenga, diſrtibuyendolo por libranças, buena cuenta, y razon: y aſimiſmo las eſcrituras, y recaudos por donde conſtare de ſu caudal, y efectos." (Recopilación de Indias 1680, II, at f. 201v–202)

See also Dougnac Rodríguez 1994, p. 330.

548 Storni 1997, p. 20.

549 Arena 1974, p. 53.

550 Arena 1974, p. 54.

551 Arena 1974, p. 55.

552 Arena 1974, p. 55.

553 Expedition to Illinois 1767, p. 19.

554 Expedition to Illinois 1767, p. 17. See also Arena 1974, p. 56.

As mentioned, *propios* existed in Louisiana,[555] and the profit from those holdings could be used to pay the salaries of public officials.[556] It is interesting to mention that even after the Louisiana Purchase, scholars kept referring to *propios* in Louisiana. For example, in his *The Civil Law of Spain and Mexico* (1851), Gustavus Schmidt suggested that a civil code should include references to *propios*.[557] That projected code was not aimed to Louisiana, which already had a civil code since 1825, yet—in the words of the author—"the recent acquisition [by the US] of California and New Mexico will probably render the work at present of some practical utility to the legal profession; and [...] to men of business having dealings with the republics of South America."[558] Finally, the land of Native American groups was also respected in Louisiana. The previously mentioned *Regulations on Land Grants* of 1799 by Ventura Morales stated in article 31 that "Indians who possess lands within the limits of the government shall not in any manner be disturbed; on the contrary, they shall be protected and supported, and to this the commandants, syndic, and surveyors ought to pay the greatest attention to conduct themselves in consequence."[559]

Chile, likewise, welcomed communal allocation. Therefore, in the present-day territory of Chile, *comunales* and *propios* existed.[560] For example, documents in the *cabildo* of Santiago indicated that the *ejido* would welcome the horses of the poorest neighbors, while in the *dehesa* all other neighbors could keep their horses.[561] Furthermore, the documents stated that only neighbors—*i.e.*, members of that specific universality—could benefit from the *dehesa*, unless a special privilege was given to neighbors from other cities.[562] Communal holdings extended over woodlands and pastures in Chile, *inter alia*.[563] Regulations on those common holdings had been imposed by the *Audiencia*

555 Arena 1974, p. 56.

556 Arena 1974, p. 56.

557 The reference of Gustavus Schmidt was included in article 184 of his proposed civil code. That article stated that "Inhabitants of towns own likewise fields, vineyards, gardens, &c., which produce an income, and which is called town property (*proprios de los pueblos*,) the use and advantages of which are not allowed to individuals, but are governed by special laws." (Schmidt 1851, p. 44)

Schmidt correctly referred to law 10, Title 28, *Partida* 3 in a note to that article.

For more information on the work of Schmidt, see Parise 2009a.

558 Schmidt 1851, at *Preface*.

559 Regulations of Ventura Morales 1799, p. 734. See also Arena 1974, p. 56.

560 Góngora 1951, p. 141.

561 Góngora 1951, p. 141.

562 Góngora 1951, p. 141.

563 Guzmán Brito 1982, p. 69.

of Lima in proceedings dealing with the lands of Talagante already by 1556.[564] Around that same time, the proceedings of the *cabildo* of Santiago mentioned several *mercedes* that included limitations dealing with the communal holding of pastures.[565] However, an earlier document of the *cabildo* of Santiago, dated July 26, 1549, stated that de Valdivia recognized the right of landowners to enclose their lands for pasture, somehow neglecting communal holdings.[566] That would change with time, nevertheless, as illustrated by a *merced* granted by Governor Martín Ruiz de Gamboa, dated February 13, 1593, stating that "pastures are communal."[567] *Propios* were similarly welcomed in Chile. For example, the governor agreed to grant *propios* in 1549, allowing non-neighbors to benefit from the woodlands, after paying a fee.[568] Furthermore, towards the end of the sixteenth century, the treasury of the *cabildo* benefited from the lease of *propios*.[569] Even when Native American groups in Chile were more individualistic than in other regions of the Americas, and hence reluctant to live in towns of Native Americans, the Crown undertook unsuccessful efforts to implement communitarian allocation between 1580 and the end of the eighteenth century.[570] In Chile, the towns of Native Americans did not flourish as agricultural communities, mainly due to the small population of Native Americans.[571] There were, however, several towns established. For example, the town of Chada had in 1616 a chief of the group (*cacique*), a church, and it cultivated and sold wheat.[572] It should be noted that the population of several towns of Native Americans was ultimately absorbed by the *haciendas*.[573]

Argentina was no exception to the implementation of communal allocation. For example, in Buenos Aires, two *Reales Cédulas* of 1546 instructed the governor to establish new settlements with "*ejidos* and lands for common pasture."[574] Also in Buenos Aires, during the second foundation of the city by

564 Borde & Góngora 1956, p. 35.

565 The importance of communities diminished with time, and records of the *cabildo* avoided references to communities of pastures after 1583. Borde & Góngora 1956, pp. 35–36.

566 Greve 1941, pp. xxiv–xxv; and Mariluz Urquijo 1978, p. 105.

567 The text in Spanish read: "[…] los pastos son comunes […]." (Greve 1941, p. xxv)

568 Góngora 1951, p. 142.

569 Góngora 1951, p. 142.

570 Dougnac Rodríguez 1994, p. 330.

571 Gallardo Fernández 2002, p. 151.

572 Góngora 1970, p. 185.

573 Gallardo Fernández 2002, p. 151.

574 The text in Spanish read: "[…] dejen ejidos y tierras para pastos comunes […]." (Mariluz Urquijo 1978, p. 116) See also Storni 2000, p. 628.

Juan de Garay in 1580, land was allocated for *ejidos*.[575] In the same city, though during the government of Hernando Arias de Saavedra (Hernandarias), the *cabildo* decided in 1608 that the woodlands could not be used by foreigners, these being subject to paying a fine and losing the timber they had collected.[576] Some years later, in 1695, another *Real Cédula*, directed to the governor, established the common use of woodlands, pastures, and water sources, hence repeating the instruction of an earlier *Real Provisión* of 1541 for Peru and its provinces.[577] *Propios* were allotted in Argentina. This was illustrated, for example, by the efforts of the *cabildo* of Buenos Aires to expand its *propios* during the first decades of the eighteenth century.[578] Córdoba likewise provided examples of communal allocation. For example, on March 12, 1574, the Governor of Córdoba, de Cabrera, instructed that a tract of land should be "*ejido* of the city [...] for now and forever after."[579] Later, another document from Córdoba stated that in 1578 lands were separated for *ejidos* and *propios* on the southern slopes, between the river and the stream named La Cañada for an extension of 23 blocks.[580] Communal holdings—not only in Argentina—could motivate conflicts amongst individuals, and society at large, who could have conflicting interests or claims.[581] Those conflicts occasionally extended to claims amongst cities, as demonstrated by confrontations between the *cabildos* of Buenos Aires, Córdoba, and Santa Fe.[582] Finally, in Argentina the Crown was likewise interested in protecting the rights of Native American groups. For example, in Salta del Tucumán, Andrés Mestre ordered the restitution of communal lands that had been taken from the Native American groups of the Beniaguas and the Tilianes.[583]

3.7.5 *Corollary*

The communal allocation of ownership responded to the different concurring interests of the different actors. Communal holdings were undertaken in European settlements and towns of Native Americans across the Americas, and therefore, in the present-day territories of Louisiana, Chile, and Argentina.

575 Mariluz Urquijo 1978, pp. 64, 116.
576 Mariluz Urquijo 1978, pp. 118–119.
577 Storni 2000, p. 629.
578 Mariluz Urquijo 1978, p. 119.
579 The text in Spanish read: "[...] exido de la dicha Ciudad [...] para agora e para siempre jamás [...]." (Luque Colombres 1958, p. 98)
580 Page 2004, p. 639.
581 Storni 2000, pp. 629–630.
582 Storni 2000, pp. 629–630.
583 Miller Astrada 2003, p. 324.

Comunales and *propios* found their origins in the Peninsula. *Comunales* included several elements, such as the *ejido* and the *dehesa*. It should be noted that in the Americas, the *ejidos* could find parallels with the Native American *mapu* of the Mapuche, the *calpulli* of the Aztec, and the *ayllu* of the Inca.[584] *Propios* included several elements, such as urban and rural dwellings, and tracts of land.

The interests of the actors did change with time, however. There was a shift from the Allocation paradigm to the Liberal paradigm. The emergence of the new paradigm during the last decades of the eighteenth century reduced the communal holdings in the Americas, both in settlements and in towns of Native Americans, yet these holdings reached the nineteenth century.[585] Towards the end of the eighteenth century the Crown started to adopt a more individualistic approach, departing from the one that had prevailed during the previous centuries, and that was incorporated into the 1680 *Recopilación*.[586] For example, in Río de la Plata, towards the middle of the eighteenth century, neighbors sensed a contradiction between the new ideology, the events in the Peninsula, and the existing legislation.[587] Only towards the end of that century did the new Liberal paradigm of ownership fully emerge.[588] Constitutions and new civil codes tended to implement in practice the new paradigm, which replaced where possible, amongst other things, the idea of communal allocation.[589] The new Liberal paradigm, together with the Bourbon Reforms, aimed to diminish the communal holdings, while activating the productivity of land and its free circulation.[590]

3.8 Closing Remarks

The Allocation paradigm was the first link in the uninterrupted chain of Ownership Paradigms that emerged in American Civil Law Jurisdictions since the arrival of European settlers in 1492. That Ownership Paradigm, which is central to this chapter, prevailed for 300 years, from the arrival of the first settlers until the American republics and states dictated their own legislation, finding an antecedent in the Bourbon Reforms of the eighteenth century.

584 Godreau & Giusti 1993, p. 431.
585 Levaggi 1987, p. 213.
586 Díaz Rementería 1995, p. 13.
587 Mariluz Urquijo 1978, pp. 127, 130.
588 Mariluz Urquijo 1978, pp. 127, 130; and Levaggi 2010b, p. 943.
589 Levaggi 2010b, p. 945.
590 Cañedo-Argüelles 1999, p. 196; and Storni 2000, p. 628.

That link extended, therefore, mainly during the time period commonly referred to as the Early Modern Period. The chapter focused on three jurisdictions (*i.e.*, the US State of Louisiana, and the republics of Chile and Argentina) that served as case studies for the analysis of the abovementioned paradigm. It should also be noticed that property was allocated to different actors within that period, reacting to their different concurring interests at different times. Additionally, it should be highlighted that American Civil Law Jurisdictions shared a common legal grounding during the entire period.

The chapter first described the different land relations of Native American groups. These groups comprised a "mosaic of different legal systems," and their land relations were marked by communal and individual control over property. Special attention was devoted to communal holdings, because these means of allotting property did prevail—with changes—during the *Indiano* period, in some jurisdictions even surviving into the post-independence periods. Native Americans were important actors in the Allocation paradigm, and understanding their land relations was very important for the Crown of Castile, which had to contemplate their preexisting precepts when translating or creating new precepts for the American territories.

The chapter further focused on the access by Spaniards to the new American territories. The main grounds for the Castilian holding of those territories were explained in the chapter. Those grounds were the capitulations, the papal bulls, and the right to conquest and just war. Special attention was devoted to the final ground, which was developed to a great extent after the efforts and writings of the members of the Spanish Scholasticism of the sixteenth century, also called Neo-Scholasticism. All grounds for the Castilian holding required a legal framework and the interplay of different actors, these being: the Crown, the Church, the Native Americans, and the European settlers. The chapter likewise demonstrated that the three case studies (*i.e.*, Louisiana, Chile, and Argentina) were parts of that Castilian holding, and they accordingly experienced the emergence of the Allocation paradigm.

The chapter then addressed the main traits of the *Indiano* legal order that applied across all American Civil Law Jurisdictions. The chapter identified the main components of the prevailing *Corpus iuris indiarum*, and placed ownership and its new paradigm within that order. It should be noted—as was reflected throughout the entire chapter—that the *Indiano* legal order aimed to allot ownership amongst the different actors: this was the paramount interest and encapsulated the main characteristic of the period. That part of the chapter confirmed that legal borrowing—achieved by means of transplantation or normative transfer—of Peninsular precepts and ideas helped develop the prevailing *corpus*, and helped to establish the resulting *Indiano* legal order.

It should be noted, however, that *Indiano* legal precepts were casuistic and they were not absolutely uniform, varying according to demographic and economic divergences.

A study of the different concurring interests that different actors had in ownership in American Civil Law Jurisdictions followed. The interests of the Castilian Crown, the Catholic Church, Native Americans, and European settlers were analyzed, while showing that interests were interconnected amongst actors, resulting ultimately in the allocation of ownership. Accordingly, settlement in the Americas was undertaken both by private and public intervention. That part of the chapter also showed that provisions on ownership were found in code-like texts (*i.e.*, *Siete Partidas*, 1680 *Recopilación*) that were fundamental elements of the *Corpus iuris indiarum*. Again, allocation necessarily required actors that would deliver and receive things, each with their own interests, both secular and spiritual.

Allocation was individual or communal, and aimed to fulfill the different interests of actors. The chapter, therefore, explained how the individual allocation of ownership was undertaken in the Americas. The explanation of the system of royal land grants, which had its origins in the Iberian Peninsula, was fundamental in that part of the chapter. References to *Indiano* documents served to illustrate that *mercedes* were implemented in a ritualistic manner (*i.e.*, petition, survey, drafting of title, entering into possession, registration in notarial act) in the Americas. In that part of the chapter, most examples were extracted from Argentine documents, yet references were made to documents from Chile and Louisiana, aiming to make manifest that the royal land grants applied across the Americas. The chapter showed that the implementation of *mercedes* resulted in joint efforts between the monarchs who granted those documents and the different settlers who aimed to secure their interests.

The chapter finally explained how the communal allocation of ownership was instrumented. That allocation was undertaken in European settlements and in towns of Native Americans across the Americas, therefore, reaching the present-day territories of Louisiana, Chile, and Argentina. That final part of the chapter helped in demonstrating that a paradigm shift started to take place towards the end of the eighteenth century, when the Bourbon Reforms, which found similar movements in parts of Europe, started to erode the main traits of the Allocation paradigm, to assist in the adoption of a new Liberal paradigm of ownership, where individual ownership prevailed over the interests of society at large.

The chapter, above all, aimed to show that American Civil Law Jurisdictions shared the Allocation paradigm of ownership. That long-lived paradigm—being the longest that existed in American Civil Law Jurisdictions—was implemented mainly through the precepts of the *Indiano* legal order and the activities and interests of the different actors. The first link (*i.e.*, Allocation paradigm) in the uninterrupted chain of Ownership Paradigms was followed by the Liberal paradigm, which was then followed by the Social Function paradigm. The effects of the first link should never be underestimated, and the comprehension of its components is essential for the full understanding of the subsequent (and current) paradigms and their effects.

CHAPTER 4

The Liberal Paradigm of Ownership in American Civil Law Jurisdictions

4.1 Introduction

The nineteenth century experienced a change in the Ownership Paradigm in American Civil Law Jurisdictions. These jurisdictions indeed incorporated provisions on ownership within their civil codes. Even when codification started and was developed in Europe, the New World was not foreign to the phenomenon, being fertile ground for codification endeavors. The Modern Period welcomed the development of a Liberal paradigm of ownership, which replaced an Allocation paradigm that included, amongst other characteristics, a decomposition of ownership in *directum* and *utile*.[1] American Civil Law Jurisdictions gradually shifted to that new Liberal paradigm, and consequently made manifest its adoption in local nineteenth-century civil codes.[2] That century has been deemed "the codification century of civil law"[3] and all private law tended to revolve around the new codes.[4] No full grasp of ownership can be attained when the codification phenomenon is not fully understood. That scenario helps explain why tracing changes mainly in those texts may help explain the shifts in Ownership Paradigms. These new texts embraced the liberal ideal of an absolute, unique, and perpetual real right of ownership, subject to the will of a single owner, but limited by some conditions determined by law that related to social responsibilities.[5]

Together with the new century, reforms to those codes incorporated elements that further considered social responsibilities and highlighted a social function for property, and that is central to the next chapter of this book.

1 Levaggi 2001, p. 413. See on the understanding of *dominium duplex* during the sixteenth century, amongst the copious literature, the interesting approach in Grossi 1992b. For more information on *dominium duplex,* see Grossi 1992c, pp. 637–648; Grossi 1992a; and Feenstra 1998. On a current approximation to *dominium duplex,* see Heirbaut 2003.

2 Levaggi 2001, p. 413.

3 Rivera 2013, p. 7.

4 It should be noted that in some jurisdictions, such as Louisiana, the code persists in being the center even during the twenty-first century. See Parise 2013b, p. 453.

5 Levaggi 2001, p. 419.

 | DOI 10.1163/9789004338203_005

The current harmonization of private laws and the exploration of changes in existing civil codes motivate a look at the scenario in American Civil Law Jurisdictions. Understanding the dynamics there will provide an enriching comparative approach for jurists in Europe and the Americas, contributing to the attempts towards harmonization and recodification, and confirming the statement that American Civil Law Jurisdictions are *a comparativist's dream*.[6]

A study in different jurisdictions will demonstrate that the resulting Ownership Paradigms in American Civil Law Jurisdictions can be linked to Europe and can be shared amongst jurisdictions in the Americas. An in-depth focus on three jurisdictions and their civil codes will serve as case studies: the US State of Louisiana (1825), Chile (1857), and Argentina (1871). As mentioned in Chapter 1 of this book, the selected jurisdictions could be deemed representative American Civil Law Jurisdictions, because they developed a vast scholarly production on the topic from an early period on and their codified provisions served as models. Before the end of the nineteenth century, most jurisdictions across the continent had transplanted provisions on ownership to be found in one of those three civil codes. Yet, those three codes borrowed or transplanted their provisions mainly from Europe (*v.gr. Code Napoléon*), blending them also with local elaborations that responded to local culture.

The chapter is divided into six parts. Firstly, the chapter describes how first-generation codification developed during the nineteenth century. Special attention is devoted to the value of studies on comparative legislation as means to promote the emergence of first-generation codes. Secondly, the chapter analyzes the paths followed towards the adoption of the civil codes of Louisiana, Chile, and Argentina. Thirdly, the chapter studies the way in which ownership provisions were codified, offering a framework for that property law institution. The European origins and the transplantation of provisions are addressed, together with the interest of scholars for formal sources on both sides of the Atlantic. Fourthly, the chapter addresses individually how ownership provisions were encapsulated within the civil code of the three jurisdictions. Accordingly, constitutional and codified protections are analyzed, together with the sources of the codified texts. Fifthly, the chapter specifies how other American Civil Law Jurisdictions adopted ownership provisions from one of the three abovementioned codes by means of pollination. This aims to demonstrate that jurisdictions shared an Ownership Paradigm. Sixthly, the chapter concludes by presenting some aspects of second-generation codes. That final

6 Rosenn 1971, p. 692. See also Kleinheisterkamp 2008, p. 300. The reference in the latter source is to Latin America, and is extended in application in this book to American Civil Law Jurisdictions.

part also shows that there is a common understanding of ownership that can be traced back to European codes and to local cultural developments. The chapter, above all, aims to show that ownership cannot be regarded as merely a European construct, and that local developments played a role in the shaping of the resulting Ownership Paradigm, being shared across American Civil Law Jurisdictions.

4.2 Emergence of First-Generation Codes[7]

Codification, as understood today, finds its origins in Europe, where it experienced a significant development during the eighteenth and nineteenth centuries.[8] A scientific revolution led the way for codification, originated in Enlightened and Humanistic ideas, and followed by Rationalistic Natural Law theorizing.[9] This revolution advocated for a new presentation of laws that replaced existing provisions,[10] while grouping different areas in an organic, systematic,[11] clear, and complete way.[12] In addition, codification suggested the laying out of a plan with terminology and phraseology[13] in a single-fabric consolidated way.[14]

Endeavors on codification spread throughout the Western Hemisphere, reaching the Americas. Those endeavors many times built on European sources, though on occasion resulted from pollination by American texts. American Civil Law Jurisdictions were not immune to codification movements. All jurisdictions adopted civil codes that aimed to regulate their private law needs. That adoption was made in a two-tier system: first generation and second generation.[15] All jurisdictions achieved their first-generation codes, while many

7 See generally Parise 2014b, pp. 318–319.

8 See generally Levasseur 1970; and Bergel 1988. For a complete study of the previous period, see Vanderlinden 1967.

9 Levaggi 1996b, p. 185.

10 Díez-Picazo & Gullón 1982, p. 51.

11 Alessandri Rodríguez & Somarriva Undurraga 1945, p. 49.

12 Carrió 1981, p. 993.

13 Bergel 1988, pp. 1084–1085.

14 Stone 1955, p. 305.

15 The two-tier generation used in this chapter found inspiration in Guzmán Brito 2000, p. 328. The Chilean jurist used the term "second generation" when referring to a second wave of influence that the *Code Napoléon* had in Europe, and eventually, in the Americas. The work of Alejandro Guzmán Brito has been of constant reference by the author of this book.

have mutated those original texts and adopted second-generation codes. The two generations are distinguishable because of content, time of enactment, and the reasons that motivated them.

First-generation civil codes were enacted during the period 1825–1889.[16] They resulted from the independence from European control in American Civil Law Jurisdictions, and from the need to enact local private law provisions. Comprehensive attempts towards codification were made in the Americas.[17] There was interest in the region for grasping the panorama of civil law legislation in a succinct and comprehensive way. There was also a demand for examination of the ideas that existed in other civilized states that had reached codification.[18] By replicating European events, many American jurisdictions started to replace their versions of *ius commune* with codified systems of national laws,[19] a process that would be completed with second-generation civil codes.

Structure and content of first-generation civil codes in American Civil Law Jurisdictions showed a harmony amongst different codes. The structure of most codes followed the model provided by the *Code Napoléon* (1804). With the turn of the century, the *Bürgerliches Gesetzbuch* (1900) and other European civil codes would also have a considerable impact on codes, though the impact would be mainly sensed later in second-generation texts.

4.2.1 *Studies on Comparative Legislation*

First-generation codification, however, was not limited to the impact of the French text. Studies on comparative legislation motivated an interest in other

16 The list of American Civil Law Jurisdictions and the years of effect of their first-generation civil codes reads as follows: Louisiana, 1825; Haiti, 1826; Bolivia, 1831; Peru, 1836; Costa Rica, 1841; Dominican Republic, 1844; Chile, 1857; El Salvador, 1860; Panama, 1860; Ecuador, 1861; Venezuela, 1862; Uruguay, 1868; Argentina, 1871; Mexico, 1871; Nicaragua, 1871; Colombia, 1873; Guatemala, 1877; Paraguay, 1877; Honduras, 1880; Cuba, 1889; and Puerto Rico, 1889.

It should be noted that some jurisdictions replaced their first generation codes by codes of second generation already before 1889. That is the case, for example, of Costa Rica, which adopted a second generation code in 1888. It should be also noted that the codes implemented in Puerto Rico and Cuba in 1889 are to be considered first generation codes only once these two jurisdictions gain independence from Spain.

As indicated in 4.3.1 of this book, Louisiana adopted a Digest in 1808, paving the way for the 1825 enactment.

17 Parise 2008b, p. 831.

18 Stone 1955, p. 307; cited also in Cairns 2015, p. 17.

19 Bravo Lira 1989, p. 54.

codification works, and they started to gain momentum towards the middle of the nineteenth century. Those comparative works were essential tools for the drafters of civil codes around the world.[20] In Europe, yet even more in American Civil Law Jurisdictions, it was very expensive to hold a private law library that would fully cover comparative legislation.[21] Important libraries were therefore few, and were mainly in hands of the Church or universities.[22] In Argentina, for example, law libraries of significant size did exist during the nineteenth century,[23] though it was more common for practitioners to have smaller personal libraries.[24] There, members of the Church held the two largest private law libraries, these being Manuel Azamor y Ramírez with 1,069 titles, and Juan Baltasar Maziel with 423 titles.[25] That scenario, together with other reasons, motivated the development of works of legislative concordances, where authors would draw parallels and differences amongst the different legislation. Furthermore, these comparative volumes would reduce the number of books needed.

The nineteenth century welcomed works of concordances amongst different civil codes being drafted in Europe and in the Americas. Those works were handy tools for codifiers when drafting civil codes. They were also useful for lawyers, judges and law professors, in their daily activities. Amongst the works of concordances it is possible to mention *Concordance entre les Codes civils étrangers et le Code Napoléon* (1840),[26] in French and by Fortuné Anthoine de Saint-Joseph (French Concordance); the previously mentioned *The Civil Law of Spain and Mexico* (1851),[27] in English and by Schmidt; the *Concordancias, Motivos y Comentarios del Código Civil Español* (1852),[28] in Spanish and by Florencio García Goyena (Spanish Concordance); and the *Jurisprudencia Civil Vigente Española y Estranjera* (1861),[29] in Spanish and by Juan Antonio Seoane.

---

20 See generally Knütel 1996.

21 For information about libraries in Río de la Plata, see Castán Vázquez 1984, p. 74. See also Tau Anzoátegui 1977b, pp. 275–281, where it is indicated that there was more access to French literature.

For information about libraries in Louisiana, see Combe 1996.

22 Castán Vázquez 2000, p. 523.

23 Castán Vázquez 2000, p. 523; and Torre Revello 1965, pp. 47–63.

24 See generally Luque Colombres 1945; Furlong 1944; and Cornejo 1946.

25 Rípodas Ardanaz 1984, p. 311.

26 Saint-Joseph (de) 1840. There was an 1856 edition in four volumes; see Saint-Joseph (de) 1856.

27 Schmidt 1851.

28 García Goyena 1852.

29 Seoane 1861.

The works of Schmidt and Seoane had relevance in the Americas. For example, the book of Schmidt—who lived in Louisiana—was one of the first works of its kind accessible to English readers. For that reason, courts and scholars referred to it early and for many years, beyond the legal community of the US.[30] The book had influence in Europe. Schmidt's brother circulated copies of the book to newspapers and law journals in Sweden.[31] Schmidt furthermore sent copies of his book to his brother to distribute them to scholars around Europe.[32] One of the addressees was Friedrich Carl von Savigny in Berlin.[33] The book by Seoane, published in Madrid, was well circulated in American Civil Law Jurisdictions, reaching, for example, Río de la Plata.[34] The book assisted in the study of foreign doctrines and legal solutions by providing the elucidations followed by other legal systems, even by those foreign to the Romanist tradition.[35] For example, when looking at other legal systems, Seoane classified his study in five main divisions: civil (*civilismo*), Slav (*eslavismo*), Germanic (*germanismo*), Oriental (*orientalismo*) and Roman (*romanismo*).[36] When addressing the main aspects of ownership, Seoane dealt with the topic in China, India, and in territories that followed Muhammad's postulates,[37] stating clearly that his study was, therefore, not limited to the Western world.

The French Concordance facilitated largely the activities of drafters of civil codes and the activities of those interested in comparative law because it provided a panorama of universal legislation.[38] It enjoyed a remarkable success, and copies were quickly made available worldwide. The work dedicated 126 pages to a chart that included and helped to compare, whenever possible, the texts of the *Code Napoléon* with the texts of the civil codes of Austria, Bavaria, Holland, Louisiana, the Kingdom of the Two Sicilies, Sardinia, Prussia, and Vaud.[39] Accordingly, article 544 of the *Code Napoléon*—which was seminal when dealing with ownership, and that will be addressed in-depth

30 Parise 2009a, p. 186, 191.

31 Modéer 2006, p. 64.

32 Modéer 2005, p. 252.

33 Modéer 2005, p. 252.

34 See generally Salerno 1969; and Tau Anzoátegui 1977b, p. 276.

35 Tau Anzoátegui 1977b, p. 275.

36 Seoane 1861, p. ix. See Parise 2012b, p. 80.

37 Seoane 1861, pp. 169–170.

38 León 1946, p. 42.

39 Saint-Joseph (de) 1840; and Parise 2008b, p. 825.

In addition, the first edition included, in 146 pages, diverse extracts of the texts of the civil codes of Aargau, Baden, Berne, Fribourg, Haiti, and Sweden. The first edition further included, in nineteen pages, a chart with the relevant articles on mortgages from the civil codes of Fribourg, Geneva, Greece, Saint Gallen, Sweden, and Württemberg.

infra—found parallels with articles 483 of Louisiana, 439 of Sardinia, 345 of Vaud, 625 of Holland, and 354–362 of Austria.[40] It should be noted that the first edition had a historical introduction on every code it included, which in Saint-Joseph's words, was a fundamental reading for a better understanding and interpretation of the legal texts.[41] The second edition of the French Concordance was published in 1856 and included many additions. Arthur de Saint-Joseph, son of the author of the first edition, was able to expand the work from one to four volumes. Volume I included an introduction,[42] a historical account on European codification,[43] and a preliminary note on the legal texts it included.[44] In addition, a chart included and helped to compare the texts of the *Code Napoléon* with those of six other contemporary legal texts.[45] Volumes III[46] and IV[47] also included references to a variety of codes, however, without the use of comparative charts and through autonomous transcriptions. Volume II followed the same format as the just-mentioned volumes, and included the text of the civil code of Louisiana[48] together with that of a variety of legal texts.[49] Drafters seeking sources that dealt with ownership could find indeed a universal panorama inside the French Concordance.

The Spanish Concordance resulted from the codification efforts undertaken by the Spanish administration. A draft of a civil code for Spain (Spanish Project) was completed in May 1851.[50] The work had been led by García

---

40 Saint-Joseph (de) 1840, p. 28.

41 The text in French read: "[…] cet historique des codes étrangers était un avant-propos indispensable pour préparer à leur intelligence […]." (Saint-Joseph (de) 1840, p. viii)

42 Saint-Joseph (de) 1840, pp. v–xcviii.

43 Saint-Joseph (de) 1840, pp. xcix–cxl.

44 Saint-Joseph (de) 1840, pp. cxli–cxlvii

45 The chart included the texts from Austria, the Kingdom of the Two Sicilies, Bavaria, Vaud, and Sardinia; and provisions from, what the author called, the German common law. Saint-Joseph (de) 1856, I, pp. 1–239.

46 The volume included the texts from Norway; Parma, Piacenza, and Guastalla; Poland; Portugal; Prussia; Russia; Saxony; Saxe-Weimar; Serbia; Sweden; and Switzerland, which was divided into the cantons of Appenzell and Aargau. Saint-Joseph (de) 1856, III, pp. 1–580.

47 The volume included the texts from the cantons of Basel, Bern, Fribourg, Geneva, Glarus, Grisons, Lucerne, Neuchâtel, Saint Gallen, Solothurn, Ticino, Valais, and Zurich. That volume also included texts from Tuscany, Turkey, Venezuela, and Württemberg. Saint-Joseph (de) 1856, IV, pp. 1–611.

48 Saint-Joseph (de) 1856, II, pp. 459–573.

49 The volume included texts from Baden, Belgium, Bolivia, Brazil, Brunswick, Denmark, Frankfurt am Main, Great Britain, Greece, Haiti, Hamburg, Hanover, Holland, Ionian Islands, Malta and Modena, Roman states, South America, Spain (with a reference to the Spanish Concordance), and the US. Saint-Joseph (de) 1856, II, pp. 1–458, 574–640.

50 Antequera 1895, p. 488.

Goyena, had 1,992 articles,[51] and was said to follow the model of the *Code Napoléon*.[52] Although the Spanish Project never reached the status of law, it was a cornerstone for the civil code of Spain of 1889.[53] The Spanish Concordance, one of the most important Spanish-language scholarly legal productions of the nineteenth century, followed the Spanish Project. In 1852, García Goyena found grounding for its publication in the discussions and debates that took place during the drafting of the Spanish Project.[54] The aim of the Spanish Concordance was to include the legal-historical background for each proposed article.[55] They guided the reader through the text of the Spanish Project, which was completely transcribed, and scholarly analysis followed each article. The work was presented in four volumes.[56] García Goyena made references to several civil codes and legislation.[57] For example, in the note to his leading article on ownership—numbered 391—he indicated parallels with articles 544 of the *Code Napoléon*, 439 of Sardinia, 345 of Vaud, 625 of Holland, and 354 of Austria.[58] García Goyena worked with the French Concordance when drafting his Spanish Concordance, and this explains the similarity in sources included in both works.[59]

---

51 García Goyena 1852, IV, p. 341 The Spanish Project contained a Preliminary Title "Of laws [legislative acts] and their effects, and of the general rules for their application" (*De las leyes y sus efectos, y de las reglas generales para su aplicación*). The Preliminary Title was followed by three books: Book I "Of persons" (*De las personas*), Book II "Of the division of things and of ownership" (*De la división de los bienes y de la propiedad*), and Book III "Of the modes of acquiring ownership" (*De los modos de adquirir la propiedad*). Each book was divided into titles, chapters, sections, and where relevant, paragraphs.

52 García-Gallo 1977, at § 261.

53 See generally Gaya Sicilia 2010.

54 Sánchez Román 1899, p. 529.

55 García Goyena 1852, I, p. 5.

56 The first three included appendices that further developed scholarly elaborations, while the fourth included both an alphabetical index of the topics covered throughout the four volumes (García Goyena 1852, IV, pp. 361–479) and an outline of the Spanish Project (García Goyena 1852, IV, pp. 345–358).

57 The most frequent references were made to the civil code of Louisiana; the civil codes of Austria, Bavaria, Holland, the Kingdom of the Two Sicilies, Prussia, Sardinia, Vaud, and Württemberg; the *Code Napoléon*; the proceedings of the Council of Trent; the *Corpus iuris civilis*; the *Fuero Juzgo;* the *Fuero Real*; the Institutes of Gaius; the *Siete Partidas;* the *Novísima Recopilación*; the project of a Spanish civil code of 1821, the *Recopilación*, the Spanish constitution of 1837, and the civil code of Württemberg. See Parise 2008b, p. 842.

58 García Goyena 1852, I, p. 352.

59 For example, the note to article 743 of the Spanish Project in an English translation read: "In the work entitled 'Concordance between Foreign Civil Codes and the Code Napoléon' [*i.e.*, Concordance] can be read that […]." (García Goyena 1852, II, p. 166)

The works of Saint-Joseph and García Goyena indeed had a significant impact on the codification efforts that emerged across the Americas. The Spanish Concordance were very well circulated in Spain and in American Civil Law Jurisdictions.[60] In American Civil Law Jurisdictions, the Spanish Concordance was an inspiration for codifiers such as Vélez Sarsfield and Bello. Vélez Sarsfield made express references to the Spanish Concordance, both in the notes to the different articles of the Argentine Code[61] and in the 1865 accompanying letter of transmission of the First Book of his code to the Minister Eduardo Costa.[62] The Civil Code of Chile of 1855 also found inspiration in the Spanish Concordance, where the Venezuelan jurist Bello followed closely the provisions of the Spanish Concordance when drafting.[63] As already mentioned, those codes from Argentina and Chile were a source of inspiration for many codification endeavors that took place in American Civil Law Jurisdictions and that replicated their provisions.[64]

Drafters of civil codes in American Civil Law Jurisdictions valued and used those two works of concordances, and ownership provisions migrated with the assistance of those works. Codification endeavors many times built on previous experiences that had proved to be successful. It has been said, furthermore, when referring to codification, that choosing correctly is to create,[65] and that drafters use the knowledge that humanity treasured.[66] A less elegant statement was provided by Frederick Parker Walton in 1916:

> Codifiers are arrant thieves, and every new civil code ought to contain some articles which the legislators of other countries will make up their minds to steal so soon as a favorable opportunity occurs. Unlike other thieves, codifiers try to improve what they steal, and if they have any success in doing this they will have justified their existence.[67]

4.3 First-Generation Codes across the Americas

First-generation civil codes encapsulated the Liberal paradigm of ownership. These texts also found sources of inspiration within the American continent.

60 See generally Parise 2008b.

61 *V.gr.*, note to article 186 of the Argentine Code. See Código Civil Argentina 1871, p. 526.

62 Levaggi 2005b, p. 310.

63 Pescio Vargas 1978, p. 115.

64 See generally Parise 2008b.

65 Machado 1898, p. xvi.

66 Colmo 1961, p. 350. See Parise 2012b, p. 75.

67 Walton 1916, p. 116.

The civil codes of Louisiana, Chile, and Argentina served as ways of spreading codification in the region. Interestingly enough, those three codes offered resistance to be replaced by codes of second generation. The Argentine text was adopted by Paraguay (1877) and was influential in the drafting of other American Civil Law Jurisdictions. The influence of the text of Chile was, however, much more significant than that of its sister states: many civil codes adopted that text entirely or subject to changes.[68]

The motivation for the first generation of texts connected many of the resulting codes. One motivation may be found in the intention to break with the past and with the Spanish presence.[69] The recently independent jurisdictions aimed to end the normative subjugation that had existed during the previous period. Another motivation for civil codes, which relates to the previous one, may be found in seeing the codes as a constitutive element of the new republics and states. Jurisdictions included within their legislative agendas the need to promulgate codes as a kind of constitutive element, some including references to codification even in their constitutions.[70] First-generation civil codes aimed to project a sense of differentiation between the Old and the New World, between former dependence and empire.

Some jurisdictions enacted a multiplicity of civil codes that preserved a first-generation status.[71] First-generation codes, therefore, are not necessarily associated with the first enacted code. First generation may also associate with a series of civil codes that do not reach the status of second generation, though when even altering the text of the original enactments. Accordingly, the adoption of two or more intermediate codes can be needed to achieve a complete mutation to second generation.

68 *V.gr.*, Colombia, Ecuador, El Salvador, Honduras, Nicaragua, and Venezuela.

69 A degree of variation can be found in the codification experience in Louisiana. In that US state, subjugation to the prior power was not challenged, and codifiers tried to preserve the Spanish and French civilian tradition within their civil codes. See Moréteau & Parise 2009, pp. 1161–1162.

70 The Argentine Constitution of 1853 stated in article 64, paragraph 11 that the National Congress had to enact, amongst other things, a national civil code. See the text of the Constitution of 1853, available at Constitución Argentina 1853.

71 Venezuela may serve as illustration. This country adopted its first-generation code in 1862. The second-generation code was adopted in Venezuela only in 1942, after a multiplicity of codes had been enforced in the country during those eighty years. For more information on codification in Venezuela, see Moréteau & Parise 2009, pp. 1140–1141.

4.3.1 *Louisiana*

Civil law codification had an early start in the newly created territory.[72] In December 1804, the Legislative Council of the Territory of Orleans[73] appointed a committee to draft a civil code.[74] Later, in June 1806, James Brown and Louis Moreau-Lislet were appointed to draft a project of a civil code.[75] In February 1808, the different books of the projected text were presented by the committee before the local legislature.[76] Finally, in March 1808, the legislature promulgated the *Digest of the Civil Laws now in force in the territory of Orleans* (Digest of 1808).[77] The Digest of 1808 comprised 2,160 articles and was divided into a Preliminary Title *of the general definitions of rights and the promulgation of the laws*, and three books: Book I *of persons*, Book II *of things or estates*, and Book III *of the different manners of acquiring the property of things*.[78] The Digest of 1808 was drafted in French and then translated into English.[79]

The Digest of 1808 did not completely repeal the civil laws that had existed in Louisiana.[80] Interpretation by the courts showed that there was uncertainty about the preservation of the Spanish, French, and Roman laws.[81] This uncertainty encouraged the local legislature to resolve in March 1822 that "three jurisconsults be appointed [...] to revise the [Digest of 1808]."[82] That same month, the attending members of the legislature appointed attorneys Pierre Derbigny, Edward Livingston, and Moreau-Lislet to draft a revision.[83]

72 See generally Parise 2014c, pp. 315–317.

73 On April 30, 1812—at the time of the ninth anniversary of the Louisiana Purchase—Louisiana was admitted as the eighteenth state of the Union. See Davis 1978, p. 136.

74 Wallach 1960, p. 46.

75 Resolution 1806, p. 214.

76 Dargo 1970, p. 321.

77 Act for Promulgation 1808, p. 122. See generally Digest of Laws 1808.

According to the 1808 act, the complete title in English read "Digest of the Civil Laws now in force in the territory of Orleans, with alterations and amendments, adapted to its present system of government;" while the complete title in French read "digeste des lois civiles actuellement en force dans le territoire d'Orléans, avec des changemens et améliorations, adaptés à son présent système de gouvernement." Act for Promulgation 1808, pp. 122–123.

78 The text of the Digest of 1808 is available digitally at Digest Online.

79 See Dubuisson 1924, p. 144; and Shuey 1941, p. 452.

80 Kilbourne 1987, p. 62.

81 Herman *et al.* 1981, p. 26.

82 Resolution 1822.

83 Journal House of Representatives 1822, p. 73; and Flory 1936, p. 53.

The work on a revised text of the Digest of 1808 was immediately started. In February 1823, the three attorneys presented their Preliminary Report before the local legislature,[84] and their revised text resulted in a civil code. On April 12, 1824, the local legislature ordered the printing and promulgation of the revised text with the proposed changes.[85] The new text had 3,522 articles, and was entitled *Civil Code of the State of Louisiana*[86] (Louisiana Code). The structure of the Louisiana Code was similar to the one of the Digest of 1808, having a Preliminary Title *of the general definitions of rights and the promulgation of the laws*; and three books: Book I *of persons*; Book II *of things and of the different modifications of property*, and Book III *of the different modes of acquiring the property of things*.[87]

4.3.2 *Chile*

Civil law codification endeavors started shortly after independence was declared.[88] In July 1822 the Supreme Director, Bernardo O'Higgins, stated publicly the need for the adoption of the five[89] traditional codes.[90] The following decade, in June 1833, Manuel Vial submitted to the House of Representatives a draft[91] which advocated for the compilation of the dispositive parts of Spanish and *Patrio* laws in a clear and concise manner.[92] He also advocated for the references to rules by glossators and scholars, and references to the sources for each article.[93] The draft of Vial was not adopted, however.[94]

Codification soon welcomed another central figure in Chile: a scholar who would shape civil law across the Americas. Bello, a native of Venezuela, had been working privately on his draft of a civil code for Chile, and by 1835 had accomplished one-third of his project.[95] The years that followed were marked

84 Livingston *et al.* 1937, p. lxxxvi.

85 Act for Printing and Promulgation 1824; and Wallach 1960, p. 48.

86 See generally Civil Code Louisiana 1825.

87 Civil Code Louisiana 1825.

88 See the detailed study on the early interest for consolidation and codification of the law in Chile. Guzmán Brito 1982, pp. 160–225.

89 *I.e.*, civil, civil procedure, commercial, criminal, and criminal procedure.

90 Guzmán Brito 2000, pp. 350–351.

91 For detailed information on the draft, see Guzmán Brito 1982, pp. 231–236.

92 Guzmán Brito 2000, p. 357.

93 Guzmán Brito 2000, p. 357.

94 Guzmán Brito 2000, p. 359.

95 Alessandri Rodríguez & Somarriva Undurraga 1945, p. 59.

by the work of Bello together with that of special commissions.[96] Starting in 1847, Bello, however, undertook the drafting autonomously.[97] In 1853, the project was published, and subjected to review by a special commission.[98] Finally, the project was sent to the National Congress, which approved it *in totum*.[99]

The *Código Civil de la República de Chile* (Chilean Code) was approved by the National Congress on December 14, 1855.[100] It took effect on January 1, 1857,[101] and has been one of the most influential civil codes for American Civil Law Jurisdictions. The code had 2,524 articles, and was divided into a Preliminary Title (*Título Preliminar*) and four books; Book I *of persons* (*de las personas*); Book II *of things and the dominium, possession, use and enjoyment of them* (*de los bienes y de su dominio, posesión, uso y goce*); Book III *of successions* mortis causa *and of donations* inter vivos (*de la sucesión por causa de muerte y de las donaciones entre vivos*); and Book IV *of obligations in general and contracts* (*de las obligaciones en general y de los contratos*).[102]

Bello found inspiration in a multiplicity of sources. He benefited from, amongst others, the *Code Napoléon* and its commentators,[103] the works of García Goyena and Saint-Joseph,[104] and of nineteenth-century civil codes that were modern at that time.[105] The work of Bello was grounded in the old law, but restated accordingly to the modern codification techniques. It included the provisions of the juridical liberalism of that time, while following the Roman and Spanish provisions. Bello, who was also known as a distinguished linguist, was able to maintain a perfect harmony between extension and development for each article of his code, making his work not only an example of law drafting but also of linguistics.[106]

---

96 Guzmán Brito 1982, pp. 306–336.

97 Guzmán Brito 1982, pp. 337–343.

98 Alessandri Rodríguez & Somarriva Undurraga 1945, p. 63. See the detailed study in Guzmán Brito 1982, pp. 366–382.

99 Approved by law dated December 14, 1855. Alessandri Rodríguez & Somarriva Undurraga 1945, p. 63.

100 Guzmán Brito 2000, p. 368. See also Moréteau & Parise 2009.

101 Código Civil Chile 1857, p. 632.

102 See generally Código Civil Chile 1857.

103 For additional information regarding the use of the *Code Napoléon*, see Mirow 2001.

104 See also Knütel 1996, pp. 1452–1459.

105 Pescio Vargas 1978, p. 115.

106 Guzmán Brito 2000, p. 373.

4.3.3 *Argentina*[107]

The first attempts towards civil law codification[108] were undertaken in 1852.[109] At that time, the head of the executive power, Justo José de Urquiza, delivered a decree ordering the appointment of drafters who would work on the civil, commercial, criminal, and procedural codes.[110] Lorenzo Torres was appointed to draft the civil code, though due to health problems he had to decline, and was replaced by Vélez Sarsfield, who at that time did not advance with a draft.[111] In addition, one year later, the Argentine Constitution stated that the national legislative branch should deliver civil, commercial, criminal, and mineral codes.[112] That first codification attempt in the area of civil law was interrupted because the province of Buenos Aires seceded from the rest of Argentina.[113]

A reunion of the province of Buenos Aires and the rest of Argentina would be reflected some years later through the constitutional reform of 1860.[114] However, in the period of secession, the province of Buenos Aires had autonomously renewed efforts towards civil law codification.[115] In 1857, the executive power of Buenos Aires had authorized the allotment of financial resources for the drafting of the civil, criminal, and procedural codes.[116] Marcelo Gamboa and Mercelino Ugarte had been appointed to draft the first of those codes, and the latter jurist started to draft a project, which due to financial constraints was soon interrupted.[117] The main sources of inspiration for Ugarte were the project of a civil code for Uruguay of 1852 by Eduardo Acevedo and the work of concordances by García Goyena.[118]

The completion of a civil code was delayed until the following decade. In 1864, Vélez Sarsfield was appointed to draft a project of a civil code for Argentina.[119] The project he drafted was approved without parliamentary

107 See generally Parise 2014b, pp. 324–325; Marotta & Parise 2014, pp. 241–242; and Parise 2012b, p. 81.

108 Previous efforts were undertaken in the area of commercial law in 1824, with the drafting of a project of a commercial code. See Tau Anzoátegui 1977b, p. 125.

109 Levaggi 1987, p. 265.

110 Levaggi 1987, p. 265.

111 Levaggi 1987, p. 265.

112 Section 64, paragraph 11 of the Argentine Constitution of 1853, available at Constitución Argentina 1853, p. 21. See Tau Anzoátegui 1977b, p. 319.

113 Levaggi 1987, p. 265.

114 Tau Anzoátegui 1977b, p. 340.

115 Tau Anzoátegui 1977b, pp. 324–340.

116 Levaggi 1987, p. 265.

117 Levaggi 1987, p. 265. See also Zorraquín Becú 1954.

118 Levaggi 1987, p. 265.

119 Levaggi 1987, p. 266.

debate (*libro cerrado*)[120] by the National Congress on September 25, 1869, and took effect as the *Código Civil de la República Argentina* (Argentine Code) on January 1, 1871.[121] The Argentine Code had 4,051 articles and was divided into two preliminary titles and four books: Book I *of persons* (*de las personas*), Book II *of personal rights in civil relations* (*de los derechos personales en las relaciones civiles*), Book III *of real rights* (*de los derechos reales*), and Book IV *of real and personal rights-dispositions in common* (*de los derechos reales y personales—disposiciones communes*).[122] Differently from the Louisiana Digest of 1808, the Argentine Code overruled all related prior laws that had developed during the Spanish period and the early independence period (*v.gr.*, *Indiano* and *Patrio* laws).[123]

The official publication of the Argentine Code, unlike the codes of Chile[124] and Louisiana, included notes for many of its articles. Those notes are not part of the law, and intend to inform the reader about the genesis of the thoughts of Vélez Sarsfield.[125] They help understand articles, in a similar way as legislative history or *exposé des motifs*.[126] The notes are useful as an additional element for interpretation of codified provisions,[127] and serve as guides when studying articles.[128]

Vélez Sarsfield had an eclectic approach to law,[129] and therefore identified materials from many sources. He worked with legislative acts, drafts of codes, codes, and doctrine that served him as guides.[130] As other drafters, he used the ideas and codes that existed at the time.[131] He was especially interested—as were Bello in Chile and Moreau-Lislet in Louisiana—in the jurists and works that theorized on modern law while building from Roman law principles.[132] Finally, Vélez Sarsfield added to those materials the identification of local customs.[133]

---

120 Levaggi 1987, p. 269. See also the complete study in Cabral Texo 1920, pp. 156–178.

121 Código Civil Argentina 1871. See Moréteau & Parise 2009, pp. 1143–1145; and Levaggi 1987, p. 266.

122 Código Civil Argentina 1871.

123 See article 22 of the Argentine Code available at Código Civil Argentina 1871, p. 508.

124 Guzmán Brito 2005, p. 66. The draft of 1853 included notes for some of its articles.

125 Moisset de Espanés 1981, p. 448.

126 Levaggi 2005b, p. 209.

127 Cobas & Zago 1991, pp. 146–147.

128 Rivarola 1901, p. 12.

129 Guzmán Brito 2000, p. 453.

130 Parise 2012b, p. 75. See also Salvat 1913, p. 436.

131 Levaggi 2005b, p. 180.

132 Levaggi 2005b, p. 180.

133 Salvat 1950, p. 132.

4.4 Codifying the Liberal Paradigm of Ownership

American Civil Law Jurisdictions gradually shifted from the Allocation paradigm towards the Liberal[134] paradigm of ownership.[135] That shift was consequently present within the provisions of first-generation codes:[136] which could be deemed as encapsulating the universe of private law. The new paradigm advocated for an absolute right of ownership, yet subject to the limitations established by law.[137] First-generation codes were, therefore, consistent with liberalism and with the gradual abolishment of the Spanish past.[138] The idea of the free circulation of property spread across the continent, while the idea of entailments started to be rejected.[139] Eighteenth-century ideas such as those of de Jovellanos in Spain[140] started to percolate in society, and were in harmony with nineteenth-century products such as the French *Code Napoléon*.[141] In American Civil Law Jurisdictions, however, the new paradigm did not fully eliminate the social responsibility of owners, departing therefore from the traditional liberal economy doctrine.[142]

4.4.1 *Origins*

Ownership was traditionally governed by provisions found within civil codes, originally in Europe. American Civil Law Jurisdictions found the French model the most appealing.[143] Accordingly, the new American jurisdictions turned towards the model provided by the *Code Napoléon*, especially in the area of property, which was a symbol of modernity and liberalism.[144] Property law occupied, indeed, a central place in the French code.[145] Article 544 of the *Code Napoléon* was present, *verbatim* or by substantive adaptation, in many of the resulting civil codes. That article was located in Book II, Title II of the French code, and read in an English translation: "ownership is the right to enjoy and

134 That paradigm is also referred to in the literature as liberal-individualistic, Napoleonic-Pandectist, or Bourgeois Property. See Levaggi 1999, p. 60.

135 Levaggi 2001, p. 413.

136 Levaggi 2001, p. 413.

137 Levaggi 2001, p. 419.

138 Mirow 2004, p. 133.

139 Levaggi 1999, p. 52.

140 See generally 3.5.1 of this book.

141 Lira Urquieta 1944, p. 167.

142 Levaggi 2001, p. 419.

143 Karst & Rosenn 1975, p. 45.

144 Halpérin 2008, p. 266.

145 Halpérin 2000, p. 37.

dispose of things in the most absolute manner, provided they are not used in a way prohibited by law or by regulations."[146] That text provided the paramount example of the new paradigm;[147] and it assisted in the distinction between ownership and usufruct, and in the eradication of any potential feudal reminiscence.[148] The definition in that article was prepared after the proposals included in the drafts by Jean-Jacques-Régis de Cambacérès[149] of 1793,[150] 1794,[151] and 1796,[152] and also found an antecedent in the *Projet* of 1800.[153] There is no certainty on which of the four commissioners appointed by Napoleon I drafted the final language.[154]

The conceptualization provided by article 544 resulted from a prolonged process that ultimately left behind many of the feudalistic limitations on property.[155] It was a product of the work by Romanists that reached its clearest expression with the writings of Robert-Joseph Pothier:[156] who should perhaps be seen as the last of the "old" writers rather than the first of the "new."[157] Immediately after the enactment of the *Code Napoléon*, a relationship was claimed between the French article and parts of the *Corpus iuris civilis*,[158] yet that relationship encountered limitations because the Liberal paradigm was foreign to Roman law,[159] even though many scholars claim that ownership was

---

146 That article in French read: "La propriété est le droit de jouir et disposer des choses de la manière la plus absolue, pourvu qu'on n'en fasse pas un usage prohibé par les lois ou par les règlemens." (Code Civil 1804, p. 100)

147 Gambaro 2011, p. 237.

148 Halpérin 2000, p. 38.

149 Halpérin 2008, p. 192.

150 Article 1, Title 2, Book 2 in French read: "La propriété d'un bien est le droit qu'a celui en qui elle réside de jouir et de disposer de ce bien." (Fenet 1827, I, p. 39)

151 Article 71, Title 1, Book 2 in French read: "La propriété est le droit de jouir et de disposer conformément à la loi." (Fenet 1827, I, p. 116)

152 Article 415, Title 1, Book 2 in French read: "Le propriétaire a droit de jouir et de disposer à son gré, en se conformant aux lois établies pour la nécessité commune." (Fenet 1827, I, p. 243)

153 Article 1, Title 2, Book 2 in French read: "La pleine propriété donne le droit de jouir et disposer de sa chose, de la manière la plus absolue, pourvu qu'on n'en fasse pas un usage prohibé par les lois ou par les réglemens." (Projet de Code Civil 1800, p. 166)

154 Halpérin 2008, p. 193.

155 Lira Urquieta 1944, p. 166.

156 Halpérin 1996, p. 25.

157 Álvarez Alonso 1999, p. 57, 59.

158 For example, in 1805, Henri-Jean-Baptiste Dard stated the relevance of *Leg. 21, Cod. Mandate. Leg. 1, § 4 et 13, ff. de aqua et aquae pluviae arcendae.* See Dard 1805, p. 104.

159 Tomás y Valiente 1997c, p. 1414.

an absolute and indivisible right in Roman law.[160] The definition of article 544 did echo concepts of the French Revolution, however.[161] This could help explain why Jean-Étienne-Marie Portalis stated, as part of the *exposé des motifs* for the corresponding title, that ownership was the fundamental right on which all social institutions rested.[162] This could help explain the resemblance to principles included in article 17 of the *Déclaration des droits de l'homme et du citoyen* of 1789,[163] which referred to ownership as an inviolable and sacred right.[164]

Bartolus de Saxoferrato deserves special attention due to his role in shaping the understanding of ownership, not only during the Middle Ages but also in the modern period, on both sides of the Atlantic. His celebrated understanding of ownership as *ius perfecte disponendi de re corporali nisi lege prohibeatur*[165] was regarded by future scholars,[166] and influenced property law, ever since its conception in the fourteenth century.[167] For example, Gregorio Lopez, when undertaking his seminal gloss of the *Siete Partidas*,[168] likewise followed the criteria of commentators such as Bartolus in which ownership meant the right to dispose of or to sell a corporeal thing when facing no prohibition by law.[169] That gloss was able to adapt the text of the *Siete Partidas* to the highest production of the commentators.[170] Spanish Scholasticism (*v.gr.*, de Molina) returned—with some nuances—to the definition of Bartolus.[171] That understanding of Bartolus was indeed replicated almost *verbtim* by the architects of *Code Napoléon*,[172] and from there was projected across the Atlantic.

160 Rüfner 2010, p. 128.
161 Tunc 1955, p. 448. See also Sagnac 1898, pp. 57–244, 330–354, cited likewise by André Tunc.
162 Jean-Étienne-Marie Portalis in French claimed: "[…] droit fundamental sur lequel toutes les institutions sociales reposent." (Fenet 1827, XI, p. 132)
163 Halpérin 2008, p. 192.
164 That article in French read: "La propriété étant un droit inviolable et sacré, nul ne peut en être privé, si ce n'est lorsque la nécessité publique, légalement constatée, l'exige évidemment, et sous la condition d'une juste et préalable indemnité." (Assemblée Nationale 1789, p. 489)
165 This expression was coined in a comment of Bartolus to Digest 41, 2, 17, I, n. 4. See Grossi 1992d, p. 368.
166 See de los Mozos 1993, p. 36; and Rüfner 2010, p. 127.
167 Rüfner 2010, p. 127.
168 See generally 3.4.2 of this book.
169 Sánchez Bella *et al.* 1992, p. 343.
170 Guzmán Brito 2000, p. 160.
171 de los Mozos 1993, pp. 36–38.
172 Rüfner 2010, p. 127.

Borrowing was not a blind activity in American Civil Law Jurisdictions. Around the second half of the nineteenth century, an ideological maturity already existed and enabled eclectic approaches to codification.[173] Accordingly, the early codification endeavors aimed to copy the *Code Napoléon*, while, with time, local lawyers started to make manifest a resistance against that simplistic adoption of foreign law.[174] In Chile, for example, there was no intention to entirely copy foreign codes, and there were aims towards achieving a change that adapted to social reality.[175]

4.4.2 *Formal Sources*[176]

Codifiers made different use of sources dealing with ownership when incorporating them into their drafts. Levaggi explained that distinction by stating that material sources (also called ideological or indirect) differ from formal sources (also called literal or direct).[177] The first type encompasses doctrines, ideas, or solutions that may be expressed in archaic or modern terminology. The second type encompasses formulas that limit themselves to expressing or simply translating those ideas. For example, in Argentina, material sources could be extracted from the *Corpus iuris civilis* and the *Siete Partidas*. Those ideas were not incorporated into the Argentine Code with their original wording, however. They were incorporated with refurnished words, taken many times from contemporary works that served as formal sources. On many occasions, therefore, formal sources "dressed" with modern language the material ideas that were considered universal.[178]

Scholars in American Civil Law Jurisdictions traced formal sources of their civil codes, and ownership provisions were subject to that veneration. There was a Pan-American interest in that treasure trove of European formal sources. On occasion, initially the drafters, and those tracing formal sources soon after, welcomed the association with the prestige held by transferred elaborations in their jurisdictions of origin. Many times, nineteenth-century scholars worked on glossed editions of codes, in which formal sources were only pinpointed. Codifiers, like builders of monuments, took in hand the best materials provided by the legal science of their time.[179] The annotation or glossing of codes

173 Tau Anzoátegui 1977b, p. 288.
174 Kleinheisterkamp 2012, p. 1033; and Kleinheisterkamp 2008, pp. 271–285.
175 Tau Anzoátegui 1977b, p. 292.
176 See generally Parise 2014b, pp. 317, 345–352.
177 Levaggi 2005b, p. 181.
178 Levaggi 2005b, p. 181.
179 Rodríguez 1938, p. 189.

helped identify those materials, and provided motives and the resulting concordances. Some nineteenth-century codifiers had incorporated annotations to their drafts (*v.gr.*, Argentina, Brazil, Chile, New York, and Uruguay).[180] In the Iberian Peninsula, Spain had provided the already mentioned work by García Goyena, which was considered a seminal glossed edition. García Goyena said that each article of the Spanish project would include a reference to corresponding provisions of other legislative works (*concordancias*), motives (*motivos*), and commentaries (*comentarios*).[181] That way, he said, readers would have almost universal knowledge of the legislation on that topic with just a simple glance.[182] That trend to provide glossed editions of codes would soon spread throughout both sides of the Atlantic, benefiting those seeking ownership provisions.

American Civil Law Jurisdictions provided several examples of glossed editions of codes. In Argentina, Luis V. Varela, Lisandro V. Segovia, Baldomero Llerena, and José Olegario Machado undertook that path.[183] Their focus, as that of other commentators, was initially on European sources mainly, both legislative and doctrinal.[184] The Argentine Code provided an example of the reception of foreign laws, which after adaptation were considered local.[185] In Chile, soon after 1856, the codifier Bello envisioned a glossed edition of his code with notes for each article. Though never completed, his projected edition was to be built on the notes that he included in his 1853 draft.[186] Such a work would have been useful in Chile, where law was taught according to the letter and structure of the local code.[187] In Uruguay, codifiers were likewise expected to explore an array of legislation and doctrinal works while looking for material sources[188] on ownership. Their works were then more about selection than creation.[189] In the early twentieth century, Rafael Gallinal provided for Uruguay a glossed edition of the local civil code.[190] Also in Uruguay, though in 1851, Acevedo, the drafter of a civil code project, made an early approach to

180 Abásolo 2004, p. 423.
181 Parise 2008b, p. 841.
182 García Goyena 1852, I, p. 9.
183 Tau Anzoátegui 1977c, pp. 113–114; and generally Parise 2014b.
184 Cabral Texo 1919, p. 26.
185 Zorraquín Becú 1976, pp. 350, 359.
186 Guzmán Brito 2005, p. 66.
187 See *Advertencia*, in Lastarria 1864.
188 Peirano Facio 2008, p. 65.
189 Peirano Facio 2008, p. 65.
190 Gallinal 1911–1912.

the distinction of formal and material sources that applies to many American codification endeavors. He stated that,

> having used for our work writings by French authors [...] it will be questioned why we have not cited them, especially since on occasions we borrowed their words. However, that was necessary because we imposed ourselves to provide a national character to the work, removing all foreign scent that would be reproached. Furthermore, many times an article that had been triggered by reading [the French] Toullier found support on an opinion by [the Spaniard] Sala [...], which, although identical in substance, lacked the fundamentals that made it more acceptable.[191]

Very early during the nineteenth century, in Louisiana, some copies of the Digest of 1808—the predecessor of the Louisiana Code—included manuscript glosses that related to its different titles and articles.[192] Later, the codifiers of the influential civil code of Louisiana drafted a project including glosses with references to many authorities.[193] In 1838, Wheelock Upton and Needler Jennings published a well-circulated edition of the code with glosses.[194] They referred to related legislation,[195] doctrinal works,[196] and court decisions.[197] Their work would "fill a void in the libraries of the gentlemen of the Bar"[198] and "render unnecessary those laborious researches, the prosecution of which often require extended and thorough knowledge of the annals of jurisprudence."[199] Those texts were naturally embellished with information dealing with the seminal articles on ownership and their resulting concordances.

Yet glossed editions were not limited to American Civil Law Jurisdictions. North American jurisdictions provided examples of glossed editions of codes. In Quebec, for example, glossed editions were welcomed soon after the code

191 Acevedo & Palomeque 1908, p. 342. See also Guzmán Brito 2000, pp. 461–62; and Moréteau & Parise 2009, p. 1146.

192 See the complete study in Cairns 2009.

193 See generally Louisiana *Projet* 1823.

194 Upton & Jennings 1838.

195 See the reference to a Louisiana Act of 1828 in the note to article 263 (Upton & Jennings 1838, p. 39).

196 See the reference to the work of Jean Domat in the note to article 263 (Upton & Jennings 1838, p. 39).

197 See the reference to the case *Proctor v. Richardson* in the note to article 301 (Upton & Jennings 1838, p. 44).

198 Upton & Jennings 1838, p. iii.

199 Upton & Jennings 1838, p. iii.

was adopted. Those glosses referred to sources, while dealing mainly with the reporting of local decisions.[200] Thomas McCord, one of the secretaries of the Codifying Commission, worked on an edition that included references to the authorities cited in the Reports together with tables of concordances with the *Code Napoléon* and the *Code de commerce*.[201] Those glosses included references for "notaries, clergymen, physicians, merchants, real estate owners, and persons out of Lower Canada."[202] Also in Canada, in the early 1870s, Charles-Chamilly de Lorimier started to work in Quebec on what he called the *library of the civil code* (*bibliothèque du Code Civil*). In that twenty-one-volume work he provided, amongst others, the transcription of authorities used when drafting the Quebec civil code.[203] Examples of glossed editions were provided by US states. The State of New York provided the Americas with glosses. David Dudley Field worked on a project of a civil code for that state.[204] His 1865 project had notes for two-thirds[205] of its articles,[206] and indicated references to, amongst others, related court decisions,[207] revised statutes,[208] the *Code Napoléon*,[209] and the Louisiana Code.[210] Even though the project was never the law of New York,[211] its drafts were influential,[212] and its provisions about the law of contracts were adopted by several states (*v.gr.*, California, Montana).[213] Additionally, in the State of California, during the early 1870s, the local Code Commissioners provided in their work annotations that significantly replicated the glosses by Field.[214]

200 Howes 1989, p. 139.

201 McCord 1870, pp. 466–475.

202 See the cover page of McCord 1870.

203 Parise 2014b, p. 316.

204 See Civil Code New York 1865.

205 Batiza 1986, p. 803.

206 The project referred to sections and not to articles.

207 For example, the note to article 443 of the project read: "Halsey v. Mc. Cormick, 18 N.Y., 147." (Civil Code New York 1865, p. 135)

208 For example, the note to article 523 of the project read: "R.S., 758, § 12." (Civil Code New York 1865, p. 156)

209 For example, the note to article 444 of the project read: "This and the four sections following are similar to those of the Code Napoleon, art. 559–563." (Civil Code New York 1865, p. 135)

210 For example, the note to Chapter 2, Title 3, Part 4, Division 2 of the project read: "The provisions of this chapter, except § 455, are similar to those of the Code Napoleon and the Code of Louisiana." (Civil Code New York 1865, p. 136) See also Herman 1996, p. 423.

211 Field 1898, p. 88.

212 Extracts Field 1894, p. 39.

213 Herman 1996, p. 425.

214 Parma 1929, p. 19.

Positivistic approaches to the study and understanding of law gained popularity during the nineteenth century in Europe and the Americas.[215] Several schools of thought evolved from nineteenth-century European positivism. Some of those, and their leading representatives, had significant impact on the drafting of codes in the Americas, and therefore, in the evolution of Ownership Paradigms. Examples of these schools are: Legal Positivism (*v.gr.*, Jeremy Bentham); the French Exegetical School (*v.gr.*, Jean-Charles Demolombe); and the German Historical School, which in part developed into Scientific Positivism (*v.gr.*, von Savigny), and ultimately into Conceptual Jurisprudence (*v.gr.*, Bernhard Windscheid).[216] The impact of positivism in the Americas was sensed especially during the last decades of the nineteenth century.[217]

The French Exegetical School occupied the paramount position in the codification projects in the Americas. In France, soon after the adoption of the *Code Napoléon,* scholars and judges interpreted code provisions by closely following their language (literal meaning)[218] and in light of their preparatory works (*v.gr.*, Pothier, Jean Domat).[219] Their interpretations were published as commentaries to the different articles,[220] and ownership provisions were subject to that scrutiny. The exegesis was both a way of presenting and of teaching law,[221] and Demolombe, regarded as the *prince of exegesis,* advocated, as other representatives, for the supremacy of written codified law.[222] Accordingly, articles would be stated individually, with no references to philosophical or historical argumentations.[223] The look into history was done, however, when searching for support for a certain interpretation, when reconstructing the "pedigree" of a provision.[224] The Exegetical School followed the *Code Napoléon,* and its representatives were read together with the code,[225] even motivating translations into vernacular languages.[226] Exegesis was therefore well received in the Americas,[227] even in Louisiana, where codifiers seemed to adhere to

215 See generally Bobbio 1996.
216 Levaggi 2005b, p. 219; Díaz Couselo 2003, p. 371; and Tau Anzoátegui 1977c, p. 105.
217 Tau Anzoátegui 1977a, p. 423.
218 Salerno 1992, p. 228.
219 Yiannopoulos 1977, p. 58.
220 Yiannopoulos 1977, p. 58.
221 Petit 2001, p. 69.
222 Levaggi 1979, p. 29.
223 Ramos Núñez 1997, p. 234.
224 Ramos Núñez 1997, p. 233.
225 Díaz Couselo 2009, pp. 17–18.
226 Aragoneses 2009, p. 80.
227 Levaggi 1979, p. 30.

the school.[228] The reconstruction of "pedigree" took place too, where the trove was for European authors, and legislative productions required references to, for example, French, German, or Italian scholars.[229] Ownership developed within this context, and the knowledge of code provisions was paramount for the full understanding of that area of property law.

The exegetical approach limited the creativity of scholars and judges, however.[230] In France first, and after in the Americas, the exegetical approach was replaced by interpretations that responded more to social reality.[231] François Gény, in France, explored the legislation that had grown outside the *Code Napoléon*, together with customs, court decisions, and social sciences.[232] His Free Scientific Research approach departed from the exegetical interpretation, and gave significant space for other sources of law (*v.gr.*, customs) that gained gravitation in civil law jurisdictions.[233] Another reaction came mainly from Germany, where the Historical School, and later Scientific Positivism, advocated for customs and traditions and for objective interpretation of the law, srespectively. Both German and French ideas would react against the supremacy of the letter of the law,[234] having ultimately an impact on the paradigm shift from the Liberal to the Social Function.

The Exegetical School prevailed, however, in law teaching, in scholarly works, and in court decisions[235] well into the twentieth century. For example, the Argentine Code triggered exegetical approaches to the law. Positivistic approaches, mainly those from the Exegetical School,[236] were present in the works of scholars and judges during the second half of the nineteenth century and extended, though at a slower pace, well into the next century.[237] These tried to identify the intention of the codifier,[238] and promoted the study of the letter of the law and its sources.[239] A *culture of the code* developed, and was reflected in scholarly writings and judicial interpretations that turned

228 Yiannopoulos 1977, p. 48.

229 Ramos Núñez 1997, p. 235.

230 Ramos Núñez 1996, p. 10.

231 Ramos Núñez 1997, p. 233.

232 Yiannopoulos 1977, pp. 58–59.

233 Yiannopoulos 1977, p. 48.

234 Ramos Núñez 1997, p. 237.

235 Ramos Núñez 1997, p. 237.

236 Esborraz 2007, pp. 34–35; and Ramos Núñez 1997, p. 200.

237 Seoane 1981, p. 68.

238 Vernengo 1977, p. 77.

239 Tau Anzoátegui 2011, p. 72.

the code into a repository of legal science[240] with absolute value:[241] ownership was what the code stated. The code was also the central figure in law teaching, together with the work of exegetical scholars.[242] Teaching followed the structure of the code until 1910,[243] and a breakdown of articles was done for their study throughout the years of law school.[244] The legislator's intention was looked for in the notes,[245] which opened the way to studies on comparative legislation.[246] Other positivistic approaches, such as the ideas of von Savigny[247] and Scientific Positivism,[248] were also welcomed and, though in cases language barriers needed to be bridged, they helped develop an eclectic legal thought.[249] The work of scholars was therefore eclectic, including exegetical and scientific approaches.[250] The new century brought criticisms to extreme positivistic approaches, however.[251] Social sciences liberated law from the narrow exegetical approach, and began to open the way to more scientific approaches that advocated for their inclusion in the study of law.[252] These approaches, presented in, for example, the seminal work of Gény,[253] placed the code in the paramount position, yet, when interpreting provisions, likewise used doctrine, court decisions, comparative legislation, customs, and other social elements.[254] The Liberal paradigm of ownership was affected in American Civil Law Jurisdictions by that context.

4.4.3 *Transplantation and Development of Common Sources*

American Civil Law Jurisdictions turned to transplantation when creating their systems of law.[255] That transplantation benefited from European sources, and

240 Tau Anzoátegui 2007, pp. 19–20.

241 Tau Anzoátegui 1998, pp. 543–544.

242 Martínez Paz 2000, p. 350; Salerno 2004, p. 149; Tau Anzoátegui 1977c, p. 113; Salerno 1993, p. 123; and Tau Anzoátegui 2007, p. 162.

243 Salerno 1974, p. 205.

244 Tau Anzoátegui 2007, p. 162; and Cháneton 1937, p. 344.

245 Levaggi 2005b, p. 247; and Salerno 1974, p. 207.

246 Cháneton 1937, p. 344.

247 Levaggi 1979, p. 78; and Tau Anzoátegui 1977b, p. 278.

248 Levaggi 1979, pp. 84–85; and Tau Anzoátegui 1988, p. 623.

249 Tau Anzoátegui 1977b, pp. 277, 282.

250 Tau Anzoátegui 1977c, pp. 114–115.

251 Tau Anzoátegui 1974, p. 241.

252 Tau Anzoátegui 2007, p. 20; Tau Anzoátegui 2008, p. 21; and Tau Anzoátegui 2011, p. 99.

253 Tau Anzoátegui 1977c, p. 141; Levaggi 1979, p. 120; Levaggi 2005b, p. 249; and Díaz Couselo 2009, pp. 1–2.

254 Tau Anzoátegui 1977c, p. 141.

255 Mirow 2004, p. 133.

eventually developed into a common set of secondary sources and methodologies for the endeavors in civil law.[256] In former Spanish territories, however, the adoption of code provisions from other American Civil Law Jurisdictions was also very common,[257] resulting in pollination,[258] such as the ones experienced by borrowings from the civil codes of Louisiana, Chile, and Argentina.

The main two nineteenth-century works of legislative concordances reflected the liberal understanding of ownership, and contributed to that pollination. García Goyena, in line with the *Code Napoléon,* stated in article 391 of his project that "ownership is the right to enjoy and dispose of a thing with no other limitation than those derived from law or regulations."[259] Accordingly, the Spanish scholar referred to absolute ownership, and distinguished it from imperfect ownership (*dominio menos pleno*), which related to emphyteusis and superficies.[260] As already mentioned, in his commentary García Goyena indicated the concordance with, amongst others, article 544 of the *Code Napoléon* and *Partida* III, Title 28, Law 1.[261] Saint Joseph, in the introduction to the 1856 edition of his French concordance, stated that ownership, in its broadest sense, was the right to enjoy and dispose of a thing,[262] and also an essential element of civil society.[263] His comparative chart showed the influence of article 544 of the *Code Napoléon,* indicating the concordance of that article with those of other transcribed civil codes.[264]

4.5 Encapsulation of the New Paradigm across the Americas

The three jurisdictions subject to study welcomed the Liberal paradigm, and the European background of ownership in those three codes cannot be challenged. The civil codes of Louisiana, Chile and, Argentina incorporated, to a large degree, the principles embodied in article 544 of the *Code Napoléon.*

256 Mirow 2004, p. 142.

257 Bravo Lira 1989, p. 51.

258 Guzmán Brito 2000, pp. 252–254.

259 That article in Spanish read: "la propiedad es el derecho de gozar y disponer de una cosa sin mas limitaciones que las que previenen las leyes ó reglamentos." (García Goyena 1852, I, p. 351)

260 García Goyena 1852, I, p. 352.

261 García Goyena 1852, I, p. 352.

262 Saint-Joseph (de) 1856, I, p. xxxviii.

263 Saint-Joseph (de) 1856, I, p. xlv.

264 See note 40 of this chapter and accompanying text.

Some codes repeated similar wordings, while others limited themselves to replicating the liberal and individualistic components of ownership.

4.5.1 *Louisiana*

The Louisiana Code presented a positive balance between enlightened conservatism and prudent liberalism.[265] It was gestated at a time of ideological certainty, when no doubts existed on the absolute character of property rights.[266]

4.5.1.1 Constitutional Protection

Constitutional rights also protected private property in Louisiana. The first Louisiana Constitution was approved by the US Congress in April 1812.[267] That constitution contained no bill of rights, and made no references to property rights.[268] Louisiana is subject to the supremacy of federal law, however, as is any other state in the Union. Louisiana therefore found limitations to disposing of property rights within the US Constitution, which were mainly located in the Fifth[269] and Fourteenth[270] Amendments.[271] Accordingly, the US Constitution could be interpreted as advocating for the establishment of safeguards for property, sensing the indissoluble link between property rights and liberty.[272]

4.5.1.2 Codified Protection

The codes in Louisiana always dealt with ownership in Book II.[273] However, property law was not dealt with exclusively in that book, because, *v.gr.*, possession was addressed in Book III.[274] Robert A. Pascal stated that Book II deals with the objects of the law and "describes the interest in things permissible by law."[275] The Digest of 1808 preliminary dealt with ownership in Book II, Title 2,

265 Yiannopoulos 2001, p. 16.

266 Cairns 2015, p. 503.

267 Davis 1978, p. 135.

268 Morgan 1975, p. 10.

269 The Fifth Amendment in its relevant part read: "No person shall [...] be deprived of life, liberty, or property, without due process of law; nor shall private property be taken for public use, without just compensation." (US Constitution 1789)

270 The Fourteenth Amendment in its relevant part read: "[...] nor shall any State deprive any person of life, liberty, or property, without due process of law; nor deny to any person within its jurisdiction the equal protection of the laws." (US Constitution 1789)

271 Riddick 2008, p. 4.

272 Ely 2005, p. 40.

273 Yiannopoulos 2001, pp. 9–11.

274 Yiannopoulos 2001, p. 11.

275 Pascal 1998, pp. 303–304.

Chapter 1. Article 1 of that chapter provided the universal principle regarding absolute ownership (*pleine propriété*), being a right to enjoy and dispose of property within the limitations of the laws.[276] The Louisiana Code, which was influential for other American Civil Law Jurisdictions, dealt preliminarily with ownership in Book II, Title 2, Chapter 1.[277] Articles 480 to 484 provided the general principles for the understanding of ownership, either perfect or imperfect.[278] In Louisiana, ownership was deemed an absolute right within the limitations of the laws.[279] Article 480 stated that "ownership is the right

276 Article 1 in English read: "Art. 1. Absolute ownership gives a right to enjoy, and to dispose of one's property in the most unlimited manner, *provided* one does not use the same in a way prohibited by the laws."

That same article in French read: "Art. I. La pleine propriété donne le droit de jouir et de disposer de sa chose de la manière la plus absolue, *pourvu* qu'on n'en fasse pas un usage prohibé par les lois."

Two other articles comprised that chapter, and in English they read:

"Art. 2. No one can be compelled to part with his property, unless by reason of public utility and on consideration of an equitable and previous indemnification.

Art. 3. The right of accession is a consequence of the right of ownership.

The right of accession is the right which the owner of a thing has to what such thing produces, and to what unites itself to the same by a kind of accessory incorporation whether naturally or artificially."

Those two same articles in French read:

"Art. II. Nul ne peut être contraint de céder sa propriété, si ce n'est pour cause d'utilité publique et moyennant une juste et préalable indemnité.

Art. III. Le droit d'accession est une suite du droit de propriété.

On appelle ainsi le droit que le propriétaire d'une chose a sur ce qu'elle produit et sur ce qui s'y unit accessoirement, soit naturellement, soit artificiellement." (Digest of Laws 1808, pp. 102–103)

277 The chapter comprised ten articles.

278 Civil Code Louisiana 1825, pp. 146–148.

279 Those articles in English read:

"Art. 480. Ownership is the right by which a thing belongs to some one in particular, to the exclusion of all other persons.

Art. 481. The ownership of a thing is vested in him who has the immediate dominion of it, and not in him who has a mere beneficiary right in it.

Art. 482. Ownership is divided into perfect and imperfect.

Ownership is perfect, when it is perpetual, and when the thing, which is the subject of it, is unincumbered with any charges towards any other person than the owner.

On the contrary, ownership is imperfect, when it is to terminate at a certain time or on a condition, or if the thing, which is the subject of it, being an immoveable, is charged with any real right towards a third person, as an usufruct, use or service.

[...]

by which a thing belongs to some one in particular, to the exclusion of all other persons;"[280] while article 483, in harmony with article 544 of the *Code Napoléon*, further stated that "absolute ownership gives the right to enjoy and to dispose of one's property in the most unlimited manner, provided it is not used in a way prohibited by laws or ordinances."[281] Drafters were aware of the

---

Art. 483. Absolute ownership gives the right to enjoy and to dispose of one's property in the most unlimited manner, provided it is not used in a way prohibited by laws or ordinances.

Persons who reside out of the State, cannot dispose of the property they possess here, in a manner different from that prescribed by its laws.

Art. 484. Imperfect ownership only gives the right of enjoying and disposing of property, when it can be done without injuring the rights of others, that is, of those who may have real or other rights to exercise upon the same property."

Those same articles in French read:

"Art. 480. La propriété est le droit par lequel une chose appartient à quelqu'un en propre, et exclusivement à tous autres.

Art. 481. La propriété d'une chose est dite appartenir à celui qui en a le domaine direct, et non à celui qui n'en a que le domaine utile.

Art. 482. La propriété se distingue en propriété pleine et parfaite, et en propriété imparfaite.

Une propriété est pleine et parfaite, lorsqu'elle est perpétuelle, et que la chose n'est chargée d'aucun droit réel envers d'autres personnes que le propriétaire.

Au contraire la propriété est imparfaite, lorsqu'elle doit se résoudre au bout d'un certain temps, ou par l'évènement d'une certaine condition, ou si la chose qui est l'objet de la propriété est un immeuble qui soit chargé envers un tiers de quelque droit réel, comme d'usufruit, d'usage ou de servitude.

[...]

Art. 483. La pleine propriété donne le droit de jouir et de disposer de sa chose, de la manière la plus absolue, pourvu qu'on n'en fasse pas un usage prohibé par les lois ou par les règlemens.

En conséquence les personnes mêmes qui résident hors de cet Etat, ne peuvent disposer des biens qu'elles y possèdent, d'une manière contraire à ce qui est prescrit par ses lois.

Art. 484. La propriété imparfaite ne donne le droit de jouir et de disposer de sa chose, qu'autant que par cette disposition on ne nuit pas aux droits d'autrui, c'est-à-dire, de ceux qui peuvent avoir des droits réels ou autres à exercer sur cette chose." (Civil Code Louisiana 1825, pp. 146–148)

280 Civil Code Louisiana 1825, p. 146.

281 Civil Code Louisiana 1825, p. 148.

The text in French read: "La pleine propriété donne le droit de jouir et de disposer de sa chose de la manière la plus absolue, pourvu qu'on n'en fasse pas un usage prohibé par les lois ou par les règlemens." (Civil Code Louisiana 1825, p. 149)

need for limitations, having mentioned it already in the 1823 project, as part of the comment that followed the to-be article 483, and which stated that limitations could exist when the use was injurious to the rights of third parties (*i.e.*, neighborhood or the public).[282]

Transplantation was massive in Louisiana,[283] and the sources of civil code provisions have been subject to study. The Digest of 1808 did not include an *exposé des motifs* explaining its sources.[284] Nevertheless, an uncertain number of copies contain interleaves with manuscript notes dictated by Moreau-Lislet, or in some cases, even written by him.[285] One of these manuscripts, the de la Vergne copy, includes references to Roman and Spanish materials linked to titles and articles.[286] The manuscript also includes references to French texts of Roman grounding, such as the works of Pothier and Domat.[287] The manuscript note for the abovementioned Article 1 of the Digest of 1808 relates to Spanish sources: *Partida* III and the second volume of the work on contracts by Febrero.[288]

Interest for Spanish law was not a rarity at that time in Louisiana.[289] Moreau-Lislet and Henry Carleton translated in 1818 the titles of the *Siete Partidas* on obligations (*Partida* V, Title 11), sale and purchase (*Partida* V, Title 5) and exchange (*Partida* V, Title 6).[290] In 1820, following a resolution of the local legislature,[291] Moreau-Lislet and Carleton further translated into English the remaining laws of the *Siete Partidas*[292] that had not been expressly repealed by the local legislature and that were not repugnant to the Louisiana and US

282 That comment read: "We have added to this article after the words *prohibited by the laws*, the words, *or ordinances*, thinking that a *law* was not always necessary to limit the exercise of the right of property; as it is limited by *police regulations*, whenever the use one makes of his property is injurious to his neighborhood or the public." (Louisiana *Projet* 1823, p. 43)

283 Watson 1974, p. 104.

284 Dainow 1958, p. 43.

285 Cairns 2009, p. 74.

286 See the text of the *avant-propos* at Digest Online. See also Cairns 2009, pp. 76–77.

287 In addition, 645 articles do not have corresponding notes. See Palmer 2003b, p. 337.

288 See the manuscript note in the interleaves of pages 104 and 105 of the de la Vergne copy of the Digest of 1808, available at Digest Online.

The note for article 1 read: "Art. I.—Partida 3, Title 2, Law 27 and Febrero, Contratos, Volume 2, Chapter 7, § 2, n. 80."

289 See generally Parise 2014c, pp. 318–322.

290 Moreau Lislet & Carleton 1818.

291 Act for Translation 1819.

292 Moreau Lislet & Carleton 1820a.

constitutions.[293] A footnote included by the authors of that translation indicated the concordance of the abovementioned Article 1 of the Digest of 1808 with *Partida* III, Title 28, Law 1.[294]

The content of the de la Vergne manuscript was tested in 1971 by Rodolfo Batiza.[295] He claimed to have identified the textual origins of 2,081 articles.[296] He concluded that approximately 85% of the text of the articles had been extracted from French texts (*v.gr. Code Napoléon*, *Projet* of 1800, French commentators).[297] In 1972, Pascal published a reply[298] claiming that French law, composed after elements from Roman, Romanized Frankish, Burgundian, and Visigothic origin, habitually resembled the Spanish law that derived from Roman or Roman-Visigothic origins.[299] He understood that the *Code Napoléon* provided a mine of texts written in French.[300] Thus, the drafters used French texts that contained or could be modified to contain in substance the Spanish-Roman law then in force in Louisiana.[301] The work of Batiza and Pascal reflected that whether French, Spanish, or Roman, the laws were mainly taken from the Continental European system, and that the Digest of 1808 was not a mere copy of the *Code Napoléon* nor of a single text.[302] As reflected in the study of Batiza, the wording of the abovementioned Article 1 of the Digest of 1808 was an almost *verbatim* extraction from article 544 of the *Code Napoléon*,[303] finding its origins in the *Projet* of 1800.[304]

4.5.1.3 Sources of the Provisions

The sources of the Louisiana Code provisions on ownership have also been of interest for scholars. As early as 1838, Upton and Jennings published the

---

293 Moreau Lislet & Carleton 1820b, p. xxiv. See also Dart 1931, p. 88.

294 Moreau Lislet & Carleton 1820a, p. 334.

295 Batiza 1971.

296 Batiza 1971, p. 11.

297 Batiza 1971, p. 12.

298 Pascal 1972.

299 Pascal 1972, p. 605.

300 Pascal 1972, p. 605.

301 Pascal 1972, p. 606.

302 Herman 1993, p. 32.

303 Batiza 1971, p. 39, 63 (art. 1, p. 102). Rodolfo Batiza stated that article I was taken almost *verbatim* from article I (page 102) of the *Projet* of 1800 and article 544 of the *Code Napoléon*.

304 The text of the Digest of 1808 and of the *Projet* of 1800 were identical, with the exception of a comma. The text of 1800 in French read: “La pleine propriété donne le droit de jouir et de disposer de sa chose, de la manière la plus absolue, pourvu qu'on n'en fasse pas un usage prohibé par les lois ou par les règlemens.” (*Projet* of 1800, p. 166)

already mentioned edition of the Louisiana Code with glosses.[305] In the comment to article 483 of the Louisiana Code the authors directed readers to, amongst others, article 544 of the *Code Napoléon* and to the work of Pothier on Ownership.[306] The nineteenth-century works of legislative concordances provided information on the sources of the Louisiana Code. Saint-Joseph, in his 1856 edition, mentioned the concordance between articles 480 and 483 of Louisiana with article 544 of the *Code Napoléon*.[307] He stated that in Louisiana there was a distinction between perfect and imperfect ownership.[308] Early twentieth-century studies, sponsored by the Louisiana State Law Institute, also indicated the concordance between article 544 of the *Code Napoléon* and article 483 of the Louisiana Code.[309] Later, in the 1970s, Batiza[310] noted that articles 480–484 of the Louisiana Code were almost *verbatim* extractions or had been substantially influenced by the first part of the work of Pothier on Ownership, from the Digest of 1808, and from the Digest of Justinian.[311]

4.5.1.4 Corollary

The Louisiana Code used both material and formal sources that captured the principles of the Liberal paradigm. Drafters in the jurisdiction had Spanish and French sources at hand, and used them when elaborating provisions. Accordingly, ownership in the Louisiana Code was, as it is today, unquestionably expressed in a language, form, and conceptualization consistent with that of other civil codes.[312] Athanasios N. Yiannopoulos stated that the civil law tradition flourished in the area of property law in Louisiana, mainly due to the local and conservative characteristics of property institutions and the adequacy of the Louisiana Code.[313]

---

305 Upton & Jennings 1838, p. 72.

306 Upton & Jennings 1838, pp. 71–72.

307 Saint-Joseph (de) 1856, II, p. 479.

308 Saint-Joseph (de) 1856, I, pp. xxxviii–xxxix.

309 Comparative Table 1937, p. 12; and Concordance Tables 1942, p. 2046.

310 Batiza 1972.

311 On that occasion Rodolfo Batiza stated the following relations:

"Art. 480.—Almost *verbatim* (in part) from Pothier, Propriété, Part. I, Chap. I, n. 4 (5) (P).

Art. 481.—Substantially influenced by Digest 4.2.12 (P); Pothier, Propriété, Part. I, Chap. I, n. 3 (3) (s).

Art. 482.—Almost *verbatim* (in part) from Pothier, Propriété, Part. I, Chap. I, ns. 6, 8 (8,10) (P).

Art. 483.—Almost *verbatim* (new par. added) from Digest of 1808, II, II, I (am'd).

Art. 484.—Substantially influenced by Pothier, Propriété, Part. I, Chap. I, ns. 12, 13 (12) (P)." (Batiza 1972, p. 38)

312 Smith 1973, p. 120.

313 Yiannopoulos 2001, p. 12.

4.5.2 *Chile*

The Chilean Code inclined in a moderate way towards the new paradigm of ownership.[314] Bello welcomed the liberal doctrine of the *Code Napoléon*, believing it provided a strong element for progress.[315] He aimed towards a free ownership, yet subject to divisions, and not bound to archaic and demanding ties.[316] Bello, therefore, advocated for the limitation of entailed estates,[317] while the ties of ownership could only last for a lifetime, aiming to avoid a complete cut with tradition and customs.[318] Bello defended the free circulation of things, not in the hands of a few, but as a way to promote economic progress for society.[319] Another example of the moderate approach to the Liberal paradigm was found in the adoption of the principles of juridical liberalism regarding ownership, real rights, and contracts, yet not adopted in the area of successions.[320]

4.5.2.1 Constitutional Protection

Constitutional rights also protected private property in Chile. The fundamental text of 1833, following the tenets of liberalism, welcomed protection of ownership in paragraph 5 of article 12.[321] This article stated the "inviolability of all property" for the inhabitants of the young republic.[322] That provision was in harmony with liberal ownership, being understood as an absolute right, and, after the adoption of the Chilean Code, being in harmony with the codified text.[323]

---

314 Levaggi 2001, p. 414.
315 Lira Urquieta 1981, p. xxxi.
316 Lira Urquieta 1981, p. xxxi.
317 Mirow 2005, p. 311.
318 Lira Urquieta 1981, p. xxxi.
319 Guzmán Brito 1982, p. 455.
320 Guzmán Brito 2008, p. 99.
321 Cordero Quinzacara 2006, pp. 129–130.
322 That article in Spanish read: "La Constitución asegura a todos los habitantes de la República: 5° La inviolabilidad de todas las propiedades, sin distinción de las que pertenezcan á particulares ó comunidades, y sin que nadie pueda ser privado de la de su dominio, ni de una parte de ella por pequeña que sea, ó del derecho que á ella tuviere, sino en virtud de sentencia judicial; salvo el caso en que la utilidad del Estado, calificada por una lei, exija el uso o enajenación de alguna; lo que tendrá lugar dándose previamente al dueño la indemnización que se ajustare con él, ó se avaluare á juicio de hombres buenos." (Chile Constitución Política 1833, pp. 6–7)
323 Cordero Quinzacara 2006, pp. 129–130.

4.5.2.2 Codified Protection

The Chilean Code dealt with ownership in Book II, Title 2. In the period 1843–1847, Bello had completed the different titles of what would be Book II, except for the title on servitudes.[324] Article 686 of the 1853 project stated that ownership was the real right to enjoy and dispose of a corporeal thing as "we wished" (*a nuestro arbitrio*) and not contrary to law or the rights of third parties.[325] That conceptualization would be finally incorporated into the Chilean Code as article 582, yet with slightly different language. This article read in its first paragraph: "ownership (also called property) is the real right in a corporeal thing to enjoy and dispose thereof *as the owner wishes*, provided that it is not contrary to the law or the rights of a third party."[326] Readers should note that even the drafter of the Chilean Code acknowledged the interchangeability of terms, and he referred in his seminal provision to ownership and property as synonyms.[327] The narration in the first person had been rejected in an intermediate draft, known as the Unpublished Draft, that preceded the publication of the Chilean Code.[328] Article 582 of the Chilean Code welcomed the Liberal paradigm of ownership. It reflected the subjective right to enjoy and dispose arbitrarily of a thing as stated in article 544 of the *Code Napoléon*.[329] Together with six other articles of Title 2, which are still in effect in Chile,[330] article 582 provided basic tenets for the understanding of ownership.[331]

---

324 Guzmán Brito 1982, p. 391.

325 That article in Spanish read: "El *dominio* (que se llama tambien *propiedad*) es el derecho real en una cosa corporal, para gozar i disponer de ella a nuestro arbitrio, no siendo contra lei o contra derecho ajeno."

In addition, article 687 in Spanish read "La propiedad separada del goce de la cosa, se llama *mera* o *nuda propiedad*." (Project Civil Code Chile 1853, p. 157)

326 Civil Code Chile 2008, p. 94.

That article, in its first paragraph, in Spanish read: "El *dominio*, (que se llama tambien *propiedad*), es el derecho real en una cosa corporal, para gozar i disponer de ella arbitrariamente; no siendo contra lei o contra derecho ajeno." (Código Civil Chile 1857, p. 147)

327 Alessandri Rodríguez *et al.* 2010, p. 35.

328 See Unpublished Draft Code 1890, p. 153; Amunátegui Perelló 2009, p. 509; Amunátegui Perelló 2012, p. 87; and Correlación de Artículos 1981, p. 1083.

329 Guzmán Brito 1982, p. 455.

330 See the current text of the Chilean civil code available at Texto Refundido del Código Civil 2015.

331 The remaining five articles in Spanish read:

"Art. 583. Sobre las cosas incorporales hai también una especie de propiedad. Así el usufructuario tiene la propiedad de su derecho de usufructo.

Art. 584. Las producciones del talento o del injenio son una propiedad de sus autores. Esta especie de propiedad se rejirá por leyes especiales.

4.5.2.3 Sources of the Provisions

The sources of the Chilean Code provisions have also been subject to study. Differently to Vélez Sarsfield and to Moreau-Lislet, Bello never indicated the sources he used when drafting his leading article on ownership, nor did he ever explain it.[332] There are only references to his understanding during his participation in the National Congress, while debating the law of *mayorazgos*,[333] where Bello stated that ownership was an absolute right.[334] Soon after 1856, Bello envisioned the already mentioned glossed edition of his code with notes for each article. Though never completed, his projected edition was to be built on the notes that he included in his 1853 project.[335] That project did not include a note for article 686 (to-be article 582).[336] The Unpublished Draft also dealt with the definition of ownership in article 686, and did not include notes by Bello.[337]

Bello acknowledged legal transplantation in the *exposé des motifs* of the Chilean Code. On that occasion he stated that it was worth using modern

---

Art. 585. Las cosas que la naturaleza ha hecho *comunes* a *todos los hombres*, como la alta mar, no son susceptibles de dominio, i ninguna nacion, corporacion o individuo tiene derecho de apropiárselas.

Su uso i goce son determinados entre individuos de una nacion por las leyes de esta, i entre distintas naciones por el Derecho Internacional.

Art. 586. Las cosas que han sido consagradas para el culto divino, se rejirán por el Derecho Canónico.

Art. 587. El uso i goce de las capillas i cementerios, situados en posesiones de particulares i accesorios a ellas, pasarán junto con ellas i junto con los ornamentos, vasos i demas objetos pertenecientes a dichas capillas o cementerios, a las personas que sucesivamente adquieran las posesiones en que están situados, a menos de disponerse otra cosa por testamento o por acto entre vivos.

Art. 588. Los modos de adquirir el dominio son la ocupacion, la accesion, la tradicion, la sucesion por causa de muerte, i la prescripcion.

De la adquisicion de dominio por estos dos últimos medios se tratará en el libro *De la sucesion por causa de muerte*, i al fin de este Código." (Código Civil Chile 1857, pp. 147–149)

332 Brahm García 1996, p. 11.

333 For more information on *mayorazgos*, see generally 3.5.1 of this book.

334 Brahm García 1996, p. 11.

335 Guzmán Brito 2005, p. 66.

336 Project Civil Code Chile 1853, p. 157; and Caldera 1981, p. 409.

337 That article in Spanish read:

"El *dominio* (que se llama también *propiedad*), es el derecho real en una cosa corporal, para gozar i disponer de ella arbitrariamente; no siendo contra lei o contra derecho ajeno.

La propiedad separada del goce de la cosa, se llama *mera* o *nuda propiedad*." (Unpublished Draft Code 1890, p. 153)

codes, yet preserving the peculiar circumstances of Chile.[338] Guzmán Brito, in his authoritative work, stated that the notes by Bello could be placed within two clusters of sources.[339] Firstly, those sources extracted from local law, *v.gr. Indiano*. This cluster encompassed, amongst others, the *Siete Partidas*, the *Corpus iuris civilis*, and the different compilations (*i.e., recopilaciones*). It also included doctrinal works, such as those by de Hevia Bolaños.[340] Secondly, those sources extracted from foreign law. Here, the main source mined was the *Code Napoléon*, though Bello sometimes departed from it and followed its commentaries, such as those by Claude Etienne Delvincourt.[341] To access the texts of many codes, Bello used the concordance of Saint-Joseph, of which he mainly cited the texts of Austria and Louisiana, and the Spanish concordance by García Goyena.[342] Bello likewise followed doctrinal writings, mainly by the already mentioned Pothier and Delvincourt, while he also cited works by Arnold Vinnius and von Savigny.[343] The influence of Pothier was very significant in the Chilean Code, being sensed in the areas of obligations and possession.[344]

The Chilean Code combined the French model with other European influences.[345] Accordingly, it could be expected that article 582 of Chile would borrow the definition from article 544 of the *Code Napoléon*.[346] Scholars indeed identified a concordance between articles 582 and 544.[347] For example, in 1871, Miguel Elizalde published a work of legislative concordances between the Chilean Code and the *Code Napoléon*.[348] That work, which provided a glossed edition of the American text, indicated parallels between article 582 of Chile and the following articles of the "French Code 537, 543 et seq., 644, 647, 651, 672, 674, 678."[349] The French and Chilean articles indeed resemble each other significantly, though some differences of dogmatic interest are worth

338 That note in Spanish read: "Desde luego concebiréis que no nos hallábamos en el caso de copiar a la letra ninguno de los códigos modernos. Era menester servirse de ellos sin perder de vista las circunstancias peculiares de nuestro país." (Montt *et al.*, p. 4)

339 Guzmán Brito 1982, p. 413.

340 Guzmán Brito 1982, pp. 413–421.

341 Guzmán Brito 1982, p. 422.

342 Guzmán Brito 1982, p. 423.

343 Guzmán Brito 1982, pp. 424–425.

344 Domínguez Águila 2005, pp. 62–63.

345 Halpérin 2008, p. 266.

346 Halpérin 2008, p. 266.

347 See, for example, Caldera 1981, p. 409.

348 Elizalde 1871.

349 See the gloss to article 582 in Elizalde 1871.
The text in Spanish read: "[...] C.F. 537, 543 i sigts., 644, 647, 651, 672, 674, 678."

mentioning.[350] Firstly, the *Code Napoléon* did not expressly mention a *corporeal thing*. The inclination towards corporeal in Chile could be found, perhaps, in a closer resemblance with the ideas of Bartolus and those who replicated his *corporeal* requirement or in the *Siete Partidas*.[351] Secondly, the reference to the right to enjoy and dispose in "the most absolute manner" was replaced in Chile by the right to enjoy and dispose "as the owner wishes."[352] Thirdly, the limitation by "law or by regulations" was extended to include in Chile limitations deriving from "the rights of a third party."[353]

The rights of third parties added a second limitation to ownership. That limitation, included in the Chilean Code, was not common at that time,[354] yet it may be found both in French and in Spanish law. The source of this limitation can be found in the work of Pothier on Ownership,[355] a work that was likewise used in Louisiana during the drafting of the corresponding articles. Pothier included a double limitation to ownership: the laws and the rights of third parties.[356] Article 544 of the *Code Napoléon* only welcomed the limitation by laws, and therefore excluded the second limitation advocated by Pothier.[357] Spanish law also provided for a limitation regarding the rights of third parties, as recognized in the *Siete Partidas*.[358] For example, *Partida* III, Title 32, Law 13 stated that "as was said by the ancient sages, although a man has the power to do what he pleases, upon his own ground, yet he ought to do it in such a manner, as to cause no damage, or harm, to any other person."[359] Therefore, Bello

350 Amunátegui Perelló 2012, p. 81.

351 Readers should note that article 583 of the Chilean Code welcomed a "kind" of ownership on incorporeal things, making a special reference to usufruct. See Código Civil Chile 1857, p. 148.

An extensive elaboration on the topic is available at Claro Solar 1979, pp. 325–334.

352 Amunátegui Perelló 2012, p. 81.

353 Amunátegui Perelló 2012, p. 81; and Amunátegui Perelló 2009, p. 506.

354 Amunátegui Perelló 2009, p. 506.

355 Amunátegui Perelló 2009, p. 508.

356 That passage in French read: "Le droit de disposer á son gré d'une chose, sans donner néanmoins atteinte au droit d'autrui, ni aux Loix; Jus de re libere disponendi, ou jus utendi & abutendi." (Pothier 1772, p. 6) See also Amunátegui Perelló 2009, p. 508.

357 Amunátegui Perelló 2009, p. 508.

358 Amunátegui Perelló 2009, p. 509.

359 English translation extracted from Moreau Lislet & Carleton 1820a, p. 440.

That law in Spanish read: "[...] Ca ſegund que dixeron los ſabios antiguos, maguer el ome aya poder defazer en lo ſuyo lo que quiſiere. Pero deue lo fazer de manera que non ſaga daño, nin tuerto a otro." (Siete Partidas 1587, p. 184) See also Amunátegui Perelló 2009, p. 509.

may have borrowed that limitation from the *Siete Partidas* and from Pothier, rather than simply from the *Code Napoléon*.[360]

4.5.2.4 Corollary

The Chilean Code, either by means of material or formal sources, captured the Liberal paradigm. The provisions of the code, therefore, recognized European Enlightened ideas.[361] Those provisions, however, did preserve traditional property expectations that were part of the local society and family structure.[362] The Chilean Code was a blend of liberal and conservative principles: property tended to be liberal, while family and dispositions of family property were more traditional, in line with pre-independence society.[363]

4.5.3 *Argentina*

The Argentine Code welcomed the Liberal paradigm, being in harmony with the tenets that existed in the region since the early nineteenth century.[364] Vélez Sarsfield acted in accordance with the local political tradition.[365] The adoption of the liberal model was therefore absolute in Argentina,[366] while in other jurisdictions the codes included some traditional institutions that were rooted in their societies.[367] If compared to Bello, Vélez Sarsfield seemed to be more receptive of the French doctrines of the *Code Napoléon*.[368] It was even claimed that Vélez Sarsfield adopted a more absolutist approach than Roman law.[369] Vélez Sarsfield was also an economist, and this could explain the modern approach he gave to ownership in his code.[370] He, accordingly, defended that the free circulation of property was the only efficient way to increase public and private wealth.[371] In Argentina, *mayorazgos* had been abolished,

---

360 Amunátegui Perelló 2009, p. 509. Readers should note that the position of Carlos Felipe Amunátegui Perelló, indicated in this chapter, is not followed by all Chilean scholars.

361 Mirow 2001, p. 292.

362 Mirow 2001, p. 292.

363 Mirow 2001, p. 302.

364 Cháneton 1937, p. 245.

365 Cháneton 1937, p. 246.

366 Levaggi 2001, p. 419; and Levaggi 1982, p. 112.

367 Levaggi 2001, p. 419.

368 Ramos Núñez 1997, p. 201.

369 Levaggi 1982, p. 114.

370 Levaggi 2001, p. 416.

371 Levaggi 1982, p. 114.

and "dead hands" were therefore limited to the property of the Church and of Native American communities.[372] That meant that the adoption of the Liberal paradigm did not immediately eliminate all institutions from the previous regime, some prevailed for some time, such as Native American communal property.[373]

4.5.3.1 Constitutional Protection

Constitutional rights also protected private property in Argentina. An Argentine Constitution was signed in 1853[374] and was based on, amongst others, Spanish antecedents and US constitutional principles.[375] Articles 14 and 17 of that constitution expressly dealt with the Liberal paradigm of ownership. The first article stated that all inhabitants should enjoy the right to dispose of their property;[376] while the second article stated that ownership was inviolable, and that inhabitants could be deprived of it only when decided by a ruling based on existing laws.[377] The Argentine Code, which took effect after the constitution, was in accordance with articles 14 and 17.[378]

372 Levaggi 2001, p. 418.

373 Levaggi 2007, p. 122.

374 A constitutional reform took place in 1860, and amongst other things, helped reflect the reunion of the seceded province of Buenos Aires and the rest of Argentina. See Tau Anzoátegui 1977b, p. 340.

375 Kluger 2009, p. 216.

376 Article 14 in Spanish read: "Todos los habitantes de la Confederación gozan de los siguientes derechos conforme a las leyes que reglamenten su ejercicio; a saber: de trabajar y ejercer toda industria licita; de navegar y comerciar; de peticionar a las autoridades; de entrar, permanecer, transitar y salir del territorio argentino; de publicar sus ideas por la prensa sin censura previa; de usar y disponer de su propiedad, de asociarse con fines útiles; de profesar libremente su culto; de enseñar y aprender." (Constitución Argentina 1853, p. 11)

377 Article 17 in Spanish read: "La propiedad es inviolable, y ningún habitante de la Confederación puede ser privado de ella, sino en virtud de sentencia fundada en ley. La expropiación por causa de utilidad pública, debe ser calificada por ley y previamente indemnizada. Sólo el Congreso impone las contribuciones que se expresan en el art. 4°. Ningún servicio personal es exigible, sino en virtud de ley o de sentencia fundada en ley. Todo autor o inventor es propietario exclusivo de su obra, invento o descubrimiento, por el término que le acuerde la ley. La confiscación de bienes queda borrada para siempre del código penal argentino. Ningún cuerpo armado puede hacer requisiciones, ni exigir auxilios de ninguna especie." (Constitución Argentina 1853, p. 12)

378 Levaggi 2007, p. 122.

4.5.3.2 Codified Protection

The code in Argentina dealt with ownership mainly in Book III, Title 5.[379] The general principles were dealt with in articles 2506 to 2524 of that title,[380] while Titles 6 and 7 also dealt with ownership, though with restrictions and imperfect ownership.[381] Limitations to ownership were therefore found in Title 6, and were developed in a detailed way that exceeds the wording of article 544 of the *Code Napoléon*.[382] Article 2506 of the Argentine Code, located in Title 5, preliminarily stated that "ownership is the real right by means of which one thing is subject to the will and action of a person."[383] The article that followed, 2507, similarly to the Louisiana Code,[384] divided ownership into either perfect or imperfect.[385] Ownership in the Argentine Code followed the *Code Napoléon* conception, and welcomed the Liberal paradigm.[386] It was therefore deemed exclusive, perpetual, and absolute.[387] Article 2508[388] of the Argentine Code stated that ownership was an exclusive right. It was also perpetual, according to article 2510;[389] while, in line with article 544 of the *Code Napoléon,*

---

379 Código Civil Argentina 1871, pp. 738–748.

380 Código Civil Argentina 1871, pp. 738–740.

381 Salvat 1962, p. 4.

382 Salvat 1962, p. 16.

383 Article 2506 in Spanish read: "El dominio es el derecho real en virtud del cual una cosa se encuentra sometida a la voluntad y a la acción de una persona." (Código Civil Argentina 1871, p. 738)

384 Vélez Sarsfield even mentioned article 482 of Louisiana in the note to his article. Código Civil Argentina 1871, p. 738.

385 Article 2507 in Spanish read: "El dominio se llama pleno o perfecto, cuando es perpetuo, y la cosa no está gravada con ningún derecho real hacia otras personas. Se llama menos pleno o imperfecto, cuando debe resolverse al fin de un cierto tiempo o al advenimiento de una condición o si la cosa que forma su objeto es un inmueble, gravado respecto de terceros con un derecho real, como servidumbre, usufructo, etcétera." (Código Civil Argentina 1871, p. 738)

386 Levaggi 2001, p. 417.

387 See Levaggi 2001, pp. 416–418; and Adrogué 1991, p. 36.

388 Article 2508 in Spanish read: "El dominio es exclusivo. Dos personas no pueden tener cada una en el todo el dominio de una cosa; mas pueden ser propietarias en común de la misma cosa, por la parte que cada una pueda tener." (Código Civil Argentina 1871, pp. 738–739)

389 Article 2510 in Spanish read: "El dominio es perpetuo y subsiste independiente del ejercicio que se pueda hacer de él. El propietario no deja de serlo, aunque no ejerza ningún acto de propiedad, aunque esté en la imposibilidad de hacerlo, y aunque un tercero los ejerza con su voluntad o contra ella, a no ser que deje poseer la cosa por otro, durante el tiempo requerido para que éste pueda adquirir la propiedad por la prescripción." (Código Civil Argentina 1871, p. 739)

article 2513[390] stated the absolute character of ownership. Finally, article 2514[391] stated that the right would not be restricted even if depriving third parties of advantages, as long as their own right was not violated.

4.5.3.3 Sources of the Provisions

The sources of the Argentine Code have been subject to study. Vélez Sarsfield facilitated the work of scholars by accompanying notes to many of his articles. These can provide assistance in identifying sources for articles. The notes were an important addition that the drafters in Louisiana and Chile did not provide in their resulting codes. Notes on ownership provided fertile ground for analysis.

In the note to article 2506,[392] Vélez Sarsfield defended that ownership should be defined according to economic relations. He started by transcribing definitions and references to ownership that were available in the *Siete*

390 Article 2513 in Spanish read: "Es inherente a la propiedad, el derecho de poseer la cosa, de disponer o de servirse de ella, de usarla y gozarla según la voluntad del propietario. El puede desnaturalizarla, degradarla o destruirla; tiene el derecho de accesión, de reivindicación, de constituir sobre ella derechos reales, de percibir todos sus frutos, prohibir que otro se sirva de ella o perciba sus frutos; y de disponer de ella por actos entre vivos" (Código Civil Argentina 1871, p. 739)

391 Article 2514 in Spanish read: "El ejercicio de estas facultades no puede serle restringido porque tuviera por resultado privar a un tercero de alguna ventaja, comodidad o placer, o traerle algunos inconvenientes, con tal que no ataque su derecho de propiedad." (Código Civil Argentina 1871, pp. 739–740)

392 The note to article 2506 in Spanish read:

"La L. 1, tít. 28, part. 3ª, define el dominio o la propiedad: "poder que ome ha en su cosa de facer de ella o en ella lo que quisiere, segun Dios e según fuero;" pero otra ley dice: "maguer el home haya poder de facer en lo suyo lo que quisiere, pero débelo facer de manera que non faga daño ni tuerto a otro." L. 13, tít. 32, Part. 3ª. El cód. francés, art. 544, define la propiedad diciendo que: "la propiedad es el derecho de gozar y de disponer de las cosas de la manera más absoluta." Este artículo, en lugar de dar una verdadera definición, hace más bien por una enumeración de los principales atributos de la propiedad, una descripción de ese derecho. Los romanos hacían una definición empírica de la propiedad, "jus utendi et abutendi," definición que no tiene relación, sino con los efectos y no con las causas, ni con los orígenes, porque ellos debían ocultar los orígenes de sus propiedades.

La propiedad debía definirse mejor en sus relaciones económicas: el derecho de gozar del fruto de su trabajo, el derecho de trabajar y de ejercer sus facultades como cada uno lo encuentre mejor. Para la legislación aceptamos la definición de los jurisconsultos Aubry y Rau, § 190." (Código Civil Argentina 1871, p. 738)

Partidas,[393] and that had been likewise referred to by García Goyena in his Spanish concordance and by Moreau-Lislet in his English translation for Louisiana. Vélez Sarsfield also reproduced parts of article 544 of the *Code Napoléon*, and criticized the French definition, because it simply provided an enumeration of the principal elements of ownership.[394] In that same note, Vélez Sarsfield stated that Romans had developed an empirical definition of ownership.[395] Finally, Vélez Sarsfield acknowledged to have followed the writings of Charles Aubry and Charles Rau when drafting his article,[396] though he omitted some parts of the text of the French jurists.[397] The Argentine codifier, differently from the French jurists, did not include in his definition, amongst others, references to the most complete juridical power (*pouvoir juridique le plus complet*) over a thing and to the absolute and exclusive manner (*absolue et exclusive*) of subjection of the thing.

The notes to articles 2510[398] and 2508[399] are also of interest. In the note to the first article, Vélez Sarsfield stated that ownership was exclusive, within the

---

393 *I.e.*, law 1, Title 28, *Partida* 3; and law 13, Title 32, *Partida* 3.

394 See Mariani de Vidal 2004, p. 279.

395 Vélez Sarsfield stated in Latin: *jus utendi et abutendi.*

396 The opening paragraph of that section of the work by Aubry and Rau in French read: "La propriété, dans le sens propre de ce mot (*dominium*), exprime l'idée du pouvoir juridique le plus complet d'une personne sur une chose, et peut se définir, le droit en vertu duquel une chose se trouve soumise, d'une manière absolue et exclusive, à la volonté et à l'action d'une personne." (Aubry & Rau 1863, p. 151, at § 190)

397 Salvat 1962, pp. 21–22.

398 The note to article 2510 in Spanish read: "Cód. de Luisiana, art. 488. L. 44, Dig. "De adq. rer. dom.". Pothier, "De la propiedad," núm. 277. Demolombe, t. 9, núm. 546. Aubry y Rau, § 191." (Código Civil Argentina 1871, p. 739)

399 The note to article 2508 in Spanish read:

"L. 5, § 15, tít. 6, lib. 13, Dig. Esta es una de las diferencias entre el derecho real y el personal. Muchas personas pueden ser, cada una por el todo, acreedoras de una misma cosa, sea por una misma obligación, cuando ha sido contratada para con muchos acreedores solidarios, sea por diferentes obligaciones de un mismo deudor o de diferentes deudores. La razón es, porque es imposible que lo que me pertenece en el todo, pertenezca al mismo tiempo a otro; pero nada impide que la misma cosa que me es debida, sea también debida a otro. Pothier, "De la propiedad," núm. 16.

Decimos que el derecho de propiedad es exclusivo. El propietario puede impedir a cualquiera disponer de la cosa que le pertenece; pero la manifestación de este poder puede ser modificada de diferentes maneras. Es posible desmembrar ciertas manifestaciones y erigirlas en derechos separados, los cuales, llamados "jura in re," nos dan el poder de disponer de una manera más o menos extensa de la cosa de otro, como cuando tenemos el uso o el usufructo de la cosa ajena. Pero estas desmembraciones no hacen partícipe al que

limits and conditions established by law. That limitation aimed to position the general interest over the individual interest, being an essential consideration for society. The note to article 2510 merits special attention. In that note, Vélez Sarsfield provided a reference to article 488 of the Louisiana Code, the North American article being a formal source for the Argentine text. The French concordance by Saint-Joseph did not reproduce the entire text of article 488;[400] while García Goyena, in his Spanish concordance, did not refer to article 488. Therefore, it could be concluded that Vélez Sarsfield necessarily had in his library a copy of the text of the Louisiana Code.

Articles 2513 and 2514 are important, especially because they played a special role in the paradigm shift towards the Social Function during the following century.[401] The note to article 2513[402] mentions the works of Pothier, Demolombe, and Karl Eduard Zachariae. In that note, Vélez Sarsfield stated the need to acknowledge that absolute ownership conferred the right to destroy the thing. He added that any preventive restriction would present more dangers than benefits, and he closed his note by indicating that—as Thomas Reynal[403] had claimed—if the state became judge of the abuse of rights, it would soon become judge of the use, and the true ideas of ownership and

las obtiene de la propiedad de la cosa, ni el propietario es privado por ellas de disponer de su propiedad.

Cuando establecemos que el dominio es exclusivo, es con la reserva que no existe con este carácter, sino en los límites y bajo las condiciones determinadas por la ley, por una consideración esencial a la sociedad: el predominio, para el mayor bien de todos y de cada uno, del interés general y colectivo, sobre el interés individual." (Código Civil Argentina 1871, pp. 738–739)

400 Saint-Joseph (de) 1840, p. 29; and Saint-Joseph (de) 1856, II, p. 479.

401 See generally 5.4.5.1 and 5.4.5.2 of this book.

402 The note to article 2513 in Spanish read: "Pothier, "De la propiedad," núm. 5. Demolombe, t. 9, desde el núm. 543. Zachariæ, § 277. Importa, sin embargo, observar que los excesos en el ejercicio del dominio son en verdad la consecuencia inevitable del derecho absoluto de propiedad, pero no constituyen por sí mismos un modo del ejercicio de este derecho que las leyes reconocen y aprueban. La palabra "abuti" de los romanos expresaba solamente la idea de la disposición y no de la destrucción de la cosa. "Expedit Reipublicæ," dice la Instituta, "ne sua re quis male utatur" (§ 2, de "his qui sui, vel alien."). Pero es preciso reconocer que siendo la propiedad absoluta, confiere el derecho de destruir la cosa. Toda restricción preventiva tendría más peligros que ventajas. Si el Gobierno se constituye juez del abuso, ha dicho un filósofo, no tardaría en constituirse juez del uso, y toda verdadera idea de propiedad y libertad sería perdida." (Código Civil Argentina 1871, p. 739)

403 Mariani de Vidal 2004, p. 279.

liberty would perish. Finally, the note to article 2514[404] referred to Roman law, indeed one of the main pillars when drafting the Argentine Code. In that note the Argentine drafter highlighted that water wells could be dug even when interrupting the flow of water towards a neighboring tract of land.

The study of the sources of the Argentine Code did not limit itself to the analysis of the notes by Vélez Sarsfield. As already mentioned, scholars in American Civil Law Jurisdictions showed a Pan-American interest in the treasure trove of European formal sources. The tracing of sources was many times pursued by means of glossed editions of codes. For example, soon after the adoption of the code, Segovia indicated in his gloss that article 2513 of the Argentine Code was inspired by articles 4214 to 4216 of the *Esboço* by Augusto Teixeira de Freitas for Brazil.[405] The latter articles do refer to the exclusiveness of ownership and belong to the section on the effects of acquiring perfect ownership.[406]

4.5.3.4 Corollary

The Argentine Code used material and formal sources that assisted in the construction of provisions that encapsulated the Liberal paradigm. Vélez Sarsfield, similarly to Juan Bautista Alberdi, believed that ownership should have an absolute character, fully armored on all its sides, to avoid being merely an illusion.[407] That right was unlimited in private law, though not in public law,[408] where, for example, in administrative law some limitations existed to protect the general interest.[409] No criticisms were immediately made to the adoption of that paradigm, because it was still well received at the time the code was adopted.[410] The paradigm was also ratified by other jurists in the decades that

404 The note to article 2514 in Spanish read: "[…] La ley romana dice que puedo abrir un pozo en mi casa, aunque por eso se corten las aguas que filtran al fundo vecino, y le traiga el perjuicio de secar los pozos o las fuentes de la propiedad contigua. L. 24, § 12, tít. 2, lib. 39, Dig. […]." (Código Civil Argentina 1871, p. 740)

405 Segovia 1881, II, p. 80.

In 1859, Freitas was appointed to elaborate a draft of a civil code, which did not turn out to be the law of Brazil. In 1872, the Brazilian government terminated the contract with Freitas because he had changed his plan of work. Freitas had also published part of his work in the shape of a sketch (*Esboço*), which was strongly influential in the civil codification works of other countries, amongst those, Argentina. See Moréteau & Parise 2009, p. 1131.

406 Freitas 1860, pp. 1448–1449.

407 Zarrilli 1993, p. 235.

408 Levaggi 2001, p. 417.

409 Levaggi 2007, p. 122.

410 Levaggi 2007, p. 122.

followed.[411] Criticism to the Liberal paradigm would wait mainly until the 1910s in Argentina.[412]

4.6 Pollination of Ownership in the Americas

Codification many times resulted from pollination of codes previously adopted by other American Civil Law Jurisdictions. First-generation codes, such as the ones of Louisiana, Chile, and Argentina, contributed to that transfer of code provisions by acting as examples of successful codification. In addition, codifiers turned to drafts of codes, such as the works by Freitas for Brazil or by Field for New York.[413] All those American sources were handy tools at the time of drafting first-generation codes, and provided models to follow, while enabling a quick adoption of local codes. The Liberal paradigm of ownership, as presented in the three nineteenth-century codes subject to analysis, spread across the continent as a result of pollination. Before the turn of the century, most jurisdictions adopted ownership provisions that derived from one of those three texts.

Some jurisdictions adopted the Liberal paradigm, though, by following closer to other nineteenth-century wordings. For example, the *Code Napoléon* was a source of inspiration in the Americas. The codes of Haiti (1826), Bolivia (1831), Peru (1836), Costa Rica (1841), and Dominican Republic (1844) benefited by borrowing the wording originated in France and that encapsulated the Liberal paradigm.[414] The civil code of Spain of 1889 also served as an important model. Article 348 of the Spanish code read in English that "ownership is the right to enjoy and dispose of a thing with no other limitations than those established by law,"[415] and replicated the tenets of the French model. The codes of Cuba (1889) and Puerto Rico (1889) indeed adopted that Spanish wording.[416] The nineteenth-century works of legislative concordances served as sources

411 Levaggi 2007, p. 122.

412 Levaggi 2007, p. 131.

413 Article 1680 of the Argentine Code is a translation of article 1324 of the project of a civil code of the state of New York. The Argentine note referred exclusively to the North American draft. See Código Civil Argentina 1871, p. 666.

414 Guzmán Brito 2000, p. 605.

415 Article 348 of the Spanish civil code, in its first paragraph, in Spanish read: "La propiedad es el derecho de gozar y disponer de una cosa, sin más limitaciones que las establecidas en las leyes." (Código Civil España 1889, p. 70)

416 The Spanish civil code of 1889 took effect in the Philippines, Cuba, and Puerto Rico by means of a *Real Decreto* on July 24, 1889. See Código Civil Puerto Rico 1984, p. 9.

of inspiration. For example, the code of Mexico (1871)[417] found an antecedent in, amongst others, the wording provided by article 391[418] of the Spanish Project.[419]

The adoption of the Liberal paradigm demonstrated that American Civil Law Jurisdictions shared a similar understanding of ownership. This was especially sensed in the adoption of first-generation codes. With time, jurisdictions reformed their first-generation codes, while pursuing their paths towards second-generation codes. These reforms altered the effects of pollination, and enabled new generation and intermediate codes to depart from the initial borrowings undertaken mainly from the provisions available in the codes of Louisiana, Chile, and Argentina.

4.6.1 *Pollination from Louisiana*

The early adoption of the Louisiana Code enabled it to be an obvious reference for other codes. The Louisiana Code was influential mainly due to its inclusion in the two works of legislative concordances. Saint-Joseph, in the 1840 edition of the French concordance, placed Louisiana in the paramount position. The North American text often occupied the first column in the comparative chart, immediately to the right of the *Code Napoléon*.[420] The Louisiana Code seemed to lose gravitation in the 1856 edition, when moved to the second volume. However, that is not necessarily a correct indication, because in the second volume the Louisiana text was reproduced *in extenso*.[421] While in the 1840 chart the text of article 480 was reproduced entirely and the text of 483 was not transcribed,[422] in the second volume of 1856 both articles were reproduced in their entirety.[423] The Spanish concordance by García Goyena also devoted significant attention to the Louisiana Code. The Louisiana Code occupied an important place in the drafting of the Spanish Project, and drafters in Spain considered—by following or rejecting—the Louisiana text. The Spanish Project did not refer directly to article 480 or 483 of the Louisiana Code, however. The work of García Goyena did refer, however, to the Louisiana Code for almost all areas of law that were covered in the Spanish Project. In addition, the impact of the Louisiana text was demonstrated through the following

417 Article 827 of Mexico in Spanish read: "La propiedad es el derecho de gozar y disponer de una cosa, sin mas limitaciones que las que fijan las leyes." (Código Civil México 1871, p. 280)

418 See note 259 of this chapter and accompanying text.

419 Batiza 1979, p. 95.

420 See, for example, Saint-Joseph (de) 1840, p. 32.

421 Saint-Joseph (de) 1856, II, pp. 459–573.

422 Reference was to the concordance of articles 483 and 544. See Saint-Joseph (de) 1840, p. 28.

423 Saint-Joseph (de) 1856, II, p. 479.

statistics: (i) 1,103 articles of the Louisiana Code were mentioned in the comments to the 1,992 articles of the Spanish Project; (ii) 24 comments to the Spanish Project made general references to the Louisiana Code; (iii) the structure of the Louisiana Code and the Spanish Project were almost identical, and even the names of many books, titles, chapters, sections, and paragraphs were the same; and (iv) only eight titles, 32 Chapters, 24 Sections, 29 paragraphs, and one preliminary title of the Louisiana Code were not mentioned in the comments to the Spanish Project.[424]

Other events help explain the pollination of the Louisiana text across the Americas. The Louisiana text of 1825 was the first code amongst American Civil Law Jurisdictions, and was regarded as a successful example of codification throughout the continent.[425] The text of the Louisiana Code was also included in European periodicals. The latter included the Louisiana text fragmentarily,[426] and many of those European publications made their way to the Americas, where jurists started to become aware of the contents of the North American text. There is uncertainty on the number of copies of the Louisiana Code that reached other parts of the continent, though it is certain that some effectively did so. For example, in 1836, even before the publication of the works of legislative concordance, the legislature in Guatemala instructed the drafters of a projected civil code to follow the model provided by the Louisiana Code. However, that drafting did not prosper in Guatemala.[427] Another example is provided by Costa Rica, where a group of jurists analyzed the possibility of adopting foreign codes, and in the period 1834 to 1837, they explored the possibility of adopting the Louisiana Code.[428]

The Louisiana Code was directly influential in the drafting of the civil codes of Chile and Argentina.[429] There are no doubts that Bello used the Louisiana Code when projecting his text for Chile. In 1837, Bello stated that the *Code Napoléon* and the Louisiana Code were rightly praised and that they were mines of rich and abundant materials.[430] Also, in the 1853 project, the notes

424 Parise 2008b, p. 847.

425 Knütel 1996, pp. 1451–1452. The text of the civil code of Haiti took effect on May 1, 1826. See Thalès 1933, p. 279.

426 *V. gr.* the French journal *Thémis* reproduced in 1826 some passages from the Louisiana Code. See Thémis 1826a; and Thémis 1826b. See also Pizarro 1950, p. 16.

427 Guzmán Brito 2000, p. 345.

428 Guzmán Brito 2000, pp. 318–319.

429 See generally Knütel 1996.

430 Andrés Bello in Spanish stated: "[…] el código civil francés y los códigos de la Luisiaina tan justamente alabados […] mineros de donde podemos sacar ricos y abundantes materiales." (Guzmán Brito 1982, p. 422)

referred occasionally to the North American code.[431] There are, however, no references to the Louisiana Code in the notes for the provisions on ownership that eventually were incorporated into the Chilean Code.[432] There are no doubts that Vélez Sarsfield used the Louisiana Code when drafting his text for Argentina. This was addressed earlier in this chapter, when stating that article 488 of the Louisiana Code was a formal source for article 2510 of the Argentine Code.[433] In addition, Vélez Sarsfield referred to the Louisiana Code in 295 notes to the articles of the Argentine Code.[434] The analysis of those notes shows that the Louisiana Code had a significant presence within the Argentine text.[435] According to the early glossed edition by Segovia, most references to Louisiana were made in Book III *of real rights* of the Argentine text.[436] Recent studies, such as those by Rolf Knütel, also noted that the influence of Louisiana was mainly in the area of real rights.[437] Knütel explained that Vélez Sarsfield used the Louisiana text because regulations in that area were extracted mainly from the *Projet* of 1800, which followed the casuistry of Roman law. Accordingly, "the majority of the concepts which found their way into the Argentine Civil Code

---

A similar claim to "mining fields of rich and abundant materials" was made in Louisiana some years before by the drafters of the 1823 project. When submitting their Preliminary Report before the local legislature they stated: "In the execution of the work we shall keep a reverent eye on those principles, which have received the sanction of time, and on the labors of the great Legislators, who have preceded us. The Laws of the Partidas, and other Statutes of Spain, the existing digest [of 1808] of our own Laws, the abundant stores of the English Jurisprudence, the comprehensive Codes of France, are so many rich mines from which we can draw treasures of Legislation; and where they differ, and we doubt we shall apply to that oracle to which an eloquent writer asserts: "All nations yet appeal, and from which all receive the answers of eternal truth;" to those inspirations of prophetic Legislation, which enabled the Roman Jurists to foresee almost every subject of civil contention, and to establish principles for the decision of Cases, which could only arise in a state of Society different from their own, and maxims applicable to all nations, at all times and under every form of Government." (Livingston *et al.* 1937, pp. lxxxix–xc)

431 For example, the notes to articles 78 and 1343 of the Chilean draft referred to Louisiana. See Project Civil Code Chile 1853, pp. 25, 315–316.

432 See generally Project Civil Code Chile 1853, p. 157.

Recent studies aimed to indicate that Andrés Bello borrowed several provisions from the Louisiana Code. Examples were found in the articles on interpretation of the law for the Chilean Preliminary Title. See Guzmán Brito 2009, p. 191. See also Ramos Núñez 1997, p. 185.

433 See note 399 of this chapter and accompanying text.

434 Parise 2012b, p. 88.

435 Parise 2012b, p. 88.

436 See generally Segovia 1881, I–II.

437 Knütel 1996, pp. 1464–1465.

through the Louisiana codification are ideas developed in Roman law, ideas garbed in modern linguistic dresses."[438]

4.6.2 *Pollination from Chile*

The Chilean Code provides a second example of pollination in the Americas.[439] It became a blueprint for many first-generation codification projects in American Civil Law Jurisdictions, and it can be therefore considered as a legal *corpus* with a projection across the Americas.[440] Jurisdictions made use of the Chilean Code in three different manners. A first group adopted the code *in totum*, without creating a new code, and simply made minor changes that would make the code operational in the new jurisdictions. A second group used the Chilean Code as a model, though creating a new code that was closely linked and dependent to that of Chile. A third group only found inspiration in the Chilean Code, and borrowed isolated elements from the work of Bello.[441] Three elements may explain the widespread borrowing of the Chilean Code in American Civil Law Jurisdictions: the shared historical background, the existing geographical similarities, and the uniformity of romance languages.[442] Finally, it must be noted that differently from the Louisiana Code, the Chilean text was not included in the two works of legislative concordances, yet it soon spread across the continent.

The Liberal paradigm of ownership was encapsulated in article 582 of the Chilean Code. The wording of article 582, defining ownership as an absolute right, "provided that it is not contrary to the law or the rights of a third party,"[443] was replicated throughout the continent. Several jurisdictions adopted that Chilean wording when they borrowed the provisions of the Chilean Code. For example, the civil codes of El Salvador (1860),[444] Panama (1860),[445]

---

438 Knütel 1996, pp. 1466–1467.

439 See generally Guzmán Brito 2000, pp. 374–425.

440 Guzmán Brito 2008, p. 100.

441 Bravo Lira 1982, pp. 93–94.

442 Moréteau & Parise 2009, p. 1123. The authors in that paper provided that understanding beyond the scope of the Chilean Code.

443 Código Civil Chile 1857, p. 147.

444 Article 608 of El Salvador, in its first paragraph, in Spanish read: "El dominio, que se llama tambien propiedad, es el derecho real en una cosa corporal, para gozar y disponer de ella arbitrariamente; no siendo contra ley ó contra derecho ajeno." (Código Civil El Salvador 1880, p. 71)

445 Article 732 of Panama, in its first paragraph, in Spanish read: "*Dominio* (que tambien se llama *propiedad*) es el derecho real en una cosa corporal, para gozar i disponer de ella arbitrariamente, no siendo contra lei o contra derecho ajeno." (Código Civil Panamá 1861, p. 87)

Ecuador (1861),[446] Venezuela (1862),[447] Nicaragua (1871),[448] Colombia (1873),[449] and Honduras (1880)[450] all adopted an almost *verbatim* version of the Chilean wording.

The work of Bello could be deemed the most influential code in the Americas.[451] His code was influential in the drafting of the civil codes of Uruguay and Argentina. In Uruguay, a report drafted in 1867 by a Codifying Commission mentioned as its sources, amongst others, the "codes of Europe, those of America, and specially the correctly praised code of Chile [...], [which] have been the precedents upon which the work we have reviewed, discussed, and approved has been elaborated."[452] Also in Uruguay, the 1868 code showed influences from Chile in the area of ownership, with article 438 of the Uruguayan Code being an almost *verbatim* copy of article 582.[453] The Chilean influence in Argentina is likewise sensed. In June 1865, Vélez Sarsfield

446 Article 571 of Ecuador, in its first paragraph, in Spanish read: "El *dominio* (que se llama tambien *propiedad*) es el derecho real en una cosa corporal, para gozar y disponer de ella arbitrariamente, no siendo contra ley ó contra derecho ageno." (Código Civil Ecuador 1871, p. 110)

447 Article 1, law 1, Title 2, Book 2 of Venezuela, in its first paragraph, in Spanish read: "El *dominio* (que se llama tambien *propiedad*), es el derecho real en una cosa corporal, para gozar y disponer de ella arbitrariamente, no siendo contra lei ó contra derecho ageno." (Código Civil Venezuela 1862, p. 77)

448 Article 582 of Nicaragua, in its first paragraph, in Spanish read: "El *dominio,* (que se llama tambien *propiedad*), es el derecho real en una cosa corporal, para gozar y disponer de ella arbitrariamente, no siendo contra ley ó contra derecho ajeno." (Código Civil Nicaragua 1871, p. 76)

449 Article 669 of Colombia, in its first paragraph, in Spanish read: "El *dominio* (que se llama también *propiedad*) es el derecho real en una cosa corporal, para gozar y disponer de ella arbitrariamente, no siendo contra ley ó contra derecho ajeno." (Código Civil Colombia 1895, p. 108)

450 Article 661 of Honduras, in its first paragraph, in Spanish read: "El *dominio*, que se llama tambien *propiedad*, es el derecho real en una cosa corporal, para gozar i disponer de ella arbitrariamente, no siendo contra lei o contra derecho ajeno." (Código Civil Honduras 1880, p. 158)

451 Mirow 2004, p. 137.

452 Parise 2008b, pp. 850–851.

The report by the Codifying Commission in Spanish read: "[...] Los Códigos de Europa, los de América, y con especialidad el justamente elogiado de Chile, los más sabios comentadores del Código Napoleón, el proyecto del doctor Acevedo, el del señor Goyena, el del señor Freitas, el del doctor Vélez Sarsfield, han sido los antecedentes sobre que se ha elaborado la obra que hemos revisado, discutido y aprobado [...]." (Araújo *et al.* 1949, p. xxiii)

453 Article 438 of Uruguay in Spanish read: "El dominio (que se llama tambien propiedad) es el derecho de gozar y disponer de una cosa arbitrariamente, no siendo contra ley ó contra derecho ageno." (Código Civil Uruguay 1868, p. 84)

presented the First Book of his draft, and the already mentioned accompanying letter of transmission read in part that "for this work I have considered all the codes published in Europe and America [...]. I have used mainly the Spanish Project of Mr. Goyena, [and] the Code of Chile, that much surpasses the European codes [...]."[454] Vélez Sarsfield even cited the Chilean Code in several articles of his code. There are references to Chile, which relate to ownership, in, for example, Chapter 1, Title 5, Book III on acquisition (*apropiación*) of the Argentine Code. That chapter included references to the Chilean Code in articles 2538, 2540, 2545, and 2546.[455] All those notes included references to the *Siete Partidas*, while the note to article 2538 included in addition notes to the *Novísima Recopilación* and the draft by Field.[456]

4.6.3 *Pollination from Argentina*

The Argentine Code provides a third example of pollination in the Americas. The resulting pollination was limited if compared with that derived from the work of Bello.[457] Nevertheless, the work of Vélez Sarsfield, which captured the Liberal paradigm of ownership, was considered by drafters of civil codes in American Civil Law Jurisdictions. Accordingly, first generation-codes could receive the influence of the Argentine text. For example, the Uruguayan Code (1868) benefited from the Argentine text.[458] The already mentioned report of 1867 by a Codifying Commission also mentioned amongst its sources the project of "doctor Vélez Sarsfield,"[459] which was not yet the law in Argentina. When the drafting of the Uruguayan Code was completed, Vélez Sarsfield had only made public the drafts of his two first books (*i.e.*, Book I *of persons*, and Book II *of personal rights in civil relations*). Therefore, the influence of Argentina in Uruguay could not have reached the area of ownership, which was developed in Book III of the Argentine Code.[460]

454 Parise 2008b, pp. 848–849.
That letter in Spanish read: "Para este trabajo, he tenido presente todos los Códigos publicados en Europa y América, y la legislación comparada del Sr. Seoane. Me he servido principalmente del Proyecto de Código Civil para España del Sr. Goyena, del Código de Chile, que tanto aventaja á los códigos europeos, y sobre todo, del Proyecto de Código Civil que está trabajando para el Brasil el Sr. Freitas, del cual he tomado muchísimos artículos." (Levaggi 2005b, p. 310)

455 Código Civil Argentina 1871, pp. 741–742.

456 Código Civil Argentina 1871, pp. 741–742.

457 See generally Guzmán Brito 1999.

458 Moréteau & Parise 2009, p. 1147.

459 Parise 2008b, pp. 850–851. See also Araújo *et al.* 1949, p. xxiii.

460 Guzmán Brito 1999, p. 266.

The Liberal paradigm of ownership as included in the Argentine Code was welcomed by first-generation codes. An example was provided by the enactment of the Paraguayan Code (1877). On August 19, 1876, Paraguay adopted the Argentine Code.[461] Accordingly, that code reproduced and adopted the provisions on ownership that had been included by Vélez Sarsfield. The adoption of a liberal code in Paraguay motivated a complete change in the ownership of land, where land shifted from being mainly state owned to being exposed to private owners.[462] The Argentine Code was replaced in Paraguay by a new one only in 1987, when that jurisdiction adopted its second-generation code, which again found inspiration in the nineteenth-century Argentine Code.[463]

The influence of the Argentine Code was reflected with more intensity in second-generation codes. This was expected, especially, because when the Argentine Code was enacted, only a handful of American Civil Law Jurisdictions had not adopted yet their first-generation codes (*v.gr.*, Paraguay, Guatemala, Honduras, and several Mexican states).[464] In addition, the two works of legislative concordances had already been published. Accordingly, the impact of the Argentine Code was especially sensed in second-generation codes, where, for example, the model was valued by drafters of the codes of Nicaragua (1904),[465] Panama (1917),[466] and Cuba (1987).[467] The influence of the work of Vélez Sarsfield, therefore, did not find time limitations, acting as source for codes even during the century that followed.

4.7 Introduction to Second-Generation Codes

This chapter focused on the adoption of first-generation codes by American Civil Law Jurisdictions. It further analyzed the place of ownership provisions within three nineteenth-century civil codes. Codification kept evolving during the twentieth century, however.[468] Jurisdictions kept amending and replacing

---

461 The code was effective since January 1, 1877. See Sapena Pastor 1986, p. 1; Levaggi 1996b, p. 241; and Moréteau & Parise 2009, p. 1125.

462 Guzmán Brito 2000, p. 457.

463 Moréteau & Parise 2009, p. 1126.

464 Guzmán Brito 1999, p. 264.

465 Moréteau & Parise 2009, p. 1139.
Claims have been made that the Nicaraguan text borrowed 878 articles from the Argentine Code. See Kleinheisterkamp 2008, p. 283.

466 Moréteau & Parise 2009, p. 1160.

467 Moréteau & Parise 2009, p. 1127.

468 See in general the complete study by Guzmán Brito 2000. See also the survey and references available at Murillo 2001; and Pérez-Perdomo 2006, pp. 61–67.

the texts of their existing codes, adapting them to their particular societies. A number of American Civil Law Jurisdictions replaced their first-generation codes[469] by adopting codes of second generation during the twentieth century,[470] though also during the nineteenth century.[471] Some replacements took place shortly after the first-generation codes were enacted,[472] while others required several decades to be achieved.[473]

Structure and content of second-generation codes in American Civil Law Jurisdictions showed a harmony amongst the different texts. That identity was also shaped by the new social aspects of legislation, which had developed especially since the adoption of the Mexican (1917) and the Weimer (1919) constitutions. Second-generation codes, however, were more eclectic than their predecessors. When looking for sources, drafters of second-generation codes did not ignore the developments of the law in Europe[474] and the Americas.[475] While looking for sources in foreign codes, drafters did not ignore their own court judgments, legislation, and doctrine, thus giving a more distinctive national identity to their texts. Second-generation codes were able to incorporate elements of local law that the different jurisdictions had been developing since their first codes were enacted.

Second-generation codes found more mature societies seeking their own identities. American Civil Law Jurisdictions found in their codes a means to differentiate themselves. Accordingly, second-generation codes gave identity to jurisdictions that had adopted texts borrowed from other American Civil Law codes—mainly the text of Chile—and to jurisdictions that aimed to renovate texts that no longer represented the local *ethos*. As a corollary, these new codes aimed to project a sense of differentiation between jurisdictions, between the different parts of the New World.

Changes were also sensed in the provisions of second-generation codes that related to ownership. These changes, however, exceed the scope this chapter.

469 The list of American Civil Law Jurisdictions and the years of effect of their second-generation civil codes reads as follows: Costa Rica, 1888; Puerto Rico, 1902; Nicaragua, 1904; Honduras, 1906; Panama, 1917; Mexico, 1932; Peru, 1936; Venezuela, 1942; Guatemala, 1963; Bolivia, 1976; Cuba, 1987; and Paraguay, 1987.

470 *V.gr.*, Mexico, 1932.

471 *V.gr.*, Costa Rica, 1888.

472 *V.gr.*, Puerto Rico adopted its first-generation code in 1889, and replaced that code for one of second generation in 1902.

473 *V.gr.*, Paraguay adopted its first-generation code in 1877, and replaced that code for one of second generation in 1987.

474 *V.gr.*, civil code of Switzerland, 1912; and civil code of Italy, 1942.

475 *V.gr.*, civil code of Peru, 1936; and civil code of Venezuela, 1942.

The next chapter will address the spreading across the continent of the idea of a social function of property, and the corresponding changes in the wording in many code articles. These would include necessary references to the responsibility that derived from the ownership and control of property. Changes found a triggering point in the 1910s, at the time when Léon Duguit lectured at the University of Buenos Aires and advocated for that awareness.[476]

4.8 Closing Remarks

Codification in American Civil Law Jurisdictions provided fertile ground for an exercise of comparative legal history. The exercise aimed to provide a Pan-American perspective that would help to better understand the development of ownership at the time when first-generation codes were enacted. As indicated in this chapter, ownership as incorporated in first-generation civil codes was, in American Civil Law Jurisdictions, an absolute right that followed the tenets of the Liberal paradigm. The chapter focused mainly—as other parts of this book—on legislative enactments. Civil codes provided the center for private law provisions, and encapsulated the seminal property law institutions. Codification developed within social and legal contexts that were replicated throughout different parts of the Americas. There was a circulation of legal ideas and a flow of paradigms that linked jurisdictions within the continent. Different political and social backgrounds provided different scenarios for codification, however. There are common legal bases and temporal parallels amongst jurisdictions, yet each jurisdiction merits its own study.[477] This chapter focused on salient similarities between the development and application of ownership in Louisiana, Chile, and Argentina, and the jurisdictions that found inspiration for their provisions in one of those three codes. There are differences that ought to be subject to further study.[478]

The chapter covered several events that took place mainly during the nineteenth century, yet that have had effects in the centuries that followed. Firstly, the chapter addressed the adoption of first-generation codes in Louisiana, Chile, and Argentina. It showed that codification took place within a Pan-American context that sought the adoption of codes. Secondly, the chapter studied the codified provisions that offered a framework for ownership. That right was considered absolute in the three jurisdictions, and was in accordance

476 See, amongst others, Mirow 2010; and Mirow 2011.

477 Tau Anzoátegui 2008, p. 16.

478 See generally Parise 2014b, pp. 352–353.

with the Liberal paradigm as encapsulated in the *Code Napoléon*. The chapter highlighted the main provisions in each of the three codes, and showed how the wording of those articles many times benefited from material or formal sources that could be traced back to Europe. Thirdly, the chapter specified how other American Civil Law Jurisdictions adopted ownership provisions from one of the three abovementioned codes. The Chilean Code was clearly a blueprint for the Americas, while the codes of Louisiana and Argentina likewise played a relevant role in the pollination of ownership provisions. The chapter demonstrated that jurisdictions shared a similar understanding of ownership. The study of the pollination helped demonstrate that interest was not limited to Europe, and that when drafting in the Americas jurists also looked at vernacular sources. Fourthly, the chapter presented some reflections to help better understand second-generation codes. Those reflections indicate that codification was not static, and that ownership kept evolving in American Civil Law Jurisdictions. This last point seems to indicate that an in-depth study of that new generation of codes is needed. As a corollary, it can be claimed that there is a Pan-American understanding of ownership in first-generation codes. That understanding can be traced back to European codes and to American elaborations. Accordingly, ownership cannot be regarded as merely a European construct, because local developments played a role in its shaping, being shared across American Civil Law Jurisdictions.

The exercise of comparative legal history helped create awareness on the use that American jurists made of European and American sources. Their resulting codes became owners of the sources that were transferred, because they forced interaction with local *ethos*. Imported elaborations were absorbed by local legal structures, many times as a result of pollination. Those sources had mutated to become part of the local *ethos* even when they could be traced, in some cases, back to Europe or to other corners of the American continent. Even when there was interest in producing autonomous codifications, the interest for foreign sources had a Pan-American scope. It must be noted, however, that codification was not limited to normative transfers in the Americas, it also extended to intellectual challenges regarding creation and adaptation.[479]

479 See generally Parise 2014b, pp. 353–354.

CHAPTER 5

The Social Function Paradigm of Ownership in American Civil Law Jurisdictions

5.1 Introduction

The twentieth century experienced a change in the Ownership Paradigm in American Civil Law Jurisdictions. The Liberal paradigm of ownership was gradually replaced by one that advocated for the social function of property. The Social Function paradigm spread across the continent, and motivated corresponding changes in the wording of constitutions and civil codes, while it also included changes in the interpretation by courts and in the development of special legislation that advocated for the new approach to ownership. The idea of a social function, though popular amongst jurists in Continental Europe and in most American Civil Law Jurisdictions, seems not to be fully explored yet within the English-language legal discourse.[1]

This chapter will study the shift from the Liberal to the Social Function paradigm in three jurisdictions. It will aim to show that the resulting Ownership Paradigm in American Civil Law Jurisdictions can be shared amongst jurisdictions. The three selected jurisdictions are again the US State of Louisiana, the Republic of Chile, and the Republic of Argentina. As explained in other chapters, they can be deemed representative American Civil Law Jurisdictions, because they developed a vast scholarly production on the topic from an early period on, and their changes illustrate the shift in Ownership Paradigms, moving from the Liberal paradigm to the Social Function paradigm.

This chapter is divided into four parts. Firstly, the chapter addresses the early developments of the Social Function paradigm, focusing mainly on the European gestation as part of the doctrinal debates. It deals with that aspect of the gestation of this third paradigm, taking a more detailed approach than the one taken for the gestation in the previous two chapters, since in this third

1 See, for example, Ankersent & Ruppert 2006, p. 119; and Davidson 2011, p. 1069.
It should be noted that volume 80 of the *Fordham Law Review* (2011) offered a notable English-language collection of papers on the Social Function paradigm. The papers included in that volume were recently published in Argentina in Bonilla Maldonado 2013, offering a Spanish translation that added an interesting perspective to the existing Spanish literature.

 | DOI 10.1163/9789004338203_006

paradigm the doctrinal debates were patently present when the manifestations took place. Secondly, the chapter focuses on the reception of the new paradigm within the constitutions of the US State of Louisiana and the constitutions of the republics of Chile and Argentina. Thirdly, the chapter discusses the reception of the new paradigm within the civil codes of the already mentioned three jurisdictions. Finally, the chapter directs readers to the analysis of the special legislation that developed outside of the codes and that aimed to welcome that new paradigm, namely, the development of agrarian reform legislation. All parts will demonstrate that American Civil Law Jurisdictions abandoned the Liberal paradigm and incorporated the tenets of the Social Function paradigm within their legal frameworks.

5.2 Social Function Understanding

Private law experienced a socialization process in the period 1890–1930,[2] since the Liberal paradigm had offered few limitations to the right of ownership. Gradual changes started to occur in society–as explained *infra*–regarding the extent of that right, and the Social Function paradigm started to develop across the Western Hemisphere. That approach entailed a less "egoistic" understanding of ownership.[3] Changes had occurred in the social and economic structures of different jurisdictions, with massive migrations into cities and the effects of the Industrial Revolution.[4] Accordingly, the crude individualistic paradigm started to be challenged as a reaction to the social problems that were developing across the Western Hemisphere.[5]

5.2.1 *Global Emergence*

The change was sensed early with the revolutionary events of 1848[6] and with the writings of, amongst others, Pierre-Joseph Proudhon,[7] Karl Heinrich Marx,[8] and Auguste Comte.[9] In 1851, Comte had already stated that ownership had a social function that aimed to shape and administer the goods for subsequent

2 Halpérin 1996, p. 186.
3 Areán 1994, p. 188.
4 Cordero Quinzacara 2008, p. 503.
5 Azcárate (de) 1879–1883, III, pp. 357–453.
6 Azcárate (de) 1879–1883, III, p. 359.
7 Peset 1999, pp. 443, 449.
8 Adrogué 1991, p. 32.
9 Ankersent & Ruppert 2006, p. 95; Bergel 1994, p. 18; and Adrogué 1991, p. 34.

generations.[10] Changes in the understanding of ownership therefore started to develop in academic circles, followed by decisions by courts and by the implementation of changes in the positive laws, both in Europe and in the Americas. The idea of a social function, it should be noted, was not limited to property law, being present to different extents in other areas of the law,[11] amongst which, family law, successions,[12] and civil procedure.[13] Those advocating for the adoption of a broad Social Function paradigm could aim to find in the legal provisions a replication of social reality,[14] where law should be a product of reality.[15] Therefore, the social function could be subject to alterations, according to the mutations in the social circumstances of different societies at different times.[16]

Advocates for a change in paradigm soon emerged throughout Continental Europe, not limited to socialist scholars and their writings.[17] Spain, being particularly important for American Civil Law Jurisdictions due to historical relations, welcomed the new paradigm of a social service or function.[18] As early as 1883, Gumersindo de Azcárate had highlighted the existence of a social function, because ownership entailed duties linked with personality, such as morals, religion, science, art, and industry.[19] Later, the new paradigm would

10 An illustrative passage in French read: "Dans tout état normal de l'humanité, chaque citoyen quelconque constitue réellement un fonctionnaire public, dont les attributions plus ou moins définies déterminent à la fois les obligations et les prétentions. Ce principe universel doit certainement s'étendre jusqu'à la propriété, où le positivisme voit surtout une indispensable fonction sociale, destinée à former et à administrer les capitaux par lesquels chaque génération prépare les travaux de la suivante. Sagement conçue, cette appréciation normale ennoblit sa possession, sans restreindre sa juste liberté, et même en la faisant mieux respecter." (Comte 1851, p. 156)

See also Camps y Arboix (de) 1953, p. 200.

That statement was later used by Léon Duguit in a lecture delivered in Paris on March 11, 1908. See Duguit 1908, p. 149.

11 See, for example, Lloredo Alix 2012, p. 214.

12 Caroni 2012, pp. 340–341; and Caroni 2013, pp. 89–99. The latter work addressed the social function in the law of successions in Switzerland.

13 Verkerk 2010, pp. 257–277.

14 Hernández Gil 1969, p. 74.

15 Keiser 2005, p. 162.

16 Ruíz B. 1964, p. 39.

17 Castán Tobeñas 1963, p. 63; and Bolgár 1960, p. 288.

18 See, for example, the claim of the development of an early school of thought in Spain available at Casso y Romero (de) 1923, pp. 29–30.

19 Azcárate (de) 1879–1883, III, p. 268, and generally pp. 267–275.

be especially reflected in the writings of José María de Semprún y Gurrea.[20] German-speaking jurisdictions were represented by, amongst others, Otto von Gierke, who advocated against the egoism of the previous paradigm,[21] and by Anton Menger, who advocated from a more socialist standpoint.[22] In a lecture delivered in 1889, von Gierke defended that "our [German] private law will be more social, or it will not exist."[23] France was well represented by Duguit, being the globalizer[24] and paladin of the Social Function paradigm, and by Henri Hayem, whose 1910 doctoral dissertation[25] was very influential in the writings of the former jurist.[26] All approaches to the new paradigm agreed that owners, to some extent, had to share the benefits produced by their goods with other members of society.[27]

Heinrich Ahrens, of German origin though active during a period at the French-speaking Free University of Brussels (*Université Libre de Bruxelles*), deserves special attention.[28] Ahrens looked early at social problems and noted that private property had two elements: one individual and the other social.[29]

20 José M. de Semprún y Gurrea built upon the social function of Léon Duguit in his 1933 PhD dissertation (See Semprún y Gurrea (de) 1933). That work included several references to the French author (*i.a.*, pp. 120–122, 135, 330–331). The Spaniard, however, claimed that the meaning of the social function should be changed for one of rational-logical function (p. 5).

See also Carretero Sánchez 1994, p. 117.

21 Carretero Sánchez 1994, p. 117; and Caroni 2013, p. 95.

On the reception of the social function in nineteenth-century Germany, see generally Repgen 2001.

22 Lira Urquieta 1944, p. 172.

See, for example, Menger 1905. That 1905 edition indicated that the work of Anton Menger had been translated into French, Russian, and Spanish (p. v). See also Cordero Quinzacara 2008, p. 506.

23 Von Gierke in German stated: "unser Privatrecht wird sozialer sein, oder es wird nicht sein." (Gierke (von) 1889, p. 45)

24 French-speaking jurists were considered the globalizers of the new paradigm. See Kennedy 2006, p. 37.

25 Hayem 1910.

Henri Hayem stated in the introduction to that work that private property was certainly one of the topics that raised the most passion during the nineteenth century and would surely raise even more passion during the twentieth century (Hayem 1910, p. 1). He stated that "there is a social function that consists of being the owner." That expression in French read: "Il y a une fonction sociale, qui consiste à être propriétaire." (Hayem 1910, p. 324)

26 Mirow 2010, p. 216.

27 Alessandri Rodríguez *et al.* 2010, p. 41.

28 Welzel 1953, p. 113.

29 Colina Garea 1995, p. 289.

This precursor claimed in his well-circulated *Cours de droit naturel* (1838) that "property, [being] one of the main objects of the law, also contains a set of conditions for the physical and intellectual development of men."[30] He also excelled in disseminating the ideas of his mentor Karl Christian Friedrich Krause amongst the Spanish-speaking discourse.[31] The *Cours* of Ahrens was immediately translated into Spanish,[32] and was adopted as teaching material in several American universities as early as 1843.[33]

The need for change was also present in English-speaking jurisdictions, though not necessarily along the same lines or to the same extent as in Continental Europe.[34] In the UK, courts during the late nineteenth century addressed the limitation of landowners' freedom on ethical grounds.[35] At that same time, authors in the UK and US addressed the matter. For example, James Barr Ames, Oliver Wendell Holmes, Jr., and Sir Frederic Pollock all discussed the matter in their writings.[36] In addition, Benjamin Nathan Cardozo stated that "property, like liberty though immune under the Constitution from destruction, is not immune from regulation essential for the common good."[37] Even citing Duguit, he then indicated that "men are saying today that property, like every other social institution, has a social function to fulfill."[38] Another example of a movement towards change was provided by Richard Theodore Ely, who claimed that:

> there are two sides to private property, and that both sides are so essential, that if either one is removed the right of private property must cease. Not only is it true that if the individual side is removed private property ceases, but it is just as true, though generally this is not fully understood, that if the social side of private property ceases to exist, the right must

---

30 That expression in French read: "La propriété, l'un des objets principaux du Droit, renferme aussi un ensemble de conditions pour le développement physique et intellectuel de l'homme." (Ahrens 1838, p. 57)
See also Levaggi 2007, p. 125.

31 Levaggi 1996b, p. 248. See generally Stoetzer 1998.

32 See generally Ahrens 1841.

33 Roig 1969, p. 43.

34 See, for example, the contemporary comparison between the limitations to ownership in Germany and the US, which touch upon the new paradigm. See generally Lubens 2007.

35 Simpson 1998, p. 27.

36 Simpson 1998, p. 28.

37 Cardozo 1946, p. 87.

38 Cardozo 1946, pp. 87–88.

> likewise cease to exist because private property then becomes an impossibility, inasmuch as it would destroy social life.[39]

According to the English-speaking advocates for change, landowners' rights in common law jurisdictions had to be limited, to some extent, in defense of public interest.[40] A closer example is found in the 1950s, when the literature referred to a property-obligation theory. That theory rapidly developed because of the crowded living conditions that resulted in awareness on the use of property by neighbors.[41]

5.2.2 *Social Doctrine of the Church*

The new paradigm was also present in the writings of the Roman Catholic Church,[42] which did not deny the existence of both a social and an individual character for ownership.[43] The Church therefore recognized an intrinsic social function for private ownership,[44] since all goods should be oriented towards the sustainability of humankind.[45] Accordingly, the Church dealt with basic tenets of property law, aiming to protect the most vulnerable groups.[46] A social doctrine of the Church was developed, and aimed to humanize property,

---

39 Ely 1914, p. 165.

40 Simpson 1998, p. 27.

41 Cox 1959, p. 868.

42 Adrogué 1991, p. 34.

43 See, for example, the statement of Pope Pius XI in the encyclical *Quadragesimo anno*: "First, then, let it be considered as certain and established that neither Leo nor those theologians who have taught under the guidance and authority of the Church have ever denied or questioned the twofold character of ownership, called usually individual or social according as it regards either separate persons or the common good. For they have always unanimously maintained that nature, rather the Creator Himself, has given man the right of private ownership not only that individuals may be able to provide for themselves and their families but also that the goods which the Creator destined for the entire family of mankind may through this institution truly serve this purpose. All this can be achieved in no wise except through the maintenance of a certain and definite order." (Encyclical Quadragesimo anno 1931 (English), at § 45)

44 See, for example, the statement of Pope Saint John XXIII in the encyclical *Mater et magistra*: "Our predecessors have insisted time and again on the social function inherent in the right of private ownership, for it cannot be denied that in the plan of the Creator all of this world's goods are primarily intended for the worthy support of the entire human race." (Encyclical Mater et magistra 1961 (English), at § 119)

45 Areán 1994, p. 188.

46 Alessandri Rodríguez *et al.* 2010, p. 42.

being a natural right, burdened with a *social hypoteque*.[47] Origins of that social doctrine can be traced back to the *Sermon on the Mount*,[48] and to the writings of Saint Basil, Saint Ambrose,[49] Saint Augustine, and Saint Thomas Aquinas.[50] For example, Aquinas stated that the Church recognized that property law was part of natural law. However, private property only derived from natural law, being deduced directly by use of reason.[51]

More recent precedents of the social doctrine of the Church can be found in a selection of nineteenth- and twentieth-century encyclicals.[52] These are important documents, because they tend to define long-term papal policies.[53] The following encyclicals are central components of the social doctrine: *Rerum*

---

47 Expression coined by Pope Saint John Paul II. See Adrogué 1991, p. 34.

The expression *social mortgage* is found in the literature, yet not within the social doctrine of the Church. *Social mortgage* may be applied when "the use of the land is bound to various limitations and privileges that come with it because of the applicability of common property rules and customs often typical in a local context." (Dekker 2003, p. 34)

48 See Mathew 5–7.

49 Castán Tobeñas 1963, p. 76.

50 Adrogué 1991, p. 35.

See, for example, the late nineteenth-century lecture by Simon Deploige at the University of Leuven on the theory of Aquinas on property. Deploige 1895.

51 Alessandri Rodríguez *et al.* 2010, p. 42.

52 The social doctrine is present in other Church documents, however. For example, the pastoral constitution *Gaudium et spes* (1965), of Pope Paul VI, in part read: "[…] it is the right of public authority to prevent anyone from abusing his private property to the detriment of the common good." (Encyclical Gaudium et spes 1965 (English), at § 71) See also de los Mozos 1993, p. 169.

The social doctrine was recognized in more recent texts. For example, the encyclicals *Laborem exercens* (1981) and *Centesimus annus* (1991) of Pope Saint John Paul II addressed the social doctrine. In *Centesimus annus* the Pope stated that there was a "necessity [for] and therefore the legitimacy of private ownership, as well as the limits which are imposed on it." (Encyclical Centesimus annus 1991 (English), at § 30) See also Alessandri Rodríguez *et al.* 2010, p. 43.

A more recent example was provided by the apostolic exhortation *Evangelii gaudium* (2013), of Pope Francis. That text in part read: "Solidarity is a spontaneous reaction by those who recognize that the social function of property and the universal destination of goods are realities which come before private property. The private ownership of goods is justified by the need to protect and increase them, so that they can better serve the common good; for this reason, solidarity must be lived as the decision to restore to the poor what belongs to them […]." (Apostolic Exhortation Evangelii gaudium 2013 (English), at § 189)

53 Alessandri Rodríguez *et al.* 2010, p. 42.

novarum[54] (1891), of Pope Leo XIII; *Quadragesimo anno*[55] (1931), of Pope Pius XI; *Mater et magistra*[56] (1961), of Pope Saint John XXIII; and *Populorum progressio*[57] (1967), of Pope Paul VI.[58] In the encyclical *Rerum novarum,* Pope Leo XIII was clear in defending the inviolability of private property and in rejecting socialist ideas.[59] Pope Pius XI later declared in *Quadragesimo anno* that the Church never denied the social and individual aspect of ownership,[60] and stated that

> [...] men must consider in this matter not only their own advantage but also the common good. To define these duties in detail when necessity requires and the natural law has not done so, is the function of those in charge of the State. Therefore, public authority, under the guiding light always of the natural and divine law, can determine more accurately upon consideration of the true requirements of the common good, what is permitted and what is not permitted to owners in the use of their property [...].[61]

---

54 See generally Encyclical Rerum novarum 1891 (English).

55 See generally Encyclical Quadragesimo anno 1931 (English).

56 See generally Encyclical Mater et magistra 1961 (English).

57 See generally Encyclical Populorum progressio 1967 (English).

58 Adrogué 1991, p. 35; and Calvo San José 2000, p. 43.

59 For example, the encyclical read: "[...] it is clear that the main tenet of socialism, community of goods, must be utterly rejected, since it only injures those whom it would seem meant to benefit, is directly contrary to the natural rights of mankind, and would introduce confusion and disorder into the commonweal. The first and most fundamental principle, therefore, if one would undertake to alleviate the condition of the masses, must be the inviolability of private property [...]." (Encyclical Rerum novarum 1891 (English), at § 15)

See also Castro Mayer (de) *et al.* 1963, p. 70.

60 Castán Tobeñas 1963, p. 27.

61 English text extracted from Encyclical Quadragesimo anno 1931 (English), at § 49. See also Alessandri Rodríguez *et al.* 2010, p. 43.

The text in Latin read: "Re vera hominibus hac in re non solum sui proprii commodi, sed etiam communis boni esse rationem habendam, ex ipsa dominii quam diximus indole individuali simul et sociali deducitur. Officia vero haec singillatim definire, ubi id necessitas postulaverit neque ipsa lex naturalis praestiterit, eorum est qui rei publicae praesunt. Quapropter quid, considerata boni communis vera necessitate, eis qui possident liceat, quid illicitum sit in suorum bonorum usu, publica auctoritas, lege naturali et divina semper praelucente, sciscere potest accuratius [...]." (Encyclical Quadragesimo anno 1931 (Latin), at II)

He claimed that "[…] certain kinds of property, it is rightly contended, ought to be reserved to the State since they carry with them a dominating power so great that cannot without danger to the general welfare be entrusted to private individuals."[62]

Another important precedent is the *Social Code of Mechelen* (1927). That text took its inspiration and foundations directly from the encyclicals and the interpretations made by the episcopate.[63] That code offered a synthesis of the Social Doctrine of the Church, and naturally dealt with ownership.[64] The second edition of the Social Code, dated 1933, stated in article 94 that property had a two-fold aspect: one individual and private, and another social and public.[65] The Belgian text was even considered a *vade mecum* for all Catholics interested in social matters,[66] being drafted and disseminated by the Intentional Union of Social Studies of Mechelen.[67] The combination of the encyclicals and the postulates of the Social Code showed that the Church advocated for a right of ownership that predated the creation of the states, a natural right that was also inviolable.[68]

5.2.3 *Duguit: The Paladin of the Social Function Paradigm*

Duguit was the paladin of the Social Function paradigm,[69] claiming early that the Liberal paradigm was in extinction.[70] Born in France in 1859 and deceased in 1928, Duguit held teaching positions at several universities in France, and also taught in Bucharest, Cairo, Coimbra, and New York.[71] He was very much

---

62 English text extracted from Encyclical Quadragesimo anno 1931 (English), at § 114. See also Alessandri Rodríguez *et al.* 2010, p. 43.

The text in Latin read: "[…] Etenim certa quaedam bonorum genera rei publicae reservanda merito contenditur, cum tam magnum secum ferant potentatum, quantus privatis hominibus, salva re publica, permitti non possit […]." (Encyclical Quadragesimo anno 1931 (Latin), at 111)

63 Código Social de Malinas 1949, p. 13.

64 Código Social de Malinas 1949, p. 8.

65 Código Social de Malinas 1947, p. 41.

66 Código Social de Malinas 1949, p. 14.

67 Código Social de Malinas 1949, p. 8.

68 Calvo San José 2000, p. 45.

69 On the life and work of Léon Duguit, see generally the commemorative volume in Melleray 2011; and Calvo González & Monereo Pérez 2005.

On the general tenets of Léon Duguit, see Claro Solar 1979, pp. 409–412; and Réglade 1932.

70 Duguit 1912b, p. 155.

71 Mirow 2010, pp. 197–198.

influenced by the writings of Comte,[72] while he further found grounding for his works in the sociological postulates of Émile Durkheim,[73] of whom he was an acquaintance.[74] Some of the writings of Duguit were available in American Civil Law Jurisdictions, being translated, for example, into Spanish by Carlos González Posada[75] and into English by Harold Joseph Laski.[76]

5.2.3.1 Postulates

Duguit claimed that ownership *entailed* a social function, or furthermore, ownership *was* a social function.[77] A status of isolation was considered fictional,[78] and he therefore defended that the holder of a thing should fulfill a social function, and if the holder fulfilled the mission, the activities of the holder would be protected by law. However, if the holder did not fulfill the mission, the state could intervene and assure that the holder used the thing according to its purpose and in benefit of all society members.[79] The French publicist popularized the term "social function" (*fonction sociale*) in 1905,[80] at a lecture in the *Congrès National de la Propriété Batie*.[81] On that occasion he referred to a social mission,[82] role,[83] and function.[84] A few years later, in August and September 1911, he delivered a series of six lectures[85] at the University of Buenos

72 Calvo San José 2000, p. 43.
73 Halpérin 2008, p. 220.
74 Mirow 2010, p. 198.
75 Duguit 1912a.
76 Mirow 2010, p. 196.
77 Areán 1994, p. 189; and Ruíz B. 1964, p. 43.
78 Bonilla 2011, p. 1155.
79 Duguit 1912b, p. 21, cited also by Alessandri Rodríguez *et al.* 2010, p. 41.
80 Halpérin 1996, p. 197.
81 Cordero Quinzacara 2008, p. 509.
82 For example, Léon Duguit stated in French that: "[…] Le droit ainsi compris s'impose, dis-je, à chacun et à tous; il s'impose à l'Etat et l'oblige à faire tour ce qui est en son pouvoir pour permettre à chacun de remplir sa mission sociale." (Duguit 1905, p. 9)
83 For example, Léon Duguit stated in French that: "Propriétaires d'immeubles bâtis, vous remplissez donc un rôle social que nul ne peut remplir mieux que vous." (Duguit 1905, p. 16)
84 For example, Léon Duguit stated in French that: "Tout législateur manque à son devoir rigoureux, qui impose aux propriétaires urbains des prestations trop lourdes sous une forme quelconque, et les met alors dans l'impossibilité de remplir leur fonction sociale, et il arrive indirectement, mais sûrement, à frapper surtout ceux-là mêmes qui ont toutes ses sympathies, les ouvriers." (Duguit 1905, pp. 20–21)
85 On the content of the six lectures, see also Mirow 2010, pp. 203–209.

Aires,[86] where he advocated for the social function in private law,[87] upon reflecting on the changes experienced in private law since the adoption of the *Code Napoléon*. Those lectures resulted from early efforts to establish cultural links between Argentina and Europe.[88] Duguit then transcribed the Buenos Aires Lectures, and published them in Paris in 1912, making them available to French readers.[89] A second edition was published in 1920, also in Paris,[90] showing the significant impact and circulation of the first edition. During the following decade, in the period 1920–1921, Duguit delivered a series of lectures at Columbia University (US) on freedom and sovereignty.[91] On that occasion, he emphasized that there was a solidary conception of freedom, by which freedom was a duty and not a right.[92] At Columbia he strongly defended that men were social beings by nature.[93]

The French publicist highlighted that property had to be destined towards the collective interest.[94] He made it clear to readers of his lectures, however, that he was against class conflict or class struggle.[95] In the second Buenos Aires lecture, he stated that men and society did not have rights, yet "every individual ha[d] a certain function to fulfill in society, a certain task to undertake."[96] In the sixth lecture, dealing mainly with the social function of property, he indicated that ownership was subject to socialization, implying two things: "that individual ownership [was] no longer an individual right, and was transform[ed] into a social function; and second, that there [was] an increase in the number of cases of wealth allocated to collectivities, that [should] be subject to juridical

86 Mirow 2010, p. 198; and Duguit 1912b, p. I.

87 For a study on the impact of the postulates of Léon Duguit on private law, see generally Morin 1932.

88 See Duguit 2011.

For additional information on the gestation and development of the conferences, see Levaggi 2010a, pp. 205–208.

89 Mirow 2010, p. 199.

90 Duguit 1920. See also Mirow 2010, p. 199.

91 Duguit 1922.

92 Léon Duguit stated in French that: "[…] la liberté n'est plus un droit, elle est un devoir." (Duguit 1922, p. 141)

93 Léon Duguit stated in French that: "[…] l'homme est par nature un être social […]." (Duguit 1922, p. 142)

94 Mariani de Vidal 2004, p. 270.

95 Duguit 1912b, p. 161.

96 Léon Duguit stated in French that: "Mais tout individu a dans la société une certaine fonction à remplir, une certaine besogne à exécuter." (Duguit 1912b, p. 24)

protection."[97] Duguit also stated that owners could use things as long as they fulfilled a social function. They had to undertake three duties:[98] (i) to enjoy things when satisfying individual or collective needs;[99] (ii) not to leave things without use or exploitation;[100] and (iii) to allow the use of things when aiming to fulfill social interests.[101] The author addressed the existence of subjective rights, and defended that "ownership [was] therefore not the subjective right of the owner, it [was] the social function of the holder of the wealth."[102] Duguit even indicated correctly that the Liberal paradigm was present in article 17 of the Argentine Constitution of 1853.[103] Readers were warned, however, that in the early twentieth century, American Civil Law Jurisdictions were at the doorsteps of the Social Function paradigm.[104]

5.2.3.2 Impact on the Legal Discourse

The ideas and writings of Duguit triggered debate and further studies.[105] He could have been considered an iconoclast, seen as someone breaking with the symbols of the past.[106] Duguit was criticized because property should *have* a social function and not *be* a social function.[107] Scholars, many being trained in the civil law,[108] claimed that the subjective right of holders should be acknowledged and not denied.[109] Accordingly, the argumentation of Duguit was

97 Léon Duguit stated in French that: "[…] d'abord que la propriété individuelle cesse d'être un droit de l'individu pour devenir une fonction sociale, et en second lieu que les cas d'affectation de richesse à des collectivités, qui doivent être juridiquement protégés, deviennent de plus en plus nombreux." (Duguit 1912b, pp. 148–149)

98 Duguit 1912b, pp. 165–166, cited also by Alessandri Rodríguez *et al.* 2010, pp. 41–42. See also Salvat 1962, p. 17.

99 Duguit 1912b, pp. 165–166.

100 Duguit 1912b, pp. 166–167.

101 Duguit 1912b, pp. 168–169.

102 English text extracted from Mirow 2010, p. 207.
Léon Duguit stated in Frencht that: "La propriété n'est plus le droit subjectif du propriétaire; elle est la fonction sociale du détenteur de la richesse." (Duguit 1912b, p. 158)

103 Duguit 1912b, p.152.

104 Léon Duguit referred to Latin American jurisdictions, and not to American Civil Law Jurisdictions. See Duguit 1912b, p. 150.

105 On the different degrees of acceptance and rejection of the ideas of Léon Duguit, see the detailed study in Hakim 2011.

106 Hakim 2011, p. 101.

107 Alessandri Rodríguez *et al.* 2010, p. 42; and Castán Tobeñas 1963, p. 79.

108 Halpérin 1996, p. 187.

109 Alessandri Rodríguez *et al.* 2010, p. 42.

not welcomed favorably by some scholars, because it implied a rejection of the subjective right of ownership, and the owner was therefore simply a functionary.[110] However, his ideas did generate awareness of the need for ownership to comply both with collective and individual needs.[111] In France, his ideas did not succeed in breaking with the movements that advocated for the preeminence of private property,[112] yet they continued circulating during the inter-war period, as demonstrated by the work of Georges Renard and Louis Trotabas.[113] Duguit continued to be a subject of study in France after his death, as a 1933 Ph.D. dissertation recognized when focusing on his social doctrine.[114] In Spain, scholars regarded Duguit's work,[115] yet some with reservations due to the socialist tint they might have perceived, as indicated by Emilio Miñana y Villagrasa in a 1917 lecture.[116] His ideas even reached the English-language legal discourse,[117] being discussed, for example, in Australia and in the UK by William Jethro Brown.[118] They were discussed early in the US literature, as demonstrated in a 1917 note published in the *Harvard Law Review*[119] and in writings by Roscoe Pound.[120] Duguit's ideas, moreover, had some influence in the drafting of the civil code in Russia after the Bolshevik Revolution and in the allotment of vacated lands after WWI.[121] With time, the perception and reception of the ideas of Duguit were altered. In the 1930s, scholars considered the ideas of Duguit also from a social doctrine perspective, enlarging the audience and the degree of acceptance.[122]

---

110 Calvo San José 2000, p. 42.

111 Calvo San José 2000, p. 42.

112 Halpérin 2008, p. 221.

113 Renard & Trotabas 1930. See also Halpérin 1996, p. 197.

114 See generally Markovitch 1933.

115 See generally Fernandez 2011.

116 Emilio Miñana y Villagrasa spoke of a "[…] brand new concept of ownership, that because of its socialist tinge, may be repugnant to some […]."

That expression in Spanish read: "[…] novísimo concepto del derecho de propiedad, que por su tinte socialista podía repugnar á algunos[…]." (Miñana y Villagrasa 1917, p. 19)

117 See generally Harlow 2011.

118 Harlow 2011, pp. 232–234.

119 See Laski 1917. See also Mirow 2010, p. 196; and Harlow 2011, p. 235.

120 Roscoe Pound referred to the Buenos Aires Lectures of Léon Duguit in one of the lectures that he delivered at Cambridge (UK) in 1922, and that were published in the US. See Pound 1923, pp. 86–87.

121 Halpérin 2008, p. 221.

122 Cordero Quinzacara 2008, p. 511.

The postulates of Duguit were welcomed in American Civil Law Jurisdictions, especially after his Buenos Aires Lectures.[123] Those lectures were translated into Spanish[124] and into English,[125] showcasing them in the Americas. The lectures indeed circulated in France, Spain, the US, and in American Civil Law Jurisdictions.[126] In Mexico, for example, the French publicist was often used as a way to support a local decision, as a way to illustrate how a potential change in Mexico had been already welcomed in the legal discourse of other jurisdictions.[127] In Colombia, in the 1930s, the writings of Duguit were known by the members of the judicial, legislative, and executive branches.[128]

The reception of the Social Function paradigm was not limited to the first decades of the twentieth century or to the European legal discourse.[129] A series of social and ideological twentieth-century shifts (*i.a.*, WWI, WWII, the Mexican Revolution) also had an impact on the reshaping of ownership.[130] The paradigm was welcomed in legislation and scholarly writings throughout the entire century, entering even into the twenty-first century. A diversity of legal provisions reflected a departure from the Liberal paradigm. For example, at the European level, Article 1 of Protocol 1 to the *Convention for the Protection of Human Rights and Fundamental Freedoms* (1952) referred to limitations due to public interest.[131] Similarly, the *American Convention on Human Rights*

123 Keiser 2012, p. 269.

124 See Duguit 1912a.

125 An English translation of the six lectures was published as Chapter 3 of volume XI of *The Continental Legal History Series*. See generally Duguit 1918.

126 Mirow 2010, p. 199.

127 Keiser 2012, p. 269.

128 Bonilla 2011, p. 1154; and Karst & Rosenn 1975, pp. 286–287.

129 See also Mirow 2010, p. 196.

As an example, it can be noted that South Africa was not immune to the need for change. See, for example, van der Walt 2009.

130 Ramella 2007, p. 320.

131 Article 1 of Protocol 1 to the *Convention for the Protection of Human Rights and Fundamental Freedoms* read:

"Every natural or legal person is entitled to the peaceful enjoyment of his possessions. No one shall be deprived of his possessions except in the public interest and subject to the conditions provided for by law and by the general principles of international law.

The preceding provisions shall not, however, in any way impair the right of a State to enforce such laws as it deems necessary to control the use of property in accordance with the general interest or to secure the payment of taxes or other contributions or penalties." (Protocol 1952, p. 31)

(1969) addressed a social interest for property.[132] A diversity of authors, likewise, made manifest a departure from the traditional Liberal paradigm. For example, in the US, contemporary authors refer to the renaissance of a new and social paradigm that departs from the Liberal paradigm.[133] Accordingly, Joseph William Singer speaks of a social relations model, which "reconceptualizes property as a social system composed of entitlements which shape the contours of social relationships,"[134] being able to include relations between people "both at the level of society as a whole (the macro level) and in the context of particular relationships (the micro level)."[135] Other US scholars also speak of a social-obligation theory.[136] For example, Gregory S. Alexander addresses an approach to the social-obligation theory that focuses on human flourishing.[137] He defends that "an owner is morally obligated to provide to the society of which the individual is a member those benefits that the society reasonably regards as necessary for human flourishing."[138] All these notions can be traced back to the Social Function paradigm that took force during the period 1890–1930.

5.2.4 *Corollary*

American Civil Law Jurisdictions, as already mentioned, experienced the reception of the new paradigm. That reception took place mainly during the first decades of the twentieth century, though some recent texts still incorporate the idea of a social function.[139] Jurisdictions during the early twentieth century

---

132 Article 21 of the *American Convention on Human Rights* read:
"Right to Property
1. Everyone has the right to the use and enjoyment of his property. The law may subordinate such use and enjoyment to the interest of society.
2. No one shall be deprived of his property except upon payment of just compensation, for reasons of public utility or social interest, and in the cases and according to the forms established by law.
3. Usury and any other form of exploitation of man by man shall be prohibited by law."
(American Convention on Human Rights 1969)
See also Arcán 1994, p. 189.

133 Mirow 2010, p. 194.

134 Singer 1996, p. 78.

135 Singer 1996, p. 78.

136 See generally Alexander 2011.

137 See generally Alexander 2009; and Alexander 2013. See also Mirow 2010, p. 194.

138 Alexander 2009, p. 774.

139 For example, article 56, paragraph 1 of the 2009 Political Constitution of Bolivia referred to the social function of property. That article read that "[...] everyone has a right to individual or collective private property, as long as it fulfills a social function."

were many times marked by an inequitable distribution of land, which converged with the new ideas developed in Europe.[140] For example, the Mexican Revolution was mainly a result of the need to terminate the unequal distribution of lands, and found in the Social Function paradigm a means to justify state intervention.[141] The three jurisdictions subject to study experienced, with different degrees, the reception of the Social Function paradigm. The reception, as will be reflected *infra*, was sensed in the text of constitutions, civil codes, and special legislation. In Argentina and Chile the term "social function" (*función social*) was explicitly referred to in the literature. In Louisiana, however, the literature included isolated references to the term "social function,"[142] while in US legislation no legal provision refers explicitly to that term in the context of ownership.[143]

5.3 Reception in Constitutions

The new Social Function paradigm was encapsulated early within the constitutions of different jurisdictions. These new ideas were first welcomed in the Mexican Constitution of 1917 and in the social ideas included in the Weimar Constitution of 1919. These constitutions included references to the responsibility that derived from the ownership and control of property. The reception of the paradigm was ignited by those two constitutions; and starting with the 1917 Mexican Constitution, the Duguitian idea was soon welcomed by other

That text in Spanish read: "Toda persona tiene derecho a la propiedad privada individual o colectiva, siempre que ésta cumpla una función social." (Constitución Bolivia 2009)

140 Ankersent & Ruppert 2006, p. 88.

141 Ankersent & Ruppert 2006, p. 88.

142 For example, in the 1940s, the *Louisiana Law Review* published an article by Ernst Rabel indicating that in Germany some aspects of private law (*i.a.*, family law, property law) were altered to delimit their social function. See Rabel 1950, p. 267.

At the same time, the *Tulane Law Review* published an article by J. Walter Jones referring to the "duty of neighbourliness," even citing Léon Duguit. See Jones 1947, p. 92.

143 A search undertaken in the databases of Westlaw (September 11, 2014) showed that the term was used, in a somehow related context, in Section 701, Chapter 13, Title 76 of the Montana Code, which read: "The legislature finds that public forests in Montana should be sustainably managed to maintain biodiversity, productivity, regeneration capacity, vitality, and potential to fulfill relevant ecological, economic, and social functions."

See also Foster & Bonilla 2011, p. 1008.

constitutions of Europe and of American Civil Law Jurisdictions.[144] The reception of the new paradigm within the text of constitutions increased during the inter-war period,[145] yet it continued throughout the entire century. The new paradigm ultimately represented a mentality and ideal that soon predominated across the Western Hemisphere.[146]

5.3.1 *American Origins: Social Constitutionalism in Mexico*

Mexico provided the first social constitution.[147] The 1917 Constitution defended the democratic means of government presented in the 1857 Constitution, yet it modified individual rights by including a shift in social rights and state obligations.[148] Those shifts contemplated the adoption of land reform, together with education and labor reforms.[149] The new Mexican text was drafted within the context of the Revolution, aiming to achieve a radical subversion of the preexisting agrarian regime and achieving a new social structure.[150] It has also been claimed that the 1917 Constitution was the "first coherent expression of ideology emerging from the 1910 Revolution."[151] Changes in property law were mainly included in article 27 of the new Constitution, which resembled a codified text by providing solutions for single practical problems.[152] The third paragraph of that article read in part:

> The Nation shall have at all times the right to impose on private property the modalities that the public interest may demand, as well as the right to regulate the use of natural elements subject to appropriation, to undertake an equitable distribution of public wealth and to secure their conservation. According to that objective, the necessary measures will be dictated for the fragmentation of the *latifundios* [...] and [to] avoid the destruction of natural elements and damages that property may suffer in detriment of society.[153]

144 Ankersent & Ruppert 2006, p. 96.
The effective extent to which the Mexican Constitution helped in disseminating the new paradigm in American Civil Law Jurisdictions has been challenged by some authors. See Mirow 2011, p. 1215.

145 Ruíz-Giménez 1961, p. 118.

146 Ramella 2007, p. 319.

147 Ankersent & Ruppert 2006, p. 96.

148 Duncan 1963, pp. 307–308.

149 Duncan 1963, pp. 307–308.

150 Camps y Arboix (de) 1953, p. 211.

151 Duncan 1963, p. 303.

152 Keiser 2012, p. 265.

153 See also the translation by Browning 1965, p. 3.

The new wording converted private property into a privilege instead of a right.[154] That idea was further present in the first and fourth paragraphs of article 27, which read that "ownership of land and water corresponded originally to the Nation, who had and has the right to transfer dominium to individuals, creating therefore private property"[155] and that "direct ownership of all natural resources [was] vested on the Nation."[156] That new privilege enabled state relocation of goods in defense of public interests.[157] In addition, the expression "direct ownership" resembled the decomposition of ownership in *directum*ww

---

The first four paragraphs of that long article in Spanish read:

"La propiedad de las tierras y aguas comprendidas dentro de los límites del territorio nacional, corresponde originariamente a la Nación, la cual, ha tenido y tiene el derecho de transmitir el dominio de ellas a los particulares, constituyendo la propiedad privada.

Esta no podrá ser apropiada sino por causa de la utilidad pública y mediante indemnización.

La Nación tendrá en todo tiempo el derecho de imponer a la propiedad privada las modalidades que dicte el interés público, así como el de regular el aprovechamiento de los elementos naturales suceptibles de apropiación, para hacer una distribución equitativa de la riqueza pública y para cuidar de su conservación. Con este objeto se dictarán las medidas necesarias para el fraccionamiento de los latifundios; para el desarrollo de la pequeña propiedad; para la creación de nuevos centros de población agrícola con las tierras y aguas que les sean indispensables; para el fomento de la agricultura y para evitar la destrucción de los elementos naturales y los daños que la propiedad pueda sufrir en perjuicio de la sociedad. Los pueblos, rancherías y comunidades que carezcan de tierras y aguas, o no las tengan en cantidad suficiente para las necesidades de su población, tendrán derecho a que se les dote de ellas, tomándolas de las propiedades inmediatas, respetando siempre la pequeña propiedad. Por tanto, se confirman las dotaciones de terrenos que se hayan hecho hasta ahora de conformidad con el Decreto de 6 de enero de 1915. La adquisición de las propiedades particulares necesarias para conseguir los objetos antes expresados, se considerará de utilidad pública.

Corresponde a la Nación el dominio directo de todos los minerales o substancias que en vetas, mantos, masas o yacimientos, constituyan depósitos cuya naturaleza sea distinta de los componentes de los terrenos, tales como los minerales de los que se extraigan metales y metaloides utilizados en la industria; los yacimientos de piedras preciosas, de sal de gema y las salinas formadas directamente por las aguas marinas. Los productos derivados de la descomposición de las rocas, cuando su explotación necesite trabajos subterráneos; los fosfatos susceptibles de ser utilizados como fertilizantes; los combustibles minerales sólidos; el petróleo y todos los carburos de hidrógeno sólidos, líquidos o gaseosos." (Constitución México 1917, p. 150)

154 Haber *et al.* 2008, pp. 13–14.

155 See paragprah 1 at Constitución México 1917, p. 150.

156 See paragprah 4 at Constitución México 1917, p. 150.

157 Haber *et al.* 2008, p. 24.

and *utile,* returning to the Allocation paradigm.[158] The Mexican government aimed therefore to project an image of being the legitimate owner,[159] inspired in the *señorío* that the Castilian Crown had had over American territories before the independence movements.[160] That new *señorío* would give ample power for the government to protect the public interest and introduce the Social Function paradigm. The 1917 text, after numerous modifications, is still the constitution of Mexico.

5.3.2 *European Origins: Social Constitutionalism in Germany*

Germany provided another early and influential constitutional text that welcomed the new paradigm of ownership. After WWI, Germany opted for a social democracy,[161] and as its 1917 Mexican predecessor, the 1919 Constitution of the Weimar Republic resulted from a consolidation period that followed the downfall of a government.[162] The 1919 text introduced the social function dimension, defending that owners should fulfill certain obligations and accept a number of limitations to their rights.[163] Accordingly, individual ownership was preserved, yet it lost its absolute character, welcoming a more social conception of law.[164] The tenets of this new paradigm were present mainly in two articles: on the one hand, in paragraph 3 of article 153, which in an overt form stated that "property obliges" (*Eigentum verpflichtet*), and then declared that property should also be used for the common good;[165] on the other hand, in paragraph 1 of article 155, which read in part that the "distribution and use of land [was] controlled by the Nation in a manner that prevent[ed] the abuse and secure[ed] healthy housing for all German families,"[166] and in paragraph

158 Keiser 2012, p. 264.

159 Keiser 2012, p. 265.

160 González 2009, p. 210.

161 Durán Bernales 1966, p. 167.

162 Keiser 2012, p. 266.

163 Halpérin 2008, p. 325.

164 Salvat 1962, p. 19.

165 Paragraph 3 of article 153 in German read: "Eigentum verpflichtet. Sein Gebrauch soll zugleich Dienst sein für das Gemeine Beste." (Verfassung des Deutschen Reichs 1919, p. 1412)

166 Paragraph 1 of article 155, in a more extensive transcription, in German read: "Die Verteilung und Nutzung des Bodens wird von Staats wegen in einer Weise überwacht, die Mißbrauch verhütet und dem Ziele zustrebt, jedem Deutschen eine gesunde Wohnung und allen deutschen Familien, besonders den kinderreichen, eine ihren Bedürfnissen entsprechende Wohn- und Wirtschaftsheimstätte zu sichern [...]." (Verfassung des Deutschen Reichs 1919, p. 1413)

3 of the same article, which read that the "exploitation and use of the land [was] an obligation of the landowner with the community."[167] The German text characterized the social content of ownership.[168] The new text fell within the creeds of the social state under the rule of law (*Sozialer Rechtsstaat*) understanding, which assumed the development of a collective responsibility for the moral, economic, and social existence of citizens, yet guaranteeing private rights.[169] Even though not fully developed, the Social Function paradigm was encapsulated in the Weimar Constitution, preparing the ground for its development in other constitutions around the globe.[170]

5.3.3 *Global Contagion of Constitutions*

Several European jurisdictions adopted the new paradigm in their constitutions.[171] In the inter-war period, for example, Estonia (1919), Poland (1921), Danzig (1922), and Lithuania (1928) imposed limitations on individual property in their fundamental laws.[172] Spain also received influences from the Weimar text.[173] Article 44 of the 1931 Constitution stated that property could be socialized and that all wealth was subject to the interests of the national economy.[174] The new paradigm was likewise adopted in common law jurisdictions, when the Republic of Ireland adopted a constitution in 1937.[175] That text is of special interest, due to the place of the Church in Irish society, welcoming parallels with American Civil Law Jurisdictions. Other European jurisdictions incorporated the new paradigm into their post-WWII texts,[176] when the social function of property was revamped in the different constitutions.[177] Examples of these last texts are found in the constitutions of Yugoslavia (1953)[178] and Portugal (1953).[179] Earlier examples are found in the Italian Constitution (1947)

167 Paragraph 3 of article 155 in German read: "Die Bearbeitung und Ausnutzung des Bodens ist eine Pflicht des Grundbesitzers gegenüber der Gemeinschaft [...]." (Verfassung des Deutschen Reichs 1919, p. 1413)
168 Ankersent & Ruppert 2006, p. 98.
169 Cordero Quinzacara 2008, p. 511.
170 Camps y Arboix (de) 1953, p. 212.
171 See, for example, Legón 1942, p. 264.
172 Ramella 2007, p. 318.
173 Ruíz-Giménez 1961, p. 118.
174 Camps y Arboix (de) 1953, p. 212.
175 See generally Walsh 2011.
176 Cordero Quinzacara 2008, p. 511.
177 Castán Tobeñas 1963, p. 64.
178 Ruíz-Giménez 1961, p. 116.
179 Ruíz-Giménez 1961, p. 120.

and in the Basic Law for the Federal Republic of Germany (*Grundgesetz für die Bundesrepublik Deutschland*) (1949). Article 42 of the Italian text expressly referred to social function,[180] and aimed at the equitable division of land and the establishment of proper social relations.[181] The German text, in paragraph 2 of article 14, also stated that "property obliges," as the Weimar precedent had done in 1919.[182]

American Civil Law Jurisdictions were not immune to the reception of the new paradigm within the texts of their constitutions. Most constitutions there incorporated explicitly the Social Function paradigm[183] during the first half of the twentieth century. Drafters in the Americas found grounding in the writings of Duguit for the changes in their constitutions,[184] and they benefited from the texts that had been drafted in other parts of the Western Hemisphere. A *contagion*[185] of constitutions developed in the region, and increased during the post-WWII period. Examples of constitutions that resulted from that *contagion* and that incorporated the Social Function paradigm are found in the texts of Bolivia (1938 and 1947), Colombia (1936 and 1945), Nicaragua (1939), Paraguay (1940), Guatemala (1946), Ecuador (1946), Panama (1941 and 1946), Peru (1947), Venezuela (1947), El Salvador (1950), and Honduras (1957).[186] For example, the 1946 Constitution of Panama read in article 45 that private

---

180 Ramella 2007, p. 319.

181 Article 42 of the constitution in Italian read:

"La proprietà è pubblica o privata. I beni economici appartengono allo Stato, ad enti o a privati.

La proprietà privata è riconosciuta e garantita dalla legge, che ne determina i modi di acquisto, di godimento e i limiti allo scopo di assicurarne la funzione sociale e di renderla accessibile a tutti.

La proprietà privata può essere, nei casi preveduti dalla legge, e salvo indennizzo, espropriata per motivi d'interesse generale.

La legge stabilisce le norme ed i limiti della successione legittima e testamentaria e i diritti dello Stato sulle eredità." (Costituzione Italiana 1947, p. 5)

See also Camps y Arboix (de) 1953, p. 216; Allende 1967, p. 379; Mariani de Vidal 2004, p. 307; and Halpérin 2008, p. 325.

182 See paragraph 2 of article 14 of the constitution. See also Carretero Sánchez 1994, p. 120; Alessandri Rodríguez *et al.* 2010, p. 44; Halpérin 2008, p. 325; and Cordero Quinzacara 2008, p. 512.

183 Ankersent & Ruppert 2006, p. 99.

184 Mirow 2010, p. 195.

185 This term is borrowed, *mutatis mutandis*, from Colley 2014.

186 Ramella 2007, p. 318; Legón 1942, p. 264; Ankersent & Ruppert 2006, pp. 96, 99; Allende 1967, p. 377; and Castán Tobeñas 1963, p. 102.

property implied obligations for the owner due to the social function it should fulfill;[187] while the 1940 Constitution of Paraguay read in article 21 that the contents and limitations of private property would be established by law dealing with the social function.[188]

The three jurisdictions subject to study (*i.e.*, Louisiana, Chile, and Argentina) experienced, with different degrees, the reception of the Social Function paradigm into their constitutional texts. Even when the three jurisdictions may be considered very conservative, the presence of the new paradigm cannot be denied.

5.3.4 *Louisiana*

Louisiana modified its constitution on numerous occasions since its first enactment in 1812.[189] The current Louisiana Constitution dates from 1974,[190] while its three immediate predecessors date from 1898, 1913, and 1921. The texts of 1913 and 1921 were tinted with progressive reform ideas, as were other US constitutional reforms across the different states,[191] yet to a lesser extent.[192] At the

187 Article 45 of the constitution in Spanish read:

"Se garantiza la propiedad privada adquirida con arreglo a la ley por personas jurídicas o naturales, la cual no podrá ser desconocida ni vulnerada por leyes posteriores.

La propiedad privada implica obligaciones para su dueño por razón de la función social que debe llenar." (Constitución Panamá 1946, p. 4)

See also Allende 1967, p. 376; and Mariani de Vidal 2004, p. 307.

188 Article 21 of the constitution in Spanish read: "La Constitución garantiza la propiedad privada, cuyo contenido y límites serán fijados por la ley, atendiendo a su función social. Nadie puede ser privado de su propiedad sino en virtud de sentencia fundada en ley. La propiedad de toda clase de bienes podrá ser transformada jurídicamente mediante la expropiación por cause de utilidad social definida por la ley, la que determinará asimismo la forma de indemnización. La ley podrá fijar la extensión máxima de tierras de que puede ser dueño un solo individuo o sociedad legalmente constituida y el excedente deberá venderse en subasta pública o expropiarse por el Estado para su distribución." (Constitución Paraguay 1940, p. 12)

See also Allende 1967, p. 377; and Mariani de Vidal 2004, p. 307.

189 The text of the constitution was modified in 1845, 1852, 1861, 1864, 1868, 1879, 1898, 1913, 1921, and 1974. Additional information on the history of the different constitutions of Louisiana is available at Powell 1954.

190 The text of the current constitution is available at Louisiana Constitution 1974.

191 Windell 1993, pp. 110, 122; and Schott 1993, p. 140.

192 It has been claimed that Louisiana had been "relatively untouched by twentieth-century progressivism." (Schott 1993, p. 140)

turn of the nineteenth century, state constitutions in the US were considered too long and detailed, while depriving local governments of the required flexibility to adapt to changes in circumstances.[193] Louisiana constitutions provided a good example of those texts, and even when constitutional conventions aimed at changes in that respect, they were not able to succeed.[194]

5.3.4.1 Social Context

A look into the society of the early twentieth century may help explain the changes in the constitutions of Louisiana.[195] Several political and social reforms took place during the first years of the new century.[196] For example, there were some agrarian protests already at the end of the previous century,[197] and the Democrats were willing to include agrarian reforms in the 1898 Constitution.[198] Organized labor, however, did not present a serious peril for the *status quo* during the first fifty years of the twentieth century.[199] The 1920 US census did not include questions regarding religion. It is known, however, that Louisiana was solidly Christian, with similar numbers of Catholics and Protestants,[200] with the south of the state being more Catholic and north more Protestant. Society was marked by segregation. At that time, Jim Crow laws resulted in a systematic segregation of Black citizens, in Louisiana and across the US.[201] Huey Pierce Long, Jr., who was state governor and US senator in the 1920s and 1930s, took the stage at a time when class conflicts were growing in Louisiana.[202] He developed an egalitarian depression-era "Share Our Wealth"[203] campaign that concerned Franklin Delano Roosevelt in the prelude to the 1936 presidential election.[204] In that same decade, Louisiana introduced

193 Hargrave 1991, p. xxi.

194 Hargrave 1991, p. xxi.

195 Randall Lesaffer correctly indicated that "[…] in trying to reconstruct the historical meaning of a rule or dogma, the scholar should not to understand it not only within the setting of the legal system it pertained to, but also within its broad societal setting." (Lesaffer 2011, p. 149)

196 Grantham 2000, p. 62.

197 Sindler 1956, p. 19.

198 Sindler 1956, p. 21.

199 Becnel 2000, p. 575.

200 Sindler 1956, p. 31.

201 Billings 1993, p. 5.

202 Sindler 1956, p. 26.

203 The campaign was summarized by opponents as a "hillbilly's paradise—$5,000 capital endowment without work, a radio, washing machine, and automobile in every home." (Schlesinger 2001, p. 60)

204 Hockett 2005, p. 10, n. 26.

social security and unemployment compensation,[205] together with other federal programs aimed at the entire nation.[206]

5.3.4.2 Reception

Protection of private property, together with its limitations, was addressed in the three Louisiana constitutions of the turn of the century. Those three constitutions predated the *contagion* of constitutions that developed in other American Civil Law Jurisdictions. Two provisions illustrated the extent of the protection of private property within the 1898 and 1913 constitutions. Article 2, being part of the bill of rights, read that "No person shall be deprived of life, liberty or property, except by due process of law."[207] Article 167, being part of the general provisions of the constitution, read that "Private property shall not be taken nor damaged for public purposes without just and adequate compensation being first paid."[208] Those two articles, with the exact same wording and numbering, were repeated in the 1913 Constitution.[209] Changes took place with the adoption of the 1921 Constitution, where several public policy issues were addressed, yet where no changes were made in the structure of government.[210] On that occasion, the wording of the former articles 2 and 167 was merged into a single article, being placed within the bill of rights.[211] Accordingly, Section 2 of article I, being part of the bill of rights, read that: "No person shall be deprived of life, liberty or property, except by due process of law. Except as otherwise provided in this Constitution, private property shall not be taken or damaged except for public purposes and after just and adequate compensation is paid."[212] That merger of texts and new dominant position seemed to provide more visibility to the public interest or welfare of society. The privileged location within the bill of rights highlighted the acknowledgment of the interests of society.

The 1921 Constitution addressed other points that may be seen as showing the reception of the new paradigm. For example, Section 2 of article IV read that "mineral rights on any and all property sold by the State shall be reserved,"[213] enabling parallels with the text of the 1917 Mexican Constitution.

205 Sindler 1956, p. 130.
206 Some of the different programs are described in Field 2001, pp. 7–9.
207 Louisiana Constitution 1898, p. 5.
208 Louisiana Constitution 1898, p. 71.
209 Louisiana Constitution 1913, pp. 2, 56.
210 Hargrave 1991, p. 13.
211 See the chart at Powell 1954, p. 545.
212 Louisiana Constitution 1921, p. 1.
213 Louisiana Constitution 1921, p. 13. See also Hargrave 1991, p. 14.

Another example was provided by Sections 1 to 6 of article XVI, which stated for the first time in Louisiana that compensation was to be given to owners who had their property appropriated for the levees that regulated the water levels of rivers and lakes.[214] Also, for the first time in the history of the state, the local legislature was instructed to pass laws that would protect and conserve natural resources.[215] Finally, several important changes took place in education, and more state funds were allocated for schools from the property tax.[216]

5.3.4.3 Constitutional Proceedings

Even though the proceedings of the constitutional convention seem to include no references to the works of Duguit, nor to the terms *social function* or *social obligation*,[217] they assist in unveiling the extent to which the new paradigm may have been received. It is known, for example, that some lobbyists came also from organized labor to represent their interests.[218] In addition, the proceedings indicated, in one of the 500 ordinances passed,[219] that a Department of Housing was needed because committee members recognized "that the housing of population is a necessary [sic] of life, and is a fundamental factor in the social order and a matter of governmental concern."[220] There were also proposals to create an Office of Social Aid, where the head had to have served as US ambassador to a South American republic.[221] There was, furthermore, a petition by the Louisiana Farmers' Union and Louisiana Dairymen's Association for the convention to adopt a text as short and concise as possible that would enable understanding by the "common yeomanry."[222]

5.3.5 *Chile*

Chile also modified its constitution on numerous occasions, since the enactment of an early regulation for the executive authority in 1811.[223] The current

214 Hargrave 1991, p. 15.
215 Powell 1954, p. 479.
216 Powell 1954, p. 490.
217 See generally Proceedings Constitutional Convention Louisiana 1921.
218 Powell 1954, p. 471.
219 Powell 1954, p. 496.
220 See, for example, *Ordinance 482* by Ethelred Macaulay Stafford, at Proceedings Constitutional Convention Louisiana 1921, p. 731.
221 Powell 1954, p. 472.
222 Powell 1954, p. 469.
223 Muñoz León 2005, p. 247.
Chile adopted regulations in 1811, 1812, and 1814; a project of provisional constitution in 1818; a political constitution in 1822; two regulations in 1823; political constitutions in

Chilean Constitution dates from 1980, while its immediate predecessors date from 1833 and 1925. Several reforms were incorporated into those three texts, however.[224] Two of those reforms, which took place in 1963 and in 1967, incorporated elements of land reform.[225] The first by allowing expropriation of property that was abandoned or not subject to adequate exploitation, while the second by replacing the wording of paragraph 10 of article 10 of the Constitution–which referred to *social function*–and by paving the way for the implementation of Law 16640 on land reform.[226]

5.3.5.1 Social Context

Depicting some aspects of Chilean society during the early twentieth century may help explain the changes in the constitutions of the republic.[227] For example, there were some agrarian and labor protests[228] already at the beginning of the century, which were seen as a threat by part of the large landholders.[229] The 1920 Chilean census indicated that 95.8% of inhabitants in Chile were Catholics;[230] followed by Protestants, who represented 1.44% of the population.[231] In the political arena, President Arturo Fortunato Alessandri Palma had gone into exile in Italy, as a result of a *coup d'état*, and returned to Chile in 1925.[232] He then called for a plebiscite in which the inhabitants opted for a presidential system, departing from the parliamentary system that had applied in Chile since 1891.[233] In 1928, during the presidency of Carlos Ibañez del Campo, one of the first steps was taken towards socializing property, with the creation of the Fund for Agricultural Colonization (*Caja de Colonización Agrícola*).[234] Pursuant to a later law,[235] that Fund aimed to break down large

1823 and 1828; and political constitutions in 1833, 1925, and 1980. See generally Carrasco Delgado 2002.

See also the repository of primary sources available at Textos Constitucionales Chilenos 2015.

224 Muñoz León 2005, pp. 263–269; and Carrasco Delgado 2006, p. 322.

225 Muñoz León 2005, p. 269.

226 Muñoz León 2005, p. 269. See generally 5.5.3 of this book.

227 For a comprehensive view of Chile during the turn of the century and until the 1930s, see Blakemore 1998.

228 Mirow 2011, p. 1187.

229 González Terán 2010, p. 79.

230 Censo 1920, p. 575.

231 Censo 1920, p. 573.

232 Muñoz León 2005, p. 266.

233 Muñoz León 2005, pp. 266–267.

234 Brahm García 2012, p. 250; and Claro Solar 1979, pp. 406–408.

235 See Ley 5604 (1935).

landholdings, transforming them into medium and small tracts, aiming, therefore, to increase the number of landholders.[236] Property in Chile then started to experience a long socializing process that also regarded European models.[237] That socializing process experienced a peak that jeopardized private property during the presidency of Salvador Guillermo Allende Gossens (1970–1973).[238]

5.3.5.2 Reception

Protection of private property, together with its limitations, was addressed in the 1925 Constitution. That text resulted from the *contagion* of social constitutions that took place after the Mexican and Weimar enactments.[239] It may have found inspiration in the latter,[240] though most probably it found inspiration in the writings of Duguit.[241] The Chilean text dealt with property and its limitations in paragraph 10 of article 10, which assured:

> The inviolability of all property without any distinction.
>
> No one may be deprived of the property of his dominion, or any part thereof, or of the right to which he has, unless by virtue of judicial sentence or of expropriation for reason of public utility, described by law. In this case, prior indemnification shall be paid to the owner that he agrees to or that is determined by corresponding judgment.
>
> The exercise of the right of property is subject to the limitations or rules that the maintenance of the progress of the social order require, and in this sense, law may impose on it obligations or servitudes of public utility in favor of the general interests of the State, of the health of citizens and of the public well-being.[242]

---

236 Durán Bernales 1966, p. 329.

237 Brahm García 1999, p. 349; and Brahm García 2012, p. 254.

238 Brahm García 1999, p. 349.

239 Cordero Quinzacara 2006, p. 131.

240 Durán Bernales 1966, p. 166.

241 Mirow 2011, pp. 1183–1184.

242 English translation extracted from Mirow 2011, p. 1205.
The original text in Spanish read:
"La inviolabilidad de todas las propiedades, sin distinción alguna.
Nadie puede ser privado de la de su dominio, ni de una parte de ella, o del derecho que a ella tuviere, sino en virtud de sentencia judicial o de expropiación por razón de utilidad pública, calificada por una ley. En este caso, se dará previamente al dueño la indemnización que se ajuste con él o que se determine en el juicio correspondiente.
El ejercicio del derecho de propiedad está sometido a las limitaciones o reglas que exijan el mantenimiento y el progreso del orden social, y, en tal sentido, podrá la ley

Therefore, the 1925 text preserved–for the first part–the liberal wording of the 1833 Constitution, and later welcomed the new paradigm, yet without including specific references to the term *social function*.[243] The already mentioned reform of 1967, implemented by Law 16615, included the specific reference to *social function* in that part of the Constitution.[244] The new paragraph 10 of article 10 read in its relevant part that:

> [...] the law will establish the means of acquiring, using, enjoying and disposing of property, and the limitations and obligations that assure its social function and make it accessible to all. The social function of property includes all that is required by the general interest of the State, the public use and well-being, the better use of sources and production energies for the collective service, and the improvement of life conditions of all inhabitants [...].[245]

imponerle obligaciones o servidumbres de utilidad pública en favor de los intereses generales del Estado, de la salud de los ciudadanos y de la salubridad pública; [...]." (Constitución Chile 1925, p. 10)

243 See also Mirow 2011, p. 1205.

244 See Ley 16615 (1967). See also Cordero Quinzacara 2006, pp. 130–131.
Matthew Mirow indicated that the term was added only in 1976, at the time of Augusto Pinochet. See Mirow 2011, pp. 1212–1213.

245 The entire text in Spanish read:
"El derecho de propiedad en sus diversas especies.
La ley establecerá el modo de adquirir la propiedad, de usar, gozar y disponer de ella y las limitaciones y obligaciones que permitan asegurar su función social y hacerla accesible a todos. La función social de la propiedad comprende cuanto exijan los intereses generales del Estado, la utilidad y salubridad públicas, el mejor aprovechamiento de las fuentes y energías productivas en el servicio de la colectividad y la elevación de las condiciones de vida del común de los habitantes.
Cuando el interés de la comunidad nacional lo exijan, la ley podrá reservar al Estado el dominio exclusivo de recursos naturales, bienes de producción u otros, que declare de importancia preeminente para la vida económica, social o cultural del país. Propenderá, asimismo, a la conveniente distribución de la propiedad y a la constitución de la propiedad familiar.
Nadie puede ser privado de su propiedad sino en virtud de ley general o especial que autorice la expropiación por causa de utilidad pública o interés social, calificada por el legislador. El expropiado tendrá siempre derecho a indemnización cuyo monto y condiciones de pago se determinarán equitativamente tomando en consideración los intereses de la colectividad y de los expropiados. La ley determinará las normas para fijar la indemnización, el tribunal que conozca de las reclamaciones sobre su monto, el que en todo caso fallará conforme a derecho, la forma de extinguir esta obligación, y las oportunidades y modo en que el expropiador tomará posesión material del bien expropiado.

The 1925 Constitution included other provisions that may also indicate the presence of the Social Function paradigm in Chile.[246] For example, paragraph 7 of article 10 highlighted the importance of providing education.[247] This importance was addressed in the 1833 Constitution, though it was dispersed in articles 153 and 154.[248] That new paragraph even made primary education mandatory. Another example is provided by paragraph 14 of article 10 of the 1925 Constitution, which stated a succession of social concerns.[249] Accordingly, the 1925 text had to assure protection of work, industry, and social security. The aim was mainly to provide healthy habitation and economic conditions for life. Homestead (*propiedad familiar* or *bien de familia*) was likewise introduced in Chile. Furthermore, the state had to safeguard the public health and the hygienic well-being of the country, while funds should be allotted towards the operation of a National Health Service.[250]

5.3.5.3 Constitutional Proceedings

The proceedings of the reform commission referred extensively to the social function of property. Most members of the study sub-committee believed that certainty on the right of property affected the economy of the country.[251] Mirow indicated in a study that the constitutional understanding of property

---

Cuando se trate de expropiación de predios rústicos, la indemnización será equivalente al avalúo vigente para los efectos de la contribución territorial, más el valor de las mejoras que no estuvieren comprendidas en dicho avalúo, y podrá pagarse con una parte al contado y el saldo en cuotas en un plazo no superior a treinta años todo ello en la forma y condiciones que la ley determine.

La ley podrá reservar al dominio nacional de uso público todas las aguas existentes en el territorio nacional y expropiar, para incorporarlas a dicho dominio, las que sean de propiedad particular. En este caso, los dueños de las aguas expropiadas continuarán usándolas en calidad de concesionarios de un derecho de aprovechamiento y sólo tendrán derecho a la indemnización cuando, por la extinción total o parcial de ese derecho, sean efectivamente privados del agua suficiente para satisfacer, mediante un uso racional y beneficioso, las mismas necesidades que satisfacían con anterioridad a la extinción.

La pequeña propiedad rústica trabajada por su dueño y la vivienda habitada por su propietario no podrán ser expropiadas sin previo pago de indemnización." (Ley 16615 (1967))

246 To see more on the reception of the new paradigm, yet in the 1980 Constitution, see Ríos Álvarez 2010, p. 124.

247 Constitución Chile 1925, p. 9.

248 Constitución Chile 1833, pp. 43–44.

249 Constitución Chile 1925, pp. 10–11.

250 Constitución Chile 1925, pp. 10–11.

251 González Terán 2010, p. 77.

was at the heart of the debates.[252] He pointed out that during the debates, President Alessandri Palma even used the words of Duguit, when he claimed that "the concept of property as a subjective right disappears, to be replaced by the concept of property as a social function."[253] According to the acts of the reform commission, Alessandri Palma used the words of Duguit to "somehow dissipate the fears that some experience when property law is addressed."[254] Radicals welcomed the social function and Conservatives were reluctant to change, while other members aimed for a compromise in Chile. For example, a representative of the first group, José Guillermo Guerra, charged against the *latifundios*, and also claimed that the new conception of property should speak of it as being a social function.[255] Representatives from the second group, Romualdo Silva Cortés and Francisco Vidal Garcés, indicated that compensation would proceed in "[…] very limited cases when referring to a measure of particular character, that would imply an almost absolute depravation of the enjoyment, and in that case falling within expropriation […]."[256] The acts of the reform commission also indicated references to legislative texts of other jurisdictions, such as Argentina, showing a pollination of ideas across the continent.[257] It cannot be denied that the new paradigm was present in Chilean constitutionalism, experiencing an early start, and linking ideas developed both in Europe and in the Americas.

5.3.6 *Argentina*

Argentina modified the text of its constitution on several occasions,[258] since the enactment of a first federal constitution in 1853.[259] The current Argentine

252 Mirow 2011, p. 1189

253 Mirow 2011, pp. 1183, 1200–1202.

254 The text in Spanish read: "Para ir disipando un poco los temores que algunos sienten cuando se trata del derecho de propiedad […]." (Actas Oficiales Proyecto Constitución 1925, p. 114) See also Mirow 2011, p. 1201.

255 Mirow 2011, p. 1195.

256 The text in Spanish read: "[…] casos muy limitados y cuando se refiriera a una medida de carácter particular, que importara una privación casi absoluta del goce y que en tal caso ello tendría el alcance de una expropiación que estaría sujeta a indemnización." (Actas Oficiales Proyecto Constitución 1925, p. 136) See also Alessandri Rodríguez *et al.* 2010, p. 50.

257 See, for example, the reference to a law of the Argentine province of Entre Ríos, available at Actas Oficiales Proyecto Constitución 1925, p. 102.

258 See generally Parise 2008a.

259 Earlier texts had been adopted in 1819 and 1826. For the period before 1853, see generally Levaggi 2005a; and Ruíz Moreno 1976.

Constitution dates from 1994, and a series of texts preceded it.[260] For example, in 1949, during the presidency of Juan Domingo Perón, a reform to the constitutional text was implemented, incorporating tenets of the Social Function paradigm that had developed during the first half of that century.[261] That reform was short-lived, being overruled in 1956,[262] when the constitutional text was traced back to the pre-1949 version. In 1957, however, a constitutional reform incorporated article 14bis,[263] which still today encapsulates the main tenets of social rights. The 1957 constitutional reform therefore prevailed in reestablishing some elements of social constitutionalism that had been eliminated when the 1949 Constitutional reform of Perón was abrogated,[264] yet not including explicit references to the term *social function*.

5.3.6.1 Social Context[265]

Early twentieth century Argentine society may help explain the changes in the constitutions.[266] For example, the 1895 Argentine census indicated that

260 For example, the *de facto* regimes introduced changes to the text in 1966, 1972, and 1976. Burgos 2001, p. 72 *et seq*.

261 Burgos 2001, p. 72 *et seq*.

262 See Proclama 1956, p. 2; and Burgos 2001, p. 72 *et seq*.

263 The text of article 14bis of the Argentine Constitution in an English translation read:

"Labor in its several forms shall be protected by law, which shall ensure to workers: dignified and equitable working conditions; limited working hours; paid rest and vacations; fair remuneration; minimum vital and adjustable wage; equal pay for equal work; participation in the profits of enterprises, with control of production and collaboration in the management; protection against arbitrary dismissal; stability of the civil servant; free and democratic labor union organizations recognized by the mere registration in a special record. Trade unions are hereby guaranteed: the right to enter into collective labor bargains; to resort to conciliation and arbitration; the right to strike. Union representatives shall have the guarantees necessary for carrying out their union tasks and those related to the stability of their employment. The State shall grant the benefits of social security, which shall be of an integral nature and may not be waived. In particular, the laws shall establish: compulsory social insurance, which shall be in charge of national or provincial entities with financial and economic autonomy, administered by the interested parties with State participation, with no overlapping of contributions; adjustable retirements and pensions; full family protection; protection of homestead; family allowances and access to a worthy housing." (Constitución Argentina 1994)

264 Sabsay 2011, p. 339; and Gelli 2004, p. 116.

265 See generally Marotta & Parise 2014, pp. 252–253.

266 For a comprehensive view on Argentina during the turn of the century and until the 1930s, see Cortés Conde 1998; and Gallo 1998.

the country had 4.1 million inhabitants,[267] of which 24.5% were foreigners,[268] mainly migrants from Europe (*v.gr.*, France, Italy, and Spain).[269] The period 1901–1910, alone, resulted in the arrival of 1.1 million permanent immigrants.[270] No other American Civil Law Jurisdiction received more immigrants than Argentina.[271] In addition, the same census indicated that "991 out of 1000 are Catholics, seven are Protestant, and two are Israelites."[272] Early twentieth-century industrialization resulted in new interaction amongst actors, many of them being immigrant workers from Europe.[273] That new interaction lacked economic and normative frameworks, and eventually triggered social unrest and strikes.[274] Those movements pursued social justice, and motivated the creation of labor unions–some of Catholic[275] origin–and reform programs, also linked with the international discourse.[276] The living and working standards of that new urban proletariat were very similar to those experienced in Europe.[277] This new scenario motivated changes in legislation, with some lawmakers looking at European models and others neglecting their use.[278] Legislative changes took place, for example, with the enactment of Law 4144 on residence in 1902.[279] That law enabled the expulsion of foreigners who undertook activities that could be considered dangerous for national security and public order.[280] In the political arena, a series of *coups d'état* took place, and the presidencies of the charismatic leader Perón–who may resemble Long in Louisiana[281]–brought several changes to property law.[282]

267 A total of 4,094,911 inhabitants. See Censo 1895, p. cxlix.
268 A total of 1,004,527 inhabitants. See Censo 1895, p. cliii.
269 Corro 1979, pp. 81–82.
270 Miller 1997, p. 1541.
271 Castro 1991, p. 4. See also the relevant statistics in Castro 1991, p. 267.
272 See Censo 1895, p. cxxii.
273 Pérez Vichich 2004, p. 140. See also Aspell 1979, p. 12.
274 Pérez Vichich 2004, p. 140.
275 Levaggi 2013a, p. 273.
276 Levaggi 2006, p. 30.
277 Levaggi 2013a, p. 273.
278 Polotto 2012, p. 326.
279 Ley 4144 (1902). See Pérez Vichich 2004, p. 140; and Giorlandini 1986, p. 8.
On the origins of Law 4144 and on the comparative law context at the time of its enactment, see Aspell 1979, p. 54 *et seq.*
280 Pérez Vichich 2004, p. 140.
281 Schlesinger 2001, p. 64.
282 For that early period, see Rock 1987, pp. 214–320.

5.3.6.2 Reception

The *contagion* of social constitutions reached Argentina during the first half of the twentieth century. The social doctrine of the Church,[283] together with the ideas of authors such as Duguit, prevailed in the constitutional text adopted at the national level in 1949. Protection of private property, together with its limitations, was therefore addressed in the 1949 Constitution.[284] According to article 26 of the new constitutional text, all inhabitants should enjoy the right to dispose of their property. That wording was preserved almost intact from article 14 of 1853.[285] In addition, and to fully introduce the new paradigm, the new constitution dedicated an entire fourth chapter to the social function of property.[286] Article 38, being part of that chapter, read that:

> Private property has a social function and therefore is subject to the obligations towards common good established by law. The State must control the distribution and use of farmland or intervene in order to develop and enhance their productivity in the interest of the community, and ensure to all farmers or farmer-families the opportunity to become owners of the land they cultivate. Expropriation for reasons of public utility or general interest must be authorized by law and compensated. Only Congress imposes the taxes mentioned in article 4 [of this constitution]. Every author or inventor is exclusive owner of his work, invention or discovery for the term provided by law. Confiscation of property is abolished forever from Argentine legislation. No armed group can make requisitions or require assistance of any kind during time of peace.[287]

283 Ramella 2007, p. 320.

284 Giannoni 2010, pp. 284–288.

285 Ramella 2007, p. 302.

286 The chapter comprised articles 38–40.

287 Article 38 in Spanish read: "La propiedad privada tiene una función social y, en consecuencia, estará sometida a las obligaciones que establezca la ley con fines de bien común. Incumbe al Estado fiscalizar la distribución y la utilización del campo e intervenir con el objeto de desarrollar e incrementar su rendimiento en interés de la comunidad, y procurar a cada labriego o familia labriega la posibilidad de convertirse en propietario de la tierra que cultiva. La expropiación por causa de utilidad pública o interés general debe ser calificada por ley y previamente indemnizada. Sólo el Congreso impone las contribuciones que se expresan en el artículo 4°. Todo autor o inventor es propietario exclusivo de su obra, invención o descubrimiento por el término que le acuerda la ley. La confiscación de bienes queda abolida para siempre de la legislación argentina. Ningún cuerpo armado puede hacer requisiciones ni exigir auxilios de ninguna especie en tiempo de paz." (Constitución Argentina 1949, pp. 15–16)

The final part of article 38 somehow preserved the wording of article 17 of the 1853 Constitution.[288] Accordingly, the main changes were placed in the opening statement of article 38, even using the term *social function*. It should be noted that parts of that *social* wording also resembled that of the Mexican Constitution. Even though the current Argentine Constitution no longer refers to the social function of property, some Argentine provinces, following the 1949 example, adopted constitutions that explicitly refer to the social function of property. Examples are found in the provincial constitutions of Chubut (1957), La Pampa (1960), and Santa Fe (1962).[289]

The 1949 Constitution included other articles that indicated the presence of the new paradigm in Argentina.[290] For example, Chapter 4 was completed with articles 39 and 40. The first article referred to the use of capital as a means to improve social welfare and the economy of the nation;[291] while the second article, along similar lines as the Mexican and Louisiana constitutions, stated, amongst other things, that mineral rights should be owned by the state. That same article indicated that the use and organization of wealth would aim towards the well-being of the people.[292] Paragraph 16 of article 68 provided an enumeration of duties of congress that would further develop the common good. That paragraph indicated, amongst other things, that congress should provide the means to achieve the prosperity of the country, together with the needed hygiene, morality, public health, and social assistance. It also stated that congress should provide the means to colonize lands owned by the state and lands made available as a result of extinguishing *latifundios*, fostering the development and exploitation of small agricultural landholdings.[293]

5.3.6.3 Constitutional Proceedings

The proceedings of the constitutional convention referred extensively to the new paradigm. There were references to the writings of Duguit, to the ongoing social constitutionalism, and to the social doctrine of the Church. For example, Arturo Sampay, being one of the members of the convention, stated that "private property–even when preserving its individual character–assumes

288 Ramella 2007, p. 303.

289 Mariani de Vidal 2004, p. 308.

290 Ramella 2007, p. 303.

291 Constitución Argentina 1949, p. 16.

292 Constitución Argentina 1949, p. 16.

293 Constitución Argentina 1949, pp. 21–22.

a double function: personal and social."[294] His words resembled the postulates of Duguit and of the social doctrine, and he even mentioned Aquinas.[295] Another member of the convention, Rodolfo G. Valenzuela, claimed that "it must be said, together with Duguit, that the State loses its Napoleonic conception, and adopts another that is broader, more flexible, more protective, and more humane."[296] Valenzuela also showed that there was a *contagion* of social constitutions, by mentioning several constitutional precedents available in other jurisdictions, both of Europe and of the Americas (*i.a.,* Weimar, 1919; Chile, 1925, Colombia, 1936; Bolivia, 1938).[297] A third example of the reception of the new paradigm within the debates of the convention is found in the reference to the encyclical *Rerum novarum* made by Oscar S. Martini.[298] It is therefore palpable that the new paradigm was present in the Argentine constitutional discourse.

5.4 Reception in Civil Codes

Civil codes also welcomed the new paradigm. Changes started in the constitutional arena, though they soon found their way into the provisions of civil codes. Societies had changed and new ideas on property law developed and were placed within the codes.[299] Those developments were not limited to property law, however. Kenneth L. Karst and Keith S. Rosenn, authors of a 1970s widely read text, shared this view when they stated that in Latin America–which may be here extended to American Civil Law Jurisdictions–most new wordings in civil codes included: "moderate social limitations on the use of private property, protection of the obviously weaker party in certain bargaining situations, workmen's compensation for injuries without regards to fault, and an expanded protection of the rights of illegitimate children and women."[300]

294 The original text in Spanish read: "[…] la propiedad privada—no obstante conservar su carácter individual—asume una doble función personal y social […]." (Convención Nacional Constituyente 1949, p. 278) See also Ramella 2007, p. 305.

295 Convención Nacional Constituyente 1949, p. 278.

296 The original text in Spanish read: "[…] corresponde decir con Duguit que el Estado pierde su forma napoleónica para adoptar otra más amplia, más flexible, más protectora y más humana […]." (Convención Nacional Constituyente 1949, p. 315) See also Ramella 2007, p. 309.

297 Convención Nacional Constituyente 1949, p. 324.

298 Convención Nacional Constituyente 1949, p. 516.

299 Mirow 2004, p. 196.

300 Karst & Rosenn 1975, p. 47; and Mirow 2004, p. 196.

5.4.1 *Momentum in Second-generation Civil Codes*

The new paradigm was present mainly in second-generation codes or in the reformed texts of first-generation codes. However, it should be noted that civil codes had started to lose their paramount place within private law during the first decades of the twentieth century. The central stage was now shared with special legislation.

The shift from first generation to second generation takes place by legislative revision, de-codification, or re-codification.[301] *Revision* is a legislative process that results in the amendment of the text of civil codes. These amendments in the text are always segmented and limited to autonomous areas of law. They never aim to substitute the generation code *in totum* by means of a wholesale replacement. In its moderate form, revision aims to introduce isolated changes that will ultimately result in a change of a particular provision, though not necessarily in the adoption of a new-generation code. For example, the introduction of changes in property law within the civil codes of American Civil Law Jurisdictions was many times achieved by means of revision.

De-codification is a legislative process that results in the altering of the effect and scope of the text of civil codes. Those alterations, however, are always included in codes that are not part of the civil code, but that affect its content. De-codification welcomed the enactment of *satellite* codes that made civil codes necessarily dependent on them. Such a process weakens the gravitation of civil codes, although it does not necessarily reach a new generational status. Agrarian reforms in American Civil Law Jurisdictions provided an example of de-codification.

Re-codification is a legislative process that results in the adoption of an entirely new civil code that replaces an existing civil code. New-generation codes are generally reached through re-codification, although a re-codification process does not necessarily result in a new-generation code. Intense revision may ultimately result in a completely new text, and therefore, qualify as re-codification. Conversely, re-codification can also take place even when intense revision did not precede it, and can happen when a new text replaces *in totum* an existing code. Some jurisdictions perceive re-codification as a drastic break from the past and opt instead for piecemeal alterations that ultimately result in new-generation codes.

301 This chapter adopted working definitions for each external element, aiming to clarify and simplify. The existing literature on the three elements, however, is copious. See, amongst many others, Bergel 2003; Crepeau 2000; Díez-Picazo y Ponce de León 1992; Glenn 1998; Irti 1979; McAuley 2003; and Rivera 2002.

American Civil Law Jurisdictions are divided between those having first-generation codes and those having second-generation codes.[302] The current scenario enables the grouping of jurisdictions in clusters. Not all jurisdictions are clear-cut examples of a particular generation, however. A group of jurisdictions resists the adoption of second-generation codes, though it can subsequently succumb to the adoption of a new code.[303] This resistance may be motivated because of veneration to the existing first-generation codes, which were *avant-garde* at the time of enactment.[304] The resistance of members of this group may also be motivated due to a lack of consensus on what steps should be followed at the time of alteration or because of a limitation in the allocation of the required resources.[305] Changes in the texts of the civil codes of this group have taken place. Jurisdictions that still preserve their first-generation codes were able to update the texts through revision and de-codification. Several decades ago, these jurisdictions began to feel a need to adopt second-generation codes. Even if their codes may be far from changing generation, they are currently undergoing a thorough revision or entering into a de-codification process, especially with regards to family law and the prevailing patriarchal systems. The civil codes of Louisiana, Chile, and Argentina were not immune to the needs for generation shift and offered resistance.[306] Another group of jurisdictions welcomed second-generation codes.[307] The texts of first-generation codes, however, had been updated through partial revisions and de-codification, and ultimately led to the adoption of texts with second-generation status. Many of these new texts incorporated social aspects of law,[308] and their sources were more eclectic. The typifying characteristic of these codes is that they were able to incorporate local elements that distinguished them from codes of other American Civil Law Jurisdictions, while distinguishing them from the texts of their previous generation codes.

302 See generally Marotta & Parise 2014, pp. 239–241.

303 Chile, Colombia, Dominican Republic, Ecuador, El Salvador, Haiti, Louisiana, and Uruguay. It should be noted that Argentina adopted in 2015 a Civil and Commercial Civil Code. See 5.4.5 of this book.

304 *v.gr.*, civil codes of Argentina and Chile.

For example, Julio Olavarría claimed that in Chile the code is not modified due to the prestige it has gained, having inspired other jurisdictions across the continent. See Carvajal Arenas 2006, p. 50.

305 *v.gr.*, Ecuador and Dominican Republic.

306 See generally 4.3.1, 4.3.2, and 4.3.3 of this book.

307 Bolivia, Costa Rica, Cuba, Guatemala, Honduras, Mexico, Nicaragua, Panama, Paraguay, Peru, Puerto Rico, and Venezuela.

308 *v.gr.*, civil code of Mexico, 1932.

As mentioned earlier, second-generation codes found a more mature society and were able to highlight their own identity.[309]

5.4.2 *Doctrine of Abuse of Rights*

The Social Function paradigm entered the new text of first- and second-generation codes mainly through the development and reception of the doctrine of abuse of rights (*abuso del derecho, abus de droit, Rechtsmissbrauch*). This can be succinctly explained by stating that "whoever abuses his legal rights should be held liable for the consequences of such abuse."[310] According to that conception, there are no absolute rights and the enjoyment of rights should be exercised according to the spirit of the law itself.[311] The new wording in civil codes did not welcome abuses and did not refer to the absolute character of property, but not being an absolute or rigid principle, and indeed being subject to limitations.[312] The theory eventually helped to abandon the Liberal paradigm that had been encapsulated in the wording of many civil codes, because, as Yiannopoulos clarified, "the doctrine of abuse of right[s], as applied to property relations, states that a landowner is responsible for certain intentional acts that exceed the social and economic purposes for which the law recognizes ownership in immovable property."[313]

Abuse of rights opened the door for the new paradigm, and was sensed early in France, towards the end of the nineteenth century,[314] though its origins could be traced back to Roman law.[315] The theory redeveloped together with the social movements and legal innovations that followed in the nineteenth and twentieth centuries,[316] and scholarly writing in France allowed its crystallization and eventual integration into French law.[317] Accordingly, the postulates of the doctrine were found in early French writings by, amongst others, Claude Bufnoir, Léobon Larombière, and Auguste Sourdat.[318] Louis Josserand, another representative of that doctrine–perhaps being the best exponent of it–indicated, when analyzing the abuse of rights doctrine within property law, that a "desire to harm others is in essence antisocial; [and] it never may

309 See generally 4.7 of this book.

310 Bolgár 1975, p. 1015.

311 Moisset de Espanés 2001, pp. 1–2.

312 Salvat 1962, pp. 16–17.

313 Yiannopoulos 1974, p. 198.

314 Ancel & Didry 2001, pp. 52–65.

315 Yiannopoulos 2004–2012, at § 3:17.

316 Ancel & Didry 2001, pp. 52–65.

317 Ancel & Didry 2001, pp. 52–65.

318 Alessandri Rodríguez *et al.* 2010, p. 75.

represent the purpose of any legal concept."[319] That doctrine–not defended by all scholars,[320] and challenged by, for example, Marcel Planiol–germinated within American universities, and eventually reached the lawmakers.[321] Abuse of rights was not circumscribed to property law, however.[322] It was also welcomed broadly in other areas of private law and in public law, even reaching public international law.[323]

Abuse of rights was welcomed by civil codes in Europe and in the Americas. Most modern codes that welcomed the doctrine referred to the social or economic purposes of the law.[324] In Europe, abuse of rights was present in, for example, the *Bürgerliches Gesetzbuch* and in the civil codes of Switzerland (1912), Italy (1942), Greece (1946), and Portugal (1967).[325] Codes in the Americas also welcomed the doctrine.[326] For example, the civil code of Mexico (1932) incorporated ideas of social progress and social solidarity, tending to eliminate the differences between rich and poor, employee and employer, and men and women.[327] That text further described property as a social function,[328] and followed the important changes implemented by the 1917 Constitution.[329]

There is harmony between the doctrine of abuse of rights and the Social Function paradigm.[330] That harmony is reflected in the case studies that follow, where the reception of the doctrine within the legal frameworks of Louisiana, Chile, and Argentina is analyzed.

---

319 The text in French read: "La volonté de préjudicier à autrui est antisociale par essence même; jamais elle ne saurait représenter la finalité d'un concept juridique quelconque." (Josserand 1905, p. 19)

320 Moisset de Espanés 2001, p. 1.

321 de Gasperi 1955, p. 229.

322 For example, the comparatist Frederick Parker Walton stated in a Louisiana journal in 1916 that the new theory had "[…] many applications in different branches of the law of which a good summary may be found in the supplement for the year 1915 to the *Nouveau Code Civil Annoté* of Dalloz." (Walton 1916, p. 103)

323 Alessandri Rodríguez *et al.* 2010, pp. 76–77.

324 Moisset de Espanés 2001, p. 9.

325 Alessandri Rodríguez *et al.* 2010, pp. 75–76; Salvat 1962, p. 16 (n. 23); and Legón 1942, p. 115.

326 See, for example, the references to the objection to the abuse of rights in the civil codes of Uruguay, Guatemala, and Peru in Alterini & López Cabana 1990, p. 1102.

327 Moréteau & Parise 2009, p. 1138.

328 Alessandri Rodríguez *et al.* 2010, pp. 75–76; and Ankersent & Ruppert 2006, p. 101.

329 Mirow 2004, p. 196.

330 Adrogué 1991, p. 123.

5.4.3 *Louisiana*

Louisiana never adopted a second-generation code. Codification of the civil law, however, continued developing well during the rest of the nineteenth century and all of the twentieth century. Three major and comprehensive revision efforts were undertaken in 1870, 1908, and since 1970 by the Louisiana State Law Institute.[331] The text of 1825, which was central to the chapter dealing with the reception of the Liberal paradigm in Louisiana, survived without significant alterations for approximately half a century.[332]

5.4.3.1 Evolution

A new social context developed after the end of the US Civil War (*v.gr.,* abolition of slavery).[333] The requirements of the legal community created a need for changes in the statutes that had been enacted during the first years of Louisiana statehood.[334] Faced with this scenario, in 1868, the local legislature ordered that a revision of the civil code should be undertaken,[335] and John Ray was appointed to undertake the task. The results of his work were adopted in March 1870 by the legislature.[336] The liberal provisions of articles 480 and 483 of the 1825 Louisiana Code were preserved in that revision work, yet with new numbering and with very few changes in their wording.[337] That text of 1870 also preserved three articles that limited the rights of owners, and that had existed in the Digest of 1808 and in the 1825 Louisiana Code,[338] yet that had

---

331 See Parise 2010a, pp. 21–29.

332 Moréteau & Parise 2009, p. 1116.

333 Moréteau & Parise 2009, p. 1116.

334 Parise 2010a, p. 21.

335 See Act for Revision 1868.

336 The complete title in English read: "An Act to amend and re-enact the Civil Code of the State of Louisiana, including, besides all other matters embraced in said Code, the several objects set forth in the Table of Contents here annexed and made part of this title." (Revised Louisiana Code 1870, p. iii)

337 Article 480 was renumbered to 488 and read: "Art. 488–[480].–Ownership is the right by which a thing belongs to some one in particular, to the exclusion of all other persons." (Ray 1869, p. 72)

Article 483 was renumbered to 491 and read:

"Art. 491–(483.)–Perfect ownership gives the right to use, to enjoy and to dispose of one's property in the most unlimited manner, provided it is not used in a way prohibited by laws or ordinances.

Persons who reside out of the State, cannot dispose of the property they possess here, in a manner different from that prescribed by its laws." (Ray 1869, p. 72)

338 Yiannopoulos 1974, pp. 201–202; and Yiannopoulos 1994, p. 1174.

no antecedent in the *Code Napoléon*.[339] The wording of those articles found its origins in the writings of Domat and in the *Siete Partidas* and the *Fuero Real*.[340] Article 667 stated that owners could not undertake works that deprived neighbors of the liberty of enjoying their rights or that caused damage.[341] Article 668, however, did allow inconveniences on neighbors, such as blocking some light due to elevated constructions.[342] Finally, article 669 explained that the degree of inconvenience or damages should be determined by customs or by police rules.[343] These three articles provided early exceptions to the absolute character of ownership, clearly abandoning an abusive exercise of the right of ownership that would result in damages to neighbors.[344]

The dawn of the twentieth century brought light to the need for a revision of the civil code in Louisiana.[345] Conditions had been altered, and the conceptual framework implemented in 1870 had proved to be analytically deficient on occasion.[346] Therefore, in 1908, the local legislature stated the need to revise the existing 1870 text.[347] R.E. Milling, W.O. Hart, and William N. Potts worked on

339 Yiannopoulos 1974, p. 201.

It is possible to trace all previous versions of the Louisiana articles in Yiannopoulos 2008, pp. 569–571.

340 Yiannopoulos 1974, pp. 201–202; Yiannopoulos 1994, p. 1175; and Vidaurrazaga (de) 1952, p. 525.

341 Article 667 read: "Although a proprietor may do with his estate whatever he pleases, still he cannot make any work on it, which may deprive his neighbor of the liberty of enjoying his own, or which may be the cause of any damage to him." (Ray 1869, p. 97)

342 Article 668 read:

"Although one be not at liberty to make any work by which his neighbor's buildings may be damaged, yet every one has the liberty of doing on his own ground whatsoever he pleases, although it should occasion some inconvenience to his neighbor.

Thus he who is not subject to any servitude originating from a particular agreement in that respect, may raise his house as high as he pleases, although by such elevation he should darken the lights of his neighbor's house, because this act occasions only an inconvenience, but not a real damage." (Ray 1869, p. 97)

343 Article 669 read: "If the works or materials for any manufactory or other operation, cause an inconvenience to those in the same or in the neighboring houses, by diffusing smoke or nauseous smell, and there be no servitude established by which they are regulated, their sufferance must be determined by the rules of the police, or the customs of the place." (Ray 1869, p. 97)

344 Barham 1976, p. 492.

345 Moréteau & Parise 2009, p. 1116.

346 Yiannopoulos 1977, p. 36; and Moréteau & Parise 2009, pp. 1116–1117.

347 Act for Revision 1908.

the project.[348] The Louisiana Bar Association originally favored that revision work, but after a study by an internal committee, decided not to recommend the proposals it included,[349] which were ultimately never adopted by the legislature.[350] That project preserved the liberal texts of articles 480 and 483 of the 1825 Louisiana Code, yet with new numbering and with a change regarding the limitation for out-of-state residents to dispose of immovable property.[351] The project also preserved, with one minor change, the three articles that limited the rights of owners (articles 667–669).[352]

The need for reform would quickly reach again the doors of the Louisiana legislature. At the federal level, for example, the US Supreme Court had demonstrated significant shifts in zoning laws in its 1926 decision in *Euclid*,[353] which limited the freedom of action of owners who could affect the stability of neighbors and the security of other owners.[354] At the state level, a series of enactments were made aiming to deal with economic and social necessities (*v.gr.*, Trusts Act, Private Works Act, and Chattel Mortgage Act).[355]

348 See generally Revised Louisiana Code 1910.

349 See Florence 1913, p. 349; and Morrison 1937, p. 221.

350 Hood 1958, p. 19.

351 Article 488 was renumbered to 500 and read: "Art. 500 [488] (480).–Ownership is the right by which a thing belongs to some one in particular, to the exclusion of all other persons." Revised Louisiana Code 1910, p. 80.

Article 491 was renumbered to 503 and read:

"Art. 503 [491] (483).–Perfect ownership gives the right to use, to enjoy, and to dispose of one's property in the most unlimited manner, provided it is not used in a way prohibited by laws or ordinances.

Persons who reside out of the State, cannot dispose of the *immovable* property they possess here, in a manner different from that prescribed by its laws." (Revised Louisiana Code 1910, p. 80)

352 Article 667 was renumbered to 680 and preserved the exact same wording.

Article 668 was renumbered to 681 and also preserved the same wording.

Article 669 was renumbered to 682 and read:

"Art. 682 [669] (665).–If the works or materials for any manufactory or other operation, cause an inconvenience to those in the same or in the neighboring houses, by diffusing smoke or nauseous smell, and there be no servitude established by which they are regulated, their sufferance must be determined by *the police regulations*, or the customs of the place." (Revised Louisiana Code 1910, pp. 106–107)

353 See Euclid 1926.

354 Shoked 2011, p. 91.

355 Yiannopoulos 1996, p. 217.

The new scenario motivated the local legislature to create the LSLI in 1938,[356] which should be the "official advisory law revision commission, law reform agency and legal research agency"[357] of Louisiana.[358] In 1948, facing the need to update the civil law, the legislature instructed the LSLI to prepare a comprehensive revision of the 1870 text.[359] The LSLI decided to undertake a revision of the civil code on a title-by-title basis,[360] which started in the 1970s,[361] and that is still ongoing today.[362] The sources of the revisions were diverse because they resulted from partial revisions undertaken by different reporters and researchers.[363] For example, the *exposé des motifs* of the revision of the titles on property law indicated that drafters studied and consulted the texts of the civil codes of, amongst others, Germany, France, and Greece.[364] The reporter for the property law revision, Yiannopoulos, stated in his widely read treatise that "modern legislation and judicial practice exhibit a distinct tendency towards limiting the intensity of ownership in the interest of all;" and, citing the writing of the previously mentioned Ely, defended that "developments tend to indicate that ownership in contemporary civil law systems is an *exclusive* rather than an *absolute* right, with two sides to it, one *individual* and the other *social*."[365]

5.4.3.2 Instrumentation

All of Book II of the civil code of Louisiana was revised by means of a succession of legislative acts, adopted in the period 1976–1979.[366] The 1970s projected revision for property law eliminated references to the absolute character of ownership in current article 477[367] (*n.b.*, this article replaced articles 480 and

---

356 Act Designating the LSLI 1938.

357 Act Designating the LSLI 1938, p. 430.

358 Even when some states (*v.gr*, New York, New Jersey) have law revision commissions, the LSLI has a clear charge and greater role than those commissions in sister states.

359 Act Instructing the LSLI 1948.

360 Litvinoff 2004, p. 135.

361 Crawford & Haymon 2008, p. 91.

362 See Crawford & Haymon 2008, pp. 91–92; and Moréteau & Parise 2009, pp. 1118–1119.

363 For further information on the entire revision process for property law see Yiannopoulos 1996, pp. 218–233.

364 Revision Book II Louisiana Code 1980, p. 3.

365 Yiannopoulos 2001, pp. 8–9.

366 Yiannopoulos 1988, p. 213.

367 The adopted text read: "Ownership is the right that confers on a person direct, immediate, and exclusive authority over a thing. The owner of a thing may use, enjoy, and dispose of it within the limits and under the conditions established by law." (Revision Book II Louisiana Code 1980, p. 59)

483 of the 1825 Louisiana Code, which had formerly encapsulated the Liberal paradigm).[368] Following the writings of Planiol, article 477 now indicated that ownership conferred an *exclusive* authority over a thing.[369] The revision work also included two articles that were ultimately not adopted by the legislature.[370] Those two articles directly addressed the abuse of rights. Projected article 661 expressly referred to abuse of rights,[371] while projected article 662 referred to the unreasonable use of property.[372] Their rejection by the legislature resulted in an innominate doctrine of abuse of rights, which in Louisiana is grounded in the Romanist tradition and in dispersed provisions of the code[373] (*v.gr.*, articles 667–669[374]).

Compare the abovementioned text with that of articles 480–483 of the 1825 civil code. See generally 4.5.1.2 of this book.

368 The concordance amongst articles was indicated in Concordance for the 1976–2008 Revisions, p. T.55.

369 Code Revision Supplement 1984, p. 437.

370 Yiannopoulos 1994, p. 1176.

371 Projected article 661 read:

"An act, activity, or work of a property owner that, under the circumstances existing when it is done, exceeds the normal exercise of the right of ownership constitutes an abuse of the right.

An abuse of the right of ownership that may cause damage to another or deprive him of the enjoyment of his property subjects the property owner to civil responsibility." (Yiannopoulos 1994, p. 1175)

372 Projected article 662 read:

"An unreasonable use of an estate that causes damage to property or excessive discomfort to persons of normal sensibilities by the diffusion of smoke, dust, vapor, noise, heat, vibrations, odors, and the like, may be enjoined. Damages may be recovered without regard to defendant's negligence.

Whether the use of an estate is unreasonable is determined in light of the nature of the neighborhood, governmental regulations, local customs, and the attending circumstance." (Yiannopoulos 1994, p. 1176)

373 Yiannopoulos 1994, p. 1176.

374 Athanasios N. Yiannopoulos differentiated articles 667 and 668 from article 669. In the first two articles, the doctrine of abuse of rights may serve as grounding for responsibility; while in the third article, the doctrine tends to be insufficient. Yiannopoulos 2004–2012, at § 3:17.

The texts of articles 667–669 read:

"Art. 667. Although a proprietor may do with his estate whatever he pleases, still he cannot make any work on it, which may deprive his neighbor of the liberty of enjoying his own, or which may be the cause of any damage to him. However, if the work he makes on his estate deprives his neighbor of enjoyment or causes damage to him, he is

The current text of the civil code is therefore a revision of the amendments incorporated in 1870, which were a revision of the 1825 Louisiana Code. It seems clear that Louisiana used revision as a way of preserving its Continental European heritage. As already mentioned, since the early 1800s, Louisiana has been an isolated "Civil Law island" partially surrounded by a "sea of Common Law."[375] This motivated Louisianans to opt for revision and de-codification, instead of re-codification, as a way of modernizing the text of their civil code, in order to match current standards and remain competitive with the other states of the Union. A re-codification might have been perceived as a complete and drastic break with the past and, therefore, a threat to a fragile collective identity.

5.4.4 *Chile*

Chile also never adopted a second-generation code. The Republic of Chile still applies the text of the civil code of 1857.[376] Several changes, however, have been incorporated into that text through revision[377] and de-codification.[378] Differently from Louisiana, no major and comprehensive revision efforts were

---

answerable for damages only upon a showing that he knew or, in the exercise of reasonable care, should have known that his works would cause damage, that the damage could have been prevented by the exercise of reasonable care, and that he failed to exercise such reasonable care. Nothing in this Article shall preclude the court from the application of the doctrine of res ipsa loquitur in an appropriate case. Nonetheless, the proprietor is answerable for damages without regard to his knowledge or his exercise of reasonable care, if the damage is caused by an ultrahazardous activity. An ultrahazardous activity as used in this Article is strictly limited to pile driving or blasting with explosives.

Art. 668. Although one be not at liberty to make any work by which his neighbor's buildings may be damaged, yet every one has the liberty of doing on his own ground whatsoever he pleases, although it should occasion some inconvenience to his neighbor.

Thus he who is not subject to any servitude originating from a particular agreement in that respect, may raise his house as high as he pleases, although by such elevation he should darken the lights of his neighbors's [neighbor's] house, because this act occasions only an inconvenience, but not a real damage.

Art. 669. If the works or materials for any manufactory or other operation, cause an inconvenience to those in the same or in the neighboring houses, by diffusing smoke or nauseous smell, and there be no servitude established by which they are regulated, their sufferance must be determined by the rules of the police, or the customs of the place."

(Civil Code Louisiana 2015)

375 Parise 2006b, p. 14.

376 See generally Guzmán Brito 1993.

377 Pescio Vargas 1978, pp. 94–115.

378 Guzmán Brito 2000, p. 54.

undertaken in Chile to change the civil code. At least since the 1990s, politicians and academics in Chile have worked on proposals for reform[379] that could evolve into re-codification. In addition, law schools and foundations began an ongoing process of study of the civil and commercial codes, possibly resulting in a unification of both codes.[380]

5.4.4.1 Evolution

Revision had an impact on the civil code. An important step was taken in 1884 with the enactment of the *secular laws* on civil marriage, civil registry, and cemeteries.[381] Revision increased since the 1930s,[382] when an intense reform movement started, triggered by the new social context that had developed. In the area of family law changes took place, for example, with the enactment of a law on adoption (1934)[383] and with the enactment of a law that altered filiation distinctions (1935).[384] In the area of property law changes took place, for example, with the enactment of a law on condominium (1937).[385] Changes continued in the 1940s, when, for example, civil death was removed from the Chilean Code (1943).[386]

Article 582 had imposed limitations on the right of ownership in the 1857 code. That article stated that the right should be enjoyed as long as it was not contrary to the law or to the rights of a third party.[387] Several changes were made to the text of that code, though not to that seminal article. Some scholars claimed, in the 1940s, that there was a need to change the civil code provisions dealing with property, to make them match current standards.[388] Other scholars, also in the 1940s, claimed that there was no need to change the wording of article 582. They understood that after almost 100 years the only difference was that there were more limitations on that right, and that limitations would continue developing.[389] Those changes had started to develop in the 1920s, with the appearance of the Social Function paradigm.[390] Even though the wording

379 Vaughn 1992–1993, p. 588.

380 See, for example, Guzmán Brito *et al.* 2000; and also Justicia Presentará Proyecto 2009.

381 Abelik Manasevich 2001, p. 74.

382 Alessandri Rodríguez 1948, p. 40.

383 Alessandri Rodríguez 1948, p. 40.

384 Alessandri Rodríguez 1948, p. 53.

385 Alessandri Rodríguez 1948, p. 40.

386 Alessandri Rodríguez 1948, p. 43.

387 See generally 4.5.2.2 of this book.

388 Alessandri Rodríguez 1948, p. 67.

389 Lira Urquieta 1944, p. 193.

390 Isler Soto 2011, pp. 74–75.

of the article was not changed, the scope and reach of the article were reduced by de-codification that transformed the exception into the rule.[391]

5.4.4.2 Instrumentation

Abuse of rights was not formally received by legislation in Chile.[392] Its presence could be perceived, however, in legislation that resulted from de-codification and in some isolated provisions of the civil code.[393] The abovementioned law on condominium (1937) did refer to an abusive exercise of rights in article 8.[394] That article stated, amongst other dispositions, that owners should not undertake acts that would disturb the tranquility of other owners or that would threaten the security of the building.[395] That law, currently overruled, was enacted to deal with the lack of housing and to enable the middle class to acquire individual dwellings.[396] Even when the doctrine of abuse of rights was not expressly mentioned in the civil code, abusive acts were not welcomed, for

391 Cordero Quinzacara 2006, p. 131.

392 Manríquez González 2011, p. 33.

393 Isler Soto 2011, p. 66.

394 Alessandri Rodríguez 1948, p. 65.

395 The text in Spanish read:

"Cada propietario usará de su piso o departamento en forma ordenada y tranquila. No podrá, en consecuencia, hacerlo servir a otros objetos que los convenidos en el reglamento de copropiedad, o a falta de éste, a aquellos a que el edificio está destinado o que deben presumirse de su naturaleza y ubicación o de la costumbre del lugar; ni ejecutar acto alguno que perturbe la tranquilidad de los demás propietarios o que comprometa la seguridad, solidez o salubridad del edificio.

Así, por ejemplo, no podrá establecer taller, fábrica o industria si el edificio se destina a la habitación; ni emplear su piso o departamento en objetos contrarios a la moral o a las buenas costumbres; ni arrendarlo a personas de notoria mala conducta; ni provocar ruidos o algazaras en las horas que ordinariamente se destinan al descanso; ni almacenar en su piso o departamento materias húmedas, infectas o inflamables que puedan dañar los otros pisos o departamentos.

Iguales restricciones regirán respecto del arrendatario y demás personas a quienes el propietario conceda el uso o el goce de su piso o departamento.

El juez, a petición del administrador del edificio o de cualquier propietario, podrá aplicar al infractor arresto hasta de quince días o multa de ciento a cinco mil pesos, y repetir estas medidas hasta que cese la infracción. Todo lo cual se entenderá sin perjuicio de las indemnizaciones que en derecho correspondan.

La reclamación se sustanciará breve y sumariamente, pudiendo el juez apreciar la prueba en conciencia." (Ley 6071 (1937))

396 Alessandri Rodríguez 1948, p. 65.

example, in article 945 of the civil code,[397] which is currently part of the Code of Waters.[398] That article stated that owners could dig wells on their property, though if the wells did not generate benefits or if the benefits could not outweigh the damages made to others, the wells should be closed.[399] The abuse of rights would not proceed when the exercise of the right was protected by law in Chile.[400] Accordingly, a neighbor could request, for example, that branches be cut from a tree (article 942).[401] Neighboring provisions within the civil code also dealt with a use of rights that could be deemed abusive. Accordingly, furnaces should comply with ordinances (article 856),[402] running water could be diverted away from nearby walls (article 941),[403] and works that polluted the

397 Isler Soto 2011, p. 66.

398 Isler Soto 2011, p. 66.

399 Article 945 in Spanish read: "Cualquiera puede cavar en suelo propio un pozo, aunque de ello resulte menoscabarse el agua de que se alimenta otro pozo; pero si de ello no reportare utilidad alguna, o no tanta que pueda compararse con el perjuicio ajeno, será obligado a cegarlo." (Código Civil Chile 1857, p. 238)

Compare that text with the note to article 2514 of the Argentine Code. See generally 4.5.3.2 of this book.

400 Alessandri Rodríguez *et al.* 2010, p. 82.

401 Article 942 in Spanish read:

"Si un árbol estiende sus ramas sobre suelo ajeno, o penetra en él con sus raices, podrá el dueño del suelo exijir que se corte la parte escedente de las ramas, i cortar él mismo las raices.

Lo cual se entiende aun cuando el árbol esté plantado a la distancia debida." (Código Civil Chile 1857, pp. 237–238)

See also Alessandri Rodríguez *et al.* 2010, p. 82.

402 Article 856 in Spanish read: "Si se trata de pozos, letrinas, caballerizas, chimeneas, hogares, fraguas, hornos u otras obras de que pueda resultar daño a los edificios o heredades vecinas, deberán observarse las reglas prescritas por las ordenanzas jenerales o locales, ora sea medianera o no la pared divisoria. Lo mismo se aplica a los depósitos de pólvora, de materias húmedas o infectas, i de todo lo que pueda dañar a la solidez, seguridad i salubridad de los edificios." (Código Civil Chile 1857, p. 215)

See also Alessandri Rodríguez *et al.* 2010, p. 103.

403 Article 941 in Spanish read:

"El dueño de una casa tiene derecho para impedir que cerca de sus paredes haya depósitos o corrientes de agua, o materias húmedas que puedan dañarla.

Tiene asimismo derecho para impedir que se planten árboles a ménos distancia que la de quince decímetros, ni hortalizas o flores a ménos distancia que la de cinco decímetros.

Si los árboles fueren de aquellos que estienden a gran distancia sus raices, podrá el juez ordenar que se planten a la que convenga para que no dañen a los edificios vecinos: el máximum de la distancia señalada por el juez será de cinco metros.

air or generated damages were not subject to prescription (article 937).[404] Yet the code, understandably, did not address all possible scenarios. Accordingly, abuse of rights could be claimed by means of article 2314, which requested compensation for a delict or cuasi-delict done to another.[405] That provision was not drafted as a consequence of the abuse of rights doctrine,[406] but could apply to different situations.

The current text of the civil code therefore includes the amendments made by revisions and by the enactment of special laws. The wording of the civil code in Chile still represents the tenets of the Liberal paradigm, yet the interplay with other legal provisions and the social context indicates that the civil code must be interpreted through a new lens, the lens of the Social Function paradigm. The first-generation code in Chile, drafted by Bello, may be subject to veneration, having been *avant-garde* at the time of enactment, and still generating resistance to be replaced. Several decades ago, nonetheless, Chile began to feel a need to adopt a second-generation code, and that stage is still to be reached.

5.4.5 *Argentina*

The Argentine Code was never replaced during the period subject to study. A civil and commercial code took effect in Argentina only on August 1, 2015,[407]

Los derechos concedidos en este artículo subsistirán contra los árboles, flores u hortalizas plantadas, a ménos que la plantacion haya precedido a la construccion de las paredes." (Código Civil Chile 1857, p. 237)

See also Alessandri Rodríguez *et al.* 2010, p. 103.

404 Article 937 in Spanish read:

"Lo dispuesto en el artículo precedente se aplica no solo a las obras nuevas, sino a las ya hechas, miéntras no haya trascurrido tiempo bastante para construir un derecho de servidumbre.

Pero ninguna prescripción se admitirá contra las obras que corrompan el aire i lo hagan conocidamente dañoso." (Código Civil Chile 1857, p. 236)

See also Alessandri Rodríguez *et al.* 2010, p. 103.

405 Article 2314 in Spanish read: "El que ha cometido un delito o cuasidelito que ha inferido daño a otro, es obligado a la indemnizacion; sin perjuicio de la pena que le impongan las leyes por el delito o cuasidelito." Código Civil Chile 1857, p. 582. See also Alessandri Rodríguez *et al.* 2010, p. 82.

406 Alessandri Rodríguez *et al.* 2010, p. 82.

407 Código Civil y Comercial Argentina 2015. The new text took effect after the submission of the PhD manuscript of this author in 2015, yet references could be included in this book.

hence replacing the Argentine Code.[408] Even though Argentina did not enact a new civil code in the period subject to study, the 1871 text was subject to many alterations.[409] Changes were introduced mainly through revision. Differently from Chile, but along similar lines as Louisiana, several major and comprehensive revision efforts were undertaken in Argentina to alter the text of the civil code. Three of those revision efforts were undertaken in 1936, 1954, and 1968, and are of interest for this chapter because they paved the way for the formal reception of the doctrine of abuse of rights within the Argentine Code.[410] That doctrine was present in the Argentine academic debates, already at the turn of the century. For example, in 1895 judge César D. Corvalán supported the doctrine and stated that even when ownership was based on personality, it should also fulfill a social mission, and that the public and immoral abuse of goods had been condemned by all civilized nations.[411]

5.4.5.1 Evolution[412]

The text of the civil code was subject to several partial revisions beginning in 1871. Similarly to Chile, *secular laws* were enacted in the 1880s. Accordingly, a law on civil marriage was adopted in 1888,[413] together with laws on civil registry that were adopted in 1884 and 1898.[414] The first decades of the new century also brought new legislation that affected the civil code. For example, the national congress adopted a law on agricultural leases in 1921[415] and a law on the rights of women in 1926.[416] Most partial reforms, however, dealt with specific areas of the civil code[417] and lacked a comprehensive approach.

At the dawn of the twentieth century, scholarly writings indicated a need to harmonize the civil code with the new context.[418] Accordingly, a first major and comprehensive revision effort was started in 1926. In July of that year,

408 Marotta & Parise 2014, p. 269.

409 Llambías 1975, pp. 199–203.

410 More recent efforts were undertaken since the 1980s. For example, drafts of civil codes were completed in 1987, 1992, 1993, 1998, and 2012. Medina 2013, p. 58.
About some of those drafts, see, amongst others, Rivera 2001; and the different approaches in Brebbia 2001.

411 Levaggi 2007, p. 130.

412 See generally Marotta & Parise 2014, pp. 243–245.

413 Cháneton 1937, p. 335.

414 Cháneton 1937, p. 336.

415 Cháneton 1937, p. 335.

416 Cháneton 1937, p. 336.

417 Levaggi 1987, p. 271.

418 Parise 2006a, p. 2.

a commission was created to draft a new civil code.[419] The codifying commission delegated to one of its members–Juan A. Bibiloni–the drafting of a pre-project of a civil code.[420] His work followed several principles of German legal science as captured by the *Bürgerliches Gesetzbuch*.[421] That pre-project did not welcome the doctrine of abuse of rights, even though the proceedings of the Civil Law Congress (*Congreso de Derecho Civil*) of that same year had condemned the absolute and individualistic character of ownership within the 1871 civil code,[422] a characteristic that Duguit had mentioned earlier in his Buenos Aires Lectures.[423] The proceedings of that same Congress also mentioned that the state should intervene to guarantee the social function of ownership.[424] Article 411 of the pre-project of Bibiloni, however, stated that rights should be exercised within the limits of the law, even if they were detrimental to third parties.[425] The work of Bibiloni preserved the text of articles 2513 and 2514 of the 1871 code, yet with new numbering (*i.e.*, 2384 and 2385).[426]

The pre-project of Bibiloni was revised by the commission, and Héctor Lafaille and Gastón Tobal undertook the final drafting of a project.[427] The project

419 Aftalión & García Olano 1939, p. 454.

A subsequent decree of July 16, 1926, appointed members. Through the ten years of its existence, the commission was composed of the following members: Juan A. Bibiloni, César de Tezanos Pinto, Mariano de Vedia y Mitre, José A. Gervasoni, Héctor Lafaille, Enrique Martínez Paz, Julián V. Pera, Juan Carlos Rébora, Roberto Repetto, Rodolfo Rivarola, Raymundo M. Salvat, and Gastón Federico Tobal. See Rébora 1937, p. 69.

420 See the outcome of that work in Bibiloni 1929–1932. See also Aftalión & García Olano 1939, p. 454.

421 Levaggi 1987, p. 272.

422 Cháneton 1937, p. 256.

423 Duguit 1912b, p. 150.

424 The statement in Spanish read:

"[…] el concepto individualista absoluto bajo el cual está organizada la institución del dominio en nuestro código civil debe ser sustituído por otro más amplio que concilie el interés social y el particular, garantizando el uso y goce de la propiedad mientras se mantenga en acción conforme a su destino. El estado debe intervenir para llenar la función social que le es propia." (Novillo Corvalán 1936, p. 62)

425 Article 411 in Spanish read: "Los derechos pueden ser ejercidos en la extensión de sus límites legales, aunque de ello resulte perjuicio a tercero." (Moisset de Espanés 2001, pp. 15–16)

426 Legón 1942, pp. 90–91.

427 Borda 1987, p. 148.

was completed in 1936, was notably brief, and was ultimately never adopted by the legislature.[428] Lafaille indicated that the commission had preferred to work with, amongst others, the Brazilian, Spanish, and Swiss civil codes, and had not excluded from their work the Chilean Code and the *Code Napoléon*.[429] The project welcomed the doctrine of abuse of rights, differently from its predecessor. The concrete applications of the doctrine were increased within the code, and the limitations for its application were removed.[430] Attempts were therefore made to modify the text of the proposed article 411 of the pre-project, yet it was ultimately eliminated from the draft.[431] In addition, the commission recommended the elimination of articles 2513 and 2514 of the 1871 text because they deemed them as representing an obsolete individualism.[432] In the words of the commission, "the social content that today emanates from the law explains the suppression [of those two articles]."[433] Social constitutionalism was also present in the work of the commission, as indicated by Lafaille, who even suggested following the tenets of the 1919 Weimer text.[434] Finally, the proceedings of the work of the commission indicated that some of its members advocated for the inclusion of an article that would specify that ownership should be exercised as if being a social function.[435]

Similarly to the developments in Chile, some Argentine scholars claimed, in the 1950s, that there was a need to change the civil code provisions dealing with property, to make them match current standards.[436] Within that scenario, a second major and comprehensive revision effort was started in 1950. It was undertaken by the Civil Law Institute (*Instituto de Derecho Civil*) of the Ministry of Justice (*Ministerio de Justicia*) of Argentina, under the leadership of

428 See Aftalión & García Olano 1939, p. 454; and Levaggi 1996b, p. 272.

429 Parise 2006a, p. 14.

430 Lafaille 1937, p. 26.

431 For example, one of the proposals recommended to add at the end of the article, "as long as there is no abuse on behalf of the agent" (*si no mediare abuso de parte del agente*). (Moisset de Espanés 2001, pp. 16–17)

432 Legón 1942, pp. 90–91.

433 The text in Spanish read: "El contenido social que hoy inspira el derecho, explica que hayamos suprimido los arts. 2513 y 2514 [...]." (Reforma Código Civil 1936, p. 151)

434 Legón 1942, pp. 90–91.

435 Allende 1967, p. 374.

The success of breaking with the Liberal paradigm was challenged by some scholars. For example, it was claimed in 1941 that the project did not fully represent the new trends. See Salas 1941, p. 41.

436 Ramella 2007, p. 308.

Jorge Joaquín Llambías.[437] The work resulted in a pre-project that welcomed the developments in the national jurisprudence, and was inspired by the codes of Italy, Peru, Switzerland, and Venezuela.[438] The pre-project was also brief, and was completed in 1954.[439] The work included an article that expressly welcomed the doctrine of abuse of rights. That article, numbered 235, read in part that "the law does not tolerate the abuse of rights" and that "the exercise of a right will be deemed abusive when it contradicts the requirements of good faith or the ends towards its recognition."[440] The extensive note to that article highlighted that the doctrine was *unequivocally* welcomed, and indicated a thorough review of foreign scholarly writings and legislation.[441] Another proposed article–numbered 236–circumscribed the limits of an abusive act, prescribing the limitations for acquiring active legal standing.[442] The note to that article cited the civil code of Peru as a source.[443] The proposals of the pre-project paved the way for the formal reception of the doctrine in the subsequent revision effort:[444] a reception that would indeed have an impact on the Ownership Paradigm.

437 Anteproyecto Código Civil 1954, p. 7. See also Levaggi 1987, p. 272.

438 Levaggi 1987, p. 272.

439 Levaggi 1987, p. 272.

440 Article 235 in Spanish read:

"La ley no tolera el abuso del derecho.

Se entenderá abusivo el ejercicio de un derecho, cuando contraríe las exigencias de la buena fe o los fines de su reconocimiento.

El ejercicio de los derechos que por su propia naturaleza o por una disposición legal, deban reputarse discrecionales, sólo será abusivo cuando tenga por fin exclusivo el perjuicio ajeno.

El daño proveniente del abuso será indemnizable." (Anteproyecto Código Civil 1954, p. 153)

See also Moisset de Espanés 2001, p. 18.

441 The note cited, amongst others, the following civil codes: BGB, arts. 226 and 826; Soviet Union, art. 1; Switzerland, art. 2; Turkey, art. 2; Uruguay, art. 1295; and Mexico, art. 1912. See Anteproyecto Código Civil 1954, pp. 153–155; and Moisset de Espanés 2001, p. 18.

442 Article 236 in Spanish read:

"Para ejercer o contestar una acción se requiere tener legítimo interés, económico o moral.

El interés moral sólo autoriza la acción cuando se refiere directamente al agente o su familia, salvo disposición expresa de la ley."

(Anteproyecto Código Civil 1954, p. 155)

See also Moisset de Espanés 2001, pp. 18–19.

443 Anteproyecto Código Civil 1954, p. 155.

444 Moisset de Espanés 2001, p. 19.

5.4.5.2 Instrumentation[445]

A third major and comprehensive revision effort was completed in 1968.[446] That effort, however, did not aim to achieve re-codification, and limited itself to achieving revision of 204 articles of the code.[447] The revision was significant, and enabled some scholars to speak of it as resulting in a *new civil code*.[448] The new texts were adopted by Law 17711,[449] and drafted by José F. Bidau, Abel M. Fleitas, and Roberto Martínez Ruiz, with the decisive participation of Guillermo Antonio Borda.[450] Their revision work introduced principles of social solidarity in a code that had been known as individualistic.[451] The 1968 revision introduced the doctrine of abuse of rights, mainly in three articles of the code (*i.e.*, 1071, 2513, and 2514).[452] Article 1071 clearly introduced the doctrine. In its previous wording it had defended that the exercise of one's rights could not turn any act illegal.[453] The new text, in radically different lines, rephrased the original wording and added a second paragraph indicating that: "the law does not protect the abusive exercise of rights. It will be deemed abusive the exercise that contradicts the aims that the law had when recognizing them or the exercise that exceeds the limits imposed by good faith, morals and good customs."[454] Borda reaffirmed his opposition to the Liberal paradigm also in other writings. For example, he stated in his widely-read treatise that in "Argentina, being inserted in the Christian civilization, ownership is the most complete and full right on a thing, yet it is not absolute."[455] Moreover, he claimed that the

445 See generally Marotta & Parise 2014, pp. 245–250.

446 Approved by Law 17711, dated April 22, 1968. See Borda 1987, p. 143.

447 See Valiente Noailles 1968, pp. 7–9; Borda 1971; and Garrido & Andorno 1971.

448 Medina 2013, p. 51.

449 Ley 17711 (1968).

450 Levaggi 1987, p. 271.

451 Levaggi 1987, p. 271.

452 Adrogué 1991, p. 119.

453 Article 1071 in Spanish read: "El ejercicio de un derecho propio, o el cumplimiento de una obligación legal no puede constituir como ilícito ningún acto." Código (Civil Argentina 1871, pp. 614–615)

454 Article 1071 in its new wording, in Spanish, read:

"El ejercicio regular de un derecho propio o el cumplimiento de una obligación legal no puede constituir como ilícito ningún acto.

La ley no ampara el ejercicio abusivo de los derechos. Se considerará tal al que contraríe los fines que aquélla tuvo en mira al reconocerlos o al que exceda los límites impuestos por la buena fe, la moral y las buenas costumbres." (Código Civil Argentina 2015)

455 That expression in Spanish read: "[Argentina], inserto en la civilización cristiana: la propiedad es el derecho más completo y pleno que se pueda tener sobra una cosa; pero no es absoluto." (Borda 2008, p. 217)

change in philosophy was mainly sensed in the alterations made to articles 2513 and 2514,[456] which simply wiped out the absolute character of ownership.[457] According to the new text of article 2513, owners should exercise their right in a regular way, and no longer be conferred the right to destroy the thing.[458] According to the new text of article 2514, that exercise should not be limited as long as it was not abusive.[459] Finally, Borda defended that exercising the right of ownership against the social function would be abusive.[460]

In Argentina–similarly to Louisiana and Chile–the text of the code included amendments made by revisions and by the enactment of special laws. The wording of the Argentine code incorporated the tenets of the Social Function paradigm. The first-generation code in Argentina, drafted by Vélez Sarsfield, may have been subject to veneration, having been *avant-garde* at the time of enactment, and had generated resistance to be replaced. However, Argentina–differently from Chile–undertook several attempts to adopt a second-generation code, which can be traced back to the first decades of the twentieth century.

5.5 Reception in Special Legislation

Jurisdictions incorporated the Social Function paradigm also within special legislation and new *satellite* codes. Those provisions developed outside civil codes and aimed to welcome the new paradigm. Special legislation pursued a shift in Ownership Paradigm. It helped depart from the liberal tenets of first-generation codes that, perhaps due to veneration to that first-generation text, were difficult to leave behind. A seminal example of special legislation is found in the land reform enactments that spread across American Civil

456 Borda 2008, p. 219.

457 Adrogué 1991, p. 123.

458 Article 2513 in Spanish read: "Es inherente a la propiedad el derecho de poseer la cosa, disponer o servirse de ella, usarla y gozarla conforme a un ejercicio regular." (Código Civil Argentina 2015) Compare with 4.5.3.2 of this book. See also Borda 2008, pp. 220, 222.

459 Article 2514 in Spanish read: "El ejercicio de estas facultades no puede ser restringido en tanto no fuere abusivo, aunque privare a terceros de ventajas o comodidades." (Código Civil Argentina 2015) Compare with 4.5.3.2 of this book. See also Borda 2008, p. 220.

460 The passage in Spanish read: "Se ha dicho ya que en el derecho moderno, la propiedad tiene una función social que cumplir. Por consiguiente, cada vez que el derecho de propiedad sea ejercido de una manera antisocial, es decir contraria a los derecho de la comunidad, ese ejercicio será abusivo y no tendrá el amparo de la ley [...]." (Borda 2008, p. 220)

Law Jurisdictions. Other examples are found in homestead enactments (*v.gr.*, Mexico, Venezuela) and in reforms to tenancy laws.[461] Special legislation contributed to creating a new *statu quo* or social dimension.[462] It introduced deep-rooted reforms to property law, transforming ownership into a right limited by the common well-being.[463] De-codification also paved the way for the incorporation of the new paradigm. Accordingly, the shift in paradigm was likewise included in *satellite* codes that were not part of civil codes, but that affected their contents. De-codification welcomed the enactment of *satellite* codes that made civil codes necessarily dependent on them. Seminal de-codification examples are the rural, labor, and family codes that were introduced during the twentieth century across many American Civil Law Jurisdictions.

5.5.1 *Land Reform*

Land-reform legislative enactments paved the way for the reception of the new paradigm in American Civil Law Jurisdictions. Land reform has been described in different ways, commonly referred to as agrarian reform,[464] and has no single meaning.[465] These reforms may be seen as historical processes that developed from hardly foreseeable political impulses, both internal and external.[466] The processes can be narrowly defined as means to provide land to inhabitants that possess none,[467] followed by a redistribution of land, tending to benefit small farmers and agricultural laborers.[468] The redistribution of land is from the landowning elite to those who have none or little access to land.[469] Yet, land reform may also be considered an element for social change that aims to eliminate rigid social structures, where actors within those contexts trigger changes.[470] In the 1960s, these reforms were described as "very complex process[es] that implie[d] substantial transformations not only of the way of life in rural areas and in the economic structure, but also in the power structure and social organization."[471]

461 de Gasperi 1955, p. 230; and Peñailillo Arévalo 2006, p. 68.

462 Cordero Quinzacara 2008, p. 504.

463 Delgado de Miguel 2002, p. 62.

464 Ankersent & Ruppert 2006, p. 71.

465 Mirow 2004, p. 219.

466 Sampaio 1993, p. 45.

467 Tai 1974, p. 11.

468 Barraclough 1973, p. 33. Warriner 1969, p. xiv, cited also by Karst & Rosenn 1975, p. 241.

469 Dekker 2003, p. 78.

470 Barraclough 1973, pp. 34–35.

471 That expression in Spanish read: "La reforma agraria es un proceso muy complejo que implica transformaciones sustanciales no sólo en los modos de vida de las zonas rurales, en la estructura de la economía, sino además, en la estructura del poder y de la organización social." (Chonchot 1965, p. 104)

Land reform varied according to the perspectives taken, and, accordingly, different actors (*v.gr., latifuindistas*, politicians, small farmers) gave different definitions and reached different understandings of the process.[472] A set of conditions are mainly necessary to trigger these reforms. The land tenure structure must be inadequate, characterized by *latifundistas* and by laborers with very limited (or no) access to land.[473] In addition, there must be notorious poverty in rural areas, where small farmers have no access to the benefits of agricultural and industrial developments.[474] Finally, political instability must accompany this scenario.[475] Land reform was many times rejected by *latifundistas*, however, who controlled large tracts of land.[476] In this chapter, land-reform legislative enactments will encompass those provisions that emanated from legislatures, aiming to alter the existing distribution of land within a jurisdiction and to make the ownership of the existing land available to those members of society who had been traditionally denied the ability or right to own. As a corollary, those new provisions assisted in shifting from the Liberal to the Social Function paradigm.

5.5.1.1 Global Evolution

Efforts towards achieving land reform spread across the world, experiencing a significant development during the second half of the twentieth century.[477] Early precedents in the Americas had followed the Mexican Revolution, while in Europe several jurisdictions had implemented land reforms after WWI[478] (*v.gr.*, Spain, 1930s).[479] Land-reform legislative enactments were present in American Civil Law Jurisdictions, and developed with different degrees of success in Europe, Africa, Asia,[480] and later in Australia,[481] reaching, amongst

472 Barraclough 1965, p. 127.

473 Barraclough 1965, p. 145.

474 Barraclough 1965, p. 145.

475 Barraclough 1965, p. 145.

476 Lapp 2004, p. 2.

477 The purpose of land redistribution can nevertheless be traced back to the ancient Greeks. Ankersent & Ruppert 2006, p. 72.

478 Durán Bernales 1966, pp. 172–174.

479 Robledo & Espinoza 1999, p. 406.

480 Dekker 2003, pp. 78, 88–102; and Halpérin 2008, pp. 312–319.

481 The main concern with land reform in Australia dealt with native title. The matter of Native Title was addressed in 1992 by the High Court of Australia in the *Mabo v Queensland [No. 2]* case. That case exceeds the time scope of this book, however. See de Villiers 2003, pp. 89–129.

others, India, Iran, Pakistan, the Philippines, and Taiwan.[482] A number of developing countries and some under reconstruction (*v.gr.*, Japan, 1940s)[483] undertook ambitious reforms–mainly during that second part of the century–aiming to achieve profound changes in the division and regime of rural lands.[484] That worldwide trend towards land reform ultimately resulted in the first United Nations *World Conference on Agrarian Reform and Rural Development*, which was held in Rome in 1979.[485]

The social function reinforced most land reform efforts in American Civil Law Jurisdictions.[486] "Social function," within the context of those jurisdictions, was an overreaching term promoting the use of land as a means to achieve social and economic progress.[487] Land reform ultimately would become an important component of property law in many American jurisdictions,[488] a group considered a leader in the unequal distribution of land,[489] where 90% of the land was owned by 10% of the population during the 1960s.[490] That traditional land tenure relationship shaped the existing social system,[491] where peasants tended to lack formal education, proper medical care, and suitable housing.[492] Furthermore, the daily existence of agricultural laborers working for a *latifundista* had not been altered with the independence from Spain in the early nineteenth century.[493] Accordingly, during the following century, reformers aimed to terminate the *latifundios* and eradicate vacated tracts,[494] while the new paradigm seemed to justify intervention to eliminate the unequal distribution of land.[495]

---

482 See generally Tai 1974; and Conesa 2012, p. 5.

483 Barraclough 1973, p. 33.

484 Halpérin 2008, pp. 312–313.

485 Parra Silva 2006, pp. 239–240.

486 Ankersent & Ruppert 2006, p. 71.

487 Hendrix 1993, p. 3.

488 Mirow 2004, p. 227.

489 Ankersent & Ruppert 2006, p. 70.

Studies that support this statement were undertaken, for example, in the 1960s by the Inter-American Committee for Agricultural Development. See Karst & Rosenn 1975, p. 242.

490 Lapp 2004, p. 2.

491 Barraclough 1973, p. 40.

For a sociological analysis of agrarian reform in Latin America, see the seminal works of Antonio García (*v.gr.*, García 1973).

492 Alexander 1974, p. 101.

493 Mirow 2004, p. 219.

494 Ankersent & Ruppert 2006, p. 100.

495 Ankersent & Ruppert 2006, p. 119.

5.5.1.2 American Evolution

Land reform took place in most American Civil Law Jurisdictions. The first experience took place in Mexico, starting in 1915, soon after the Revolution.[496] Mexico adopted an array of decrees, codes, and laws that were relevant for achieving reform.[497] As previously stated,[498] the 1917 Mexican Constitution welcomed elements of land reform, mainly in article 27.[499] Further steps towards reform were taken in 1934, through de-codification, when the Agrarian Code was enacted in Mexico.[500] That Code stimulated the creation of the *ejido*,[501] where land could be cultivated collectively or distributed amongst holders.[502] Several jurisdictions followed Mexico on the path towards land reform during the next half-century,[503] though some jurisdictions seem to have not demanded reform (*v.gr.*, Argentina and Uruguay).[504] A *contagion* of land reform legislative enactments took place in the region. Examples of the first land-reform legislative enactments[505] are found in Colombia (1936), Venezuela (1940), Puerto Rico (1941), Guatemala (1952), Bolivia (1953), Cuba (1959), Dominican Republic (1961), Chile (1962), Costa Rica (1962), Honduras (1962), Panama (1962), Paraguay (1963), Peru (1963), Ecuador (1964), Nicaragua (1979), and El Salvador (1980).[506] Land reform experienced a peak in the 1960s[507] and slowed down in the 1980s.[508] It has even been claimed that changes in the agrarian structures of those jurisdictions were greater during the period 1930–1980 than they were during the prior 400 years.[509]

---

496 Halpérin 2008, pp. 313–314; and Assies & Duhau 2009, pp. 359–360. See generally Mirow 2004, pp. 219–222.

497 Hernández Gaona 1991, p. 93.

498 See generally 5.3.1 of this book.

499 Mirow 2004, p. 206; Halpérin 2008, pp. 313–314; and Alexander 1974, p. 25.

500 Hernández Gaona 1991, p. 88; and Meyer 1998, p. 187.

501 The *ejido* existed before the independence period. See generally 3.7.1 of this book. For more information on the *ejido*, stretching beyond the first half of the twentieth century, see generally Duhau 2009.

502 Alexander 1974, p. 26.

503 See generally Alexander 1974.

504 Lapp 2004, p. 14.

505 Some jurisdictions enacted multiple laws on land reform. For example, Colombia enacted land reform laws in 1936, 1961, and 1980. Sampaio 1993, p. 10.

506 Sampaio 1993, p. 10; Zoomers & van der Haar 2000, p. 19; Chonchot 1965, p. 100; Halpérin 2008, pp. 314–315; Alexander 1974, p. 40; de Janvry *et al.* 2001, p. 279; Lapp 2004, p. 13; Rosenn 1963, p. 335; and Wilkie 1974, p. 1.

507 Tai 1974, p. 15.

508 García 1985, p. 120.

509 Long & Roberts 1994, p. 325.

Reforms varied significantly to the extent they restructured land tenure and production.[510] The measures required, amongst other things, the setting of limitations on privately held ownership and the expropriation of large tracts of land.[511] The programs varied in scope: some granted practically all land individually to be cultivated as family farms; others opted for mixed systems, welcoming cooperative agriculture and private landholding; while others opted for the socialization of land, as was the case in Cuba.[512] The Cuban land reform experience of 1959 was radical,[513] and was undertaken as part of the communist revolution.[514] It triggered concerns in the US, which fueled reforms across the jurisdictions by means of the *Alliance for Progress*[515] program of President John Fitzgerald Kennedy.[516] That program advocated for progressive reforms that would help prevent additional revolutions across the continent,[517] and transformed the idea of land reform, from something considered subversive into something considered a general commitment of jurisdictions that aimed towards a respectable goal.[518] The enactment of law reform legislation, however, did not necessarily mean that land reform did take place.[519] Even though it can certainly be claimed that the land reform enactments ultimately did not alter substantially the agrarian structure of the region,[520] or were in some

510 Long & Roberts 1994, p. 362.

511 Zoomers & van der Haar 2000, p. 19.

512 Alexander 1974, p. 58.

513 Sampaio 1993, p. 11.

514 Alexander 1974, p. 37.

515 A charter established the Alliance, and was signed in Punta del Este (Uruguay) in 1961. Title 1 in part read: "The American Republics agree to work toward the achievement of the following fundamental goals in the present decade: [...] 6. To encourage, in accordance with the characteristics of each country, programs of comprehensive agrarian reform leading to the effective transformation, where required, of unjust structures and systems of land tenure and use, with a view to replacing latifundia and dwarf holdings by an equitable system of land tenure so that, with the help of timely and adequate credit, technical assistance and facilities for the marketing and distribution of products, the land will become for the man who works it the basis of his economic stability, the foundation of his increasing welfare, and the guarantee of his freedom and dignity." (Charter of Punta del Este 1961)

See also Karst & Rosenn 1975, p. 275.

516 Sampaio 1993, p. 11.

517 Chonchot 1965, p. 102; Long & Roberts 1994, p. 361; Carroll 1970, p. 126; Sampaio 1993, p. 33; and Lapp 2004, pp. 28–29.

518 Alexander 1974, p. 23, 42.

519 Karst & Rosenn 1975, p. 274.

520 Sampaio 1993, p. 15.

jurisdictions *no more than a gesture*,[521] they did assist in welcoming the reception of the new paradigm. Those enactments joined the efforts that had been made in constitutions and in civil codes. The enactment of special legislation and the introduction of the social function resulted in eliminating the unitarian understanding of ownership.[522]

5.5.2 *Louisiana*

Louisiana incorporated aspects of the Social Function paradigm also within special legislation. It can be claimed that land-reform legislative enactments affected the land tenure in Louisiana during the twentieth century.

5.5.2.1 Evolution

The first decades of the twentieth century still showed a state that was mainly rural and agricultural.[523] In 1900, Louisiana was marked by agrarian monopoly, and at the US level it was a leader in the rate of absentee ownership and overseer management.[524] It could still be considered a colonial region, and due to its Creole traditions, it resembled other American Civil Law Jurisdictions.[525] Enactments affecting Louisiana took place both at the state and at the federal levels. Many of those changes were triggered in the 1930s as part of the New Deal programs of President Roosevelt. Later, in the 1960s, the legal discourse in the US and in Louisiana also dealt with property issues, mainly with regulations on land use (*i.a.*, zoning, subdivisions, building),[526] while addressing the assessment of land reform endeavors that were experiencing a peak in other jurisdictions.[527]

Louisiana was led by the idea of an *agricultural ladder*. That theoretical construct dominated the US land tenure research mainly in the period 1920–1950.[528] The classic explanation of that *ladder* was given by William J. Spillman in 1919, when he defended that:

> [...] the first rung of the agricultural ladder is represented by the period during which the embryo farmer is learning the rudiments of his trade.

521 Alexander 1974, p. 40.
522 Cordero Quinzacara 2008, p. 513.
523 Kniffen & Hilliard 1988, p. 178.
524 Shugg 1939, pp. 241–242.
525 Schlesinger 2001, p. 64.
526 Haar 1965, p. 244.
527 Delahaye 2003, pp. 456–457.
528 Kloppenburg & Geisler 1985, p. 59.

> In the majority of cases this period is spent as an unpaid laborer on the home farm.
>
> The hired man stands on the second rung, the tenant on the third, while the farm owner has attained the fourth or final rung of the ladder.[529]

The *ladder* was immediately incorporated into the theoretical framework of researchers and, for example, found its place in the analysis of the already mentioned 1920 US census.[530] It was said in an accompanying study on farm tenancy to that census that "evidence seems to prove conclusively that tenancy is generally a convenient way of approach to full ownership. It is, in fact, a part of the agricultural ladder."[531] Yet, tenancy relations in the 1930s seemed to prove the contrary, where in Louisiana, for example, having the third highest rate of farm tenancy in the US,[532] only 36% of farms were operated by owners and the number of farmers undertaking tenancy had increased during the previous decade.[533] That tenancy relation, together with the effects of the Great Depression, motivated more state intervention in agricultural affairs.[534] President Roosevelt negatively referred to the *ladder* when delivering a message to the US Congress.[535] In that 1937 message he expressed that the "American dream of the family-size farm, owned by the family which operates it, has become more and more remote. The agricultural ladder, on which an energetic young man might ascend from hired man to tenant to independent owner, is no longer serving its purpose."[536]

5.5.2.2 Implementation

A series of land-reform legislative enactments affected Louisiana, and were made both at the state and at the federal level. This chapter focuses only on two sets of enactments that were made at the federal level, and that had an impact at the state level. Those two sets provide an illustration–though not the only one–of enactments that tended to show a shift from the Liberal to the Social Function paradigm.

529 Spillman 1919, p. 170.

530 Kloppenburg & Geisler 1985, p. 61.

531 Goldenweiser & Truesdell 1924, p. 10. See also Kloppenburg & Geisler 1985, p. 61.

532 Holley 2001, p. 184.

533 Howard 2000, p. 57.

534 Delahaye 2003, p. 452.

535 Roosevelt 1937. See also Holley 2001, p. 184.

536 Roosevelt 1937. See also Kloppenburg & Geisler 1985, pp. 62–63.

A first set of land-reform legislative enactments was undertaken in the area of land use control. Early efforts were taken, for example, in the area of zoning with the drafting by the US Department of Commerce of the Standard State Zoning Enabling Act of 1924 and 1926.[537] All US states adopted acts on zoning, and Louisiana was no exception,[538] because its 1926 zoning act[539] was indeed modeled after the federal text.[540] Those regulations coexisted with the new dispositions of the already mentioned 1921 Constitution, which authorized municipalities to introduce planning and zoning ordinances.[541] Furthermore, the principle of comprehensive zoning was upheld by the US Supreme Court in the already mentioned decision in *Euclid*,[542] and was along similar lines as that incorporated across the US.[543] Another early land use control effort was made in the area of subdivisions, with the drafting by the US Department of Commerce of the Standard City Planning Enabling Act of 1928.[544] Several states followed that initiative, and Louisiana again was no exception.[545] Several decades later, already in the 1960s, land use controls had developed significantly across the US, and therefore further changes were experienced.[546]

A second set of land-reform legislative enactments was undertaken as part of the New Deal of President Roosevelt. The New Deal offered several programs that aimed to affect the farmer tenancy rate. Initially, the Agricultural Adjustment Administration was established in 1933 within the US Department of Agriculture, yet it did not favor the farm workers and tenants, being beneficial for larger farmers.[547] It mainly aimed to give better prices to farmers, and did not aim to alter agrarian social structures.[548] The Resettlement Administration program followed, and was begun in 1935.[549] It helped redistribute large plantations and tracts of land that were on the market or failing to comply with taxes.[550] That program was referred to as "America's first war on rural

537 Cunningham 1965, pp. 368–369.
538 Cunningham 1965, pp. 368–369.
539 Act Authorizing Zoning Plans 1926. See also Fordham 1946, p. 503.
540 Fordham 1946, p. 504; and Villavaso 1999, p. 660.
541 Villavaso 1999, p. 657.
542 Cunningham 1965, p. 380.
543 Villavaso 1999, p. 657.
544 Cunningham 1965, p. 415.
545 Cunningham 1965, pp. 415, 418.
546 See generally Cunningham 1965.
547 Gilbert 2003, p. 132.
548 Roth 2002, p. 2.
549 Bagdikian 1967.
550 Bagdikian 1967.

poverty,"[551] and offered rural relief and rehabilitation by means of supervised credit.[552] It also pursued land reform by acquiring lands to resettle dislocated farm families, and it aimed to achieve rural and suburban resettlement.[553] That same year the tension between Long and Roosevelt negatively affected some New Deal programs, which were delayed (*v.gr.*, housing projects in New Orleans).[554] Full benefits rolled back into the state, however, when Richard Leche was elected governor.[555] The Resettlement Administration program was transformed into the Farm Security Administration in 1937,[556] and offered "tenant purchase" programs[557] that were implemented in Louisiana.[558] Also in 1937, the US Bankhead-Jones Act[559] was passed, and enabled 249 tenant farmers in Louisiana to borrow funds for purchasing lands and undertaking repairs of buildings.[560]

Louisiana indeed benefited from the New Deal agricultural programs. Farm tenancy started to recede after reaching a peak in Louisiana in 1935.[561] In addition, forced sales of farms dropped from 75% in 1933 to 1.2% in 1939,[562] while in the period 1935–1939 a total of 1,900 farmers and tenants received financial assistance to purchase lands.[563] Nevertheless, African Americans were not fully favored by the New Deal agricultural programs,[564] including in Louisiana.[565] Yet, some succeeded in purchasing land, and several of those owners led the civil rights movement in the 1960s.[566] Ultimately, the New Deal agricultural programs were hindered by WWII,[567] though they were considered by scholars as a small land reform endeavor in rural areas of the US, which led tenants to become owners.[568]

551 Gilbert & Brown 1981, p. 360.
552 Gilbert & Wood 2004, p. 2.
553 Roth 2002, p. 18.
554 Field 2001, p. 9.
555 Field 2001, p. 10.
556 The Farm Security Administration was ultimately transformed into the Farmers Home Administration in 1946. Bagdikian 1967.
557 Gilbert 2003, p. 132; and Gilbert & Wood 2004, p. 2.
558 Moore 2001, p. 138.
559 The impact of the Act was questioned by Kloppenburg & Geisler 1985, p. 65.
560 Moore 2001, p. 138.
561 Moore 2001, p. 138.
562 Moore 2001, p. 137.
563 Moore 2001, p. 138.
564 Bagdikian 1967; and Linder 1987, p. 1371.
565 Moore 2001, p. 139.
566 Gilbert & Wood 2004, p. 1.
567 Bagdikian 1967.
568 Gilbert & Wood 2004, p. 1.

New Deal programs also aimed to benefit city dwellers. Accordingly, there were Federal programs to provide financial support for urban renewal by means of the Housing Acts of 1937, which were continued in 1949 and 1954, well beyond the presidency of Roosevelt.[569] Those acts addressed planning, redevelopment, acquisition, and clearance of land.[570] The New Deal programs granted financial aid to protect the family home for city dwellers, as reflected, for example, with the Home Owners Loan Corporation, which assisted in refinancing defaulted mortgages and in keeping homes away from foreclosure or tax sale.[571]

Louisiana took its own steps towards achieving a shift in paradigm during the New Deal. Governor Long proposed and implemented some changes within the state. For example, he called for special sessions of the local legislature in 1934–1935, and offered new benefits to Louisianans (*i.a.*, homestead tax exemption of up to $2,000).[572] In addition, his "Share Our Wealth" campaign aimed to procure a home for each American household.[573] His campaign was not to be considered communist, however, because it preserved private property and avoided a violent revolution.[574]

Louisiana reflected a shift in paradigm by means of adopting special legislation. The reception of special legislation often replicated enactments made at the federal level. US model statutes and legislative precedents turned out to be useful quarries for Louisiana legislators. As previously mentioned, a context for change in paradigm had spread across the Western Hemisphere and was not limited to American Civil Law Jurisdictions. Therefore, changes experienced in the special legislation of Louisiana would naturally be linked to changes that developed in other US states. It is undisputed that Louisiana undertook land-reform legislative enactments. Those efforts, as in other American Civil Law Jurisdictions, were not limited to the first half of the twentieth century, though they can indeed find their origins early in the century, when the shift started to be sensed.

5.5.3 *Chile*

Chile welcomed the Social Function paradigm also within special legislation. Land-reform legislative enactments in Chile had, compared with other jurisdictions, the highest degree of impact on the modernization of agriculture.[575]

---

569 Barlowe 1965, p. 355.

570 Scheuer *et al.* 1962, p. 959.

571 Field 2001, p. 8.

572 Carter 2001, p. 38.

573 Haas 2001, p. 112.

574 Haas 2001, p. 113.

575 Sampaio 1993, p. 20.

5.5.3.1 Evolution

The first decades of the twentieth century still showed that landowners strongly opposed significant land reform.[576] Similarly to other American Civil Law Jurisdictions, the land tenure structure in Chile had been inherited from the Spanish period, and continued during the first decades of the republican periods.[577] Changes were ignited during the presidency of Alessandri Palma in 1920, when the political power of landowners started to be eroded.[578] During that century, industrialization and capitalism percolated into the rural sector, triggering a weakening effect on the landowning elite.[579] The main reforms were undertaken in the 1960s and consolidated in the 1970s,[580] during the presidencies of Eduardo Nicanor Frei Montalva, Jorge Alessandri Rodríguez (*n.b.*, son of Alessandri Palma), and Allende Gossens. The rural areas of Chile, before those significant reforms, were characterized by large estate owners, who preserved an almost feudal relationship with tenants,[581] where 80% of agricultural land was divided amongst 3% of rural families.[582] There was a clear dichotomy between large landholders on *haciendas* (which comprised *latifundios*) and small farmers owning lands that hardly sufficed for subsistence (which comprised *minifundios*).[583] Even when *haciendas* seemed to be multifamily properties, they remained uniform economic units[584] and the *latifundio* was the dominant economic and social unit.[585] In Chile, during the era of revolution (1960–1980), some groups aimed to depart from capitalism and adopt socialism.[586]

Several laws have limited ownership beyond land reform in Chile since the turn of the twentieth century. For example, homestead (*propiedad familiar*), as already mentioned, was also introduced in Chile.[587] Its reception can be traced back to the 1925 Constitution and to other special laws (*v.gr.*, Law 1838 of 1906, Law 5950 of 1936, and Law 7600 of 1943).[588] Limitations were further imposed on the right of ownership, amongst others, due to public servitudes

576 Chilean Land Reform 1963, pp. 312–313.
577 Thome 1971, p. 491.
578 Thome 1971, p. 494.
579 Lapp 2004, p. 54.
580 Brahm García 2012, p. 254.
581 Barraclough 1999, p. 20.
582 Barraclough 1999, p. 21.
583 Dekker 2003, p. 7; and Barraclough 1973, pp. 133–134.
584 Becket 1965, p. 561.
585 Petras & Zeitlin 1970, p. 507.
586 Bellisario 2006, p. 169.
587 See generally 5.3.5.2 of this book.
588 Peñailillo Arévalo 2006, p. 69.

(*v.gr.*, Law 4851 of 1930),[589] urban or municipal characteristics (*v.gr.*, Decree 1472 of 1941),[590] public health (*v.gr.*, Labor Code),[591] and social utility (*v.gr.*, Decree-Law 261 of 1925[592] and Law 6844 of 1941[593]).

5.5.3.2 Implementation

A first set of reforms welcomed the Social Function paradigm and was undertaken beginning in the 1920s. The labor and land tenure structure in Chile–differently from Louisiana–indicated that no *agricultural ladder* could be envisioned, and state intervention was therefore required.[594] A *hacienda* system had developed in Chile, where a social structure of agricultural production existed, together with political power exerted by landlords over rural dwellers (*campesinos*).[595] That structure made workers, tenants and small landowners dependents of the *hacienda*, turning it into a social system rather than only a unit of production.[596] Notably, parallels can be drawn between the *hacienda* system and feudalism in Europe.[597] In 1928, during the presidency of Ibañez del Campo, the already mentioned Fund for Agricultural Colonization was established.[598] That timid land reform legislation only succeeded in distributing 10,000 units of land, not reaching the 600,000 eligible *campesinos*.[599] The resettlement activities of the Fund, however, paved the way for the reforms that followed in the 1960s and 1970s.[600]

A second set of reforms was undertaken in the 1960s,[601] when the land structure kept demanding changes in Chile. The Third Farming Census (*Tercer Censo Agropecuario*) of 1955 stated that 345,000 families lived in the Chilean

589 Lira Urquieta 1944, p. 176.
590 Lira Urquieta 1944, p. 177.
591 Lira Urquieta 1944, p. 179.
592 Lira Urquieta 1944, p. 180.
593 Lira Urquieta 1944, p. 182.
594 See the description of the structure in Barraclough 1973, pp. 139–140.
595 Bellisario 2006, p. 172.
596 Barraclough 1973, pp. 147–148.
597 Bellisario 2006, p. 172.
598 Brahm García 2012, p. 250; and Claro Solar 1979, pp. 406–408.
599 Hurtado-Edwards & Smith 1964, p. 93; and Barraclough 1999, p. 23.
The Fund ended its activities in 1962, after settling only 4,206 families. See Thome 1971, p. 495.
Authors mentioned parallels between the activities of the Fund and the land reforms implemented in Italy since the 1940s. See Durán Bernales 1966, p. 331.
600 Barraclough 1999, p. 23.
601 For more information on the reforms of the 1960s, see Mirow 2011, pp. 1209–1211.

rural areas, while 47% of those families did not own land.[602] In addition, at that time, 55% of the farmed area was divided amongst *latifundios* of more than 5,000 hectares.[603] Legislation on land reform was first enacted by means of Law 15020 of 1962,[604] which met with a favorable response,[605] yet it was considered too long and detailed, therefore presenting challenges for its implementation.[606] That initial effort was undertaken during the administration of Alessandri Rodríguez, within the context of the activities of the *Alliance for Progress*[607] and of the *Economic Commission for Latin America*,[608] and was an extension of the policies that had preexisted in Chile.[609] Law 15020 was the first land-reform legislative enactment in American Civil Law Jurisdictions, following the establishment of the *Alliance for Progress*,[610] while Chile was by 1963 amongst the principal beneficiaries of *Alliance* funds.[611] The new law, moreover, aimed to eliminate the inefficient *hacienda* system,[612] and in the words of Alessandri Rodríguez, it aimed to be "an efficient instrument for [Chile] to satisfy the just and human aspiration of those that work the land to achieve an easier means to access the ownership of land."[613] The Church also welcomed land reform in Chile,[614] advocating for change with the government of Alessandri Rodríguez.[615] Furthermore, the Church had implemented land redistribution in parts of its rural lands by 1963.[616]

---

602 Silva 1987, p. 57. See also González Terán 2010, p. 89.

603 Lapp 2004, p. 54.

604 Ley 15020 (1962).

605 Lapp 2004, p. 66.

606 The law had 104 articles, and eight transitory articles that aimed to facilitate its implementation. See Ley 15020 (1962). See also Thome 1971, p. 497.

607 Sampaio 1993, p. 70.

608 Mirow 2011, p. 1209.

For example, ECLA held a meeting in Santiago de Chile in May 1961 to specifically deal with land reform. See Brahm García 1994, p. 171.

609 Becket 1965, p. 579; and Brahm García 1994, p. 168.

610 Chilean Land Reform 1963, p. 311.

611 Chilean Land Reform 1963, p. 331.

612 Gallardo Fernández 2002, p. 61.

613 The message of Jorge Alessandri Rodríguez in Spanish read: "[…] será un instrumento eficaz para que nuestro país pueda satisfacer la aspiración humana y justa de quienes trabajan la tierra en orden a tener un más fácil acceso a la propiedad de ella […]." (Reforma Agraria Chilena 1962, pp. 5–6)

614 Tai 1974, pp. 14–15; and Mirow 2011, p. 1210.

615 Brahm García 1994, p. 173.

616 Thome 1971, p. 498; and Barraclough 1999, p. 24.

Law 15020 welcomed the social function of ownership,[617] and enabled the state expropriation of unproductive land, recognizing the social responsibility of owners.[618] Article 1 of the law indicated that ownership would be limited according to the requirements of maintenance and progress as demanded by social order.[619] In addition, article 3 stated that it was paramount, amongst the aims of the reform, to give access to ownership to those working the land.[620] Creation of institutions was required to implement land reform. Accordingly, the law established the creation of, amongst others, the Corporation for Agricultural Reform (*Corporación de Reforma Agrícola*, CORA) and the Institute for the Development of Agriculture (*Instituto de Desarrollo Agropecuario*, INDAP).[621] Article 11 of the law stated that the Fund for Agricultural Colonization would be transformed into the CORA,[622] aiming to administer the acquisition and redistribution of land. Article 12 indicated that the INDAP should,

617 Brahm García 1994, p. 163.

618 Lapp 2004, p. 66.

619 Article 1 of Law 15020 in Spanish read:

"El ejercicio del derecho de propiedad sobre un predio rústico está sometido a las limitaciones que exijan el mantenimiento y progreso del orden social. Estará sujeto, especialmente, a las limitaciones que exija el desarrollo económico nacional y a las obligaciones y prohibiciones que establece la presente ley y a las que contemplen las normas que se dicten en conformidad a ella.

Todo propietario agrícola está obligado a cultivar la tierra, aumentar su productividad y fertilidad, a conservar los demás recursos naturales y a efectuar las inversiones necesarias para mejorar su explotación o aprovechamiento y las condiciones de vida de los que en ella trabajen, de acuerdo con los avances de la técnica." (Ley 15020 (1962))

620 Article 3 of Law 15020 in Spanish read: "Con el propósito de llevar a cabo una reforma agraria que permita dar acceso a la propiedad de la tierra a quienes la trabajan, mejorar los niveles de vida de la población campesina, aumentar la producción agropecuaria y la productividad del suelo, se dictan los preceptos que a continuación se expresan." (Ley 15020 (1962))

See also Lapp 2004, p. 66.

621 Thome 1971, p. 495; and Alexander 1974, p. 83.

622 Article 11 of Law 15020–in part–in Spanish read:

"Transfórmase la Caja de Colonización Agrícola en Corporación de la Reforma Agraria. Dicha Corporación tendrá el carácter de persona jurídica de derecho público, empresa autónoma del Estado de duración indefinida, con patrimonio propio, con plena capacidad para adquirir, ejercer derechos y contraer obligaciones.

La Corporación de la Reforma Agraria será la sucesora de la Caja de Colonización Agrícola, en todos sus bienes, derechos y obligaciones." (Ley 15020 (1962))

amongst other functions, consider the financial support for small farmers.[623] Law 15020 has been deemed the most transcendental step towards the reception of the social aspect of ownership in Chile.[624] Even though it ultimately affected only 980 families and extended over 1.5% of the total surface of Chile,[625] its main effect was that it effectively introduced to the political agenda land-reform legislative enactments and highlighted the deficiencies of the Chilean agriculture sector.[626] Law 15020 was indeed an important stepping stone for the forthcoming land-reform legislative enactments.[627]

A new time of reform was ignited with Law 16640 of 1967.[628] That law resulted from drafting techniques that were interdisciplinary, involving input from lawyers, sociologists, agronomists, farmers, and economists.[629] There were at that time still concerns regarding the output of agricultural production, and the reforms of Alessandri Rodríguez seemed stagnant.[630] In addition, a rural labor movement had developed in Chile, and found support in the government of President Frei Montalva[631] who advocated for an effective agrarian reform that would end the existing structure of land tenure.[632] That rural labor

---

623 Article 12 of Law 15020–in part–in Spanish read:

"Transfórmase el Consejo de Fomento e Investigaciónes Agrícolas en Instituto de Desarrollo Agropecuario. [...] Sus funciones serán las que siguen:

a) Otorgar asistencia técnica gratuita y ayuda crediticia a los pequeños y medianos agricultores, incluyendo a los que exploten minifundios y a los indígenas, y a las respectivas cooperativas; como también fomentar las actividades de artesanía y pequeña industria en zonas rurales, especialmente las relacionadas con las complementarias de la agricultura;

b) Otorgar asistencia crediticia a dueños de minifundios de propiedades familiares agrícolas o de pequeños predios no divisibles a fin de facilitar la adjudicación de la tierra en beneficio de quien la trabaje, en casos de liquidación de herencia o comunidades; o para transformar el minifundio en unidad económica o para pagar el todo o parte del saldo de precio de un inmueble comprado con el mismo objetivo [...]." (Ley 15020 (1962))

See also Lapp 2004, p. 66.

624 Brahm García 1994, p. 163.

625 Sampaio 1993, p. 70.

626 Sampaio 1993, p. 70.

627 Thome 1971, p. 497; and Barraclough 1999, pp. 23–24.

628 Ley 16640 (1967).

629 Thome 1971, p. 497.

630 Lapp 2004, p. 70.

631 Alexander 1974, pp. 95–96.

The law was voted favorably by 93% of all members of the National Congress. See Sampaio 1993, p. 71.

632 Thome 1971, p. 489.

movement took place almost simultaneously with the land reform activities and some of its participants took active roles in the reform process.[633]

Law 16640 aimed to modernize the Chilean countryside and further establish democracy.[634] Article 2 of the law clearly welcomed the new paradigm, by expressly mentioning that expropriation was authorized because agrarian property should "fulfill a social function."[635] The new law, resembling the postulates of Duguit, indicated in article 4 that ownership could be limited if land was not used or used in a way that was not economically efficient.[636] The Communal Counsels of Farmers (*Consejos Comunales Compesinos*) played a fundamental role in that stage of the agrarian reform, mainly in the taking over of the control of *latifundios*, and their replacement with new productive units.[637] Law 16640 ultimately benefited 20,976 families[638] that received 2.6 million hectares of land,[639] while agricultural production grew at an annual rate of 2.9%.[640] More land reform efforts were still to be expected in Chile, however.

A third and more radical set of reforms was undertaken in the period 1970–1973,[641] during the presidency of Allende Gossens, and was interrupted by the military *coup d'état* by Augusto José Ramón Pinochet Ugarte.[642] Without enacting a new law, the administration of Allende Gossens aimed to accelerate and further develop land reform and to involve the state in the activities of

---

633 Alexander 1974, pp. 95–96.

634 Sampaio 1993, p. 70.

635 Article 2 of Law 16640 in Spanish read: "Con el objeto de que la propiedad agraria cumpla su función social, declárase de utilidad pública y autorízase la expropiación total o parcial de los predios rústicos que se encuentren en cualquiera de las situaciones que se expresan en los artículos 3° y 4° a 13° inclusive de la presente ley." (Ley 16640 (1967))

636 Article 4 of Law 16640 in Spanish read:

"Son expropiables los predios rústicos que se encuentren abandonados y los que estén mal explotados.

No obstante la causal de expropiación por mala explotación, sólo se aplicará después de tres años contados desde la fecha de publicación de la presente ley, respecto de aquellos predios rústicos que, desde una fecha anterior al 4 de noviembre de 1964, tengan una superficie que no exceda de 80 hectáreas de riego básicas." (Ley 16640 (1967))

See also Alexander 1974, p. 38.

637 García 1973, pp. 32–33.

638 Sampaio 1993, p. 71.

639 Lapp 2004, p. 72.

640 Sampaio 1993, p. 71.

641 For more information on the reforms of that period, see Mirow 2011, pp. 1211–1212.

642 Sampaio 1993, p. 71.

the agricultural sector.[643] Allende Gossens made clear his intention to terminate the dominance of the *latifundio*.[644] Accordingly, part of the expropriated *latifundios* continued to be transformed into cooperatives of farmers (*asentamientos*), yet with some alterations and referred to as Agrarian Reform Centers (*Centros de Reforma Agraria*),[645] resulting in the implementation of changes in the land tenure structure.[646] The aim was to socialize the means of production,[647] while also substituting the *latifundio-minifundio* dichotomy with a new structure built on state, communal, cooperative, and family land holdings.[648] The Chilean Congress would not have backed a land-reform legislative enactment by Allende Gossens, and he therefore opted to use the existing laws to their full potential, expropriating during his first year in government a similar number of hectares as Frei Montalva had done during his entire administration.[649] Expropriation grew exponentially in Chile, as sensed in the 6,297,000 hectares that were affected and that ultimately benefited 37,277 families.[650]

Chile represents one of the best examples of land-reform legislative enactments, where true change was experienced during the reform process.[651] This is reflected by the shift in the total number of landowners, which grew from 140,000 in 1924 to 317,955 by 1976.[652] The reception of the new paradigm within special legislation was also a result of the efforts of local and foreign intellectuals. These actors participated in the land reform activities in Chile by highlighting the deficiencies of the *hacienda* system and by providing comparative approaches that looked at the experiences of land reform in other jurisdictions.[653] The entire *hacienda* system was indisputably affected by

After the coup, 55% of the land that had been affected by land reform was granted to individual beneficiaries, who ultimately held 22% of the total agricultural area of Chile. See Sampaio 1993, pp. 20, 72. Matthew Mirow showed that Augusto Pinochet, nevertheless, embraced aspects of the Social Function paradigm and referred to it in legislative enactments. See Mirow 2011, pp. 1212–1214.

643 Sampaio 1993, p. 71.

644 Lapp 2004, p. 78.

645 Barraclough 1999, p. 26.

646 Cantor & Kraus 1990, p. 520.

647 Sampaio 1993, p. 71.

648 García 1973, p. 179.

649 Lapp 2004, p. 79; and Barraclough 1999, p. 25.

650 Sampaio 1993, p. 72.

651 Mirow 2004, p. 223.

652 Gallardo Fernández 2002, p. 67.

653 Barraclough 1999, p. 27.

expropriation and redistribution of land in Chile, and *latifundios* were no longer dominant in Chile.[654] This jurisdiction faced a clear dichotomy. On the one hand, a civil code that experienced little change, presenting the initial liberal tenets of ownership. On the other hand, a constitution and special legislation that clearly opened the door to the Social Function paradigm. Accordingly, Chile welcomed the means to restrict the right of ownership, departing from the paradigm that had prevailed during the nineteenth and part of the twentieth centuries.[655]

5.5.4 *Argentina*

Argentina welcomed the new paradigm within special legislation that aimed to limit the absolute scope of ownership. Land-reform legislative enactments, however, were not significant in Argentina, when compared with other American Civil Law Jurisdictions.[656]

5.5.4.1 Evolution

Land reform was not a priority for the different national administrations,[657] while colonization of land was promoted as an alternative to expropriation and land redistribution in Argentina.[658] Migration from rural to urban areas had been massive in Argentina, and by the 1960s only 28.3% of the population lived in rural areas,[659] therefore reducing the population pressure on the land.[660] At that same time, there were 465,400 farm units, and 264,200 were controlled by owners and part-owners.[661] Furthermore, the *minifundio* was not a characteristic of the Argentine rural structure, differently from other American Civil Law Jurisdictions.[662] Changes in land tenure policy and in the democratization of access to land were addressed during the first two administrations of Perón (1946–1955).[663] He had claimed in 1944 that those who “own land must

654 Gallardo Fernández 2002, pp. 61–62.

655 Matus Valencia 1958, p. 81.

656 Zoomers & van der Haar 2000, p. 19; Mirow 2004, p. 223; Durán Bernales 1966, pp. 316–317; and Lapp 2004, p. 14.

657 Barraclough 1973, p. 81.

658 Lapp 2004, p. 12.

659 Barraclough 1973, pp. 63–64.

660 On the pressure on land in Argentina since the turn of the century, see Lapp 2004, pp. 27–28.

661 Barraclough 1973, pp. 65–66.

662 Lapp 2004, p. 26.

663 Blanco 2001, p. 1.

extract its juice, because land is the wealth of the State."[664] Yet in practice, the policy shifts were less radical, and started to fade again towards the end of that decade.[665] A new time of reforms would start during the 1958–1962 administration of Arturo Frondizi, who ignited the "developing" (*desarrollista*) stage in Argentina.[666] While other American Civil Law Jurisdictions were undertaking and aiming towards land reform, Argentina at that time aimed to transform agricultural exploitation into real corporations.[667] The natural advantages of Argentina had to be augmented by means of new technologies (*v.gr.*, fertilizers, botanical techniques, and zootechnics);[668] and the social aspect of rural life had to be transformed by means of new roads, education, and the fulfillment of other basic needs.[669]

The twentieth century welcomed legislative enactments that limited ownership in Argentina, beyond land reform. For example, at the federal level there were enactments dealing with horizontal property, and urban and rural tenancy; while at the provincial and municipal levels there were enactments dealing with zoning and urban planning,[670] fields also addressed, for example, in Louisiana. Several laws were implemented in Argentina during the 1910s and 1920s, aiming to incorporate aspects of the new paradigm.[671] Already by the 1920s special legislation had altered the conditions of property rights, even when the text of the civil code was not significantly reformed.[672] Law 9080 of 1913 secured for the state the ownership of archeological findings;[673] while Laws 11156 and 11157 of 1921 established the minimum period for tenancy contracts and the maximum amount to be paid.[674] The new century also saw an early start towards the improvement of living conditions for small owners with the enactment of Law 4167 of 1902, which aimed to distribute state lands.[675] Furthermore, Law 10284 on homestead was passed in 1917,[676] continuing the

664 Blanco 2001, p. 1.
665 Blanco 2001, p. 1.
666 Monserrat Llairó 2009.
667 Monserrat Llairó 2009.
668 Monserrat Llairó 2009.
669 Monserrat Llairó 2009.
670 Adrogué 1991, p. 38.
671 Salvat 1962, p. 17.
672 Giannoni 2010, p. 230.
673 Legón 1942, p. 117.
674 Salvat 1962, p. 18.
675 The law was enacted in January 1903. See Giannoni 2010, pp. 40, 184, 194.
676 Anta 2007, p. 96; and Giannoni 2010, p. 40.

selling and land tenancy policy,[677] and offering tracts of land to settlers.[678] The 1940s saw the emergence of several special laws that could be interpreted as further developing the new paradigm. Accordingly, regulations of tenancy contracts were implemented in Argentina,[679] with specific enactments on rural tenants during 1946–1947.[680] Furthermore, Law 13246 of 1948[681] dealt with rural tenancy (*arrendamiento*), also during the administration of Perón, and in article 1 required that the land should be used for agricultural purposes.[682]

5.5.4.2 Colonization as an Alternative

Colonization of lands served as a means to avoid traditional land reform in Argentina,[683] yet still dealing with the needs of access to land.[684] Colonization had been an important element for Argentine settlement since 1876,[685] with the enactment of Law 817 on immigration and colonization. Immigration and colonization policies still required at that time the enactment of a specific national law, and Law 817 was a reaction to that need, being adopted during the presidency of Nicolás Avellaneda.[686] That 1876 law welcomed European immigration,[687] and replicated the protection of foreigners as enshrined in the Argentine Constitution.[688] Numerous legislative enactments were undertaken in Argentina to colonize and sell public lands during the period 1900–1940.[689] Colonization had been reaffirmed with the already mentioned Law 4167, which

677 Giannoni 2010, p. 213.

678 Lapp 2004, p. 166.

679 Barraclough 1973, pp. 44, 79–80.

680 Giannoni 2010, p. 276.

681 Giannoni 2010, p. 277.

682 Article 1 of Law 13246, in its first paragraph, in Spanish read: "La presente ley será aplicable a todo contrato, cualquiera sea la denominación que las partes le hayan asignado y sus distintas modalidades, siempre que conserve el carácter substancial de las prestaciones correlativas, conforme a sus preceptos, y su finalidad agroeconómica." (Ley 13246 (1948), p. 85)

683 Colonization was used in this sense by other jurisdictions. See Barraclough & Domike 1970, p. 72.

684 Other jurisdictions benefited likewise from colonization programs. See Barraclough 1973, p. 42; and Wilkie 1974, p. 2.

685 Emphyteusis had been previously used in Argentina as a means of colonization of lands. See generally Levaggi 2012.

686 On the context in which the law was enacted, see Frontera 1988.

687 Slater 2009, p. 702.

688 Hines 2010, p. 479.

689 Ramella 2007, p. 342.

authorized land grants,[690] and which resulted in the selling of approximately 3 million hectares of state lands before 1910.[691] Provinces also enacted laws at that time, such as Law 248 of Mendoza, enacted in 1902, which paved the way for systematic colonization.[692] Further colonization attempts were undertaken in the period 1916–1924, aiming to develop small farms–around urban centers and train stations–that would coexist with the *latifundio*.[693] An important step was taken in 1940 during the administration of Ramón Castillo with the enactment of Law 12636.[694] That law created the National Agrarian Council (*Consejo Agrario Nacional*), giving to that Council the control over the Lands Office (*Dirección de Tierras*).[695] Article 1 of that law did not refer explicitly to the social function, yet it welcomed clearly the new paradigm by stating that land "is subject to the limitations and restrictions established in this law according to the collective interests."[696] Law 12636 was a legislative enactment with impact on ownership, and it enabled the transferring of land to those working the land.[697] President Perón also dealt with colonization, and addressed the need as point 24 of his first Five-Year Plan (1947–1951), defending that colonization should pursue social justice, respect the national interests, and aim to improve living conditions and production.[698] Changes to regulations on colonization were implemented in 1954 with the enactment of Law 14392, which overruled Law 12636.[699] A study indicated that in the period 1940–1956 colonization affected 2,195,394 hectares,[700] though by the end of the 1960s there were still abundant lands for colonization, and colonization was an incidental activity that took place in frontier regions.[701]

Similar to many other American Civil Law Jurisdictions, Argentina subscribed to the Punta del Este Charter of the *Alliance for Progress*. The Argentine delegates actively participated in the drafting of the charter, and aimed

690 See Giannoni 2010, p. 184.
691 Giannoni 2010, p. 201.
692 Cueto 1999, p. 487.
693 Girbal de Blacha 1991, p. 211.
694 Ramella 2007, pp. 342–343.
695 Ramella 2007, pp. 342–343.
696 Paragraph 2, article 1 of Law 12636 in Spanish read: "La propiedad de la tierra queda sujeta a las limitaciones y restricciones que se determinan en esta ley de acuerdo al interés colectivo." (Ramella 2007, p. 343; and Ley 12636 (1940), p. 862)
697 Giannoni 2010, pp. 274, 287.
698 Ramella 2007, p. 345.
699 Martínez de Hoz 1961, p. 55.
700 Barraclough 1973, p. 42.
701 Barraclough 1973, pp. 78, 82.

towards a more "developing" content for the *Alliance*, even softening the references to land reform.[702] In a different context, Frondizi had already claimed that "fundamental socio-economic conditions ha[d] to be created to enable the agricultural activity to remunerate all its factors and to raise the levels of the rural society to those of the entire country."[703] A technocratic approach was therefore followed in Argentina, where dissociation existed between the land-holding structure and *latifundio*, on the one hand, and the modernization of agriculture, on the other.[704] Accordingly, Frondizi advocated for progress that went beyond the land-holding structure in Argentina, requiring an agrarian technification,[705] and therefore not enrolling in land reform movements that developed in other jurisdictions. Colonization of periphery lands was at that time also on the agendas of those advocating for a change beyond land reform.[706]

Argentina welcomed the new paradigm by means of special legislation, yet it was not a fruitful jurisdiction for land-reform legislative enactments. This is a main difference with other American Civil Law Jurisdictions, where land reform took place mainly during the 1960s. Argentina sought colonization and tenancy reforms, not being enrolled with most other jurisdictions that pursued land reform. Furthermore, Argentina developed special legislation that weakened the role of the civil code as a cornerstone for property law.[707] That special legislation joined the reforms in the constitution and in the civil code, and was able to show a shift in Ownership Paradigms.

5.6 Closing Remarks

Ownership Paradigms experienced a shift in American Civil Law Jurisdictions. This chapter illustrated how the Liberal paradigm there was replaced by one that welcomed social limitations to the right of ownership. The Social Function paradigm was shaped when things and individual actors offered a place of prominence to society at large. The chapter focused on three jurisdictions (*i.e.*, the US State of Louisiana, and the republics of Chile and Argentina) that served as case studies for the analyses of the abovementioned paradigm shift.

702 Morgenfeld 2012, p. 12.
703 Monserrat Llairó 2009.
704 García 1973, p. 131; and García 1967, p. 29.
705 García 1967, p. 30.
706 García 1973, pp. 130–131.
707 Adrogué 1991, pp. 38–39.

The chapter first demonstrated that the adoption of a new paradigm took time, starting during the second half of the nineteenth century, and experiencing a peak in the period 1890–1930. It also showed that the new paradigm developed both in Europe and in the Americas, and found reception that was not limited to English, French, German, and Spanish legal literature, and even extended to the writings of the Church. Special attention was devoted to the writings of Duguit, who may be considered the paladin of the new paradigm, and to the reception of his ideas on both sides of the Atlantic Ocean. Levaggi clearly explained–and this chapter showed–that there were three consecutive (and at times overlapping) periods in the evolution of this new paradigm.[708] Firstly, ownership was seen as having both a social and an individual purpose, as presented in the writings of Ahrens. Secondly, ownership was considered as being a social function, as defended by Duguit. Thirdly, ownership was considered as having a social function, as advocated by the detractors of Duguit and by part of the legislative enactments that took place mainly since the 1940s.

The chapter further focused on the reception of the new paradigm within constitutional texts, both of Europe and of the Americas. An in-depth focus on the changes experienced in the constitutional texts of the three studied jurisdictions demonstrated that society demanded a departure from the Liberal paradigm that had prevailed during the nineteenth century, and that legislatures were open to the reception of a new understanding of ownership. There was a *contagion* of constitutions that welcomed the new paradigm, and that was triggered after the Mexican and Weimar constitutions.

Thirdly, the chapter discussed the reception of the Social Function paradigm within the civil codes of the already mentioned three jurisdictions. The doctrine of abuse of rights served as a channel for the reception of the new paradigm, being welcomed in the civil codes of many American Civil Law Jurisdictions. A pollination of that doctrine was experienced in the Old World and in the New World, at similar time periods.

The chapter finally focused on the special legislation that developed outside the civil codes and that welcomed the new paradigm. A look into the three jurisdictions demonstrated that legislatures addressed social needs, such as land reform, colonization of lands, and regulation of tenancy contracts. Those enactments succeeded in reaching a paradigm shift, even in jurisdictions where constitutional texts or civil codes were not subject to substantive changes.

American Civil Law Jurisdictions indeed abandoned the Liberal paradigm and incorporated the tenets of the Social Function paradigm within their legal

708 This clarification was made by Abelardo Levaggi during a meeting held at the *Instituto de Investigaciones de Historia del Derecho* (Buenos Aires) on July 15, 2015.

frameworks. The degree of departure from the previous paradigm differed according to the different jurisdictions, some being more conservative than others. A group of jurisdictions welcomed the new paradigm expressly in their enactments, even referring to the term *social function*, while other jurisdictions weakened the absolute character of ownership by adopting doctrines and principles that had an indirect impact on that fundamental pillar of property law.

CHAPTER 6

Conclusions

6.1 Presentation

This book offers readers a journey across time and space. It addresses three American Civil Law Jurisdictions in three subsequent time periods. Attention is devoted to the shifts in Ownership Paradigms at every step of the journey, offering perspectives primarily on the manifestations of the shifts in Ownership Paradigms within the legislation of Louisiana, Chile, and Argentina. The journey also offers a bridge between continents, between jurisdictions in Europe and in the Americas. Historical events are traced across time and space, assisting readers in the understanding of how the different Ownership Paradigms were shaped and how shifts in paradigms occurred from Allocation to Liberal to Social Function. Looking at law in different times and jurisdictions indeed serves as a tool to understand legal changes, better explaining differences and similarities.

This chapter addresses the central and peripheral conclusions of the study. Those conclusions may be further contextualized by readers if they return to the corollaries[1] and closing remarks[2] included in the different chapters of the book. In this book, central conclusions are those that result directly from the answers to the posed research questions; while peripheral conclusions are those that do not necessarily derive from the answers to the research questions, though they still provide additional knowledge for the understanding of ownership in American Civil Law Jurisdictions. The chapter furthermore offers insight on different areas of future research. Those areas merit the attention of scholars and would likewise assist in extending the comprehension of that seminal property-law institution. The chapter closes with some final remarks that highlight the value of this comparative legal historical exercise.

6.2 Central Conclusions

This book explained the way in which American Civil Law Jurisdictions shared the evolution of the prevailing Ownership Paradigms. Legislative enactments

1 See generally 2.3.4, 3.2.3, 3.3.3, 3.4.4, 3.5.4, 3.6.4, 3.7.5, 4.5.1.4, 4.5.2.4, 4.5.3.4, and 5.2.4 of this book.

2 See generally 2.5, 3.8, 4.8, and 5.6 of this book.

 | DOI 10.1163/9789004338203_007

and social-historical events provided the main causal mechanisms that enabled readers to trace the evolution of the paradigms. A set of questions were addressed in order to enrich the referred explanation, securing that the outcome applied to all American Civil Law Jurisdictions.

6.2.1 *Visualizing Paradigms and Shifts*

The Allocation, Liberal, and Social Function are the three Ownership Paradigms that prevailed in American Civil Law Jurisdictions in the analyzed period. The book looked at causal mechanisms for the three jurisdictions (*i.e.*, Louisiana, Chile, and Argentina), and these mechanisms made manifest that the three Ownership Paradigms indeed prevailed in those parts of the Americas at different time periods.

The Allocation paradigm was the first to emerge in American Civil Law Jurisdictions. In that paradigm, individual actors and society at large offered a place of prominence to things. In this paradigm, both the individual and the communal allocation of things were experienced, and being that allocation paramount, it prevailed over the concurring interests of individual actors and of society at large. The causal mechanisms, such as the legislative enactments included in Book 4 of the 1680 *Recopilación* and in the other components of the *Indiano* legal order, certainly aimed to the allocation of things amongst different actors. Other mechanisms, such as doctrinal writings (*v.gr.*, de Solórzano Pereira), also confirmed that allocation interest. Furthermore, allocation was clearly highlighted by the implementation of the system of royal land grants. Allocation was the paramount purpose of the Spanish quest in the Americas, though each actor naturally had its own concurring interests. To achieve that purpose things could be allotted in an individual (again, royal land grants) or communal manner (*comunales* and *propios*). The efforts to allot were so clear that there was no perpetual allocation, and if things were neglected by individual actors or society at large, the allocation purpose would motivate a change in the beneficiary. It should be noted, in addition, that allocation prevailed beyond the disappearance of the Spanish administration and extended until the new Liberal paradigm was welcomed. This fact reaffirms that colonialism is not a paramount element when dealing with the Ownership Paradigm that prevailed in American Civil Law Jurisdictions before the independence movements from Spain. A triangle composed by things, individual actors, and society at large may assist in explaining the paradigm shifts. As illustrated in Figure 6.1, the Allocation paradigm secured that the apex was occupied by things.

The Liberal paradigm was the second paradigm to emerge in American Civil Law Jurisdictions. In that paradigm, things and society at large offered a place of prominence to individual actors. The nineteenth century was deemed the

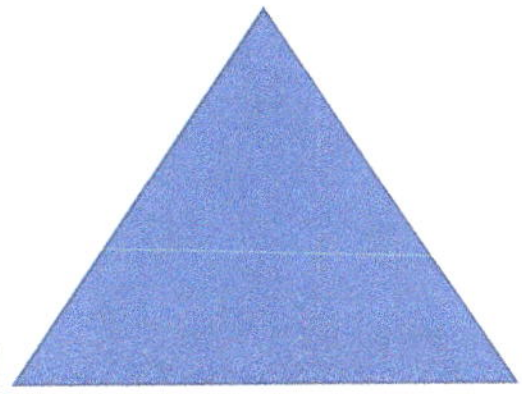

FIGURE 6.1
Allocation paradigm pyramid

century of codification, and the civil codes of American Civil Law Jurisdictions (*v.gr.*, Louisiana, 1825; Chile, 1857; and Argentina, 1871) occupied the paramount, exclusive, and exhaustive place in private law. Scholars venerated the letter of the codes, and the encapsulations of ownership in those texts were deemed authoritative. For example, the wordings in different code articles (*v.gr.*, 544, *Code Napoléon*; 483, Louisiana; 582, Chile; and 2513, Argentina) illustrated that paramount place for individual actors. Furthermore, elaborations on comparative legislation and scholarly writings by members of the Exegetical School (*v.gr.*, Demolombe, Varela, and Elizalde) further enhanced the value of codes, on both sides of the Atlantic. Codes, therefore, amounted to fundamental causal mechanisms. The different civil codes included provisions that confirmed the preeminence of individual actors, placing them well above things or society at large. As illustrated in Figure 6.2, the Liberal paradigm secured that the apex was occupied by individual actors.

The Social Function paradigm was the third paradigm to emerge in American Civil Law Jurisdictions. In that paradigm, things and individual actors offered a place of prominence to society at large. The different causal mechanisms confirmed the shift. Accordingly, looking at changes in civil codes, in constitutions, and in special legislation reaffirmed that society at large occupied the paramount position, displacing individual actors from the apex of the triangle. It should be noted that during that paradigm civil codes were no longer the main source of private law, and that other enactments took the stage, on occasion leading to reaffirming the paradigm shifts, such as the enactments dealing with land reform. Civil codes welcomed at that time the doctrine of abuse of rights (*v.gr.*, articles 1071, 2513, and 2514 of the Argentine Code), showing a paradigm shift. Furthermore, changes were sensed in constitutions, when several amendments were introduced to the existing texts (*v.gr.*, paragraph 10, article 10, Chilean Constitution; and article 38, Argentine Constitution), to provide a path towards the adoption of the new paradigm. The shift that occurred during the new paradigm is represented in Figure 6.3: a triangle that places society at large at its apex.

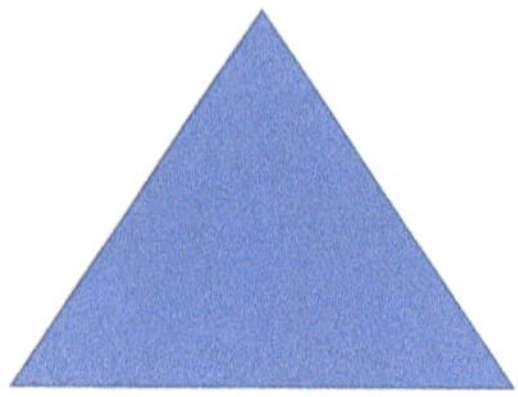

FIGURE 6.2
Liberal paradigm pyramid

FIGURE 6.3
Social function paradigm pyramid

Generalizations–as previously stated[3]–are difficult when working with case studies, since the resulting research has to demonstrate that selected cases are representative. However, a hypothesis may be generalized if it explains a hard case. Louisiana, in this book, acted as a hard case, and together with the experiences in Chile and Argentina, provided a means to elaborate a generalization that applies to all American Civil Law Jurisdictions.

6.2.2 *Circulation of Ideas and Paradigm Flows*

Shifts in Ownership Paradigms resulted from the circulation and flow of legal ideas. The book provided examples where that circulation and flow took place. Transplantation and the circulation of ideas and paradigms were fundamental aspects of this book, helping to identify foreign and vernacular creations, those that originated in Europe and those that originated in the Americas.

The three Ownership Paradigms showed a circulation of ideas and flows. The study of the Allocation paradigm reflected that legal ideas circulated across the Atlantic, from the Iberian Peninsula to the American jurisdictions. For example, the elaborations of Spanish Scholasticism were not circumscribed to Europe. Furthermore, the circulation of ideas across American Civil Law Jurisdictions, as represented in scholarly writings (*v.gr.*, de Hevia Bolaños), also helped in shaping an American *Ius commune*. A look into the Liberal paradigm showed similar results. For example, positivistic approaches to the study

3 See generally 1.5 of this book.

and understanding of law (*v.gr.*, Legal Positivism, Exegetical School, Historical School) gained popularity during the nineteenth century in Europe and in the Americas. The circulation of ideas of members of those schools had a significant impact on, amongst others, the drafting of legislation in the Americas, and therefore, in the shaping of Ownership Paradigms. Finally, the Social Function paradigm also developed within a context of circulation and flow. Examples were provided by the ideas and writings of Duguit and of the representatives of the Social Doctrine of the Church. Those ideas circulated across jurisdictions, regardless of geographic and language barriers. The tracing of paradigms assisted in showing the circulation of ideas and the flow of paradigms across the Americas, while bridging the divide between jurisdictions.

6.2.3 *Contagious Evolution across Time and Space*

The case study showed that American Civil Law Jurisdictions shared the evolution of the three Ownership Paradigms. With their own nuances, each jurisdiction shifted paradigms during the same three time periods. The book focused on the three jurisdictions that served as the case study (*i.e.*, Louisiana, Chile, and Argentina). The results of the book, however, can be applied to American Civil Law Jurisdictions at large.

A look into the paradigms again serves as illustration, this time of the contagious evolution of Ownership Paradigms across time and space. For example, Peninsular legislation was meant to apply in the new territories as part of the *Indiano* legal order, and the resulting Allocation paradigm was therefore sensed across all parts of the Americas alike. The pollination of civil code provisions (mainly from the texts included in the civil codes of the three studied jurisdictions) assisted in sharing the Liberal paradigm across American Civil Law Jurisdictions. Finally, the transatlantic contagion of constitutions and the global development of land-reform legislative enactments helped in achieving a paradigm shift: moving towards the Social Function paradigm that was shared across jurisdictions.

6.2.4 *Transplantation of Vernacular and Foreign Legal Sources*

Vernacular and foreign private law legal sources played a similar role in shaping the Ownership Paradigms in American Civil Law Jurisdictions. No single source prevailed. No claim can be made that both foreign (*v.gr.*, European) and vernacular sources autonomously shaped the paradigms. Accordingly, ownership cannot be regarded as merely an American or European construct, because local and foreign developments played a role in its shaping, being shared across American Civil Law Jurisdictions. It can be claimed, however, that transplantation was a fundamental element. American Civil Law Jurisdictions were not evolving as watertight compartments. Circulations of ideas, many times present in transplantation or normative transfers, were able to shape Ownership Paradigms.

A look into the Ownership Paradigms can reaffirm that vernacular and foreign sources played a similar role. For example, the *Siete Partidas*–yet more importantly its provisions–applied throughout the American jurisdictions. Those foreign sources had originated in the Peninsula. In addition, many provisions included in the 1680 *Recopilación* dealt with specific American needs, occasionally resulting from local request for legislation to be applied in the Americas. Ultimately, the book showed that provisions in the *Siete Partidas* and in the 1680 *Recopilación* played an important part in the instrumentation of the royal land grants. The shaping of the Liberal paradigm was also affected by the transplantation of vernacular and foreign legal sources. The seminal article 544 of the *Code Napoléon* was many times transplanted across the Americas, while the text of article 582 of the Chilean Code was replicated in most American Civil Law Jurisdictions: the influence on the resulting products was shared alike, both vernacular and foreign. The Social Function paradigm similarly reflected the interplay of the vernacular and the foreign. The changes in constitutions found their origins in the 1917 Mexican Constitution, which were soon after matched by the 1919 Weimar text. A contagion then followed, by means of the circulation of ideas and transplantation, and constitutions across the Atlantic (and beyond) welcomed the new paradigm. The claim of exclusivity is therefore impossible. No single influence prevailed. The transplantation of foreign and vernacular private law legal sources assisted in the elaboration of the legislative enactments that ultimately shaped the Ownership Paradigms. The book therefore provided perspectives on the interplay between American Civil Law Jurisdictions and European jurisdictions: an interplay that resulted in tracing the "genetic" history of the shifts in Ownership Paradigms.

6.3 Peripheral Conclusions

The book provided answers to the posed research questions. Other fruitful conclusions were reached on the path towards finding the answers to the posed questions, however. Some of those conclusions may be deemed peripheral, since they do not necessarily derive from the answers to the research questions. Peripheral conclusions are a consequence of the context-building process undertaken to address the three jurisdictions across time and space.

6.3.1 *Disciplinary Value of Comparative Legal History*

It can be briefly restated that comparative legal history is an autonomous discipline. This book demonstrated that the discipline studies external and internal aspects of the law across different time periods and jurisdictions. This book crossed the vertical and horizontal axes by looking at Ownership Paradigms in three different time periods and in three different jurisdictions. This book helped confirm that comparative legal historical studies are of special value for the understanding of the circulation of legal ideas or the flow of paradigms. The circulation of ideas implies a look into a jurisdiction of origin and a jurisdiction of destination. Furthermore, circulation requires the addressing of a shift: to study how things were *before* and *after* the idea circulated. The change can be sensed fully only by looking at two time periods: *ex ante* and *ex post*. The horizontal and vertical crossing of axes indeed provided a full (and unique) perspective on a specific aspect of the law.

The book further demonstrated that disciplinary studies share advantages and challenges when dealing with American Civil Law Jurisdictions. The advantages were confirmed when elaborating this book. For example, language uniformity is a clear advantage, as demonstrated in this book, when researchers can easily access the discourses developed in multiple jurisdictions. Examples were provided in the study of the constitutional conventions that took place in the nineteenth and twentieth centuries, when research across the proceedings could be done with no need to resort to multiple translations. In addition, the study of the pollination of civil code provisions demonstrated that the language uniformity facilitated access to the articles and to their meanings. Tracing the replication of article 582 of the Chilean Code in other codification endeavors provided a clear illustration of the referred advantage. The challenges were not sensed in the elaboration of the book. The geographical, economic, and alleged lack of innovation challenges presented no obstacle. Those disadvantages were overcome by the gathering of prior studies, by *standing on the shoulders of giants*, and hence benefiting from the rich legal historiography that developed across American Civil Law Jurisdictions during the *Indiano* and the post- independence periods.

6.3.2 *Quality of Existing Output*

The process of elaboration of this book confirmed that legal historiography is well developed in the three studied jurisdictions. Ownership has been dealt with extensively in the three jurisdictions, in the three time periods. It can also be concluded that there is, however, a *lacunae* in comparative legal historical studies that deal with ownership across American Civil Law Jurisdictions.

Previous studies, even when vernacular or segmented, served as fundamental building blocks for this exercise of comparative legal history. New research questions were indeed posed in this book, while dealing with the existing sources.

The sources used in the elaboration of this book also confirmed that American Civil Law Jurisdictions have been of interest not only for local scholars. The research boundaries are being eliminated. For example, Mirow extensively studied private law in the Americas. He likewise produced, amongst other works, authoritative works on the Social Function paradigm in Chile. Interest for these jurisdictions is likewise found in Europe. For instance, Cairns produced authoritative studies on Louisiana Law, dealing with, amongst others, the sources of the Digest of 1808, an important container of ownership provisions.

6.3.3 *Transatlantic Circulation*

There was a transatlantic circulation of ideas and flow of paradigms. The book demonstrated that the evolution of ownership was not addressed within watertight compartments on either side of the Atlantic. Ideas were indeed not circumscribed to continents. Furthermore, ideas did not circulate in a unidirectional way. Looking at Ownership Paradigms and their shifts demonstrated in this book that ideas circulated and flowed in a bidirectional manner, for example, from Europe to the Americas and from the Americas to Europe.

The transatlantic circulation was sensed when looking at the different Ownership Paradigms in American Civil Law Jurisdictions. For example, during the Allocation paradigm ideas were mainly projected from the Peninsula. Nevertheless, on occasion, as represented in some provisions of the 1680 *Recopilación*, American ideas and concerns migrated to the Old Continent, to be assessed and eventually included in legislative enactments. The Liberal paradigm presented another example. Multiple provisions of the Louisiana Code were valued by Spanish codifiers when elaborating the 1851 Spanish Project of a civil code. The migration of ideas was, in that example, eastbound. Finally, the Social Function paradigm provided perhaps the clearest example of bidirectional circulation across the Atlantic. The contagion of constitutions started after the 1917 Mexican enactment, and shifted back and forth across the Atlantic Ocean multiple times during the first half of the twentieth century.

6.3.4 *Global Undertakings*

A look into American Civil Law Jurisdictions demonstrated that some events were part of global undertakings. The book showed that some events took place across the globe at similar time periods, and that even when taking place similarly in the Americas, they were far from being unique in that part of the world.

Some events developed across the globe, and at the same time were sensed within the Ownership Paradigms that evolved in American Civil Law Jurisdictions. Those events were not exclusive of the studied jurisdictions. For example, codification was a global phenomenon, clearly not limited to the jurisdictions that are central to this book. Codification spread beyond American Civil Law Jurisdictions in the new continent. The book mentioned the codification endeavors in New York and in Quebec, and those are examples of that global undertaking. Furthermore, the book mentioned that land-reform legislative enactments were far from being exclusive undertakings of the studied jurisdictions. The need to alter land structures was present in Europe, Africa, Asia, and Australia. With different degrees of success, enactments or rulings aimed to alter land structures. Acknowledging that events may be part of global phenomena offers new perspectives on findings and helps broaden contexts of analyses.

6.4 Areas of Future Research

This book offers new areas of research that place ownership in American Civil Law Jurisdictions as the main field of study. Future studies could address some of the following areas that merit scholarly attention.

6.4.1 *Additional Sources of Law and Ownership Paradigms*

Legislative enactments across three time periods and in three jurisdictions were the main focus of this book. Other studies should focus on other sources of law (*i.a.*, customs, doctrine, jurisprudence) that deal with ownership. This book examined mainly the manifestations of the shifts in Ownership Paradigms within the legislation of Louisiana, Chile, and Argentina; while the gestation of those shifts, which many times find fundamental grounding on doctrinal elaborations and court decisions, still requires further study. The attention should be either autonomous or collective, *i.e.*, on one or multiple sources of law. Those further studies could use this book as a building block, while additionally contrasting their outcomes to the ones included in this book. Comparative legal historical studies must look into the normative framework, yet also into the application of law and the doctrinal assessment.

Other studies should deal with Ownership Paradigms in an additional time period. This book only mentioned briefly some aspects of Native American law relations, aiming to provide a basic context. However, a more focused study would be welcomed. The pre-Spanish period is likewise of interest when dealing with Ownership Paradigms. Understanding the Ownership Paradigm of Native American groups before the European arrival could provide fertile ground for analysis and offer a useful tool to contrast with the three Ownership Paradigms that followed. Tracing the background of that American paradigm would be beneficial to further understanding the interplay amongst actors, mainly with Native Americans, who are indeed important actors in American Civil Law Jurisdictions.

6.4.2 *Ecological Function of Ownership*

Ownership Paradigms evolve. Future studies, though not necessarily of a comparative legal historical nature, should deal with the current paradigms in American Civil Law Jurisdictions. Is it time to speak of a new Ownership Paradigm? Has an Ecological Function paradigm taken the stage? Society at large plays a role in preserving the environment, yet individual actors must play a specific preservation role. Preservation no longer falls within the exclusive competence of public law, being now welcomed by private law, especially by the law of property. Several governmental and non-governmental organizations have warned of the jeopardy involved in the relationship between some owners of property and the environment. Those claims have reached the legislatures, where significant efforts have canalized towards the prevention of further depletion of natural resources. This new claim stretches beyond the tenets of the Social Function paradigm, gaining paradigm status itself. No comprehensive study has been done on this new ecological function paradigm, even though the environment has a fundamental impact on the daily lives of people in all societies.

Native American groups, again, should be examined when addressing the Ecological Function paradigm. This potentially new paradigm could place Native American studies in the paramount position, where the centuries-long relationship of Native Americans with their land and their use of it may be much valued at decision-making stages of policymakers.

6.4.3 *Global Context for Ownership Paradigms*

This book extended the study of Ownership Paradigms from legal history to comparative legal history: from the vernacular level to the multi-jurisdictional level. Further studies could aim to place that multi-jurisdictional level within a global context. The evolution and shifts in Ownership Paradigms could be extended–in a very ambitious project–to another level. Comparisons could be performed, for example, with the developments in former British territories. Attention could also be devoted to events on different continents, where enriching comparisons could be made with the evolution and shifts in Africa, Asia, Australia, and Europe. The degree of development in local or comparative legal historiography will naturally dictate the path to follow in selecting the more demanding and suitable comparisons. Parallelisms or divergences could be reached, aiming towards a global context. Universal comparative legal history is impossible and not sought for, yet different building blocks (such as the one offered by this book) could be contrasted, seeking to develop further the knowledge of that property law institution within a globalized context. This could be linked to one of the peripheral conclusions of this book, namely that some events were part of global undertakings. Events that took place in the Americas were far from being unique.[4]

The proposed global approach could be likewise useful to assist in the efforts towards the harmonization of law. Learning from other experiences–as mentioned earlier in this book[5]–could therefore offer more case studies to assess the operation of legal institutions. New open laboratories for study may be identified, and globalized comparisons may present interesting features. For example, interactions may be valued by jurists who intend to implement Continental European principles while undertaking practices in the common law, and vice versa. Furthermore, the European Union is exploring changes in civil codes, and the revisions of civil codes of Member States (or the drafting of a uniform text) could benefit from the global context. A similar scenario is present in the Americas, where some jurisdictions are working in reaching harmonization of their private law provisions (*v.gr.*, Principles of Latin American Contract Law). Comparisons across time and space should be welcomed, since they are enriching, providing new perspectives and new knowledge.

6.5 Finale

Ownership Paradigms shifted in American Civil Law Jurisdictions and the comparative legal historical exercise undertaken in this book confirmed those joint shifts. This book aimed to achieve an innovative and comprehensive approach to ownership on both sides of the Atlantic. The book also aimed to incorporate American Civil Law Jurisdictions into the current literature that is developing on comparative property law, filling at the same time a gap in the existing literature of comparative legal history, expecting to offer further knowledge on that property law institution. The results are available to groups

4 See generally 6.3.4 of this book.

5 See generally 2.3.3 of this book.

working in harmonization of laws, who may then consider this American experience when elaborating the context in which their harmonizing efforts take place. Above all, the results from the book are now available to scholars that aim to understand the shifts in that fundamental pillar of law and society in American Civil Law Jurisdictions.

List of References

ABA & LSAC 2009 — American Bar Association and Law School Admission Council; *ABA-LSAC: Official Guide to ABA-Approved Law Schools—2010 Edition*. Newtown: Law School Admission Council, 2009.

Abásolo 2004 — Ezequiel Abásolo; 'Las Notas de Dalmacio Vélez Sársfield como Expresiones del "Ius Commune" en la Apoteosis de la Codificación, o de Cómo un Código Decimonónico pudo no ser la Mejor Manifestación de la "Cultura del Código"'. *Revista de Estudios Histórico-Jurídicos 26*, 2004, pp. 423–444.

Abásolo 2009 — Ezequiel Abásolo; 'Las actuales reflexiones latinoamericanas sobre historia jurídica, iluminadas por la experiencia disciplinar argentina de la primera mitad del siglo XX'. *Forum Historiae Iuris (07. Mai 2009)*. http://www.forhistiur.de/2009-05-abasolo/. Last visited on April 21, 2015.

Abásolo 2014 — Ezequiel Abásolo; 'Aportes del comparatismo jurídico al estudio de la circulación de ideas y experiencias normativas en Europa y América durante la primera mitad del siglo XX', in: Ezequiel Abásolo et al; *La cultura jurídica latinoamericana y la circulación de ideas durante la primera mitad del siglo XX: Aproximaciones teóricas y análisis de experiencias*. Buenos Aires: Instituto de Investigaciones de Historia del Derecho, 2014, pp. 11–21.

Abelik Manasevich 2001 — René Abelik Manasevich; 'Últimas modificaciones del código civil chileno. "Materia de derecho de familia y sucesorio"'. *Revista Jurídica 14*, 2001, pp. 73–80.

Acevedo & Palomeque 1908 — Eduardo Acevedo and Alberto Palomeque; *Eduardo Acevedo Años 1815–1863: Su Obra como Codificador, Ministro, Legislador y Publicista.* Montevideo: Imp. "El Siglo ilustrado," de Mariño y Caballero, 1908.

Act Authorizing Zoning Plans 1926 — 'An act authorizing the legislative body of all incorporated cities, towns and villages [...] to provide for comprehensive zoning plans [...] [July 14, 1926]', in: *Acts Passed by the Legislature of the state of Louisiana at the Regular Session*. Baton Rouge: Ramires-Jones Printing Co., 1926, pp. 412–418.

Act Designating the LSLI 1938 — 'An act designating the Louisiana State Law Institute [...]; and authorizing the printing of its recommended publications with the approval of the governor and the State printing board [July 2, 1938]', in: *Acts Passed by the Legislature of the state of Louisiana at the Regular Session 1938*. Baton Rouge: s.n., 1938, pp. 429–433.

Act for Printing and Promulgation 1824 — 'An Act to provide for the printing and promulgation of the amendments made to the civil code of the state of Louisiana [April 12, 1824]', in: *Acts passed at the Second Session of the Sixth Legislature of the State of Louisiana*. New Orleans: Peter K. Wagner, 1824, pp. 172–179.

Act for Promulgation 1808 — 'An Act Providing for the promulgation of the Digest of the Civil Laws now in force in the territory of Orleans [March 31, 1808]', in: *Acts passed at the First Session of the Second Legislature of the Territory of Orleans*, New Orleans: Bradford & Anderson Printers, 1808, pp. 120–129.

Act for Revision 1868 — 'An Act to Provide for the Revision of the Statutes of the State of a general character. [August 17, 1868]', in: *Acts passed by the General Assembly of the State of Louisiana at the First Session of the First Legislature*. New Orleans: A.L. Lee, 1868, pp. 39–40.

Act for Revision 1908 — 'An act to create a commission to revise and re-enact the Civil Code of the State of Louisiana, and to fix the compensation or salary of the members thereof, and of their clerks, pursuant to Articles 322 and 324 of the Constitution of 1898; to make an appropriation to carry out the provisions of this act. [July 2, 1908]', in: *Acts passed by the General Assembly of the State of Louisiana at the Regular Session*. New Orleans: The Daily State, 1908, pp. 216–217.

Act for Translation 1819
'An Act to authorize and encourage the translation of such parts of the Partidas as are considered to have force of law in this State [March 3, 1819]', in: *Acts passed at the First Session of the Fourth Legislature of the State of Louisiana*. New Orleans: J.C. de St. Romes, 1819, pp. 44–47.

Act Instructing the LSLI 1948
'An Act instructing the Louisiana State Law Institute to prepare a project for the revision of the Civil Code of Louisiana and the Code of Practice of Louisiana; providing the manner of submitting the same to the Legislature and the method for their enactment into law [July 6, 1948]', in: *Acts Passed by the Legislature of the State of Louisiana at the Regular Session 1948*. Baton Rouge: s.n., 1948, pp. 810–811.

Actas Oficiales Proyecto Constitución 1925
Ministerio del Interior; *Actas Oficiales de las Sesiones celebradas por la Comisión y Sub-comisiones encargadas del estudio del Proyecto de Nueva Constitución Política de la República*. Santiago: Imprenta Universitaria, 1925.

Adrogué 1991
Manuel I. Adrogué; *El Derecho de Propiedad en la Actualidad. Introducción a sus Nuevas Expresiones*. Buenos Aires: Abeledo-Perrot, 1991.

Aftalión & García Olano 1939
Enrique R. Aftalión and Fernando García Olano; *Introducción al Derecho*. 4th edition, Buenos Aires: s.n., 1939.

AHILA 2015
'Historia'. Asociación de Historiadores Latinoamericanistas Europeos. http://www.ahila.eu/historia. Last visited on April 21, 2015.

Ahrens 1838 — H[einrich] Ahrens; *Cours de droit naturel ou de philosophie du droit, fait d'après l'état actuel de cette science en Allemagne*. Brussels: Société Typographique Belge, 1838.

Ahrens 1841 — H[einrich] Ahrens; *Curso de derecho natural ó de filosofía del derecho, formado con arreglo al estado de esta ciencia en Alemania*. Translation by Ruperto Navarro Zamorano, Madrid: Boix, 1841.

AJLH 2015 — 'American Journal of Legal History'. American Journal of Legal History. http://www.temple.edu/law/ajlh/. Last visited on April 21, 2015.

Akkermans 2013 — Bram Akkermans; 'The Use of the Functional Method in European Union Property Law'. *European Property Law Journal 2*, 2013, pp. 95–118.

Alessandri Rodríguez 1948 — Arturo Alessandri Rodríguez; 'El Codigo Civil chileno y sus reformas'. *Revista de Derecho y Jurisprudencia 45:3–4*, 1948, pp. 37–67.

Alessandri Rodríguez & Somarriva Undurraga 1945 — Arturo Alessandri Rodríguez and Manuel Somarriva Undurraga; *Curso de derecho civil, basado en las explicaciones de los profesores de la Universidad de Chile*. 2nd edition, Volume I, Santiago: Editorial Nascimento, 1945.

Alessandri Rodríguez *et al.* 2010 — Arturo Alessandri Rodríguez et al; *Tratado de los Derecho Reales*. 6th edition, Volume I, Santiago: Editorial Jurídica de Chile, 2010.

Alexander 1974 — Robert J. Alexander; *Agrarian Reform in Latin America*. New York: Macmillan, 1974.

Alexander 2009 — Gregory S. Alexander; 'The Social-Obligation Norm in American Property Law'. *Cornell Law Review 94*, 2009, pp. 745–819.

Alexander 2011 — Gregory S. Alexander; 'Pluralism and Property'. *Fordham Law Review 80*, 2011, pp. 1017–1052.

Alexander 2013 — Gregory S. Alexander; 'Ownership and Obligations: The Human Flourishing Theory of

Property'. *Hong Kong Law Journal 43*, 2013, pp. 451–462.

ALI 2014 — American Law Institute; *Restatement of the Law Third: The Law of American Indians. Disucssion Draft No. 2 (April 24, 2014)*. Philadelphia: American Law Institute, 2014.

Allende 1967 — Guillermo L. Allende; *Panorama de Derechos Reales*. Buenos Aires: La Ley, 1967.

Altamira y Crevea 1890 — Rafael Altamira y Crevea; *Historia de la Propiedad Comunal*. Madrid: J. López Camacho, 1890.

Altamira y Crevea 1912 — Rafael Altamira [y Crevea]; 'Spain', in: John H. Wigmore et al (Eds.); *General Survey of Events Sources Persons and in Continental Legal History*. Volume I, Boston: Little, Brown, and Co., 1912, pp. 578–702.

Altamira y Crevea 1914 — Rafael Altamira y Crevea; *Cuestiones de Historia del Derecho y de Legislación Comparada*. Madrid: Sucesores de Hernando, 1914.

Alterini & López Cabana 1990 — Atilio Aníbal Alterini and Roberto M. López Cabana; 'El abuso del derecho. Estudio de Derecho Comparado'. *Revista Jurídica Argentina La Ley 1990-B*, 1990, pp. 1101–1117.

Alterini *et al.* 2005 — Jorge Horacio Alterini et al; *Propiedad Indígena*. Buenos Aires: Educa, 2005.

Álvarez Alonso 1999 — Clara Álvarez Alonso; *Lecciones de historia del constitucionalismo*. Madrid and Barcelona: Marcial Pons, 1999.

American Convention on Human Rights 1969 — 'American Convention on Human Rights "Pact of San Jose, Costa Rica" (B-32)'. Department of International Law. Organization of American States, Washington D.C. http://www.oas.org/dil/treaties_B-32_American_Convention_on_Human_Rights.htm. Last visited on April 21, 2015.

Amunátegui Perelló 2009 — Carlos Felipe Amunátegui Perelló; 'No siendo contra derecho ajeno: hacia la formulación de una teoría de las inmisiones en nuestro código civil'. *Revista Chilena de Derecho 36.3*, 2009, pp. 505–525.

Amunátegui Perelló 2012 — Carlos Felipe Amunátegui Perelló; 'Las relaciones de vecindad y la teoría de las inmisiones en el Código Civil'. *Revista de Derecho de la Pontificia Universidad Católica de Valparaíso 38*, 2012, pp. 77–120.

Ancel & Didry 2001 — Pascal Ancel and Claude Didry; 'L'abus de droit: une notion sans histoire? L'apparition de la notion d'abus de droit en droit français au début du XXe siècle', in: *L'abus de droit: Comparaisons franco-suisses*. Saint-Étienne: Publications de l'Université de Saint-Étienne, 2001, pp. 51–66.

Andreu Ocariz 1975 — Juan José Andreu Ocariz; *Luisiana Española*. Zaragoza: Librería General, 1975.

Ankersent & Ruppert 2006 — Thomas T. Ankersent and Thomas Ruppert; '*Tierra y Libertad*: The Social Function Doctrine and Land Reform in Latin America'. *Tulane Environmental Law Journal 19*, 2006, pp. 69–120.

Anta 2007 — Carlos Alberto Anta; 'Bien de familia y quiebra. Particularidades de dos sistemas en colisión'. *Revista Doctrina Societaria y Concursal 231*, 2007, pp. 96–114.

Anteproyecto Código Civil 1954 — *Anteproyecto de Código Civil de 1954 para la República Argentina*. [Tucumán]: Universidad Nacional de Tucumán, 1968.

Antequera 1895 — José María Antequera; *Historia de la legislación española desde los tiempos más remotos hasta nuestros dias*. 4th edition, Madrid: Imprenta de San Francisco de Sales, 1895.

Apostolic Exhortation Evangelii gaudium 2013 (English) — 'Apostolic Exhortation Evangelii gaudium of the Holy Father Francis'. The Holy See. http://w2.vatican.va/content/francesco/en/apost_exhortations/documents/papa-francesco_esortazione-ap_20131124_evangelii-gaudium.html. Last visited on April 21, 2015.

Aragoneses 2009 — Alfons Aragoneses; *Un Jurista del Modernismo: Raymond Saleilles y los Orígenes del Derecho Comparado*. Madrid: Editorial Dykinson, 2009.

Aranda 1890	Ricardo Aranda; *Colección de los tratados, convenciones capitulaciones, armisticios, y otros actos diplomáticos y políticos celebrados desde la independencia hasta el día, precedida de una introducción que comprende la época colonial.* Volume I, Lima: Imprenta del Estado, 1890.
Araújo *et al.* 1949	Orestes Araújo et al.; *Código Civil Anotado.* Volume I, Montevideo: Facultad de derecho y ciencias sociales. Universidad de Montevideo, 1949.
Arazi 1995	Roland Arazi; *Derecho procesal civil y comercial. Partes general y especial.* 2nd edition, Buenos Aires: Astrea, 1995.
Areán 1994	Beatriz Areán; *Curso de Derechos Reales: Privilegios y Derecho de Retención.* 3rd edition, Buenos Aires: Abeledo-Perrot, 1994.
Arena 1974	C. Richard Arena; 'Land Settlement Policies and Practices in Spanish Louisiana', in: John Francis McDermott (Ed.); *The Spanish in the Mississippi Valley, 1762–1804.* Urbana, Chicago, and London: University of Illinois Press, 1974, pp. 51–60.
Archivo General	Archivo General de la Nación Argentina, Sala IX-45-6-4, Buenos Aires.
Arnold 1996	Morris S. Arnold; 'Government, Law, and Politics', in: Gilbert C. Din (Ed.); *The Louisiana Purchase Bicentennial Series in Louisiana History.* Volume II, Lafayette: Center for Louisiana Studies University of Southwestern Louisiana, 1996, pp. 124–142.
ASLH 2013	'2013 Annual Meeting'. The American Society for Legal History. http://aslh.net/upcoming-conference/2013-conference/. Last visited on April 21, 2015.
ASLH 2015	'About ASLH'. The American Society for Legal History. http://aslh.net/about-aslh/. Last visited on April 21, 2015.
Asociación Argentina de Historia del Derecho 2006	'Asociación Argentina de Profesores e Investigadores de Historia del Derecho'. *Iushistoria Revista Electrónica 3*, 2006, p. 1. http://

p3.usal.edu.ar/index.php/iushistoria/issue/view/157. Last visited on April 21, 2015.

Aspell 1979 — Marcela Aspell; 'La Ley 4144 "de residencia": antecedentes—sanción—aplicación'. *Revista del Instituto de Historia del Derecho "Ricardo Levene"* 25, 1979, pp. 11–127.

Aspell 2010 — Marcela Aspell, 'Cómo enseño Historia del Derecho en las aulas de la Facultad de Derecho y Ciencias Sociales de la Universidad Nacional de Córdoba', in: Marcela Aspell et al (Coord.); *Perspectivas y desafíos de la historia del derecho argentino. I encuentro de la Asociación Argentina de Profesores e Investigadores de Historia del Derecho. Córdoba (8 y 9 de noviembre de 2007)*. Córdoba: Asociación Argentina de Profesores e Investigadores de Historia del Derecho, 2010, pp. 15–136.

Assemblée Nationale 1789 — 'Assemblée nationale. Séance du mercredi 26 aout 1789', in: J[érôme] Mavidal et al (Dir.); *Archives parlementaires de 1787 [à] 1860. Première série (1787 à 1799). Recueil complet des débats législatifs & politiques des Chambres françaises imprimé par ordre de l'Assemblée Nationale*. Volume VIII, Paris: Libraire Administrative de Paul Dupont, 1875, pp. 486–489.

Assies & Duhau 2009 — Willem Assies and Emilio Duhau; 'Land Tenure and tenure regimes in Mexico: An overview', in: Janine M. Ubink et al (Eds.); *Legalising Land Rights: Local Practices, State Responses and Tenure Security in Africa, Asia and Latin America*. Leiden: Leiden University Press, 2009, pp. 355–385.

Aubry & Rau 1863 — Charles Aubry and Charles-Frédéric Rau; *Cours de droit civil français: d'après l'ouvrage allemand de C.-S. Zachariae*. 3rd edition, Volume II, Paris: Cosse, 1863.

Australian-Canadian Legal History 2015 — 'Australian-Canadian Colonial Legal History Website'. OZCAN. http://web2.uvcs.uvic.

ca/courses/lawdemo/. Last visited on April 21, 2015.

Azcárate (de) 1879–1883 Gumersindo de Azcárate; *Ensayo sobre la historia del derecho de propiedad y su estado actual en Europa*. Volumes I–III, Madrid: Imprenta de la Revista de Legislación, 1879–1883.

Baade 1978 Hans W. Baade; 'The Formalities of Private Real Estate Transactions in Spanish North America: A Report on Some Recent Discoveries'. *Louisiana Law Review 38*, 1978, pp. 655–745.

Bagdikian 1967 Ben H. Bagdikian; 'A Forgotten New Deal Experiment in Land Reform in Mississippi'. *I.F. Stone's Weekly XV:25*, July 31, 1967, p. 3.

Bailey 1942 Joseph Kenton Bailey; *A Manual on Examination of Louisiana Land Titles*. New Orleans: Industries Publishing Co., 1942.

Barham 1976 Mack E. Barham; 'Methodology of the Civil Law in Louisiana'. *Tulane Law Review 50*, 1976, pp. 474–494.

Barlowe 1965 Raleigh Barlowe; 'Federal Programs for the Direction of Land Use'. *Iowa Law Review 50*, 1965, pp. 337–366.

Barnes 2013 Richard A. Barnes; 'The Capacity of Property Rights to Accommodate Social-Ecological Resilience'. *Ecology and Society 18(1)*: 6, 2013. http://dx.doi.org/10.5751/ES-05292-180106. Last visited on April 21, 2015.

Barraclough 1965 Solon [L.] Barraclough; '¿Qué es una reforma agraria?', in: Óscar Delgado (Ed.); *Reformas Agrarias en la America Latina: Procesos y Perspectivas*. Mexico and Buenos Aires: Fondo de Cultura Económica, 1965, pp. 127–145.

Barraclough 1973 Solon [L.] Barraclough (Ed.); *Agrarian Structure in Latin America; A Resume of the CIDA Land Tenure Studies of: Argentina, Brazil, Chile, Colombia, Ecuador, Guatemala, Peru*. Lexington: Lexington Books, 1973.

Barraclough 1999 — Solon L. Barraclough; *Land Reform in Developing Countries: The Role of the State and Other Actors*. Discussion Paper No. 101, June 1999. Geneva: United Nations Research Institute for Social Development, 1999.

Barraclough & Domike 1970 — Solon L. Barraclough and Arthur L. Domike; 'Agrarian Structure in Seven Latin American Countries', in: Rodolfo Stavenhagen (Ed.); *Agrarian Problems and Peasant Movements in Latin America*. Garden City: Anchor Books, 1970, pp. 41–94.

Barrientos Grandón 2009 — Javier Barrientos Grandón; 'Juan Sala Bañuls (1731–1806) y el "Código Civil" de Chile (1855)'. *Revista de Estudios Histórico-Jurídicos 31*, 2009, pp. 351–368.

Batiza 1962 — Rodolfo Batiza; 'The Unity of Private Law in Louisiana under the Spanish Rule'. *Inter-American Law Review 4*, 1962, pp. 139–156.

Batiza 1971 — Rodolfo Batiza; 'The Louisiana Civil Code of 1808: Its Actual Sources and Present Relevance'. *Tulane Law Review 46*, 1971, pp. 4–165.

Batiza 1972 — Rodolfo Batiza; 'The Actual Sources of the Louisiana *Projet* of 1823: A General Analytical Survey'. *Tulane Law Review 47*, 1972, pp. 1–115.

Batiza 1979 — Rodolfo Batiza; *Las fuentes del código civil de 1928: Introducción, notas y textos de sus fuentes originales no reveladas*. Mexico: Editorial Porrúa, 1979.

Batiza 1986 — Rodolfo Batiza; 'Sources of the Field Civil Code: The Civil Law Influences on a Common Law Code'. *Tulane Law Review 60*, 1986, pp. 799–819.

Beach & Pedersen 2013 — Derek Beach and Rasmus Brun Pedersen; *Process-Tracing Methods: Foundations and Guidelines*. Ann Arbor: University of Michigan Press, 2013.

Beaglehole 1935 — Ernest Beaglehole; 'Ownership and Inheritance in an American Indian Tribe'. *Iowa Law Review 20*, 1935, pp. 304–316.

Becket 1965 — James Becket; 'Problemas de la reforma agraria', in: Óscar Delgado (Ed.); *Reformas Agrarias en la America Latina: Procesos y Perspectivas*. Mexico and Buenos Aires: Fondo de Cultura Económica, 1965, pp. 559–592.

Becnel 2000 — Thomas A. Becnel; 'Louisiana Labor in the First Half of the Twentieth Century', in: Vaughan Burdin Baker (Ed.); *The Louisiana Purchase Bicentennial Series in Louisiana History*. Volume XV, Lafayette: Center for Louisiana Studies University of Southwestern Louisiana, 2000, pp. 564–577.

Beers 1989 — Henry Putney Beers; *French and Spanish Records of Louisiana*. Baton Rouge: LSU Press, 1989.

Bellisario 2006 — Antonio Bellisario; 'The Chilean Agrarian Transformation: The Pre-Agrarian Reform Period (1955–1965)'. *Journal of Agrarian Change* 6:2, 2006, pp. 167–204.

Bellomo 2003 — Manlio Bellomo; '¿Por qué un historiador del derecho europeo tiene que investigar las obras de los juristas indianos?', in: Luis E. González Vale (Coord.); *XIII Congreso del Instituto Internacional de Historia del Derecho Indiano. San Juan, 21 al 25 de mayo de 2000. Actas y Estudios*. Volume I, San Juan: Asamblea Legislativa de Puerto Rico, 2003, pp. 5–16.

Beneyto Pérez 1953 — Juan Beneyto Pérez; 'Derecho Histórico y Orden Jurídico Mundial'. *Tijdschrift voor Rechtsgeschiedenis* 21, 1953, pp. 55–58.

Bennett & Checkel 2015 — Andrew Bennett and Jeffrey T. Checkel; 'Process Tracing: From Philosophical Roots to Best Practices', in: Andrew Bennett and Jeffrey T. Checkel (Eds.); *Process Tracing in the Social Sciences: From Metaphor to Analytic Tool*. Cambridge: Cambridge University Press, 2015, pp. 3–38.

Berg 2010 — Bruce L. Berg; *Qualitative Research Methods for the Social Sciences*. 7th edition, London: Pearson Education, 2010.

Bergel 1988 Jean-Louis Bergel; 'Principal Features and Methods of Codification'. *Louisiana Law Review 48*, 1988, pp. 1073–1097.

Bergel 1994 Jean-Louis Bergel; *La Propriété.* Paris: Dalloz, 1994.

Bergel 2003 Jean-Louis Bergel; 'Les phénomènes de codification, de décodification et de recodification', in: Louis Perret and Alain-François Bisson (Eds.); *Evolution des Systemes Juridiques Bijuridsma et Commerce International.* Montreal: Wilson et Lafleur, 2003, pp. 31–42.

Berní y Catalá 1760 Joseph Berní [y Catalá]; *Instituta civil, y real, en donde con la mayor brevedad ſe explican los §§. de Justiniano, y en ſu ſeguida los caſos practicos, ſegun Leyes Reales de España, muy util, y provechoſo à los que deſean el bien comun.* Valencia: Benito Monfort, 1760.

Bibiloni 1929–1932 Juan Antonio Bibiloni; *Anteproyecto de reformas al código civil argentino: presentado a la comisión encargada de redactarlo.* Volumes I–VII, Buenos Aires: Valerio Abeledo, 1929–1932.

Billings 1983 Warren M. Billings; 'Louisiana Legal History and Its Sources: Needs, Opportunities and Approaches', in: Edward F. Haas (Ed.); *Louisiana's Legal Heritage.* Pensacola: Perdido Bay Press, 1983, pp. 189–202.

Billings 1993 Warren M. Billings; 'In Search of Fundamental Law: Constitutionalism in Louisiana', in: Warren M. Billings and Edward F. Haas (Eds.); *In Search of Fundamental Law: Louisiana's Constitutions, 1812–1974.* Lafayette: Center for Louisiana Studies, 1993, pp. 1–5.

Black's Law Dictionary 2014 'jurisdiction'. Bryan A. Garner (Ed.); *Black's Law Dictionary.* 10th edition, St. Paul: Thompson West, 2014.

Blakemore 1998 Harold Blakemore; 'Chile from the War of the Pacific to the world depression, 1880–1930', in: Leslie Bethell (Ed.); *The Cambridge History of Latin America.* Reprint, Volume V,

Cambridge and New York: Cambridge University Press, 1998, pp. 499–551.

Blanco 2001 — Mónica Blanco; 'Peronismo, mercantismo y política agraria en la Provincia de Buenos Aires (1946–55)'. *Mundo Agrario 1:2*, 2001, pp. [1–22].

Blasco 2000 — Yolanda Blasco, Juan Sala y el derecho de propiedad en México'. *Cuadernos del Instituto Antonio de Nebrija 3*, 2000, pp. 11–30.

Bloch 1952 — Marc Bloch; *Les caractères originaux de l'histoire rurale française*. New edition, Paris: Armand Colin, 1952.

Bobbio 1996 — Norberto Bobbio; *Il positivismo giuridico: Lezioni di Filosofia del Diritto raccolte dal dott. Nello Morra*. New edition, Turin: G. Giappichelli Editore, 1996.

Bobroff 2001 — Kenneth H. Bobroff; 'Retelling Allotment: Indian Property Rights and the Myth of Common Ownership'. *Vanderbilt Law Review 54*, 2001, pp. 1559–1623.

Bolgár 1960 — Vera Bolgár; 'The Magic of Property and Public Welfare'. *Inter-American Law Review 2*, 1960, pp. 283–298.

Bolgár 1975 — Vera Bolgár; 'Abuse of Rights in France, Germany, and Switzerland: A Survey of a Recent Chapter in Legal Doctrine'. *Louisiana Law Review 35*, 1975, pp. 1015–1036.

Bonilla 2011 — Daniel Bonilla; 'Liberalism and Property in Colombia: Property as a Right and Property as a Social Function'. *Fordham Law Review 80*, 2011, pp. 1135–1170.

Bonilla Maldonado 2013 — Daniel Bonilla Maldonado (Coord.); *La Función Social de la Propiedad*. Buenos Aires: Eudeba, 2013.

Borda 1971 — Guillermo A. Borda; *La reforma de 1968 al código civil*. Buenos Aires: Editorial Perrot, 1971.

Borda 1987 — Guillermo A. Borda; *Tratado de Derecho Civil Parte General*. 9th edition, Volume I, Buenos Aires: Editorial Perrot, 1987.

Borda 2008 — Guillermo A. Borda; *Tratado de Derecho Civil Derechos Reales*. 5th edition, Volume I, Buenos Aires: La Ley, 2008.

Borde & Góngora 1956 — Jean Borde and Mario Góngora; *Evolución de la propiedad rural en el Valle del Puangue*. Volume I, Santiago: Universidad de Chile, 1956.

Botero Bernal 2010 — Andrés Botero Bernal; 'Presupuestos epistemológicos y metodológicos de la iushistoria'. *Precedente—Anuario Jurídico 2010*, 2010, pp. 45–70.

Boulot 2012 — Peter Boulot; 'A New Legal Paradigm: Towards a Jurisprudence Based on Ecological Sovereignty'. *Macquarie Journal of International and Comparative Environmental Law 8*, 2012, pp. 1–15.

Brahm García 1994 — Enrique Brahm García; 'El concepto de propiedad en la Ley N° 15.020 sobre reforma agraria'. *Revista Chilena de Derecho 21:1*, 1994, pp. 159–187.

Brahm García 1996 — Enrique Brahm García; 'El concepto de propiedad en el Código Napoleónico: Una nueva interpretación de su artículo 544 en la historiografía jurídica alemana'. *Revista Chilena de Derecho 23:1*, 1996, pp. 7–12.

Brahm García 1999 — Enrique Brahm García; 'La perversión de la cultura jurídica chilena durante el Gobierno de la Unidad Popular. "Resquicios legales" y derecho de propiedad'. *Revista Chilena de Historia del Derecho 18*, 1999, pp. 335–349.

Brahm García 2012 — Enrique Brahm García; 'Algunos aspectos del proceso de socialización del derecho de propiedad en Chile durante el gobierno del general Carlos Ibañez del Campo (1927–1931)'. *Rechtsgeschichte 20*, 2012, pp. 234–256.

Brand 2007 — Oliver Brand; 'Conceptual Comparisons: Towards a Coherent Methodology of Comparative Legal Studies'. *Brooklyn Journal of International Law 32*, 2007, pp. 405–466.

Bravo Lira 1982 Bernardino Bravo Lira; 'La difusión del código civil de Bello en los países de derecho castellano y portugués'. *Revista de Estudios Histórico-Jurídicos* 7, 1982, pp. 71–106.

Bravo Lira 1989 Bernardino Bravo Lira; *Derecho Común y Derecho Propio en el Nuevo Mundo*. Santiago: Editorial Jurídica de Chile, 1989.

Bravo Lira 1993 Bernardino Bravo Lira; *Historia de las instituciones políticas de Chile e Hispanoamérica*. 2nd edition, Santiago: Editorial Jurídica de Chile, 1993.

Bravo Lira 2000 Bernardino Bravo Lira; 'Dougnac, Antonio y Vicencio, Felipe, *La escuela chile de historiadores del derecho*'. *Revista Chilena de Derecho* 27:1, 2000, pp. 621–624.

Brebbia 2001 Roberto Brebbia (Dir.); *Estudios sobre el Proyecto de Código Unificado de 1998*. Buenos Aires: Zavalía, 2001.

Brierley 1994 John E.C. Brierley; 'Reception of English Law in the Canadian Province of Quebec', in: Michel Douce and Jacques Vanderlinden (Coord.); *La réception des systèmes juridiques. Implantation et destin*. Brussels: Bruylant, 1994, pp. 103–137.

Brierley & Macdonald 1993 John E.C. Brierley and Roderick A. Macdonald (Eds.); *Quebec Civil Law: An Introduction to Quebec Private Law*. Toronto: Montgomery, 1993.

Brito Figueroa 1982 Federico Brito Figueroa; *El Cuadro Histórico de la Propiedad Territorial en las Colonias Hispanoamericanas*. Caracas: Universidad Santa Maria, 1982.

Brosman 1938 Paul Brosman; 'Editorial: A Controversy and a Challenge'. *Tulane Law Review* 12, 1938, pp. 239–242.

Browning 1965 David S. Browning; 'Historic Basis of Mexican Mining Law'. *Inter-American Law Review* 7, 1965, pp. 1–31.

Bryan 2000 Bradley Bryan; 'Property as Ontology: On Aboriginal and English Understandings of

Ownership'. *Canadian Journal of Law and Jurisprudence* 13, 2000, pp. 3–31.

Bryner 2012 — Nicholas S. Bryner; 'Brazil's Green Court: Environmental Law in the Superior Tribunal de Justiça (High Court of Brazil)'. *Pace Environmental Law Review* 29, 2012, pp. 470–537.

Bunge 1912–1913 — Carlos O. Bunge; *Historia del Derecho Argentino*. Volumes I–II, Buenos Aires: Facultad de Derecho y Ciencias Sociales, 1912–1913.

Burger & Frymer 2013 — Michael Burger and Paul Frymer; 'Property Law and American Empire'. *Roger Williams University Legal Studies Paper No. 134*, 2013. http://ssrn.com/abstract=2228418. Last visited on April 21, 2015.

Burgos 2001 — Benjamín Burgos; *Curso de derecho constitucional*. Salta: Virtudes Editorial Universitaria, 2001.

Burns 1928 — Francis P. Burns; 'The Spanish Land Laws of Louisiana'. *Louisiana Historical Quarterly* 11, 1928, pp. 557–581.

Cabral Texo 1919 — Jorge Cabral Texo; *Fuentes Nacionales del Código Civil Argentino*. Buenos Aires: Jesús Menéndez, 1919.

Cabral Texo 1920 — Jorge Cabral Texo; *Historia del Código Civil argentino*. Buenos Aires: Jesús Menéndez, 1920.

Cairns 2009 — John W. Cairns; 'The De la Vergne Volume and the Digest of 1808'. *Tulane European and Civil Law Forum* 24, 2009, pp. 31–81.

Cairns 2015 — John W. Cairns; *Codification, Transplants and History: Law Reform in Louisiana (1808) and Quebec (1866)*. Clark: Talbot Publishing, 2015.

Caldera 1981 — Rafael Caldera (Dir.); *Obras Completas de Andrés Bello*. 2nd edition, Volume XIV, Caracas: Fundación La Casa de Bello, 1981.

Calvo González & Monereo Pérez 2005 — José Calvo González and José Luis Monereo Pérez; 'Léon Duguit (1859–1928): jurista de una sociedad en transformación'. *Revista de*

Derecho Constitucional Europeo 4, 2005, pp. 483–547.

Calvo San José 2000 — María José Calvo San José; *La Función Social de la Propiedad y su Proyección en el Sistema de Compensación Urbanística*. Salamanca: Ediciones Universidad de Salamanca, 2000.

Campos Harriet 1956 — Fernando Campos Harriet; *Historia Constitucional de Chile*. Santiago: Editorial Jurídica de Chile, 1956.

Camps y Arboix (de) 1953 — Joaquín de Camps y Arboix; *La propiedad de la tierra y su función social*. Barcelona: Bosch, 1953.

Cantor & Kraus 1990 — Paul Cantor and James Kraus; 'Changing Patterns of Ownership Rights in the People's Republic of China: A Legal and Economic Analysis in the Context of Economic Reforms and Social Conditions'. *Vanderbilt Journal of Transnational Law 23*, 1990, pp. 479–538.

Cañedo-Argüelles 1999 — Teresa Cañedo-Argüelles; 'La comunidad de Itatí, un marco para el debate cultural y la afirmación identitaria en el Paraná'. *Revista Complutense de Historia de América 25*, 1999, pp. 195–217.

Cardozo 1946 — Benjamin N. Cardozo; *The Nature of the Judicial Process*. 13th printing, New Haven: Yale University Press, 1946.

Caroni 2012 — Pio Caroni; *Escritos sobre la Codificiación*. Translation by Adela Mora Cañada and Manuel Martínez Neira, Madrid: Universidad Carlos III de Madrid, 2012.

Caroni 2013 — Pio Caroni; *Lecciones de Historia de la Codificación*. Edition by Adela Mora Cañada and Manuel Martínez Neira, Madrid: Universidad Carlos III de Madrid, 2013.

Carrasco Delgado 2002 — Sergio Carrasco Delgado; *Génesis y vigencia de los textos constitucionales chilenos*. 3rd edition, Santiago: Editorial Jurídica de Chile, 2002.

Carrasco Delgado 2006 — Sergio Carrasco Delgado; 'La evolución político-constitucional de Chile'. *Estudios Constitucionales 6:2*, pp. 301–324.

Carretero Sánchez 1994 — Santiago Carretero Sánchez; *La Propiedad: Bases sociológicas del concepto en la sociedad postindustrial*. Unpublished Ph.D. thesis, Madrid: Universidad Complutense de Madrid, 1994.

Carrió 1981 — Genaro R. Carrió; 'Judge Made Law under a Civil Code'. *Louisiana Law Review 41*, 1981, pp. 993–1005.

Carroll 1970 — Thomas F. Carroll; 'Land Reform as an Explosive Force in Latin America', in: Rodolfo Stavenhagen (Ed.); *Agrarian Problems and Peasant Movements in Latin America*. Garden City: Anchor Books, 1970, pp. 101–137.

Carter 2001 — Hodding Carter; 'Huey Long: American Dictator', in: Edward F. Haas (Ed.); *The Louisiana Purchase Bicentennial Series in Louisiana History*. Volume VIII, Lafayette: Center for Louisiana Studies University of Southwestern Louisiana, 2001, pp. 27–44.

Carvajal Arenas 2006 — Lorena Carvajal Arenas; 'La unificación del derecho de las obligaciones civiles y comerciales'. *Revista de Derecho de la Pontificia Universidad Católica de Valparaíso 27*, 2006, pp. 37–53.

Casso y Romero (de) 1923 — Ignacio de Casso y Romero; *El problema de la propiedad de la tierra* (*Discurso leído en la Universidad de Sevilla en el acto de la apertura del curso académico el 1° de octubre de 1923*). Seville: Imp. y lib. de Eulogio de las Heras, 1923.

Castán Tobeñas 1963 — José Castán Tobeñas; *La propiedad y sus problemas actuales*. 2nd edition, Madrid: Reus, 1963.

Castán Vázquez 1984 — José María Castán Vázquez; 'Los Libros Jurídicos Españoles consultados por Vélez Sarsfield', in: *Estudios en Homenaje al*

Dr. Guillermo A. Borda. Buenos Aires: La Ley, 1984, pp. 73–83.

Castán Vázquez 2000 — José María Castán Vázquez; 'Vélez Sársfield, Jurista Bibliófilo', in: *Homenaje a Dalmacio Vélez Sársfield*. Volume IV, Córdoba: Academia Nacional de Derecho y Ciencias Sociales de Córdoba, 2000, pp. 519–528.

Castro 1991 — DonaldS.Castro;*TheDevelopmentandPolitics of Argentine Immigration Policy 1852–1914:* To Govern is to Populate. San Francisco: Mellen Research University Press, 1991.

Castro y Bravo (de) 1955 — Federico de Castro y Bravo; *Derecho civil de España*. 3rd edition, Volume I, Madrid: Instituto de Estudios Políticos, 1955.

Castro Mayer (de) *et al.* 1963 — Antonio de Castro Mayer et al; *Reforma Agraria: Problema de Conciencia*. Buenos Aires: Club de Lectores, 1963.

Censo 1895 — *Segundo Censo de la República Argentina. Mayo 10 de 1895. Decretado en la administración del Dr. Sáenz Peña verificado en la del Dr. Uriburu.* Volume II, Buenos Aires: Taller Tipográfico de la Penitenciaria Nacional, 1898.

Censo 1920 — Dirección General de Estadística; *Censo de Población de la República de Chile. Levantado el 15 de diciembre de 1920*. Santiago: Soc. Imp. y Litografía Universo, 1925.

Censo 2010 — 'Resultados definitivos'. Censo Argentino 2010. http://www.censo2010.indec.gov.ar/resultadosdefinitivos_totalpais.asp. Last visited on April 21, 2015.

Census 2010 — '2010 Census Data'. United States Census 2010. http://www.census.gov/2010census/data/. Last visited on April 21, 2015.

Centro de Estudios de la Educación Argentina 2015 — Centro de Estudios de la Educación Argentina; *CEA Informe 4:34*. Buenos Aires: Universidad de Belgrano, 2015.

Cerro 1979 — Ernesto Cerro, 'La migración en la República Argentina y especialmente en Tucumán entre 1869 y 1914', in: *La Inmigración en la*

Argentina. Tucumán: Universidad Nacional de Tucumán, 1979, pp. 81–88.

Chambers 1925 Henry E. Chambers; *A History of Louisiana: Wilderness, Colony, Province, Territory, State, People*. Volume I, Chicago and New York: American Historical Society, 1925.

Cháneton 1937 Abel Cháneton; *Historia de Vélez Sársfield*. Volume II, Buenos Aires: Editorial "La Facultad," 1937.

Charter of Punta del Este 1961 'The Charter of Punta del Este, Establishing an Alliance for Progress Within the Framework of Operation Pan America; August 17, 1961'. The Avalon Project: Documents in Law, History and Diplomacy. http://avalon.law.yale.edu/20th_century/intam16.asp . Last visited on April 21, 2015.

Chilean Land Reform 1963 'The Chilean Land Reform: A Laboratory for Alliance-for-Progress Techniques'. *Yale Law Journal* 73, 1963, pp. 310–333.

Chonchot 1965 Jacques Chonchot; 'Razones económicas, sociales y políticas de la reforma agraria', in: Óscar Delgado (Ed.); *Reformas Agrarias en la America Latina: Procesos y Perspectivas*. Mexico and Buenos Aires: Fondo de Cultura Económica, 1965, pp. 100–126.

Civil Code Chile 2008 Julio Romanach Jr. (Trans.); *Civil Code of Chile 2008: Translated into English with an Introduction and Index*. Baton Rouge: Lawrence Publishing, 2008.

Civil Code Louisiana 1825 *Civil Code of the State of Louisiana*. New Orleans: J.C. de St. Romes, 1825.

Civil Code Louisiana 2015 'Louisiana Civil Code'. Civil Law Online. Center of Civil Law Studies. Louisiana State University. http://lcco.law.lsu.edu/. Last visited on April 21, 2015.

Civil Code New York 1865 *The Civil Code of the State of New York: Reported Complete by the Commissioners of the Code*. Albany: Weed, Parsons & Co., 1865.

Claro Solar 1979 — Luis Claro Solar; *Explicaciones de Derecho Civil Chileno y Comparado*. Volume III:VI:I (De los bienes), Santiago: Editorial Jurídica de Chile, 1979.

Clemente Campos 1994–1995 — María Belén Clemente Campos; 'Notas sobre la subasta de bienes de propios a principios del siglo XIX'. *Anuario de la Facultad de Derecho 12–13*, 1994–1995, pp. 439–453.

Cobas & Zago 1991 — Manuel Osvaldo Cobas and Jorge Alberto Zago; 'La influencia de las 'notas' del código civil en la ciencia del derecho argentino y latinoamericano', in: Sandro Schipani (Coord.); *Dalmacio Vélez Sarsfield e il diritto latinoamericano*. Padua, CEDAM, 1991, pp. 141–148.

Code Civil 1804 — *Code civil des français. Édition originale et seule officielle*. Paris: De l'Imprimerie de la République, an XII, 1804.

Code Revision Supplement 1984 — *Civil Law Property: Code Revision Supplement*. Baton Rouge: Paul M. Hebert Law Center Publications Institute, 1984.

Código Civil Argentina 1871 — 'Ley 340 -Código Civil', in: *Anales de Legislación Argentina*. Volume 1852–1880, Buenos Aires: La Ley, 1954, pp. 496–905.

Código Civil Argentina 2015 — 'Código Civil de la Nación'. Infoleg. Ministerio de Economía y Finanzas Públicas. http://www.infoleg.gov.ar/infolegInternet/anexos/105000-109999/109481/texact.htm. Last visited on April 21, 2015.

Código Civil Chile 1857 — *Código Civil de la República de Chile*. Santiago: Imprenta Nacional, 1856.

Código Civil Colombia 1895 — *Código civil colombiano expedido por el congreso de 1873 y adoptado por la ley 57 de 1887: con un suplemento de las leyes que lo adicionan y reforman, desde 1887 hasta 1892. Edición Oficial.* Bogotá: Imprenta Nacional, 1895.

Código Civil Ecuador 1871 — *Código Civil y Código de Enjuiciamientos en Materia Civil de la República del Ecuador.*

New York: Imprenta de Hallet y Breen, 1871.

Código Civil El Salvador 1880 — *Código Civil de la República del Salvador*. 2nd edition, San Salvador: Imprenta del Comercio, 1880.

Código Civil España 1889 — *Código Civil–Edición Oficial Reformada*. Madrid: Imprenta del Ministerio de Gracia y Justicia, 1889.

Código Civil Honduras 1880 — *Código Civil de la República de Honduras. 1880*. Tegucigalpa: Tipografía Nacional, 1880.

Código Civil México 1871 — *Código Civil del Distrito Federal y Territorio de la Baja-California, mandado observar en el Estado de Hidalgo*. Mexico: Imprenta de E. Ancona y M. Peniche, 1871.

Código Civil Nicaragua 1871 — *Código Civil de la República de Nicaragua*. Managua: Imprenta de "El Centro-Americano," 1871.

Código Civil Panamá 1861 — *Código Civil del Estado de Panamá*. New York: Imprenta de Esteban Hallet, 1861.

Código Civil Puerto Rico 1984 — *Código Civil de Puerto Rico Comentado*. Orford: Equity Pub. Corp., 1984.

Código Civil Uruguay 1868 — *Código Civil para el Estado Oriental del Uruguay promulgado por el gobierno provisorio en 23 de enero de 1868 y sancionado por la Honorable Asamblea en 20 de julio de 1868*. Montevideo: Imprenta de La Tribuna, 1868.

Código Civil Venezuela 1862 — *Código Civil. Edición Oficial*. Caracas: Imprenta de El Independiente, 1862.

Código Civil y Comercial Argentina 2015 — Código Civil y Comercial de la Nación Ley 26994. Infoleg. Ministerio de Economía y Finanzas Públicas. http://www.infoleg.gob.ar/infolegInternet/anexos/235000-239999/235975/texact.htm. Last visited on August 20, 2016.

Código Social de Malinas 1947 — Unión Internacional de Estudios Sociales; *Código Social de Malinas. Esbozo de una síntesis social católica*. 2nd edition, Buenos Aires: Junta Central de la Acción Católica Argentina, 1947.

Código Social de Malinas 1949 — Unión Internacional de Estudios Sociales; *Código Social de Malinas*. Buenos Aires: Editorial Difusión, 1949.

Códigos Españoles 1847–1851 — *Los códigos españoles concordados y anotados*. Volumes I–XII, Madrid: M. Rivadeneyra, 1847–1851.

Cohen 2002 — Jean L. Cohen; *Regulating Intimacy: A New Legal Paradigm*. Princeton and Oxford: Princeton University Press, 2002.

Coing 1976 — Helmut Coing; *Aufgaben des Rechtshistorikers*. Sitzungsberichte der Wissenschaftlichen Gesellschaft an der Johann Wolfgang Goethe-Universität Frankfurt am Main, Volume 13:5, Wiesbaden: Steiner, 1976.

Colina Garea 1995 — Rafael Colina Garea; *La función social de la propiedad privada en la constitución española de 1978*. Unpublished Ph.D. thesis, La Coruña: Universidad de La Coruña, 1995.

Colley 2014 — Linda Colley; 'Empires of Writing: Britain, America and Constitutions, 1776–1848'. *Law and History Review 32:2*, 2014, pp. 237–266.

Colmo 1961 — Alfredo Colmo; *Técnica Legislativa del Código Civil Argentino*. 2nd edition, Buenos Aires: Abeledo-Perrot, 1961.

Combe 1996 — David Combe; 'The Louisiana Lawyer's Roman Law Library: Recollections of an Antiquarian Bibliophile'. *Tulane Law Review 70*, 1996, pp. 2003–2049.

Comparative Table 1937 — 'Comparative Table of Codal Articles of Civil Code of 1808, 1825, and 1870[;] The Projet and Code Napoleon', in: *Louisiana Legal Archives*. Volume II, New Orleans: Thos. J. Moran's Sons, 1937, pp. 2–68.

Comte 1851 — Auguste Comte; *Système de politique positive, ou traité de sociologie, Instituant la Religion de l'humanité*. Volume I, Paris: Librairie scientifique industrielle de L. Mathias, 1851.

Concordance for the 1976–2008 Revisions — 'Concordance for the 1976–2008 Revisions, the Civil Code of 1870, Civil Code of 1825,

Projet, Civil Code of 1808, and Code Napoléon', in: A[thanasios] N. Yiannopoulos (Ed.); *2008 Compiled Edition of the Civil Codes of Louisiana*. Volume XVIIA West's Louisiana Statutes Annotated, St. Paul: Thomson West, 2008, pp. T.54–T.106.

Concordance Tables 1942 — 'Concordance Tables for Revised Civil Code of 1870, Civil Code of 1825, Projet, Civil Code of 1808, and Code Napoleon', in: *Louisiana Legal Archives*. Volume III, Part II, Baton Rouge: The Louisiana State Law Institute, 1942, pp. 2043–2066.

Conesa 2012 — Eduardo Conesa; 'El impuesto a la tierra libre de mejoras, recursos naturales, hidrocarburos y el federalismo en la Argentina'. Portal Académico. Facultad de Derecho, Universidad de Buenos Aires, [2012], pp. 1–23. http://portalacademico.derecho.uba.ar/catedras/archivos/catedras/19/el_impuesto_tierra_libre_de_mejoras_y_a_los_recursos_naturales_en_general_en_el_regimen_federal_argentino_copia.pdf. Last visited on April 21, 2015.

Conferencia de Facultades 1961 — 'II Conferencia de Facultades Latinoamericanas de Derecho'. *Revista de Derecho Puertorriqueño 1*, 1961, pp. 93–97.

Congost 2007a — Rosa Congost; 'La "gran obra" de la propiedad. Los motivos de un debate', in: Rosa Congost and José Miguel Lana (Eds.); *Campos cerrados, debates abiertos: análisis histórico y propiedad de la tierra en Europa (siglos XVI-XIX)*. Pamplona: Universidad pública de Navarra, 2007, pp. 21–52.

Congost 2007b — Rosa Congost; *Tierras, leyes, historia: estudios sobre "la gran obra de la propiedad."* Barcelona: Crítica, 2007.

Constitución Argentina 1853 — 'Constitución de la Confederación Argentina', in: *Anales de Legislación Argentina*. Volume 1852–1880, Buenos Aires: La Ley, 1954, pp. 9–52.

Constitución Argentina 1949 — *Constitución de la Nación Argentina. La reforma de la carta magna. Aprobada y Jurada por la Convención Nacional Constituyente (16 de marzo 1949)*. Buenos Aires: Editores Ciordia & Rodríguez, 1951.

Constitución Argentina 1994 — 'República de Argentina. Argentine Republic. Constitución de 1994. 1994 Constitution'. Political Database of the Americas. http://pdba.georgetown.edu/Constitutions/Argentina/argen94_e.html. Last visited on April 21, 2015.

Constitución Bolivia 2009 — 'República del Bolivia. Republic of Bolivia. Constitución de 2009. Constitution of 2009'. Political Database of the Americas. http://pdba.georgetown.edu/Constitutions/Bolivia/bolivia09.html. Last visited on April 21, 2015.

Constitución Chile 1833 — *Constitución de la República de Chile jurada y promulgada el 25 de mayo de 1833*. [Santiago]: Imprenta de la Opinión, [1833].

Constitución Chile 1925 — *Constitución Política de la República de Chile promulgada el 18 de septiembre de 1925. Edición Oficial*. Santiago: Imprenta Universitaria, 1925.

Constitución México 1917 — 'Constitución política de los Estados Unidos Mexicanos que reforma la de 5 de febrero del 1857', in: *Diario Oficial. Órgano del Gobierno Provisional de la República Mexicana. Tomo V. 4ª Época. Número 30. Lunes 5 de febrero de 1917*, pp. 149–161.

Constitución Panamá 1946 — 'La Constitución Política de la República de Panamá', in: *Gaceta Oficial. Órgano del Estado. Año XLIII. Número 9938. Lunes 4 de marzo de 1946*, pp. 1–24.

Constitución Paraguay 1940 — 'Decreto-Ley N. 2.242. Por el cual se promulga la nueva Constitución Nacional', in: *Gaceta Oficial. Sección Registro Oficial. Asunción, Julio 12 de 1940*, pp. 9–21.

Convención Nacional Constituyente 1949 — *Diario de Sesiones de la Convención Nacional Constituyente. Año 1949. 24 de enero—16 de*

	marzo. Volume I, Buenos Aires: Imprenta del Congreso de la Nación, 1949.
Cordero Quinzacara 2006	Eduardo Cordero Quinzacara; 'La Dogmática Constitucional de la Propiedad en el Derecho Chileno'. *Revista de Derecho 19:1*, 2006, pp. 125–148.
Cordero Quinzacara 2008	Eduardo Cordero Quinzacara; 'De la propiedad a las propiedades. La evolución de la concepción liberal de la propiedad'. *Revista de Derecho de la Pontificia Universidad Católica de Valparaíso 31*, 2008, pp. 493–525.
Cornejo 1946	Atilio Cornejo; 'Bibliotecas privadas de Salta en la época colonial'. *Boletín del Instituto de San Felipe y Santiago de Estudios Históricos de Salta 4:16*, 1946, pp. 67–109.
Cornejo & Vergara 1938	Atilio Cornejo and Miguel Ángel Vergara; *Mercedes de Tierras y Solares (1583–1589)*. Salta: Imprenta San Martín, 1938.
Correlación de Artículos 1981	'Índice de Correlación de Artículos', in: Rafael Caldera (Dir.); *Obras Completas de Andrés Bello*. 2nd edition, Volume XVI, Caracas: Fundación La Casa de Bello, 1981, pp. 1065–1140.
Corrientes (Provincia de) 1877	Provincia de Corrientes; *Coleccion de datos y documentos referentes á Misiones como parte integrante del territorio de la provincia de Corrientes*. Corrientes: Imprenta de La Verdad, 1877.
Cortés Conde 1998	Roberto Cortés Conde; 'The growth of the Argentine economy, *c*. 1870–1914', in: Leslie Bethell (Ed.); *The Cambridge History of Latin America*. Reprint, Volume V, Cambridge and New York: Cambridge University Press, 1998, pp. 327–357.
Costituzione Italiana 1947	'Costituzione della Repubblica Italiana. Copia del documento firmato dal Capo Provvisorio dello Stato, Enrico De Nicola, a Palazzo Giustiniani il 27 dicembre 1947'. Senato della Repubblica. http://www.senato.it/documenti/repository/relazioni/

libreria/Costituzione_anastatica.pdf. Last visited on April 21, 2015.

Cox 1959 — James J. Cox; 'Outdoor Advertisements—Aesthetics and the "Public Right"'. *Tulane Law Review 33*, 1959, pp. 852–869.

Crawford & Haymon 2008 — William E. Crawford and Cordell H. Haymon; 'Louisiana State Law Institute Recognizes 70-Year Milestone: Origin, History and Accomplishments'. *Louisiana Bar Journal 56*, 2008, pp. 85–95.

Crepeau 2000 — Paul-A. Crepeau; 'Réflexions sur la Codification du Droit Privé'. *Osgoode Hall Law Journal 38 :2*, 2000, pp. 267–295.

Cruz Barney 2012 — Óscar Cruz Barney; *Historia del Derecho Indiano*. Valencia: Tirant lo Blanch, 2012.

Cueto 1999 — Adolfo Omar Cueto; *Historia del Proceso de Enajenación de la Tierra Fiscal en Mendoza (siglos XVI-XIX): Estudio sobre la aplicación de la Legislación Indiana en la época colonial. Su vigencia y proyección durante el siglo XIX en Mendoza.* Mendoza: Universidad Nacional de Cuyo, Facultad de Filosofía y Letras, 1999.

Cunningham 1965 — Roger A. Cunningham; 'Land-Use Control—The State and Local Programs'. *Iowa Law Review 50*, 1965, pp. 367–457.

Daggett *et al.* 1937 — Harriet Spiller Daggett et al.; 'A Reappraisal Appraised: A Brief for the Civil Law of Louisiana'. *Tulane Law Review 12*, 1937, pp. 12–41.

Dagrossa 2010 — Norberto C. Dagrossa; 'Las ideas iushistoriográficas de Ricardo Smith', in: Marcela Aspell et al (Coord.); *Perspectivas y desafíos de la historia del derecho argentino. I encuentro de la Asociación Argentina de Profesores e Investigadores de Historia del Derecho. Córdoba (8 y 9 de noviembre de 2007)*. Córdoba: Asociación Argentina de Profesores e Investigadores de Historia del Derecho, 2010, pp. 491–507.

Dainow 1958 Joseph Dainow; 'Moreau Lislet's Notes On Sources of Louisiana Civil Code of 1808'. *Louisiana Law Review 19*, 1958, pp. 43–51.

Daract 2005–2007 María Victoria Daract; 'La historia de la propiedad', in: Susana T. Ramella (Dir.); *Poder, propiedad y propiedades en Argentina. Informe final de investigación (SECyT UNCuyo 06/F184)*. Mendoza: Universidad Nacional de Cuyo, Facultad de Ciencias Políticas y Sociales, 2005–2007, pp. 16–35. http://bdigital.uncu.edu.ar/1509. Last visited on April 21, 2015.

Dard 1805 Henri-Jean-Baptiste Dard; *Code civil des Français, avec des notes indicatives des lois romaines, coutumes, ordonnances, édits et déclarations, qui ont rapport [à] chaque article; ou Conférence du Code civil avec les lois anciennes*. Paris: J.-A. Commaille, 1805.

Dargo 1970 George Dargo; *Legal codification and the politics of territorial government in Jefferson's Louisiana, 1803–1808*. S.l.: s.n. [typed edition preserved at the LSU Law Library], 1970.

Dargo 2009a George Dargo; 'Introduction to Revised Edition', in: George Dargo; *Jefferson's Louisiana: Politics and the Clash of Legal Traditions*. Revised edition, Clark: Lawbook Exchange, 2009, pp. xiii–xxix.

Dargo 2009b George Dargo; *Jefferson's Louisiana: Politics and the Clash of Legal Traditions*. Revised edition, Clark: Lawbook Exchange, 2009.

Dart 1931 Henry Plauche Dart; 'The Influence of the Ancient Laws of Spain on the Jurisprudence of Louisiana'. *Tulane Law Review 6*, 1931, pp. 83–93.

David & Brierley 1968 René David and John E. Brierley; *Major Legal Systems in the World Today: An Introduction to the Comparative Study of Law*. London: The Free Press, Collier-Macmillan, 1968.

Davidson 2011 — Nestor M. Davidson; 'Sketches for a Hamiltonian Vernacular as a Social Function of Property'. *Fordham Law Review 80*, 2011, pp. 1053–1070.

Davis 1978 — Edwin Adams Davis; *Louisiana the Pelican State.* 4th edition (reprint), Baton Rouge: Louisiana State University Press, 1978.

de Gasperi 1955 — Luis de Gasperi; 'El Futuro de la Codificación'. *Tulane Law Review 29*, 1955, pp. 223–238.

de Janvry *et al.* 2001 — Alain de Janvry et al; 'The Changing Role of the State in Latin American Land Reforms', in: Alain de Janvry et al (Eds.); *Access to Land, Rural Poverty and Public Action.* Oxford: Oxford University Press, 2001 pp. 279–303.

de la Harpe 1851 — Benard de la Harpe; 'Historical Journal of the Establishment of the French in Louisiana (circa 1723)', in: Benjamin Franklin French; *Historical Collections of Louisiana.* Volume III, New York: Appleton & Company, 1851, pp. 9–118.

de los Mozos 1993 — José Luis de los Mozos; *El derecho de propiedad: crisis y retorno a la tradición jurídica.* Madrid: Editorial Revista de Derecho Privado, 1993.

de Villiers 2003 — Bertus de Villiers; *Land reform: Issues and challenges. A comparative overview of experiences in Zimbabwe, Namibia, South Africa and Australia.* Johannesburg: Konrad-Adenauer-Stiftung, 2003.

de Vries 2013 — Ubaldus de Vries; 'Kuhn and Legal Research: A Reflexive Paradigmatic View on Legal Research'. *Recht en Methode in onderzoek en onderwijs 2013 3:1*, 2013, pp. 7–25.

Dekker 2003 — Henri A.L. Dekker; *The Invisible Line: Land Reform, Land Tenure Security, and Land Registration.* Aldershot and Burlington: Ashgate, 2003.

Del Duca & Levasseur 2010 — Louis F. Del Duca and Alain A. Levasseur; 'Impact of Legal Culture and Legal Transplants on the Evolution of the U.S. Legal System'. *The American Journal of Comparative Law 58: supplement,* 2010, pp. 1–29.

Delahaye 2003 — Olivier Delahaye; 'Réforme agraire et marché foncier: la réflexion aux États-Unis et son impact dans les institutions multilatérales de développement'. *Revue Tiers-Monde 44 :174*, 2003, pp. 449–466.

Delgado de Miguel 2002 — Juan Francisco Delgado de Miguel (Coord.); *Instituciones de Derecho Privado: Reales.* Volume II, Madrid: Civitas, 2002.

Demélas 2003 — Marie-Danielle Demélas; 'Présentation', in: Marie-Danielle Demélas and Nadine Vivier (Dir.); *Les propriétés collectives face aux attaques libérales (1750–1914): Europe occidentale et Amérique latine.* Rennes: Presses universitaires de Rennes, 2003, pp. 219–224.

Deploige 1895 — Simon Deploige; 'La théorie thomiste de la propriété'. *Revue néo-scolastique 2:5*, 1895. pp. 61–82.

Díaz Couselo 2003 — José María Díaz Couselo; 'Pensamiento Jurídico y Renovación Legislativa', in: *Nueva Historia de la Nación Argentina.* Volume V, Buenos Aires: Academia Nacional de la Historia, 2003, pp. 363–403.

Díaz Couselo 2006 — José María Díaz Couselo; 'Enrique R. Aftalión y la Historia del Derecho'. *Revista de Historia del Derecho 34*, 2006, pp. 31–65.

Díaz Couselo 2009 — José María Díaz Couselo; 'Francisco Gény en la Cultura Jurídica Argentina'. *Revista de Historia del Derecho 38*, 2009, pp. 1–18.

Díaz Couselo 2010 — José María Díaz Couselo; 'Reflexiones sobre relaciones entre la Historia del Derecho y la ciencia jurídica', in: Marcela Aspell et al (Coord.); *Perspectivas y desafíos de la historia del derecho argentino. I encuentro de la Asociación Argentina de Profesores e Investigadores de Historia del Derecho. Córdoba (8 y 9*

	de noviembre de 2007). Córdoba: Asociación Argentina de Profesores e Investigadores de Historia del Derecho, 2010, pp. 259–272.
Díaz Rementería 1990	Carlos J. Díaz Rementería; 'El patrimonio comunal indígena: del sistema incaico de propiedad al de derecho castellano', in: Abelardo Levaggi (Coord.); *El aborigen y el derecho en el pasado y el presente*. Buenos Aires: Universidad del Museo Social Argentino, 1990, pp. 105–139.
Díaz Rementería 1995	Carlos J. Díaz Rementería; 'Supervivencia y disolución de la comunidad de bienes indígena en la Argentina del siglo XIX'. *Revista de Historia del Derecho "Ricardo Levene" 30*, 1995, pp. 11–39.
Díez-Picazo & Gullón 1982	Luis Díez-Picazo and Antonio Gullón; *Sistema de Derecho Civil*. 4th edition, Volume I, Madrid: Tecnos, 1982.
Díez-Picazo y Ponce de León 1992	Luis Díez-Picazo y Ponce de León; 'Codificación, descodificación y recodificación'. *Anuario de Derecho Civil 45:2*, 1992, pp. 473–484.
Digest of Laws 1808	*A digest of the civil laws now in force in the territory of Orleans, with alterations and amendments adapted to its present system of government*. New Orleans: Bradford & Anderson, 1808.
Digest Online	'Digest Online'. Center of Civil Law Studies, LSU Law Center. http://www1.law.lsu.edu/clo/digest-online/. Last visited on April 21, 2015.
Din & Harkins 1996	Gilbert C. Din and John E. Harkins; *The New Orleans Cabildo: Colonial Louisiana's first city government: 1769–1803*. Baton Rouge and London: Louisiana State University Press, 1996.
Domínguez 1861	Luis L. Domínguez; *Historia Argentina*. Buenos Aires: Imprenta del Orden, 1861.
Domínguez Águila 2005	Ramón Domínguez Águila; 'La Influencia de la Doctrina Francesa en el Derecho Chileno',

in: Alejandro Guzmán B[rito] et al; *De la Codificación a la Descodificación.* Code Civil (*1804–2004*). *Código de Bello* (*1855–2005*). Santiago: Ediciones Universidad Diego Portales, 2005, pp. 61–80.

Donahue 1997 — Charles Donahue Jr.; 'Comparative Legal History in North America'. *Tijdschrift voor Rechtsgeschiedenis 65*, 1997, pp. 1–17.

Donlan 2012 — Seán Patrick Donlan; 'Clashes and Continuities: Brief Reflections on the "New Louisiana Legal History"'. *Journal of Civil Law Studies* 5, 2012, pp. 67–79.

Donlan & Masferrer 2013 — Seán Patrick Donlan and Aniceto Masferrer; 'Preface'. *Comparative Legal History 1:1*, 2013, p. iii.

Dougnac Rodríguez 1994 — Antonio Dougnac Rodríguez; *Manual de Historia del Derecho Indiano.* Mexico: Universidad Nacional Autónoma de México, 1994.

Dougnac Rodríguez & Vicencio Eyzaguirre 1999–2000 — Antonio Dougnac Rodríguez and Felipe Vicencio Eyzaguirre; *La Escuela Chilena de Historiadores del Derecho y los estudios jurídicos en Chile.* Volumes I–II, Santiago: Universidad Central de Chile, Facultad de Ciencias Jurídicas y Sociales, 1999–2000.

Dubuisson 1924 — E[dward] B. Dubuisson; 'The Codes of Louisiana (Originals Written in French; Errors of Translation)'. *Louisiana Bar Association Annual Report 25*, 1924, pp. 143–157.

Duguit 1905 — Léon Duguit; *Congrès national de la propriété b*[â]*tie de France. Séance d'ouverture, 13 Juin 1905. Discours.* Bordeaux: Delmas, 1905.

Duguit 1908 — Léon Duguit; *Le droit social, le droit individuel et la transformation de l'état: conférences faites à l'Ecole des hautes études sociales.* Paris: Félix Alcan, 1908.

Duguit 1912a — León Duguit; *Las Transformaciones generales del Derecho privado desde el Código de Napoleón.* Translation by Carlos G. Posada, Madrid: Francisco de Beltrán, 1912.

Duguit 1912b — Léon Duguit; *Les transformations générales du droit privé depuis le Code Napoléon*. Paris: Félix Alcan, 1912.

Duguit 1918 — Léon Duguit; 'Changes of Principle in the Field of Liberty, Contract, Liability, and Property', in: Wigmore John H. et al. (Eds.); *The Progress of Continental Law in the Nineteenth Century*. Volume XI The Continental Legal History Series, Boston: Little, Brown and Co., 1918, pp. 65–146.

Duguit 1920 — Léon Duguit; *Les transformations générales du droit privé depuis le Code Napoléon*. 2nd revised edition, Paris: Félix Alcan, 1920.

Duguit 1922 — Léon Duguit; *Souveraineté et liberté. Leçons faites à l'Université Columbia (New-York) 1920–1921*. Paris: Félix Alcan, 1922.

Duguit 2011 — 'León Duguit: a 100 años de sus conferencias en la Facultad'. *Derecho al Día X:187*. December 1, 2011. Universidad de Buenos Aires. http://www.derecho.uba.ar/derechoaldia/tapa/leon-duguit-a-100-anos-de-sus-conferencias-en-la-facultad/+4162. Last visited on April 21, 2015.

Duhau 2009 — Emilio Duhau; 'A case study on the implementation and outcomes of the 1992 reforms on the Mexican agrarian property institutions: An *ejido* in the frontier of the urbanisation process', in: Ubink Janine M. et al. (Eds.); *Legalising Land Rights: Local Practices, State Responses and Tenure Security in Africa, Asia and Latin America*. Leiden: Leiden University Press, 2009, pp. 388–407.

Duncan 1963 — W. Raymond Duncan; 'The Mexican Constitution of 1917: Its Political and Social Background'. *Inter-American Law Review* 5, 1963, pp. 277–312.

Durán Bernales 1966 — Florencio Durán Bernales; *Población, Alimentos y Reforma Agraria*. Santiago: Editorial Universitaria, 1966.

Duve 2014 — Thomas Duve; 'European Legal History–Concepts, Methods, Challenges', in: Duve Thomas (Ed.); *Entanglements in Legal History: Conceptual Approaches, Global Perspectives on Legal History*. Max Planck Institute for European Legal History, Open Access Publication, Frankfurt am Main, 2014, pp. 29–66. http://dx.doi.org/10.12946/gplh1. Last visited on April 21, 2015.

Eidenmüller *et al.* 2012 — Horst Eidenmüller et al.; 'The Proposal for a Regulation on a Common European Sales Law: Deficits of the Most Recent Textual Layer of European Contract Law'. *The Edinburgh Law Review 16.3*, 2012, pp. 301–357.

Elizalde 1871 — Miguel Elizalde; *Concordancias de los artículos del Código civil chileno entre sí i con los artículos del Código frances.* Santiago: Imprenta de la Libertad, 1871.

Ely 1914 — Richard T. Ely; *Property and Contract in their Relations to the Distribution of Wealth*. Volume I, New York: The Macmillan Company, 1914.

Ely 2005 — James W. Ely Jr.; "Poor Relation" Once More: The Supreme Court and the Vanishing Rights of Property Owners'. *Cato Supreme Court Review 2004–2005*, 2005, pp. 39–69.

Encyclical Centesimus annus 1991 (English) — 'John Paul II. Holy Father. "Centesimus Annus" Encyclical Letter'. The Holy See. http://w2.vatican.va/content/john-paul-ii/en/encyclicals/documents/hf_jp-ii_enc_01051991_centesimus-annus.html. Last visited on April 21, 2015.

Encyclical Gaudium et spes 1965 (English) — 'Pastoral Constitution on the Church in the Modern World Gaudium et spes'. The Holy See. http://www.vatican.va/archive/hist_councils/ii_vatican_council/documents/vat-ii_const_19651207_gaudium-et-spes_en.html. Last visited on April 21, 2015.

Encyclical Mater et magistra 1961 (English) — 'Mater et magistra'. The Holy See. http://w2.vatican.va/content/john-xxiii/en/encyc

	licals/documents/hf_j-xxiii_enc_15051961_mater.html. Last visited on April 21, 2015.
Encyclical Populorum progressio 1967 (English)	'Populorum progression. Encyclical of Pope Paul VI on the Development of Peoples'. The Holy See. http://www.vatican.va/holy_father/paul_vi/encyclicals/documents/hf_p-vi_enc_26031967_populorum_en.html. Last visited on April 21, 2015.
Encyclical Quadragesimo anno 1931 (English)	'Quadragesimo anno'. The Holy See. http://w2.vatican.va/content/pius-xi/en/encyclicals/documents/hf_p-xi_enc_19310515_quadragesimo-anno.html. Last visited on April 21, 2015.
Encyclical Quadragesimo anno 1931 (Latin)	'Pius PP. XI. Litterae Encyclicae. Quadragesimo anno'. The Holy See. http://www.vatican.va/holy_father/pius_xi/encyclicals/documents/hf_p-xi_enc_19310515_quadragesimo-anno_lt.html. Last visited on April 21, 2015.
Encyclical Rerum novarum 1891 (English)	'Rerum novarum. Encyclical of Pope Leo XIII on Capital and Labor'. The Holy See. http://www.vatican.va/holy_father/leo_xiii/encyclicals/documents/hf_l-xiii_enc_15051891_rerum-novarum_en.html. Last visited on April 21, 2015.
Encyclopædia Britannica 2007	'Latin America', in: *The New Encyclopædia Britannica*. 15th edition, Volume VII Micropædia, Chicago: Encyclopædia Britannica, 2007, pp. 180–181.
Esborraz 2007	David Fabio Esborraz; 'La Individualización del Subsistema Jurídico Latinoamericano como Desarrollo Interno Propio del Sistema Jurídico Romanista: (II) La Contribución de la Ciencia Jurídica Argentina en la Primera Mitad del Siglo *XX*'. *Roma e America Diritto Romano Comune 24*, 2007, pp. 33–84.
Euclid 1926	'Village of Euclid, Ohio, et al. v. Ambler Realty Co. [272 U.S. 365 (1926)]'. *Supreme Court Reporter 47*, 1926, pp. 114–122.

Expedition to Illinois 1767 — 'Ulloa sends an expedition to the (Spanish) Illinois country to establish a fort and settlement and his rules for the government of the same', in: Houck Louis (Ed.); *The Spanish regime in Missouri; a collection of papers and documents relating to upper Louisiana principally within the present limits of Missouri during the dominion of Spain, from the Archives of the Indies at Seville, etc., translated from the original Spanish into English, and including also some papers concerning the supposed grant to Col. George Morgan at the mouth of the Ohio, found in the Congressional library*. Volume I, Chicago: R.R. Donnelley & Sons Co., 1909, pp. 1–19.

Extracts Field 1894 — *Extracts from Notices of David Dudley Field.* S.l. [New York]: s.n., [1894].

Farnan 1972 — William Thomas Farnan; *Land claims problems and the federal land system in the Louisiana-Missouri Territory.* Unpublished Ph.D. thesis, Saint Louis: Saint Louis University, 1972.

Favrot Papers 1796–1799 — Louisiana Historical Records Survey; *Transcriptions of manuscript collections of Louisiana. No.I. The Favrot Papers 1796–1799.* Volume V, New Orleans: Tulane University of Louisiana, 1941.

Favrot Papers 1801–1803 — Louisiana Historical Records Survey; *Transcriptions of manuscript collections of Louisiana. No.I. The Favrot Papers 1801–1803.* Volume VII, New Orleans: Tulane University of Louisiana, 1942.

Febrero 1783 — José Febrero; *Libreria de escribanos, é instruccion juridica teorico practica de principiantes. Parte primera dividida en tres tomos. Trata de testamentos, y contratos.* 3rd edition, Volume II, Madrid: Imprenta de Don Pedro Marin, 1783.

Fedtke 2006 — Jörg Fedtke; 'Legal Transplants', in: Smits Jan M. (Ed.); *Elgar Encyclopedia of Comparative*

Law. Cheltenham: Edward Elgar Publishing Limited, 2006, pp. 434–437.

Feenstra 1998
Robert Feenstra, '*Dominium utile* est chimaera: Nouvelles réflexions sur le concept de propriété dans le droit savant (à propos d'un ouvrage récent)'. *Tijdschrift voor Rechtsgeschiedenis 66*, 1998, pp. 381–397.

Fenet 1827
P[ierre] A[ntoine] Fenet; *Recueil complet des travaux préparatoires du code civil, suivi d'une édition de ce code,* [à] *laquelle sont ajoutés les lois, décrets et ordonnances formant le complément de la législation civile de la France, et ou se trouvent indiqués, sous chaque article séparément, tous les passages du recueil qui s'y rattachent.* Volumes I and XI, Paris: Au dépôt, rue Saint-André-des-Arcs, no. 51, 1827.

Fernandez 2001
Mark F. Fernandez; 'Introduction. Louisiana Legal History: Past, Present, and Future', in: Billings Warren M. and Fernandez Mark F. (Eds.); *A Law unto Itself?: Essays in the New Louisiana Legal History*. Baton Rouge: Louisiana State University Press, 2001, pp. 1–22.

Fernandez 2011
Tomás-Ramón Fernandez; 'Duguit lu: l'Espagne', in: Melleray Fabrice (Dir.); *Autour de Léon Duguit: Colloque commémoratif du 150e anniversaire de la naissance du doyen Léon Duguit. Bordeaux, 29–30 mai 2009*. Brussels: Bruylant, 2011, pp. 255–275.

Field 1898
Henry M. Field; *The Life of David Dudley Field*. New York: Charles Scribner's Sons, 1898.

Field 2001
Betty M. Field; 'Louisiana and the Great Depression', in: Haas Edward F. (Ed.); *The Louisiana Purchase Bicentennial Series in Louisiana History*. Volume VIII, Lafayette: Center for Louisiana Studies University of Southwestern Louisiana, 2001, pp. 3–12.

Figueroa-Torres 2008
Marta Figueroa-Torres; 'Recodification of Civil Law in Puerto Rico: A Quixotic Pursuit

of the Civil Code for the New Millennium'. *Tulane European and Civil Law Forum 23*, 2008, pp. 143–166.

Fleitas Ortiz de Rozas 1967 — Abel Fleitas Ortiz de Rozas; 'Nota Bibliográfica de Mario Rotondi, Derecho Comparado'. *Lecciones y Ensayos 34*, 1967, pp. 197–198.

Florence 1913 — Ernest T. Florence; 'Report of Special Committee Revision Civil Code'. *Report of the Louisiana Bar Association for 1912–13*, 1913, pp. 345–349.

Flory 1936 — Ira Flory; 'Edward Livingston's Place in Louisiana Law'. *Louisiana Historical Quarterly 19* [reprint], 1936, pp. 3–64.

Fordham 1946 — Jefferson B. Fordham; 'Legal Aspects of Local Planning and Zoning in Louisiana'. *Louisiana Law Review* 6, 1946, pp. 495–520.

Fortier 1966–1985 — Alcée Fortier; *A History of Louisiana*. 2nd edition, Volumes I-IV, Baton Rouge: Claitor's, 1966–1985.

Foster & Bonilla 2011 — Sheila R. Foster and Daniel Bonilla; 'Symposium. The Social Function of Property: A Comparative Perspective. Introduction'. *Fordham Law Review 80*, 2011, pp. 1003–1015.

Freitas 1860 — A[ugusto] T[eixeira] de Freitas; *Codigo Civil. Esboço*. Rio de Janeiro: Typographia Universal de Laemmert, 1860.

Frontera 1988 — Carlos Guillermo Frontera; 'Las ideas sobre inmigración en el debate de la Ley No 817 y en los periódicos de la época'. *Revista de Historia del Derecho 16*, 1988, pp. 287–319.

Furlong 1944 — Guillermo Furlong; *Bibliotecas Argentinas durante la Dominación Hispánica*. Buenos Aires: Talleres Gráficos San Pablo, 1944.

Gallardo Fernández 2002 — Gloria L. Gallardo Fernández; *Communal Land Ownership in Chile: The agricultural communities in the commune of Canela, Norte Chico (1600–1998)*. Aldershot: Ashgate Publishing Limited, 2002.

Gallinal 1911–1912 — Rafael Gallinal; *Concordancias, Motivos y Comentarios del Código Civil del Uruguay.*

Volumes I-II, Montevideo: Barreiro y Ramos, 1911–1912.

Gallo 1998 Ezequiel Gallo; 'Argentina: Society and Politics, 1880–1916', in: Bethell Leslie (Ed.); *The Cambridge History of Latin America.* Reprint, Volume V, Cambridge and New York: Cambridge University Press, 1998, pp. 359–391.

Gambaro 2011 Antonio Gambaro; 'Property Rights in Comparative Perspective: Why Property Is So Ancient and Durable'. *Tulane European and Civil Law Forum 26*, 2011, pp. 205–239.

García 1953 Juan Agustín García; *La Ciudad Indiana: Buenos Aires desde 1600 hasta mediados del siglo XVIII*. Buenos Aires: Alpe, 1953.

García 1967 Antonio García; *Reforma Agraria y Economía Empresarial en América Latina.* Santiago: Editorial Universitaria, 1967.

García 1973 Antonio García; *Sociología de la reforma agraria en América latina.* Buenos Aires: Amorrortu editores, 1973.

García 1985 Antonio García; *Modelos operacionales de reforma agraria y desarrollo rural en América Latina*. Reprint, San José: Instituto Interamericano de Cooperación para la Agricultura, 1985.

García-Gallo 1977 Alfonso García-Gallo; *Manual de Historia del Derecho Español.* 7th revised edition, Volume I, Madrid: s.n., 1977.

García-Gallo 1987a Alfonso García-Gallo; 'Bases para una programación de la enseñanza de la Historia del Derecho y en especial de la del Derecho Indiano', in: García-Gallo Alfonso; *Los orígenes Españoles de las Instituciones Americanas: Estudios de Derecho Indiano*. Madrid: Real Academia de Jurisprudencia y Legislación, 1987, pp. 1069–1092.

García-Gallo 1987b Alfonso García-Gallo; 'El pluralismo jurídico en la América española', in: García-Gallo Alfonso; *Los orígenes Españoles de las Instituciones Americanas: Estudios de Derecho Indiano*. Madrid: Real Academia de Jurisprudencia y Legislación, 1987, pp. 299–310.

García-Gallo 1987c — Alfonso García-Gallo; 'Las Bulas de Alejandro VI y el ordenamiento jurídico de la expansión portuguesa y castellana en África e Indias', in: García-Gallo Alfonso; *Los orígenes Españoles de las Instituciones Americanas: Estudios de Derecho Indiano*. Madrid: Real Academia de Jurisprudencia y Legislación, 1987, pp. 313–659.

García Goyena 1852 — Florencio García Goyena; *Concordancias, motivos y comentarios del código civil español*. Volumes I-IV, Madrid: Sociedad Tipográfico-Editorial, 1852.

García Valdecasas 1983 — Guillermo García Valdecasas; *Parte general del derecho civil español*. Madrid: Civitas, 1983.

Garrido & Andorno 1971 — Roque Garrido and Luis Andorno; *Reformas al código civil*. 2nd edition, Buenos Aires: Zavalía, 1971.

Garriga 2012 — Carlos Garriga; 'La Ilustración jurídica', in: Lorente Marta and Vallejo Jesús (Coord.); *Manual de Historia del Derecho*. Valencia: Tirant lo Blanch, 2012, pp. 259–288.

Gaya Sicilia 2010 — Regina Gaya Sicilia; 'La influencia del Código Civil de Luisiana en la codificación civil española'. *Anuario de Derecho Civil* 63:2, 2010, pp. 719–752.

Gayarré 1903 — Charles Gayarré; *History of Louisiana*. Volumes I-IV, New Orleans: F.F. Hansell & Bro., 1903.

Gelli 2004 — María Angélica Gelli; *Constitución de la Nación Argentina: Comentada y Concordada*. 2nd edition, Buenos Aires: La Ley, 2004.

Giannoni 2010 — Tonya Caprarola Giannoni; *The Evolution of Property Rights in Argentina, 1853–1949*. Unpublished Ph.D. thesis, Washington: The George Washington University, 2010.

Gierke (von) 1889 — Otto von Gierke; *Die soziale Aufgabe des Privatrechts. Vortrag gehalten am 5. April 1889 in der juristischen Gesellschaft zu Wien.* Berlin: J. Springer, 1889.

Gilbert 2003 — Jess Gilbert; 'Low Modernism and the Agrarian New Deal: A Different Kind of State', in: Adams Jane (Ed.); *Fighting for the Farm: Rural America Transformed.* Philadelphia: University of Pennsylvania Press, 2003, pp. 129–146.

Gilbert & Brown 1981 — Jess Gilbert and Steve Brown; 'Alternative Land Reform Proposals in the 1930s: The Nashville Agrarians and the Southern Tenant Farmers' Union'. *Agricultural History 55:4*, 1981, pp. 351–369.

Gilbert & Wood 2004 — Jess Gilbert and Spencer D. Wood; *Rural Resettlements: New Deal Experiments in Land Reform and Racial Justice, 1935–2003.* Paper presented at the Rural Sociological Society Annual Meeting, Sacramento, CA. July 2004.

Giorlandini 1986 — Eduardo Giorlandini; 'Una historia negra: La ley de residencia'. *Todo es Historia 41:226*, 1986, pp. 8–42.

Girbal de Blacha 1991 — Noemí M. Girbal de Blacha; 'Política de tierras públicas en la Argentina (1916–1930): El caso de los territorios nacionales del Sur'. *Revista de Historia del Derecho 19*, 1991, pp. 209–243.

Glenn 1998 — H. Patrick Glenn; 'The Grounding of Codification'. *U.C. Davis Law Review 31*, 1998, pp. 765–782.

Glennan 1996 — Stuart S. Glennan; 'Mechanisms and the Nature of Causation'. *Erkenntnis 44* (*1*), 1996, pp. 49–71.

Godreau & Giusti 1993 — Michel J. Godreau and Juan A. Giusti; 'Las concesiones de la corona y la propiedad de la tierra en Puerto Rico, siglos XVI-XX: Un estudio jurídico'. *Revista Jurídica Universidad de Puerto Rico 62*, 1993, pp. 351–579.

Goldenweiser & Truesdell 1924 E[manuel] A. Goldenweiser and Leon E. Truesdell; *Farm Tenancy in the United States: An analysis of the results of the 1920 census relative to farms classified by tenure supplemented by pertinent data from other sources*. Washington: Government Printing Office, 1924.

Góngora 1951 Mario Góngora; *El estado en el derecho indiano: época de fundación (1492–1570)*. Santiago: Editorial Universidad de Chile, 1951.

Góngora 1970 Mario Góngora; *Encomenderos y Estancieros: Estudios acerca de la Constitución social aristocrática de Chile después de la Conquista 1580–1660*. Santiago: Universidad de Chile, 1970.

González 2009 María del Refugio González; 'Reformas y revoluciones en la historia del derecho en México (1810–1917)'. *Revista del Instituto Latino Americano de Historia de* [sic] *Derecho 1(1)*, 2009, pp. 190–215.

González Terán 2010 Diana Luz González Terán; *El Derecho de Propiedad Privada en el Liberalismo Individualista*. Unpublished B.Phil. thesis, Santiago: Universidad de Chile, 2010.

Gordley 2007 James Gordley; *Foundations of Private Law: Property, Tort, Contract, Unjust Enrichment*. Reprint, Oxford and New York: Oxford University Press, 2007.

Gordley 2008 James Gordley; 'Comparative Law and Legal History', in: Reimann Mathias and Zimmermann Reinhard (Eds.); *The Oxford Handbook of Comparative Law*. Oxford: Oxford University Press, 2008, pp. 754–773.

Grantham 2000 Dewey W. Grantham; 'Introduction to *Southern Progressivism: The Reconciliation of Progress and Tradition*', in: Schott Matthew J. (Ed.); *The Louisiana Purchase Bicentennial Series in Louisiana History*. Volume VII, Lafayette: Center for Louisiana Studies University of Southwestern Louisiana, 2000, pp. 62–69.

Graziadei 2008 — Michele Graziadei; 'Comparative Law as the Study of Transplants and Receptions', in: Reimann Mathias and Zimmermann Reinhard (Eds.); *The Oxford Handbook of Comparative Law*. Oxford: Oxford University Press, 2008, pp. 441–475.

Grenón 1930 — Pedro Grenón (Comp.); *Documentos Históricos de Córdoba No.19. El Libro de Mercedes*. Córdoba: Imprenta de la Penitenciaria, 1930.

Greve 1941 — Ernesto Greve; 'La Mensura General 1602–1605: antecedentes históricos', in: *Colección de Historiadores de Chile y de Documentos relativos a la Historia Nacional. Tomo 48. Mensuras de Ginés de Lillo*. Santiago: Imprenta Universitaria, 1941, pp. ix–xc.

Groner 1947 — Samuel B. Groner; 'Louisiana Law: Its Development in the First Quarter-Century of American Rule'. *Louisiana Law Review 8*, 1947, pp. 350–382.

Grossi 1976–1977 — Paolo Grossi; 'Pagina Introduttiva'. *Quaderni Fiorentini per la storia del pensiero giuridico moderno 5–6*, 1976–1977, pp. 1–4.

Grossi 1992a — Paolo Grossi; 'Ideologia e tecnica in una definizione giuridica (la definizione obertina di Feudo dai Glossatori a Cujas)," in: Paolo Grossi; *Il dominio e le cose: percezioni medievali e moderne dei diritti reali*. Milan: Giuffrè, 1992, pp. 217–246.

Grossi 1992b — Paolo Grossi; 'La categoria del dominio utile e gli *homines novi* del quadrivio cinquecentesco', in: Paolo Grossi; *Il dominio e le cose: percezioni medievali e moderne dei diritti reali*. Milan: Giuffrè, 1992, pp. 247–280.

Grossi 1992c — Paolo Grossi; 'La proprietà e le proprietà nell'officina dello storico', in: Paolo Grossi; *Il dominio e le cose: percezioni medievali e moderne dei diritti reali*. Milan: Giuffrè, 1992, pp. 603–665.

Grossi 1992d — Paolo Grossi; 'La proprietà nel sistema privatistico della Seconda Scolastica', in: Grossi Paolo; *Il dominio e le cose: percezioni medievali e moderne dei diritti reali*. Milan: Giuffrè, 1992, pp. 281–383.

Gruning 2004 David Gruning; 'Bayou State Bijuralism: Common Law and Civil Law in Louisiana'. *University of Detroit Mercy Law Review 81*, 2004, pp. 437–464.

Guzmán Brito 1982 Alejandro Guzmán Brito; *Andrés Bello codificador: Historia de la fijación y codificación del derecho civil en Chile*. Volume I, Santiago: Ediciones de la Universidad de Chile, 1982.

Guzmán Brito 1993 Alejandro Guzmán Brito; 'Codificación, Descodificación y Recodificación del Derecho Civil Chileno'. *Revista de Derecho y Jurisprudencia 90:2*, 1993, pp. 39–62.

Guzmán Brito 1999 Alejandro Guzmán Brito; 'La Influencia del Código Civil de Vélez Sarsfield en las codificaciones de Iberoamérica hasta principios del siglo XX'. *Revista Chilena de Historia del Derecho 18*, 1999, pp. 263–273.

Guzmán Brito 2000 Alejandro Guzmán Brito; *La codificación civil en Iberoamérica. Siglos XIX y XX*. Santiago: Editorial Jurídica de Chile, 2000.

Guzmán Brito 2005 Alejandro Guzmán Brito; *Historia literaria del código civil de la República de Chile*. Santiago: s.n., 2005.

Guzmán Brito 2008 Alejandro Guzmán Brito; *Vida y Obra de Andrés Bello especialmente considerado como Jurista*. Cizur Menor: Thomson-Aranzadi, 2008.

Guzmán Brito 2009 Alejandro Guzmán Brito; 'Las fuentes de las normas sobre interpretación de las leyes del "digeste des lois civiles" ("Code civil") de la Luisiana (1808/1825)'. *Revista de Estudios Histórico-Jurídicos 31*, 2009, pp. 171–195.

Guzmán Brito *et al.* 2000 Alejandro Guzmán Brito et al; *Estudios sobre reformas al Código civil y Código de comercio*. Santiago: Fundación Fernando Fueyo Laneri and Editorial Jurídica de Chile, 2000.

Haar 1965 Charles M. Haar; 'Symposium-Land Use: Foreword'. *Iowa Law Review 50*, 1965, pp. 243–244.

Haas 2001 Edward F. Haas; 'Huey Long and the Communists', in: Haas Edward F. (Ed.); *The Louisiana Purchase Bicentennial Series in Louisiana History*. Volume VIII, Lafayette: Center for Louisiana Studies University of Southwestern Louisiana, 2001, pp. 112–123.

Haba 1996 Enrique P. Haba; 'Ciencias del derecho, La controversia de paradigmas en la Teoría del Derecho contemporánea', in: Ossorio Manuel y Florit et al. (Eds.); *Enciclopedia Jurídica Omeba*. Appendix Volume VII, Buenos Aires: Driskill, 1996, pp. 107–145.

Haber *et al.* 2008 Stephen Haber et al.; *Mexico Since 1980*. New York: Cambridge University Press, 2008.

Habermas 1996 Jürgen Habermas; 'Paradigms of Law'. *Cardozo Law Review 17*, 1996, pp. 771–784.

Hakim 2011 Nader Hakim; 'Duguit et les privatistes', in: Melleray Fabrice (Dir.); *Autour de Léon Duguit: Colloque commémoratif du 150e anniversaire de la naissance du doyen Léon Duguit. Bordeaux, 29–30 mai 2009*. Brussels: Bruylant, 2011, pp. 81–114.

Hall *et al.* 1991 Kermit L. Hall et al; *American Legal History: Cases and Materials*. New York: Oxford University Press, 1991.

Halpérin 1996 Jean-Louis Halpérin; *Histoire du droit privé français depuis 1804*. Paris: Presses Universitaires de France, 1996.

Halpérin 2000 Jean-Louis Halpérin; *The Civil Code*. Translation by Gruning David W. and Levasseur Alain A., Baton Rouge: Center of Civil Law Studies, 2000.

Halpérin 2008 Jean-Louis Halpérin; *Histoire du droit des biens*. Paris: Économica, DL, 2008.

Hancké 2009 Bob Hancké; *Intelligent Research Design: A Guide for Beginning Researchers in the Social Sciences*. Oxford: Oxford University Press, 2009.

Hanke 1986 Lewis U. Hanke; 'Mi vida con Bartolomé de Las Casas, 1930–1985', in: *En el quinto centenario de Bartolomé de las Casas*. Madrid:

Ediciones Cultura Hispánica, Instituto de Cooperación Iberoamericana, 1986, pp. 11–20.

Hargrave 1991 — Lee Hargrave; *The Louisiana State Constitution: A Reference Guide*. Westport: Greenwood Press, 1991.

Harlow 2011 — Carol Harlow; 'The Influence of Léon Duguit on Anglo-American Legal Thought', in: Melleray Fabrice (Dir.); *Autour de Léon Duguit: Colloque commémoratif du 150e anniversaire de la naissance du doyen Léon Duguit. Bordeaux, 29–30 mai 2009*. Brussels: Bruylant, 2011, pp. 227–254.

Hayem 1910 — Henri Hayem, *Essai sur le Droit de propriété et ses limites*. Paris: Arthur Rousseau, 1910.

Heirbaut 2003 — Dirk Heirbaut; 'Feudal Law: the Real *Ius Commune* of Property in Europe, or: Should We Reintroduce *Duplex Dominium*?'. *European Review of Private Law 3–2003*, 2003, pp. 301–320.

Heirbaut 2011 — Dirk Heirbaut; 'European Comparative Legal History as a Necessity: The Belgian Experience', in: Modéer Kjell Å. and Nilsén Per (Eds.); *How to Teach European Comparative Legal History: Workshop at the Faculty of Law, Lund University, 19–20 August 2009*. Lund: Juristförlaget i Lund, 2011, pp. 94–105.

Hendrix 1993 — Steven E. Hendrix; *Property Law Innovation in Latin America with Recommendations*. LTC Paper 149, Madison: Land Tenure Center, 1993.

Herman 1993 — Shael Herman; *The Louisiana Civil Code: A European Legacy for the United States*. New Orleans: Louisiana Bar Foundation, 1993.

Herman 1996 — Shael Herman; 'The Fate and the Future of Codification in America'. *American Journal of Legal History 40*, 1996, pp. 407–437.

Herman *et al.* 1981 — Shael Herman et al.; *The Louisiana Civil Code: A Humanistic Appraisal*. New Orleans: Tulane Law School, 1981.

Hermes 2008 Katherine A. Hermes; 'The Law of Native Americans, to 1815', in: Grossberg Michael and Tomlins Christopher L. (Eds.); *The Cambridge history of law in America*. Volume I, Cambridge and New York: Cambridge University Press, 2008, pp. 32–62.

Hernández 1992 Ramón Hernández; 'The Internationalization of Francisco de Vitoria and Domingo de Soto'. *Fordham International Law Journal 15*, 1992 pp. 1031–1059.

Hernández Gaona 1991 Pedro Hernández Gaona; 'Evolución y proyección de la legislación agraria mexicana'. *Anuario Mexicano de Historia del Derecho III-1991*, 1991, pp. 81–94.

Hernández Gil 1969 Antonio Hernández Gil; La función social de la posesión (Ensayo de teorización sociológico-jurídica). Madrid: Alianza Editorial, 1969.

Hernández Montalbán 1999 Francisco J. Hernández Montalbán; *La abolición de los señoríos en España [1811–1837]*. Madrid: Biblioteca Nueva, 1999.

Hidalgo 1997 Jorge Hidalgo; 'The Indians of southern South America in the middle of the sixteenth century', in: Bethell Leslie (Ed.); *The Cambridge History of Latin America*. Reprint, Volume I, Cambridge and New York: Cambridge University Press, 1997, pp. 91–117.

Hines 2010 Barbara Hines; 'The Right to Migrate as a Human Right: The Current Argentine Immigration Law'. *Cornell International Law Journal 43*, 2010, pp. 471–511.

Hockett 2005 Robert Hockett; 'Whose Ownership? Which Society?'. *Cardozo Law Review 27*, 2005, pp. 1–103.

Hoeflich & Sheppard 2006 Michael H. Hoeflich and Steve Sheppard; 'Disciplinary Evolution and Scholarly Expansion: Legal History in the United States'. *The American Journal of Comparative Law 54: supplement*, 2006, pp. 23–44.

Hoffman 1992 Paul E. Hoffman; *Luisiana*. Madrid: Editorial Mapfre, 1992.

Holley 2001 — Donald Holley; 'Old and New Worlds in the New Deal Resettlement Program: Two Louisiana Projects', in: Haas Edward F. (Ed.); *The Louisiana Purchase Bicentennial Series in Louisiana History*. Volume VIII, Lafayette: Center for Louisiana Studies University of Southwestern Louisiana, 2001, pp. 184–203.

Holmes 1881 — Oliver Wendell Holmes Jr.; *The Common Law*. Boston: Little, Brown, and Company, 1881.

Hood 1958 — John T. Hood; 'The History and Development of the Louisiana Civil Code'. *Tulane Law Review* 33, 1958, pp. 7–20.

Howard 2000 — Perry Howard; 'The Populist-Republican Fusion: 1896', in: Schott Matthew J. (Ed.); *The Louisiana Purchase Bicentennial Series in Louisiana History*. Volume VII, Lafayette: Center for Louisiana Studies University of Southwestern Louisiana, 2000, pp. 25–61.

Howes 1989 — David Howes; 'The Origin and Demise of Legal Education in Quebec (Or Hercules Bound)'. *University of New Brunswick Law Journal* 38, 1989, pp. 127–149.

Hurtado-Edwards & Smith 1964 — José Luis Hurtado-Edwards and Robert Gene Smith; 'The Chilean Agrarian Reform'. *Inter-American Law Review* 6, 1964, pp. 93–137.

Husa 2013 — Jaakko Husa; 'Functional Method in Comparative Law–Much Ado About Nothing?'. *European Property Law Journal* 2, 2013, pp. 4–21.

Ibbetson 2013 — David Ibbetson; 'The Challenges of Comparative Legal History'. *Comparative Legal History* 1:1, 2013, pp. 1–11.

IHDIP 2015 — 'Objetivos'. Instituto de Historia del Derecho y las Ideas Políticas "Roberto I. Peña". http://www.psi.unc.edu.ar/acaderc/institutos/instituto-de-historia-del-derecho. Last visited on April 21, 2015.

ILAHD 2015 — 'Instituto Latino Americano de Historia del Derecho'. Instituto Latino Americano de Historia del Derecho. http://www.ilahd.org/. Last visited on April 21, 2015.

Inostroza Córdova 2011 — Iván Inostroza Córdova; 'El concepto de propiedad de la tierra en la tradición mapuche'. *Revista de Educación y Humanidades* 1:2, 2011, pp. 101–133.

Instituto Gioja 2015 — 'Publicaciones del Instituto'. Instituto de Investigaciones Jurídicas y Sociales "Ambrosio L. Gioja." http://www.derecho.uba.ar/investigacion/inv_inst_gioja_publicaciones.php#rihdrl. Last visited on April 21, 2015.

Instituto de Estudios Indígenas 2003 — Instituto de Estudios Indígenas, Universidad de la Frontera; *Los derechos de los pueblos indígenas en Chile: Informe del programa de derechos indígenas.* Santiago: LOM Ediciones, Universidad de la Frontera, Instituto de Estudios Indígenas, 2003.

Ireland 1937 — Gordon Ireland; 'Louisiana's Legal System Reappraised'. *Tulane Law Review* 11, 1937, pp. 585–598.

Irti 1979 — Natalino Irti; *L'età Della Decodificazione*. Milan: Giuffrè, 1979.

Isler Soto 2011 — Erika Isler Soto; 'La relatividad de los derechos subjetivos de los consumidores'. *Revista de Derecho* [Valdivia] 24:2, 2011, pp. 65–89.

Jones 1947 — J. Walter Jones; 'Forms of Ownership'. *Tulane Law Review* 22, 1947, pp. 82–93.

Josserand 1905 — Louis Josserand; *De l'abus des droits*. Paris: Arthur Rousseau, 1905.

Journal House of Representatives 1822 — *Journal of the Louisiana House of Representatives, during the Second Session of the Fifth Legislature of the State of Louisiana.* New Orleans: Charles St. Romes, 1822.

Jovellanos (de) 1795 — Gaspar Melchor de Jovellanos; *Informe de la Sociedad Económica de esta Corte al Real y Supremo Consejo de Castilla en el expediente de ley agraria*. Madrid: Imprenta de Sancha, 1795.

Justicia Presentará Proyecto 2009 — 'Justicia presentará en 2009 proyecto de nuevo Código Civil'. Cooperativa.cl. http://www.cooperativa.cl/p4_noticias/site/artic/20080620/pags/20080620124510.html. Last visited on April 21, 2015.

Karst & Rosenn 1975 — Kenneth L. Karst and Keith S. Rosenn; *Law and Development in Latin America: A Case Book*. Berkeley: University of California Press, 1975.

Keiser 2005 — Thorsten Keiser; *Eigentumsrecht in Nationalsozialismus und Fascismo*. Tübingen: Mohr Siebeck, 2005.

Keiser 2012 — Thorsten Keiser; 'Social conceptions of Property and Labour—Private Law in the aftermath of the Mexican Revolution and European Legal Science'. *Rechtsgeschichte 20*, 2012, pp. 258–273.

Kennedy 2006 — Duncan Kennedy; 'Three Globalizations of Law and Legal Thought: 1850–2000', in: Trubek David and Santos Alvaro (Eds.); *The New Law and Economic Development. A Critical Appraisal*. Cambridge and New York: Cambridge University Press, 2006, pp. 19–73.

Ker Texada 1968 — David Ker Texada; *The Administration of Alejandro O'Reilly as Governor of Louisiana 1769–1770*. Unpublished Ph.D. thesis, Baton Rouge: Louisiana State University, 1968.

Kilbourne 1987 — Richard Holcombe Kilbourne Jr.; *A History of the Louisiana Civil Code: The Formative Years, 1803–1839*. Baton Rouge: LSU Law Center Publications Institute, 1987.

Kleinheisterkamp 2008 — Jan Kleinheisterkamp; 'Development of Comparative Law in Latin America', in: Reimann Mathias and Zimmermann Reinhard (Eds.); *The Oxford Handbook of Comparative Law*. Oxford: Oxford University Press, 2008, pp. 261–301.

Kleinheisterkamp 2012 — Jan Kleinheisterkamp; 'Latin America, Influence of European Private Law', in:

Basedow Jürgen et al. (Eds.); *Max Planck Encyclopedia of European Private Law*. Volume II, Oxford: Oxford University Press, 2012, pp. 1032–1034.

Kloppenburg & Geisler 1985 — Jack R. Kloppenburg Jr. and Charles C. Geisler; 'The Agricultural Ladder: Agrarian Ideology and the Changing Structure of U.S. Agriculture'. *Journal of Rural Studies 1:1*, 1985, pp. 59–72.

Kluger 2009 — Viviana Kluger; 'Argentina', in: Katz Stanley N. (Ed.); *The Oxford International Encyclopedia of Legal History*. Volume I, New York: Oxford University Press, 2009, pp. 215–216.

Kniffen & Hilliard 1988 — Fred B. Kniffen and Sam Bowers Hilliard; *Louisiana: Its Land and People*. Revised edition, Baton Rouge: Louisiana State University Press, 1988.

Knütel 1996 — Rolf Knütel; 'Influences of the Louisiana Civil Code in Latin America'. *Tulane Law Review 70*, 1996, pp. 1445–1480.

Koschaker 1947 — Paul Koschaker; *Europa und das römische Recht*. Munich: Biederstein, 1947.

Kuhn 1970 — Thomas S. Kuhn; *The Structure of Scientific Revolutions*. 2nd edition, enlarged, Chicago: The University of Chicago Press, 1970.

Kunkel 1951 — Paul A. Kunkel; 'The Indians of Louisiana, about 1700-Their Customs and Manner of Living'. *Louisiana Historical Quarterly 34*, 1951, pp. 175–203.

Lafaille 1937 — Héctor Lafaille; 'Hacia el nuevo código civil'. *Jurisprudencia Argentina 58*, 1937, pp. 21–28 (sec. doct.).

Lambert 1903 — Édouard Lambert; *La fonction du droit civil comparé*. Volume I, Paris: V. Giard & E. Brière, 1903.

Land Claims in Louisiana 1859 — 'Land Claims in Louisiana', in: Dickins Asbury and Allen James C. (Eds.); *American State Papers. Documents of the Congress of the United States in relation to the Public Lands, from the First Session of the Eighteenth to the Second Session of the*

Nineteenth Congress. Volume IV, Washington: Gales & Seaton, 1859, pp. 490–519.

Lapp 2004 — Nancy D. Lapp; *Landing Votes: Representation and Land Reform in Latin America*. New York: Palgrave Macmillan, 2004.

Laski 1917 — Harold J. Laski; 'A Note on M. Duguit'. *Harvard Law Review 31*, 1917, pp. 186–192.

Lastarria 1864 — J[osé] V[ictorino] Lastarria, *Instituta del Derecho Civil Chileno*. 2nd edition, Ghent, Imprenta de Eug. Vanderhaeghen, 1864.

Lee 1935 — Bertram Tamblyn Lee (Ed.); *Libros de Cabildos de Lima. 1534–1539*. Volume I, Lima: Torres Aguirre, 1935.

Legón 1942 — Fernando Legón; *Tratado de los Derechos Reales en el Código y en la Reforma*. Volume VI, Buenos Aires: Valerio Abeledo, 1942.

León 1946 — Pedro León; *El Código de Prusia como fuente del Código Civil Argentino*. Córdoba: Imprenta de la Universidad, 1946.

León Pinelo (de) 1630 — Antonio de León Pinelo; *Tratado de Confirmaciones Reales de Encomiendas, Oficios i caſos, en que ſe requieren para las Indias Occidentales*. Madrid: Iuan Gonzalez, 1630.

Lesaffer 2009 — Randall Lesaffer; *European Legal History: A Cultural and Political Perspective*. Cambridge: Cambridge University Press, 2009.

Lesaffer 2011 — Randall Lesaffer; 'Law and History: Law between Past and Present', in: Bart van Klink and Sanne Taekema (Eds.); *Law and Method: Interdisciplinary Research into Law*. Tübingen: Mohr Siebeck, 2011, pp. 133–152.

Levaggi 1979 — Abelardo Levaggi; 'La Interpretación del Derecho en la Argentina en el Siglo XIX'. *Revista de Historia del Derecho 7*, 1979, pp. 23–121.

Levaggi 1982 — Abelardo Levaggi; *Historia del derecho de las obligaciones, contratos y cosas*. Buenos Aires: Editorial Perrot, 1982.

Levaggi 1987 — Abelardo Levaggi; *Manual de Historia del Derecho Argentino (Castellano-Indiano/*

Nacional). Volume II, Buenos Aires: Depalma, 1987.

Levaggi 1990a — Abelardo Levaggi; 'Consideraciones sobre la enseñanza de la historia del derecho'. *Revista de Historia del Derecho "Ricardo Levene"* 27, 1990, pp. 159–169.

Levaggi 1990b — Abelardo Levaggi; 'Tratamiento legal y jurisprudencial del aborigen en la Argentina durante el siglo XIX', in: Abelardo Levaggi (Coord.); *El aborigen y el derecho en el pasado y el presente*. Buenos Aires: Universidad del Museo Social Argentino, 1990, pp. 245–284.

Levaggi 1992 — Abelardo Levaggi; *Las Capellanías en la Argentina: Estudio Histórico-Jurídico*. Buenos Aires: Instituto de Investigaciones Jurídicas y Sociales "Ambrosio L. Gioja," 1992.

Levaggi 1994 — Abelardo Levaggi; 'La réception du système juridique espagnol par les systèmes indigènes en Amérique', in: Michel Doucet and Jacques Vanderlinden (Eds.); *La Réception des Systèmes juridiques: implantations et destins*. Brussels: Etablissements Emile Bruylant, 1994, pp. 331–379.

Levaggi 1996a — Abelardo Levaggi; 'Antecedentes romano-visigóticos e hispano-canarios de los tratados hispano-amerindios', in: *Homenaje al Profesor Alfonso García-Gallo*. Volume III:1, Madrid: Universidad Complutense, 1996, pp. 199–211.

Levaggi 1996b — Abelardo Levaggi; *Manual de Historia del Derecho Argentino (Castellano-Indiano/Nacional)*. 2nd edition, Volume I, Buenos Aires: Depalma, 1996.

Levaggi 1999 — Abelardo Levaggi; 'El proceso desamortizador y desvinculador de los bienes de manos muertas desde la óptica jurídica', in: Hans-Jürgen Prien y Rosa María Martínez de Codes (Coord.); *Cuadernos de Historia Lationamericana 7: El Proceso Desvinculador y Desamortizador de Bienes Eclesiásticos y*

Comunales en la América Española. Siglos XVIII y XIX. [The Netherlands]: Asociación de Historiadores Latinoamericanistas Europeos, 1999, pp. 33–60.

Levaggi 2001 Abelardo Levaggi; 'El proceso de transformación del régimen de la propiedad según la codificación iberoamericana del siglo XIX', in: Eugénio dos Santos (Ed.); *Actas do XII Congresso Internacional de AHILA*. Volume V, Porto: Faculdade de Letras da Universidade do Porto, 2001, pp. 413–421.

Levaggi 2004 Abelardo Levaggi; 'Cómo fue la relación de los indígenas con el territorio'. *Roma e America 18*, 2004, pp. 105–114.

Levaggi 2005a Abelardo Levaggi; 'Constitucionalismo Argentino 1810–1850'. *Iushistoria Revista Electrónica 5:2*, 2005, pp. 1–30. http://p3.usal.edu.ar/index.php/iushistoria/issue/view/160. Last visited on April 21, 2015.

Levaggi 2005b Abelardo Levaggi; *Dalmacio Vélez Sarsfield, Jurisconsulto*. Córdoba: Ciencia, Derecho y Sociedad, 2005.

Levaggi 2006 Abelardo Levaggi; 'Historia del Derecho Argentino del Trabajo'. *Iushistoria Revista Electrónica 3*, 2006, pp. 1–101. http://p3.usal.edu.ar/index.php/iushistoria/issue/view/157. Last visited on April 21, 2015.

Levaggi 2007 Abelardo Levaggi; 'Ideas acerca del derecho de propiedad en la Argentina entre 1870 y 1920'. *Revista Electrónica del Instituto de Investigaciones "Ambrosio L. Gioja" 1:1*, 2007, pp. 120–133.

Levaggi 2009 Abelardo Levaggi; 'Consideraciones sobre investigación en historia del derecho'. *Revista del Instituto Latino Americano de Historia de* [sic] *Derecho 1*(*1*), 2009, pp. 154–163.

Levaggi 2010a Abelardo Levaggi; 'Catedráticos europeos en la Facultad de Derecho alrededor del Centenario', in: Tulio Ortiz (Coord.); *El Bicentenario de la Revolución de Mayo*. Mar del

Plata: Facultad de Derecho Universidad de Buenos Aires, 2010, pp. 191–208.

Levaggi 2010b — Abelardo Levaggi; 'Marco jurídico de la propiedad comunal civil en hispanoamérica hasta el siglo XIX'. *Revista Chilena de Historia del Derecho* 22, 2010, pp. 939–948.

Levaggi 2012 — Abelardo Levaggi; *La enfiteusis en la Argentina (siglos XVII–XX). Estudio histórico-jurídico*. Buenos Aires: USAL, Facultad de Ciencias Jurídicas, 2012.

Levaggi 2013a — Abelardo Levaggi; *Manual de Historia del Derecho Argentino (Castellano-Indiano/Nacional)*. 3rd edition, Volume III, Buenos Aires: Abeledo Perrot, 2013.

Levaggi 2013b — Abelardo Levaggi; 'Trayectoria de la Historiografía Jurídica Latinoamericana'. Presented at the *IV Encuentro del Instituto Latino Americano de Historia del Derecho* on June 14, 2013. Unpublished manuscript, on file with the author.

Levasseur 1970 — Alain [A.] Levasseur; 'On the Structure of a Civil Code'. *Tulane Law Review* 44, 1970, pp. 693–703.

Levasseur 1994 — Alain [A.] Levasseur; 'La Réception du Système de la Common Law par le Système Législatif Français en Louisiane', in: Michel Doucet and Jacques Vanderlinden (Eds.); *La Réception des Systèmes juridiques: implantations et destins*. Brussels: Etablissements Emile Bruylant, 1994, pp. 381–409.

Levasseur 1996 — Alain A. Levasseur; *Louis Casimir Elisabeth Moreau-Lislet: Foster father of Louisiana civil law*. Baton Rouge: Louisiana State University, Law Center Publications Institute, 1996.

Levene 1934 — Ricardo Levene; *Lecciones de Historia Argentina*. 15th edition, Volume I, Buenos Aires: Lajouane, 1934.

Levene 1953 — Ricardo Levene; 'Diez años de historia jurídica argentina, 1940 a 1950'. *Tijdschrift voor Rechtsgeschiedenis* 21, 1953, pp. 108–117.

Levene 1962 — Ricardo Levene; *Manual de Historia del Derecho Argentino*. 3rd edition, Buenos Aires: Editorial G. Kraft, 1962.

Lewis 2003 — Daniel K. Lewis; *The History of Argentina*. New York: Palgrave Macmillan, 2003.

Ley 4144 (1902) — 'Ley N° 4144 Residencia de Extranjeros', in: *Anales de Legislación Argentina*. Complemento Años 1889–1919, Buenos Aires: La Ley, 1954, pp. 560–562.

Ley 5604 (1935) — 'Colonización Nacional'. Biblioteca del Congreso Nacional de Chile. http://www.leychile.cl/Navegar?idNorma=25154. Last visited on April 21, 2015.

Ley 6071 (1937) — 'Dispone que los diversos pisos de un edificio y los departamentos en que se divida cada piso podran pertenecer a distintos propietarios'. Biblioteca del Congreso Nacional de Chile. http://www.leychile.cl/Navegar?idNorma=256753&tipoVersion=0. Last visited on April 21, 2015.

Ley 12636 (1940) — 'Ley 12636—Colonización. Creación del Consejo agrario nacional', in: *Anales de Legislación Argentina*. Volume 1920–1940, Buenos Aires: La Ley, 1953, pp. 862–870.

Ley 13246 (1948) — 'Ley 13246—Arrendamientos rurales y aparcerías', in: *Anales de Legislación Argentina*. Volume VIII-1948, Buenos Aires: La Ley, 1968, pp. 85–106.

Ley 15020 (1962) — 'Reforma Agraria'. Biblioteca del Congreso Nacional de Chile. http://www.leychile.cl/Navegar?idNorma=28016&tipoVersion=0. Last visited on April 21, 2015.

Ley 16615 (1967) — 'Modifica la Constitución Política del Estado'. Biblioteca del Congreso Nacional de Chile. http://www.leychile.cl/Navegar?idNorma=130884&tipoVersion=0. Last visited on April 21, 2015.

Ley 16640 (1967) — 'Reforma Agraria'. Biblioteca del Congreso Nacional de Chile. http://www.leychile.cl/Navegar?idNorma=28596&tipoVersion=0. Last visited on April 21, 2015.

Ley 17711 (1968) 'Leyes. Reforma del Código Civil. (Ley 17.711)', in: *Anales de Legislación Argentina*. Volume XXVIII-B, Buenos Aires: La Ley, 1968, pp. 1799–1827.

LHA 2015 'History'. Louisiana Historical Association. http://www.lahistory.org/site4.php. Last visited on April 21, 2015.

LHS 2015 'Louisiana Historical Society'. Louisiana Historical Society. http://louisianahistoricalsociety.org/. Last visited on April 21, 2015.

Liebrecht 2012 Johannes Liebrecht; 'Legal History', in: Jürgen Basedow et al. (Eds.); *Max Planck Encyclopedia of European Private Law*. Volume II, Oxford: Oxford University Press, 2012, pp. 1064–1068.

Linder 1987 Marc Linder; 'Farm Workers and the Fair Labor Standards Act: Racial Discrimination in the New Deal'. *Texas Law Review* 65, 1987, pp. 1335–1393.

Lira Montt 1998 Luis Lira Montt; 'Los beneméritos de Indias y la gestación de la nobleza de América'. *Revista de Historia del Derecho* 26, 1998, pp. 233–252.

Lira Urquieta 1944 Pedro Lira Urquieta; *El Código Civil y el Nuevo Derecho*. Santiago: Imprenta Nascimento, 1944.

Lira Urquieta 1981 Pedro Lira Urquieta; 'Introducción al Código Civil de Andrés Bello', in: Rafael Caldera (Dir.); *Obras Completas de Andrés Bello*. 2nd edition, Volume XIV, Caracas: Fundación La Casa de Bello, 1981, pp. xiii–lxii.

Litvinoff 2004 Saúl Litvinoff; 'Codificación en Louisiana', in: *La Codificación: Raíces y Prospectivas II. La Codificación en América*. Buenos Aires: El Derecho, 2004, pp. 127–141.

Livingston *et al.* 1937 Edward Livingston et al.; 'Preliminary Report of the Code Commissioners. Dated February 13, 1823', in: *Louisiana Legal Archives*. Volumes I–II, New Orleans: Thos. J. Moran's Sons, 1937, pp. lxxxv–xcv.

Lizondo Borda 1936 — Manuel Lizondo Borda (Comp.); *Documentos coloniales relativos a San Miguel de Tucumán y a la gobernación de Tucumán, siglo XVI*. Volumes I-III, Buenos Aires: Imprenta López, 1936.

Llambías 1975 — Jorge Joaquín Llambías; *Tratado de Derecho Civil, Parte General*. 6th edition, Volume I, Buenos Aires: Editorial Perrot, 1975.

Lloredo Alix 2012 — Luis M. Lloredo Alix; 'Rafael Altamira y Adolfo Posada: Dos aportaciones a la socialización del derecho y su proyección en Latinoamérica'. *Rechtsgeschichte 20*, 2012, pp. 209–233.

Lobingier 1932 — Charles Sumner Lobingier; 'The Modern Expansion of the Roman Law'. *University of Cincinnati Law Review 6*, 1932, pp. 152–184.

Löhnig 2014 — Martin Löhnig; 'Comparative Law and Legal History: A Few Words about Comparative Legal History', in: Maurice Adams and Dirk Heirbaut (Eds.); *The Method and Culture of Comparative Law: Essays in Honour of Mark Van Hoecke*. Oxford and Portland: Hart Publishing, 2014, pp. 113–120.

Long & Roberts 1994 — Norman Long and Bryan Roberts; 'The agrarian structures of Latin America, 1930–1990', in: Leslie Bethell (Ed.); *The Cambridge History of Latin America*. Volume VI, Cambridge and New York: Cambridge University Press, 1994, pp. 325–390.

López 2008 — Teodoro López; 'Propiedad y dominio en Francisco de Vitoria', in: Juan Cruz Cruz (Ed.); *Ley y dominio en Francisco de Vitoria*. Pamplona: EUNSA, Ediciones Universidad de Navarra, 2008, pp. 71–91.

Louisiana Constitution 1898 — *Constitution of the State of Louisiana adopted in convention at the city of New Orleans, May 12, 1898*. New Orleans: Hearsey, Convention Printer, 1898.

Louisiana Constitution 1913 — *Constitution of the State of Louisiana adopted in convention at the city of Baton Rouge. November 22, 1913*. Baton Rouge: Ramires-Jones Printing Company, 1913.

Louisiana Constitution 1921 — *Constitution of the State of Louisiana adopted in convention at the city of Baton Rouge. June 18, 1921.* Baton Rouge: Ramires-Jones Printing Company, [1921].

Louisiana Constitution 1974 — 'Constitution of Louisiana'. Louisiana State Senate. http://senate.legis.state.la.us/documents/Constitution/. Last visited on April 21, 2015.

Louisiana *Projet* 1823 — 'Projet of the Civil Code of Louisiana of 1825', in: *Louisiana Legal Archives*. Volume I, New Orleans: Thos. J. Moran's Sons, 1937, pp. 1–428.

Louisiana Purchase Treaty 1803 — 'Louisiana Purchase Treaty; April 30, 1803'. The Avalon Project: Documents in Law, History and Diplomacy. http://avalon.law.yale.edu/19th_century/louis1.asp. Last visited on April 21, 2015.

Lubens 2007 — Rebecca Lubens; 'The Social Obligation of Property Ownership: A Comparison of German and U.S. Law'. *Arizona Journal of International & Comparative Law 24*, 2007, pp. 389–449.

Luque Colombres 1945 — Carlos Luque Colombres; *Libros de derecho en bibliotecas particulares cordobesas 1573–1810*. Córdoba: Imprenta de la Universidad, 1945.

Luque Colombres 1958 — Carlos Luque Colombres; 'Los ejidos de Córdoba y la enfiteusis'. *Revista del Instituto de Historia del Derecho 9*, 1958, pp. 97–114.

Luque Colombres 1985 — Carlos Luque Colombres; 'La Real Instrucción de 1754. Su aplicación en Córdoba del Tucumán'. *Revista Chilena de Historia del Derecho 11*, 1985, pp. 43–51.

Luque Talaván 2003 — Miguel Luque Talaván; *Un universo de opiniones. La literatura jurídica indiana*. Madrid: Consejo Superior de Investigaciones Científicas, Instituto de Historia, 2003.

Machado 1898 — José Olegario Machado; *Exposición y comentario del código civil argentino: conteniendo la edición oficial y las notas del Dr. Vélez-Sarsfield, la aplicación de los fallos de la suprema corte nacional, los de las cámaras de apelación de la capital y un estudio sobre la ley del registro civil*. Volume I, Buenos Aires: Talleres Gráficos Argentinos, 1898.

Maitland 1898 Frederic William Maitland; 'A Prologue to a History of English Law'. *The Law Quarterly Review 14*, 1898, pp. 13–33.

Maluquer de Motes 1986 Carlos J. Maluquer de Motes; 'La desamortización y la codificación civil: propiedad y persona jurídica', in: *Desamortización y Hacienda Pública*. Volume II, Madrid: Ministerio de Agricultura, Alimentación y Medio Ambiente and Ministerio de Economía y Hacienda, 1986, pp. 703–714.

Manríquez González 2011 Vicente Maximiliano Manríquez González; *Ejercicio abusivo del derecho de acción y de petición, y sus efectos en materia de libre competencia*. Unpublished LL.B. thesis, Santiago: Universidad de Chile, 2011.

Margadant 1980 Guillermo Floris Margadant; 'Official Mexican Attitudes toward the Indians: An Historical Essay'. *Tulane Law Review 54*, 1980, pp. 964–986.

Mariani de Vidal 2004 Marina Mariani de Vidal; *Derechos Reales*. 7th edition, Volume I, Buenos Aires: Zavalía, 2004.

Mariluz Urquijo 1970 José María Mariluz Urquijo; 'La propiedad en el derecho indiano'. *Revista Chilena de Historia del Derecho 6*, 1970, pp. 154–157.

Mariluz Urquijo 1978 José María Mariluz Urquijo; *El Régimen de la Tierra en el Derecho Indiano*. 2nd edition, Buenos Aires: Editorial Perrot, 1978.

Markovitch 1933 Milan P. Markovitch; *La doctrine sociale de Duguit—ses idées sur le syndicalisme et la représentation professionnelle. Thèse pour le doctorat présentée et soutenue le 6 Décembre 1933*. Paris: Éditions Pierre Bossuet, 1933.

Marks 1990 G.C. Marks; 'Indigenous Peoples in International Law: The Significance of Francisco de Vitoria and Bartolome de las Casas'. *The Australian Year Book of International Law 13*, 1990, pp. 1–51.

Marotta & Parise 2014 Julieta Marotta and Agustín Parise; 'On Codes, Marriage, and Access to Justice: Recent Developments in the Law of Argentina'. *Journal of Civil Law Studies* 7, 2014, pp. 237–269.

Marshall 1914 Thomas Maitland Marshall; *A History of the Western Boundary of the Louisiana Purchase, 1819–1841*. Berkeley: University of California Press, 1914.

Martin 1975 Francois-Xavier Martin; *The History of Louisiana From the Earliest Period*. Reprint of the 1827 edition, Gretna: Pelican Publishing Company, 1975.

Martínez de Codes 2003 Rosa María Martínez de Codes; 'Les propriétés collectives au Mexique', in: Marie-Danielle Demélas and Nadine Vivier (Dir.); *Les propriétés collectives face aux attaques libérales (1750–1914): Europe occidentale et Amérique latine*. Rennes: Presses universitaires de Rennes, 2003, pp. 229–246.

Martínez de Hoz 1961 José Alfredo Martínez de Hoz (h.); *Enfiteusis y arrendamiento vitalicio en la Argentina y Nueva Zelandia*. Buenos Aires: Abeledo-Perrot, 1961.

Martinez-Fraga 2008 Pedro J. Martinez-Fraga; 'Examining the Codification of History and the Search for First Principles in Professor Alejandro Guzmán Brito's History of the Codification of Civil Law in Iberoamerica'. *University of Miami Inter-American Law Review* 39, 2008, pp. 503–528.

Martínez Paz 2000 Enrique Martínez Paz; *Dalmacio Vélez Sarsfield y el Código Civil Argentino*. Reprint, Córdoba: Academia Nacional de Derecho y Ciencias Sociales de Córdoba 2000.

Martini & Mayorga García 2004 Mónica Patricia Martini and Fernando Mayorga García; 'Los derechos de los pueblos originarios sobre sus tierras de comunidad. Del Nuevo Reino de Granada a la República de Colombia', in: Mario G. Losano (Ed.); *Un giudice e due leggi: pluralismo normativo e conflitti agrari in sud America*. Milan: Giuffrè, 2004, pp. 35–73.

Martiré 1977 — Eduardo Martiré; *Consideraciones Metodológicas sobre la Historia del Derecho*. Buenos Aires: Editorial Perrot, 1977.

Mathew 5–7 — 'The Gospel According to Matthew [Chapters 5–7]', in: *New American Bible for Catholics: Including the Revised Psalms and the Revised New Testament Translated from the Original Languages with Critical Use of All ancient Sources*. New York: American Bible Society, 1991, pp. 959–964.

Matus Valencia 1958 — Juan G. Matus Valencia; 'The Centenary of the Chilean Civil Code'. *The American Journal of Comparative Law 7*, 1958, pp. 71–83.

McAuley 2003 — Michael McAuley; 'Proposal for a Theory and a Method of Recodification'. *Loyola Law Review 49*, 2003, pp. 261–285.

McCord 1870 — Thomas McCord; *The Civil Code of Lower Canada: Together with a synopsis of changes in the law, references to the reports of the commissioners, the authorities as reported by the commissioners, a concordance with the Code Napoleon and Code de commerce, special references for notaries, clergymen, physicians, merchants, real estate owners, and persons out of Lower Canada,–and a complete index*. 2nd edition, Montreal: Dawson Brothers, 1870.

McGinty 1951 — Garnie William McGinty; *A History of Louisiana*. 2nd edition, New York: Exposition Press, 1951.

McLaren 2003 — John McLaren; 'Internet Teaching in Reparations Law: The Ozcan Model'. *Windsor Year Book of Access to Justice 22*, 2003, pp. 201–211.

Medina 2013 — Graciela Medina; 'Argentina on the Eve of a New Civil and Commercial Code', in: Julio César Rivera (Ed.); *The Scope and Structure*

	of Civil Codes. Dordrecht, Heidelberg, New York, and London: Springer, 2013, pp. 43–66.
Melleray 2011	Fabrice Melleray (Dir.); *Autour de Léon Duguit: Colloque commémoratif du 150e anniversaire de la naissance du doyen Léon Duguit. Bordeaux, 29–30 mai 2009*. Brussels: Bruylant, 2011.
Menger 1905	Anton Menger; *Über die sozialen Aufgaben der Rechtswissenschaft. Inaugurationsrede gehalten am 24. Oktober 1895 bei Übernahme des Rektorats der Wiener Universität.* 2nd edition, Vienna and Leipzig: Wilhelm Braumüller, 1905.
Merryman 1974	John Henry Merryman; 'Ownership and Estate (Variations on a Theme by Lawson)'. *Tulane Law Review 48*, 1974, pp. 916–945.
Merryman *et al.* 1994	John Henry Merryman et al; *The Civil Law Tradition: Europe, Latin America, and East Asia*. Charlottesville: Michie Co., 1994.
Meyer 1998	Jean Meyer; 'Mexico: revolution and reconstruction in the 1920s', in: Leslie Bethell (Ed.); *The Cambridge History of Latin America*. Reprint, Volume V, Cambridge and New York: Cambridge University Press, 1998, pp. 155–194.
Michaels 2008	Ralf Michaels; 'The Functional Method of Comparative Law', in: Mathias Reimann and Reinhard Zimmermann (Eds.); *The Oxford Handbook of Comparative Law*. Oxford: Oxford University Press, 2008, pp. 339–382.
Michaels 2012	Ralf Michaels; 'Comparative Law', in: Jürgen Basedow et al (Eds.); *Max Planck Encyclopedia of European Private Law*. Volume I, Oxford: Oxford University Press, 2012, pp. 297–301.
Miller 1997	Jonathan M. Miller; 'The Authority of a Foreign Talisman: A Study of U.S. Constitutional Practice as Authority in Nineteenth Century Argentina and the Argentine Elite's

Leap of Faith'. *The American University Law Review 46*, 1997, pp. 1483–1572.

Miller 2003 Jonathan M. Miller; 'A Typology of Legal Transplants: Using Sociology, Legal History and Argentine Examples to Explain the Transplant Process'. *The American Journal of Comparative Law 51*, 2003, pp. 839–885.

Miller Astrada 1985 Luisa Miller Astrada; 'El Repartimiento de Tierras a Particulares en Salta (Siglos XVI, XVII y XVIII)'. *Revista de Historia del Derecho 13*, 1985, pp. 373–392.

Miller Astrada 2003 Luisa Miller Astrada; 'Tierras comunitarias de las parcialidades calchaquíes (Siglos XVII y XVIII)', in: Luis E. González Vale (Coord.); *XIII Congreso del Instituto Internacional de Historia del Derecho Indiano. San Juan, 21 al 25 de mayo de 2000. Actas y Estudios*. Volume II, San Juan: Asamblea Legislativa de Puerto Rico, 2003, pp. 307–325.

Miñana y Villagrasa 1917 Emilio Miñana y Villagrasa; *Conferencia del señor D. Emilio Miñana y Villagrasa. Pronunciada en la sesión pública de 27 de marzo de 1917. Tema: Bases para la transformación del régimen de la propiedad territorial.* Madrid: Establecimiento Tipográfico de Jaime Ratés, 1917.

Mirow 2000–2001 M[atthew] C. Mirow; 'Latin American Legal History: Some Essential Spanish Terms'. *Berkeley La Raza Law Journal 12*, 2000–2001, pp. 43–86.

Mirow 2001 M[atthew] C. Mirow; 'Borrowing Private Law in Latin America: Andres Bello's use of the Code Napoleon in Drafting the Chilean Civil Code'. *Louisiana Law Review 61*, 2001, pp. 291–329.

Mirow 2004 M[atthew] C. Mirow; *Latin American Law: A History of Private Law and Institutions in Spanish America*. Austin: University of Texas Press, 2004.

Mirow 2005 — M[atthew] C. Mirow; 'Individual Experience in Legal Change: Exploring a neglected factor in Nineteenth-Century Latin American Codification'. *Southwestern Journal of Law and Trade in the Americas 11*, 2005, pp. 301–321.

Mirow 2010 — M[atthew] C. Mirow; 'The Social-Obligation Norm of Property: Duguit, Hayem, and Others'. *Florida Journal of International Law 22*, 2010, pp. 191–226.

Mirow 2011 — M[atthew] C. Mirow; 'Origins of the Social Function of Property in Chile'. *Fordham Law Review 80*, 2011, pp. 1183–1217.

Mirow 2014 — M[atthew] C. Mirow; 'Teaching Latin American Legal History', in: Robert M. Jarvis (Ed.); *Teaching Legal History: Comparative Perspectives*. London: Wildy, Simmonds & Hill Publishing, 2014, pp. 235–238.

Mirow 2016 — M[atthew] C. Mirow; 'Rerum Novarum: New Things and Recent Paradigms of Property Law'. *The University of the Pacific Law Review 47*, 2016, pp. 183–197.

Moccia 2011 — Luigi Moccia; 'Réflexions sur l'idée de propriété'. *Revue internationale de droit comparé 1–2011*, 2011, pp. 7–38.

Modéer 2005 — Kjell Å. Modéer; 'Mittermaier och bröderna Schmidt—Ett bidrag till 1800-talets interkulturella juristkommunikation', in: Göran Regner et al (Eds.); *Festskrift till Hans Ragnemalm*. Lund: Juristförlaget i Lund, 2005, pp. 233–256.

Modéer 2006 — Kjell Å. Modéer; 'Carl und Gustavus Schmidt als Zeitschriftenherausgeber. Zwei schwedische Juristenbruder als Pioniere juristischer Zeitschriften im 19. Jahrhundert', in: Michael Stolleis and Thomas Simon (Eds.); *Juristische Zeitschriften in Europa*. Frankfurt am Main: Klostermann, 2006, pp. 55–66.

Modéer 2011	Kjell Å. Modéer; 'Is European Comparative Legal History Running Wild? From Function and Texts to Perspectives and Contexts', in: Kjell Å. Modéer and Per Nilsén (Eds.); *How to Teach European Comparative Legal History: Workshop at the Faculty of Law, Lund University, 19–20 August 2009*. Lund: Juristförlaget i Lund, 2011, pp. 13–19.
Modéer & Nilsén 2011	Kjell Å. Modéer and Per Nilsén; 'Introduction', in: Kjell Å. Modéer and Per Nilsén (Eds.); *How to Teach European Comparative Legal History: Workshop at the Faculty of Law, Lund University, 19–20 August 2009*. Lund: Juristförlaget i Lund, 2011, pp. 9–10.
Moisset de Espanés 1981	Luis Moisset de Espanés; 'Reflexiones sobre las notas del código civil argentino', in: *Studi sassaresi. V, Diritto romano, codificazioni e unità del sistema giuridico latinoamericano*. Milan: Giuffrè, 1981, pp. 448–476.
Moisset de Espanés 2001	Luis Moisset de Espanés; 'Introducción al abuso del derecho [2001]'. Academia Nacional de Derecho y Ciencias Sociales de Córdoba, pp. 1–30. http://www.derecho.unc.edu.ar/acaderc/doctrina/articulos/introduccion-al-abuso-del-derecho. Last visited on April 21, 2015.
Monserrat Llairó 2009	María Monserrat Llairó; 'La tierra prometida'. *Encrucijadas 46*, 2009. http://www.uba.ar/encrucijadas/46/sumario/enc46-tierraprometida.php. Last visited on April 21, 2015.
Montoya 2010	Juny Montoya; 'The Current State of Legal Education Reform in Latin America: A Critical Appraisal'. *Journal of Legal Education 59*, 2010, pp. 545–566.
Montt *et al.* 1855	Manuel Montt et al.; 'Exposición de motivos [1855]', in: Rafael Caldera (Dir.); *Obras Completas de Andrés Bello*. 2nd edition, Volume XIV, Caracas: Fundación La Casa de Bello, 1981, pp. 3–22.

Moore 2001 — John Robert Moore; 'The New Deal in Louisiana', in: Edward F. Haas (Ed.); *The Louisiana Purchase Bicentennial Series in Louisiana History*. Volume VIII, Lafayette: Center for Louisiana Studies University of Southwestern Louisiana, 2001, pp. 124–148.

Morales Padrón 1979 — Francisco Morales Padrón; *Teoría y leyes de la conquista*. Madrid: Ediciones Cultura Hispánica del Centro Iberoamericano de Cooperación, 1979.

Moreau Lislet & Carleton 1818 — L[ouis] Moreau [Lislet] and Henry Carleton; *A Translation of the titles on Promises and Obligations, sale and purchase, and exchange from the Spanish of Las Siete Partidas*. New Orleans: Roche Brothers, 1818.

Moreau Lislet & Carleton 1820a — L[ouis] Moreau Lislet and Henry Carleton; *The Laws of las Siete Partidas Which are Still in Force in the State of Louisiana*. Reprint of the 1820 edition, Volume I, Baton Rouge: Claitor's Publishing Division, 1978.

Moreau Lislet & Carleton 1820b — L[ouis] Moreau Lislet and Henry Carleton; 'Translators' Preface', in: L[ouis] Moreau Lislet and Henry Carleton; *The Laws of las Siete Partidas Which are Still in Force in the State of Louisiana*. Reprint of the 1820 edition, Volume I, Baton Rouge: Claitor's Publishing Division, 1978, pp. iii–xxv.

Moréteau 2007 — Olivier Moréteau; 'Édouard Lambert et l'enseignement du droit comme science sociale et comparative', in David Deroussin (Ed.); *Le renouvellement des sciences sociales et juridiques sous la IIIe République: la Faculté de Droit de Lyon : actes du colloque des 4 & 5 février 2004*. Paris: La mémoire du droit, 2007, pp. 193–212.

Moréteau & Parise 2009 — Olivier Moréteau and Agustín Parise; 'Recodification in Louisiana and Latin America'. *Tulane Law Review 83*, 2009, pp. 1103–1162.

Morgan 1975 — Cecil Morgan; 'Introduction', in: Cecil Morgan (Comp.); *The First Constitution of the*

State of Louisiana. Baton Rouge: Louisiana State University Press, 1975, pp. 3–30.

Morgenfeld 2012 — Leandro Morgenfeld; 'Desarrollismo, Alianza para el Progreso y Revolución Cubana: Frondizi, Kennedy y el Che en Punta del Este (1961–1962)'. *Ciclos en la historia, la economía y la sociedad 20:40*, 2012, pp. 1–29. http://www.scielo.org.ar/pdf/ciclos/v20n40/v20n40a01.pdf. Last visited on April 21, 2015.

Morin 1932 — Gaston Morin; 'L'œuvre de Duguit et le droit privé'. *Archives de Philosophie du droit et de Sociologie juridique 1–2*, 1932, pp. 153–162.

Mörner 1997 — Magnus Mörner; 'The rural economy and society of colonial Spanish South America', in: Leslie Bethell (Ed.); *The Cambridge History of Latin America.* Reprint, Volume II, Cambridge and New York: Cambridge University Press, 1997, pp. 189–217.

Morrison 1937 — James J. Morrison; 'The Need for a Revision of the Louisiana Civil Code'. *Tulane Law Review 11*, 1937, pp. 213–242.

Muñoz León 2005 — Fernando Muñoz León; 'Notas sobre la Historia constitucional de Chile: génesis y evolución entre 1810 y 1970', in: Jan Woischnik (Ed.); *Anuario de Derecho Constitucional Latinoamericano 2005.* Volume I, Montevideo: Konrad-denauer-Stiftung, 2005, pp. 245–271.

Murchison 1988 — Kenneth M. Murchison; 'The Judicial Revival of Louisiana's Civilian Tradition: A Surprising Triumph for the American Influence'. *Louisiana Law Review 49,* 1988, pp. 1–37.

Murillo 2001 — María Luisa Murillo; 'The Evolution of Codification in the Civil Law Legal Systems: Towards Decodification and Recodification'. *Journal of Transnational Law and Policy 11*, 2001, pp. 163–182.

Nelken 2003 — David Nelken; 'Comparatists and transferability', in: Pierre Legrand and Roderick Munday (Eds.); *Comparative Legal Studies: Traditions and Transitions*. Cambridge: Cambridge University Press, 2003, pp. 437–466.

Nieto 1964 — Alejandro Nieto; *Bienes comunales*. Madrid: Editorial Revista de Derecho Privado, 1964.

Niglia 2010 — Leone Niglia; 'Of Harmonization and Fragmentation: The Problem of Legal Transplants in the Europeanization of Private Law'. *Maastricht Journal of European and Comparative Law 17:2*, 2010, pp. 116–136.

Nörr 1992 — Knut Wolfgang Nörr; 'From Codification to Constitution: On the Changes of Paradigm in German Legal History of the Twentieth Century'. *Tijdschrift voor Rechtsgeschiedenis 60*, 1992, pp. 145–155.

Novillo Corvalán 1936 — Sofanor Novillo Corvalán; 'El dominio en el código civil—Hacia la verdad de su doctrina'. *Revista Jurídica Argentina La Ley 3*, 1936, pp. 61–66 (sec. doct.).

Nuttall 1921 — Zelia Nuttall; 'Royal Ordinances Concerning the Laying out of New Towns'. *Hispanic American Historical Review 4:4*, 1921, pp. 743–753.

Oliver 2003 — Paul Oliver; *Dwellings: The Vernacular House World Wide*. London and New York: Phaidon Press, 2003.

Oosterhuis 2011 — Janwillem Oosterhuis; *Specific Performance in German, French and Dutch Law in the Nineteenth Century: Remedies in an Age of Fundamental Rights and Industrialisation*. Leiden and Boston: Martins Nijhoff Publishers, 2011.

Örücü 2006 — A. Esin Örücü; 'Methodology of Comparative Law', in: Jan M. Smits (Ed.); *Elgar Encyclopedia of Comparative Law*. Cheltenham:

Edward Elgar Publishing Limited, 2006, pp. 442–454.

Osipova 2011 — Sanita Osipova; 'Europäische Rechtsgeschichte: Geopolitisch, kulturell oder historisch gebildete Wissenschaft', in: Kjell Å. Modéer and Per Nilsén (Eds.); *How to Teach European Comparative Legal History: Workshop at the Faculty of Law, Lund University, 19–20 August 2009*. Lund: Juristförlaget i Lund, 2011, pp. 77–83.

Ots Capdequí 1940 — José María Ots Capdequí; *Estudios de historia del derecho español en las Indias.* (*El derecho de propiedad. El municipio colonial. El derecho de sucesión. Condición jurídica del extranjero. Aportaciones para la historia de la iglesia. La expansión del derecho español en los territorios indianos*). Bogotá: Editorial Minerva, 1940.

Ots Capdequí 1945 — José María Ots Capdequí; *Manual de historia de derecho español en las Indias y del derecho propiamente indiano*. Buenos Aires: Editorial Losada, 1945.

Ots Capdequí 1946 — José María Ots Capdequí; *El régimen de la tierra en la América española durante el periodo colonial: Cursillo dictado en la Universidad de Santo Domingo del 27 de noviembre al 13 de diciembre de 1944*. Ciudad Trujillo [Santo Domingo]: Universidad de Santo Domingo, 1946.

Oxford English Dictionary 2015a — 'jurisdiction, n.'. OED Online. June 2016. Oxford University Press. http://www.oed.com/view/Entry/102156?redirectedFrom=jurisdiction Last visited on September 5, 2016.

Oxford English Dictionary 2015b — 'paradigm, n.'. OED Online. March 2015. Oxford University Press. http://www.oed.com/view/Entry/137329?redirectedFrom=paradigm. Last visited on April 21, 2015.

Ozcan 2000 — Ozcan; 'Webbing the Pacific: Teaching an Intercontinental Legal History Course'. *Law and History Review 18:2*, 2000, pp. 445–456.

Pagden & Lawrance 1991 — Anthony Pagden and Jeremy Lawrance (Eds.); *Vitoria: Political Writings*. Cambridge and New York: Cambridge University Press, 1991.

Page 2004 — Carlos A. Page; 'Los *ejidos* como espacio comunal de la ciudad de Córdoba del Tucumán'. *Revista de Indias 64:232*, 2004, pp. 635–650.

Palma González 2009a — Eric Eduardo Palma González, 'Historia del derecho en América Latina en el siglo XXI: el caso de Chile, Colombia y México'. *Ambiente Jurídico 11*, 2009, pp. 44–65.

Palma González 2009b — Eric Eduardo Palma González, 'Pasado, presente y futuro de la historia del derecho en Chile'. *Forum Historiae Iuris* (*30. März* 2009). http://www.forhistiur.de/2009-03-palma-gonzalez/. Last visited on April 21, 2015.

Palmer 1999 — Vernon Valentine Palmer; 'Introduction', in: Vernon Valentine Palmer (Ed.); *Louisiana: Microcosm of a Mixed Jurisdiction*. Durham, N.C.: Carolina Academic Press, 1999, pp. 3–22.

Palmer 2003a — Vernon Valentine Palmer; 'The French Connection and The Spanish Perception: Historical Debates and Contemporary Evaluation of French Influence on Louisiana Civil Law'. *Louisiana Law Review 63*, 2003, pp. 1067–1125.

Palmer 2003b — Vernon Valentine Palmer; 'The Recent Discovery of Moreau Lislet's System of Omissions and Its Importance to the Debate Over the Sources of the Digest of 1808'. *Loyola Law Review 49*, 2003, pp. 301–337.

Palmer 2006 — Vernon Valentine Palmer; 'Mixed Jurisdictions', in: Jan M. Smits (Ed.); *Elgar Encyclopedia of Comparative Law*. Cheltenham: Edward Elgar Publishing Limited, 2006, pp. 467–475.

Parise 2002a — Agustín Parise; 'La imperiosa remisión al derecho comparado en las investigaciones de carácter jurídico'. *Revista Universitaria La Ley 4:6*, 2002, pp. 36–41.

Parise 2002b — Agustín Parise; 'Un Crisol Utilizado por la Historia, el Derecho y la Ciencia del Pueblo'. *Lecciones y Ensayos 77*, 2002, pp. 201–212.

Parise 2004 — Agustín Parise; 'Mercedes de Tierras y Solares. Aspectos de la Institución en la América Hispana Meridional durante los Siglos XVI y XVII'. *Revista de Derecho Puertorriqueño 43*, 2004, pp. 181–195.

Parise 2006a — Agustín Parise; 'La Comisión de Reformas al Código Civil (1926). Aproximación histórico-jurídica a su proyección'. *Iushistoria Revista Electrónica 3*, 2006, pp. 1–26. http://p3.usal.edu.ar/index.php/iushistoria/issue/view/157. Last visited on April 21, 2015.

Parise 2006b — Agustín Parise; *Non-Pecuniary Damages in the Louisiana Civil Code Article 1928: Originality in the Early Nineteenth Century and Its Projected Use in Further Codification Endeavors*. Unpublished LL.M. thesis, Baton Rouge: Louisiana State University, 2006.

Parise 2008a — Agustín Parise, 'La Carta Fundamental de los argentinos: Desde lo intrínseco, un siglo y medio después', in: Olivier Moréteau et al (Eds.); *Essays in Honor of Saúl Litvinoff*. Baton Rouge: Claitor's Publishing Division, 2008, pp. 659–673.

Parise 2008b — Agustín Parise; 'The Place of the Louisiana Civil Code in the Hispanic Civil Codifications: Inclusion in the Comments to the Spanish Civil Code Project of 1851'. *Louisiana Law Review 68*, 2008, pp. 823–929.

Parise 2008c — Agustín Parise; 'The Valladolid Controversy Revisited: Looking Back at the Sixteenth-Century Debate on Native Americans While Facing the Current Status of Human Embryos'. *Journal of Civil Law Studies 1*, 2008, pp. 107–138.

Parise 2009a Agustín Parise; 'Gustavus Schmidt, The Civil Law of Spain and Mexico'. *Journal of Civil Law Studies* 2, 2009, pp. 183–193.

Parise 2009b Agustín Parise; 'Las bibliotecas jurídicas como herramientas fundamentales del Derecho Comparado: El caso de Schmidt en la Luisiana del siglo XIX'. *Revista de Derecho Comparado* 15, 2009, pp. 195–241.

Parise 2010a Agustín Parise; 'A Constant Give and Take: Tracing Legal Borrowings in the Louisiana Civil Law Experience'. *Seton Hall Legislative Journal* 35, 2010, pp. 1–35.

Parise 2010b Agustín Parise; 'Las Revistas Jurídicas en el Ámbito Universitario: Foros de Expresión y Laboratorios de Escritura'. *Academia. Revista sobre Enseñanza del Derecho* 15, 2010, pp. 123–132.

Parise 2011a Agustín Parise; 'George Dargo, Jefferson's Louisiana: Politics and the Clash of Legal Traditions'. *Journal of Civil Law Studies* 4, 2011, pp. 631–637.

Parise 2011b Agustín Parise; 'Sobre el estudio comparado de la Historia del Derecho'. *Revista de Historia del Derecho* 42, 2011, pp. 212–218.

Parise 2012a Agustín Parise; 'Codification of the Law in Louisiana: Early Nineteenth-Century oscillation between Continental European and Common Law Systems'. *Tulane European & Civil Law Forum* 42, 2012, pp. 133–164.

Parise 2012b Agustín Parise; 'Legal Transplants and Codification: Exploring the North American Sources of the Civil Code of Argentina (1871)', in: Jorge A. Sánchez Cordero (Ed.); *Legal Culture and Legal Transplants. La culture juridique et l'acculturation du droit.* Volume I, Mexico: IACL, UNAM, and CMDU, 2012, pp. 71–121.

Parise 2013a Agustín Parise; *Historia de la Codificación Civil del Estado de Luisiana y su Influencia en el Código Civil Argentino*. Buenos Aires: Eudeba, 2013.

Parise 2013b — Agustín Parise; 'Private Law in Louisiana: An Account of Civil Codes, Heritage, and Law Reform', in: Julio César Rivera (Ed.); *The Scope and Structure of Civil Codes*. Dordrecht, Heidelberg, New York, and London: Springer, 2013, pp. 429–453.

Parise 2014a — Agustín Parise; 'Civil Law Codification in Latin America: Understanding First and Second Generation Codes', in: J. Michael Milo et al (Eds.); *Tradition, Codification and Unification: Comparative-Historical Essays on Developments in Civil Law*. Cambridge, Antwerp, and Portland: Intersentia, 2014, pp. 183–193.

Parise 2014b — Agustín Parise; 'Libraries of Civil Codes as Mirrors of Normative Transfers from Europe to the Americas: The Experiences of Lorimier in Quebec (1871–1890) and Varela in Argentina (1873–1875)', in: Thomas Duve (Ed.); *Entanglements in Legal History: Conceptual Approaches, Global Perspectives on Legal History*. Max Planck Institute for European Legal History, Open Access Publication, Frankfurt am Main, 2014, pp. 315–384. http://dx.doi.org/10.12946/gplh1. Last visited on April 21, 2015.

Parise 2014c — Agustín Parise; 'Translators' Preface to the Laws of *Las Siete Partidas* which are Still in Force in the State of Louisiana'. *Journal of Civil Law Studies* 7, 2014, pp. 311–353.

Parma 1929 — Rosamond Parma; 'The History of the Adoption of the Codes of California'. *Law Library Journal* 22, 1929, pp. 8–21.

Parra Silva 2006 — Rogelio Parra Silva; 'Conferencia internacional sobre reforma agraria y desarrollo rural'. *Estudios Agrarios* 31, 2006, pp. 239–253.

Pascal 1972 — Robert A. Pascal; 'Sources of the Digest of 1808: A Reply to Professor Batiza'. *Tulane Law Review* 46, 1972, pp. 603–627.

Pascal 1998 — Robert A. Pascal; 'Of the Civil Code and Us'. *Louisiana Law Review* 59, 1998, pp. 301–324.

Peirano Facio 2008 — Jorge Peirano Facio; *Tristán Narvaja: Un Jurista Rioplatense en Tiempos de la Codificación.* Buenos Aires: Instituto de Investigaciones de Historia del Derecho, 2008.

Peñailillo Arévalo 2006 — Daniel Peñailillo Arévalo; *Los Bienes: la Propiedad y otros Derechos Reales.* 4th edition, Santiago: Editorial Jurídica de Chile, 2006.

Pérez-Perdomo 2006 — Rogelio Pérez-Perdomo; *Latin American Lawyers: A Historical Introduction.* Stanford: Stanford University Press, 2006.

Pérez Vichich 2004 — Nora Pérez Vichich; 'Los trabajadores migrantes en la nueva ley de migraciones: De objeto de normas a sujetos de Derecho', in: Rubén Giustiniani (Ed.); *Migración: Un derecho humano.* Buenos Aires: Prometeo, 2004, pp. 137–157.

Pérez y López 1791–1798 — Antonio Xavier Pérez y López; *Teatro de la legislacion universal de España é Indias: por orden cronológico de sus cuerpos y decisiones no recopiladas: y alfabético de sus títulos y principales materias.* Volumes I–XXVIII, Madrid: [publishers differ in the volumes], 1791–1798.

Pescio Vargas 1978 — Victorio Pescio Vargas; *Manual de Derecho Civil.* 2nd edition, Volume I, Santiago: Editorial Jurídica de Chile, 1978.

Peset 1999 — Mariano Peset; 'Fundamento ideológico de la propiedad', in: Salustiano de Dios et al (Coord.); *Historia de la Propiedad en España siglos XV–XX. Encuentro Interdisciplinar. Salamanca, 3–6 de junio de 1998.* [Madrid]: Centro de Estudios Registrales, 1999, pp. 441–470.

Petit 1995 — Carlos Petit; 'Absolutismo jurídico y derecho comparado. Método comparativo y sistema de fuentes en la obra de Édouard Lambert', in Paolo Cappellini et al; *De la Ilustración al Liberalismo. Symposium en honor al Profesor*

Paolo Grossi. Madrid: Centro de Estudios Constitucionales, 1995, pp. 121–137.

Petit 2001 — Carlos Petit; 'Lambert en la *Tour Eiffel*, o el derecho comparado de la *Belle Époque*', in Antonio Padoa-Schioppa (Ed.); *La comparazione giuridica tra Otto e Novecento: In Memoria di Mario Rotondi*. Milan: Istituto Lombardo di scienze e lettere, 2001, pp. 53–98.

Petras & Zeitlin 1970 — James Petras and Maurice Zeitlin; 'Agrarian Radicalism in Chile', in: Rodolfo Stavenhagen (Ed.); *Agrarian Problems and Peasant Movements in Latin America*. Garden City: Anchor Books, 1970, pp. 503–531.

Phillipson 1915 — Coleman Phillipson; 'Franciscus a Victoria (1480–1546)'. *Journal of the Society of Comparative Legislation, new series, 15*, 1915, pp. 175–197.

Pihlajamäki 2011 — Heikki Pihlajamäki; 'When Small is Beautiful: Teaching Comparative Legal History in the Periphery', in: Kjell Å. Modéer and Per Nilsén (Eds.); *How to Teach European Comparative Legal History: Workshop at the Faculty of Law, Lund University, 19–20 August 2009*. Lund: Juristförlaget i Lund, 2011, pp. 39–45.

Pihlajamäki 2014 — Heikki Pihlajamäki; 'Comparative Contexts in Legal History: Are We All Comparatists Now?', in: Maurice Adams and Dirk Heirbaut (Eds.); *The Method and Culture of Comparative Law: Essays in Honour of Mark Van Hoecke*. Oxford and Portland: Hart Publishing, 2014, pp. 121–132.

Pizarro 1950 — Néstor A. Pizarro; *El Código Civil Argentino y el Código de Luisiana* (*Estudio sobre las Fuentes Legislativas del Código Civil*). Córdoba: Imprenta de la Universidad, 1950.

Plato 1852 — Plato; 'The Laws', in: George Burges, *The Works of Plato: A New and Literal Version, chiefly from the Text of Stallbaum*. Volume V, London: Henry G. Bohn, 1852, pp. 1–548.

Polotto 2012 — María Rosario Polotto; 'Argumentación jurídica y trasfondo ideológico. Análisis del debate legislativo sobre prórroga de alquileres en argentina a principios del siglo XX'. *Rechtsgeschichte 20*, 2012, pp. 309–327.

Pothier 1772 — Robert-Joseph Pothier; *Traité du droit de domaine de propriété*. Volume I, Paris and Orléans: Debure and Rouzeau-Montaut, 1772.

Pound 1923 — Roscoe Pound; *Interpretations of Legal History*. New York: The Macmillan Company, 1923.

Powell 1954 — Alden L. Powell; 'A History of Louisiana Constitutions', in: *Projet of a Constitution for the State of Louisiana with Notes and Studies*. Volume I, Part I, Baton Rouge: Louisiana State Law Institute, 1954, pp. 271–553.

Prevedello 1992 — Nora Lilí Prevedello; 'La lengua en el "Libro de las mercedes de tierras" (1573–1600): Notas para una historia del español de Córdoba (Argentina)'. *Thesaurus: Boletín del Instituto Caro y Cuervo 47:3*, 1992, pp. 605–628.

Proceedings Constitutional Convention Louisiana 1921 — *Official Journal of the proceedings of the Constitutional Convention of the State of Louisiana. Begun and Held in the City of Baton Rouge. March 1, 1921. And calendar.* [Baton Rouge]: Ramires-Jones Printing Co., [1921].

Proclama 1956 — 'Proclama del 27 de abril de 1956', in: *Anales de Legislación Argentina*. Volume XVI-A, Buenos Aires: La Ley, 1956, pp. 1–2.

Project Civil Code Chile 1853 — *Obras Completas de Don Andrés Bello: Proyecto de Código Civil (1853)*. Volume XII, Santiago: Impreso por Pedro G. Ramírez, 1888.

Projet de Code Civil 1800 — *Projet de code civil, présenté par la commission nommée par le gouvernement*. Paris: de l'imprimerie de la république, Ventôse an IX [February, 1801].

Protocol 1952 — 'Protocol', in: *European Convention on Human Rights*. European Court of Human

Rights—Council of Europe, pp. 31–37. http://www.echr.coe.int/Documents/Convention_ENG.pdf. Last visited on April 21, 2015.

Puig Brutau 1987 — José Puig Brutau; *Compendio de derecho civil*. Volume I, Barcelona: Bosch, 1987.

Rabalais 1982 — Raphael J. Rabalais; 'The Influence of Spanish Laws and Treatises on the Jurisprudence of Louisiana: 1762–1828'. *Louisiana Law Review 42*, 1982, pp. 1485–1508.

Rabel 1950 — Ernst Rabel; 'Private Laws of Western Civilization'. *Louisiana Law Review 10*, 1950, pp. 265–275.

Rabinovich-Berkman 1990 — Ricardo David Rabinovich[-Berkman]; 'El publicismo como característica del derecho del Tawantinsuyu', in: Abelardo Levaggi (Coord.); *El aborigen y el derecho en el pasado y el presente*. Buenos Aires: Universidad del Museo Social Argentino, 1990, pp. 9–22.

Rabinovich-Berkman 2006 — Ricardo D[avid] Rabinovich-Berkman; *Principios generales del derecho latinoamericano*. Buenos Aires: Astrea, 2006.

Ramella 2007 — Susana T. Ramella; 'Propiedad en función social en la Constitución de 1949: Una "mentalidad" del Antiguo Régimen representada en el constitucionalismo social de la época'. *Revista de Historia del Derecho 35*, 2007, pp. 297–354.

Ramos Núñez 1996 — Carlos Ramos Núñez; *Codificación, Tecnología y Postmodernidad*. Lima: Ara Editores, 1996.

Ramos Núñez 1997 — Carlos Ramos Núñez; *El Código Napoleónico y su Recepción en América Latina*. Lima: Pontificia Universidad Católica del Perú, 1997.

Ray 1869 — John Ray; *The Civil Code of the State of Louisiana, Revised, Arranged and Amended*. Monroe: Office of the "Louisiana Intelligencer," 1869.

RChHD 2015 — 'Portada'. Revista Chilena de Historia del Derecho. http://www.historiadelderecho.uchile.cl/. Last visited on April 21, 2015.

Real Cédula 1591 — 'Real cédula de composición y restitución de tierras a la Corona'. Asociación para el Fomento de los Estudios Históricos en Centroamérica. http://www.afehc-historia-centroamericana.org/index.php?action=fi_aff&id=1288. Last visited on April 21, 2015.

Rébora 1937 — Juan Carlos Rébora; 'Informe anexo a la nota de 10 de octubre de 1936'. *Revista Jurídica Argentina La Ley 5*, 1937, pp. 69–85 (sec. doct.).

Recopilación de Indias 1680 — *Recopilacion de Leyes de los Reynos de las Indias*. Volumes I–IV, Madrid: Ivlian de Paredes, 1681.

Reforma Agraria Chilena 1962 — *La Reforma Agraria Chilena. Ley 15.020*. Santiago: El Diario Ilustrado, [1962].

Reforma Código Civil 1936 — *Reforma del Código Civil. I. Antecedentes—II. Informe. III. Proyecto*. Buenos Aires: Kraft, 1936.

Réglade 1932 — Marc Réglade; 'Théorie générale du droit dans l'œuvre de L. Duguit'. *Archives de Philosophie du droit et de Sociologie juridique 1–2*, 1932, pp. 21–67.

Regulations of Ventura Morales 1799 — 'General regulations and instructions of Morales for conceding lands', in: Asbury Dickins and John W. Forney (Eds.); *American State Papers. Documents of the Congress of the United States in relation to the Public Lands, from the First Session of the Twentieth to the Second Session of the Twentieth Congress*. Volume V, Washington: Gales & Seaton, 1860, pp. 731–734.

Reich 1964 — Charles A. Reich; 'The New Property'. *Yale Law Journal 73*, 1964, pp. 733–787.

Reich 2007 — Peter L. Reich; '*Siete Partidas* in My Saddlebags: The Transmission of Hispanic Law from Antebellum Louisiana to Texas and California'. *Tulane European and Civil Law Forum 22*, 2007, pp. 79–88.

Reimann & Levasseur 1998 — Mathias Reimann and Alain Levasseur; 'Comparative Law and Legal History in the United States'. *The American Journal of Comparative Law 46: supplement,* 1998, pp. 1–15.

Reinsch 1907 — Paul Samuel Reinsch; 'The English Common Law in the Early American Colonies', in: John H. Wigmore et al (Eds.); *Selected Essays in Anglo-American Legal History.* Volume I, Boston: Little, Brown, and Company, 1907, pp. 367–415.

Renard & Trotabas 1930 — Georges Renard and Louis Trotabas; *La fonction sociale de la propriété privée.* Paris: Sirey, 1930.

Renoux-Zagamé 1987 — Marie-France Renoux-Zagamé; *Origines théologiques du concept moderne de propriété.* Geneva: Librairie Droz, 1987.

Repgen 2001 — Tilman Repgen; *Die soziale Aufgabe des Privatrechts: Eine Grundfrage in Wissenschaft und Kodifikation am Ende des 19. Jahrhunderts.* Tübingen: Mohr Siebeck, 2001.

Resolution 1806 — 'A Resolution relative to the formation of a civil code [June 7, 1806]', in: *Acts passed at the First Session of the First Legislature of the Territory of Orleans.* New Orleans: Bradford & Anderson, 1807, pp. 214–219.

Resolution 1822 — 'Resolutions [March 14, 1822]', in: *Acts passed at the Second Session of the Fifth Legislature of the State of Louisiana.* New Orleans: J.C. de St. Romes, 1822, pp. 108.

Revised Louisiana Code 1870 — *The Revised Civil Code of the State of Louisiana.* New Orleans: Office of the Republican, 1870.

Revised Louisiana Code 1910 — *The Revised Civil Code of the State of Louisiana 1910.* Baton Rouge: The New Advocate, 1910.

Revision Book II Louisiana Code 1980 — *Civil Law Property: Revision of Book II of the Louisiana Civil Code with the drafter's comments.* Baton Rouge: Paul M. Hebert Law Center Publications Institute, 1980.

Richert & Richert 1973 — John Richert and Suzanne Richert; 'The Impact of the Civil Code of Louisiana upon the Civil Code of Quebec of 1866'. *Revue juridique Thémis de l'université de Montréal 8*, 1973, pp. 501–520.

Riddick 2008 — Winston W. Riddick; 'Economic Development and Private Ownership of Immovable Property: A Comparison of Louisiana and Haiti'. *Electronic Journal of Comparative Law 12:1*, 2008, pp. 1–12. http://www.ejcl.org/121/art121-22.pdf. Last visited on April 21, 2015.

Riley 2013 — Angela R. Riley; 'The History of Native American Lands and the Supreme Court'. *Journal of Supreme Court History 38*, 2013, pp. 369–385.

Ríos Álvarez 2010 — Lautaro Ríos Álvarez; 'El principio constitucional de la función social de la propiedad', in: Raúl Tavolari Oliveros (Dir.); *Revista de Derecho y Jurisprudencia. Edición Bicentenario. Doctrinas Esenciales. Derecho Civil. Bienes*. Volume I, Santiago: Jurídica de Chile, 2010, pp. 111–136.

Rípodas Ardanaz 1984 — Daisy Rípodas Ardanaz; 'La Biblioteca de Mariano Izquierdo. Un repositorio jurídico atípico en el Buenos Aires finicolonial'. *Revista de Historia del Derecho 12*, 1984, pp. 303–336.

Rivarola 1901 — Rodolfo Rivarola; *Instituciones del Derecho Civil Argentino: Programa de una nueva exposición del derecho civil*. Volume I, Buenos Aires: Imprenta de Peuser, 1901.

Rivera 2001 — Julio César Rivera; 'El Proyecto de Código Civil para la República Argentina'. *Revista Jurídica Universidad Interamericana de Puerto Rico 35*, 2001, pp. 381–442.

Rivera 2002 — Julio César Rivera; 'La recodificación. Un estudio de derecho comparado'. *Revista Jurídica del Perú LII:41*, 2002, pp. 83–130.

Rivera 2013 — Julio César Rivera; 'The Scope and Structure of Civil codes. Relations with Commercial

Law, Family Law, Consumer Law and Private International Law. A Comparative Approach', in: Julio César Rivera (Ed.); *The Scope and Structure of Civil Codes*. Dordrecht, Heidelberg, New York, and London: Springer, 2013, pp. 3–39.

Robinson *et al.* 2000 — O[livia] F. Robinson et al; *European Legal History: Sources and Institutions*. 3rd edition, London; Butterworths, 2000.

Robledo & Espinoza 1999 — Ricardo Robledo and Luis Enrique Espinoza; 'La Reforma Agraria en la II República: El Proceso de Asentamiento de Comunidades de Campesinos en la Provincia de Salamanca', in: Salustiano de Dios et al (Coord.); *Historia de la Propiedad en España siglos XV–XX. Encuentro Interdisciplinar. Salamanca, 3–6 de junio de 1998*. [Madrid]: Centro de Estudios Registrales, 1999, pp. 403–439.

Rocca Mones-Ruiz 2009 — Gabriel Rocca Mones-Ruiz; 'Fuentes clásicas de la historia del derecho hispanoamericano en formato digital: Romanas'. *Iushistoria Revista Electrónica 6*, 2009, pp. 105–121. http://p3.usal.edu.ar/index.php/iushistoria/issue/view/132. Last visited on April 21, 2015.

Rock 1987 — David Rock; *Argentina, 1516–1987: From Spanish colonization to Alfonsín*. Revised edition, Berkeley: University of California Press, 1987.

Rodríguez 1938 — Carlos J. Rodríguez; 'La Redacción de los Códigos: Necesidad de la Indicación de la Fuente de sus Artículos'. *Revista del Colegio de Abogados de Buenos Aires 17:16*, 1938, pp. 187–198.

Roig 1969 — Arturo Andrés Roig; *Los Krausistas argentinos*. Puebla: Editorial J.M. Cajica, 1969.

Rojas 2002 — Hugo Rojas; 'Cambios Sociales y Cambios Jurídicos en Chile: Construyendo Nuevos Puentes entre Sociología y Derecho en la Promoción del Realismo Jurídico

Latinoamericano'. *Berkeley La Raza Law Journal 13*, 2002, pp. 453–487.

Roosevelt 1937 — Franklin D. Roosevelt; 'Message to Congress on Farm Tenancy'. February 6, 1937. Online by Gerhard Peters and John T. Woolley, *The American Presidency Project*. http://www.presidency.ucsb.edu/ws/?pid=15362. Last visited on April 21, 2015.

Rosenn 1963 — Keith S. Rosenn; 'Puerto Rican Land Reform: The History of an Instructive Experiment'. *Yale Law Journal 73*, 1963, pp. 334–356.

Rosenn 1971 — Keith S. Rosenn; 'Teaching Latin American Law'. *The American Journal of Comparative Law 19*, 1971, pp. 692–699.

Rosti 2004 — Marzia Rosti; 'Gli indios e la terra nell'attuale Costituzione argentina', in: Mario G. Losano (Ed.); *Un giudice e due leggi: pluralismo normativo e conflitti agrari in sud America*. Milan: Giuffrè, 2004, pp. 75–116.

Roth 2002 — Dennis Roth; 'The New Deal', in: Dennis Roth et al; *Federal Rural Development Policy in the Twentieth Century*. Beltsville: USDA, National Agricultural Library, Rural Information Center, 2002, pp. 1–25 (Chapter 2).

Rotondi 1968 — Mario Rotondi; 'Technique du droit, dogmatique et droit comparé'. *Revue internationale de droit comparé 20:1*, 1968, pp. 5–18.

Rüfner 2010 — Thomas Rüfner; 'The Roman Concept of Ownership and the Medieval Doctrine of Dominium Utile', in: John W. Cairns and Paul J. du Plessis (Eds.); *The Creation of the* Ius Commune*: From* Casus *to* Regula. Edinburgh: Edinburgh University Press, 2010, pp. 127–142.

Ruíz B. 1964 — Gil A. Ruíz B.; *La función social de la propiedad agrícola en la ley de reforma agraria venezolana de 1960*. [Caracas]: [Ministerio de Agricultura y Cría], [1964].

Ruíz-Giménez 1961 — Joaquín Ruíz-Giménez; *La Propiedad. Sus Problemas y su Función Social*. Volume I,

Salamanca and Madrid: Ediciones Anaya, 1961.

Ruíz Moreno 1976 — Isidoro J. Ruíz Moreno; *La Lucha por la Constitución (1820–1853)*. Buenos Aires: Astrea, 1976.

Sabsay 2011 — Daniel A. Sabsay; *Manual de Derecho Constitucional*. Buenos Aires: La Ley, 2011.

Sacco 1991a — Rodolfo Sacco; 'Legal Formants: A Dynamic Approach to Comparative Law (Installment I of II)'. *The American Journal of Comparative Law* 39, 1991, pp. 1–34.

Sacco 1991b — Rodolfo Sacco; 'Legal Formants: A Dynamic Approach to Comparative Law (Installment II of II)'. *The American Journal of Comparative Law* 39, 1991, pp. 343–401.

Sagnac 1898 — Philippe Sagnac; *La législation civile de la Révolution Française (1789–1804): Essai d'histoire sociale*. Paris: Hachette, 1898.

Saint-Joseph (de) 1840 — Anthoine de Saint-Joseph; *Concordance entre les codes civils étrangers et le Code Napoléon*. Paris: Charles Hingray, 1840.

Saint-Joseph (de) 1856 — Anthoine de Saint-Joseph; *Concordance entre les codes civils étrangers et le Code Napoléon ouvrage terminé et publié par M.A. de Saint-Joseph*. Volumes I–IV, Paris: Cotillon, 1856.

Sala 1803 — Juan Sala; *Ilustración del derecho real de España*. Volume I, Valencia: Imprenta de Joseph de Orga, 1803.

Salas 1941 — Acdeel Ernesto Salas; 'La Reforma del Código Civil Argentino por Ángel Ossorio'. *Jurisprudencia Argentina* 74, 1941, pp. 41–42 (sec. bibl.).

Salerno 1969 — Marcelo Urbano Salerno; 'La legislación comparada del señor Seoane, fuente del código civil argentino'. *Revista del Instituto de Historia del Derecho "Ricardo Levene"* 20, 1969, pp. 311–318.

Salerno 1974 — Marcelo Urbano Salerno; 'Aporte de Héctor Lafaille a la Enseñanza del Derecho Civil'. *Revista de Historia del Derecho* 2, 1974, pp. 199–224.

Salerno 1992 — Marcelo Urbano Salerno; 'Un Retorno a las Fuentes del Código Civil Argentino: La Doctrina Francesa', in: Abelardo Levaggi (Coord.); *Fuentes Ideológicas y Normativas de la Codificación Latinoamericana*. Buenos Aires: Universidad del Museo Social Argentino, 1992, pp. 217–240.

Salerno 1993 — Marcelo Urbano Salerno; 'Argentine', in: *La Circulation du Modèle Juridique Français*. Paris: Litec, 1993, pp. 121–124.

Salerno 2004 — Marcelo Urbano Salerno; 'El Código de Vélez Sársfield', in: Jorge H. Alterini et al; *La Codificación: Raíces y Prospectiva II La Codificación en América*. Buenos Aires: EDUCA, 2004, pp. 143–158.

Salvat 1913 — Raymundo [M.] Salvat; 'El Código Civil Argentino (Estudio General). Historia, Plan o Método y Fuentes'. *Revista Argentina de Ciencias Políticas VII*, 1913, pp. 420–437.

Salvat 1950 — Raymundo M. Salvat; *Tratado de Derecho Civil Argentino: Parte General*. 9th edition, Volume I, Buenos Aires: Tipográfica Ed. Argentina, 1950.

Salvat 1962 — Raymundo M. Salvat; *Tratado de Derecho Civil Argentino: Derechos Reales*. 5th edition, Volume II, Buenos Aires: Tipográfica Ed. Argentina, 1962.

Sampaio 1993 — Plinio Sampaio; *La Reforma Agraria en America Latina. RLAC/93/10—DERU-46*. Santiago: Organización de las Naciones Unidad para la Agricultura y la Alimentación. Oficina Regional de la FAO para America Latina y el Caribe, 1993.

Sánchez Albornoz 1983 — Claudio Sánchez Albornoz; *La edad media española y la empresa de América*. Madrid: Ediciones Cultura Hispánica del Instituto de Cooperación Iberoamericana, 1993.

Sánchez Bella 1958 — Ismael Sánchez Bella; 'Book Reviews'. *Hispanic American Historical Review 38:3*, 1958, pp. 400–401.

Sánchez Bella 1989 — Ismael Sánchez Bella; 'Las ordenanzas de Felipe II sobre nuevos descubrimientos

(1573), consolidación de la política de penetración pacífica'. *Anales de la Universidad de Chile* 20, 1989, pp. 533–549.

Sánchez Bella *et al.* 1992 — Ismael Sánchez Bella et al; *Historia del Derecho Indiano*. Madrid: Editorial MAPFRE, 1992.

Sánchez Echevarría 2014 — Ada Inés Sánchez Echevarría; '*Legal transplants*: una propuesta metodológica para el derecho comparado', in: Abásolo Ezequiel et al.; *La cultura jurídica latinoamericana y la circulación de ideas durante la primera mitad del siglo XX: Aproximaciones teóricas y análisis de experiencias*. Buenos Aires: Instituto de Investigaciones de Historia del Derecho, 2014, pp. 45–60.

Sánchez Román 1899 — Felipe Sánchez Román; *Estudios de derecho civil: según los principios, los precedentes y cuerpos legales del antiguo derecho de Castilla, las leyes civiles generales, las especialidades de las legislaciones forales, la jurisprudencia del Tribunal Supremo de Justicia y el Código civil, é historia general de la legislación española*. 2nd edition, Volume I, Madrid: Est. tipográfico "Sucesores de Rivadeneyra" 1899.

Santa Fe Capitulations 1492 — 'Santa Fe Capitulations'. Memory of the World, UNESCO. http://www.unesco.org/new/en/communication-and-information/flagship-project-activities/memory-of-the-world/register/full-list-of-registered-heritage/registered-heritage-page-8/santa-fe-capitulations/. Last visited on April 21, 2015.

Sapena Pastor 1986 — Raúl Sapena Pastor; *Fuentes Próximas del Código Civil*. Asunción: Editorial el Foro, 1986.

Savigny (von) 1840 — Friedrich Carl von Savigny; *Vom Beruf unserer Zeit für Gesetzgebung und Rechtswissenschaft, Erste Beylage, Stimmen für und wider neue Gesetzbücher*. 3rd edition, Heidelberg: J.C.B. Mohr, 1840.

Sato 1976 — Akio Sato; *Legal Aspects of Landownership in Colonial Spanish America*. Tokyo: Institute of Developing Economies, 1976.

Scheuer *et al.* 1962 — James H. Scheuer et al; 'Disposition of Urban Renewal Land—A Fundamental Problem in the Rebuilding of Our Cities'. *Columbia Law Review* 62, 1962, pp. 959–991.

Schimmelfennig 2015 — Frank Schimmelfennig; 'Efficient Process Tracing: Analyzing the Causal Mechanisms of European Integration', in: Andrew Bennett and Jeffrey T. Checkel (Eds.); *Process Tracing in the Social Sciences: From Metaphor to Analytic Tool*. Cambridge: Cambridge University Press, 2015, pp. 98–125.

Schlesinger 2001 — Arthur M. Schlesinger Jr.; 'The Messiah of the Rednecks', in: Haas Edward F. (Ed.); *The Louisiana Purchase Bicentennial Series in Louisiana History*. Volume VIII, Lafayette: Center for Louisiana Studies University of Southwestern Louisiana, 2001, pp. 45–65.

Schmidt 1841 — Gustavus Schmidt; 'Ancient Jurisprudence of Louisiana'. *The Louisiana Law Journal* 1:2, 1841, pp. 1–65.

Schmidt 1851 — Gustavus Schmidt; *The civil law of Spain and Mexico. Arranged on the principles of the modern codes, with notes and references. Preceded by a historical introduction to the Spanish and Mexican law; and embodying in an appendix some of the most important acts of the Mexican Congress*. New Orleans: Thomas Rea, 1851.

Schott 1993 — Matthew J. Schott; 'A Legal Monstrosity? The Constitution of 1921', in: Warren M. Billings and Edward F. Haas (Eds.); *In Search of Fundamental Law: Louisiana's Constitutions, 1812–1974*. Lafayette: Center for Louisiana Studies, 1993, pp. 124–140.

Schultz 2014 — Thomas Schultz; *Transnational Legality: Stateless Law and International Arbitration*. Oxford: Oxford University Press, 2014.

Schwartz 1974 — Bernard Schwartz; *The Law in America: A History*. New York: McGraw-Hill, 1974.

Scott 1928 — James Brown Scott; 'Asociación Francisco de Vitoria'. *The American Journal of International Law* 22, 1928, pp. 136–139.

Seckinger 1984 — Ron Seckinger; *The Brazilian Monarchy and the South American Republics, 1822–1831: Diplomacy and State Building*. Baton Rouge: Louisiana State University Press, 1984.

Secretaría de Políticas Universitarias 2009 — Secretaría de Políticas Universitarias 2008; Anuario 2008 de Estadísticas Universitarias, Buenos Aires, 2009. http://repositorio.educacion.gov.ar:8080/dspace/bitstream/handle/123456789/97105/Anuario_2008.pdf?sequence=1. Last visited on April 21, 2015.

Segovia 1881 — Lisandro Segovia; *El Código civil de la República Argentina (cópia de la edición oficial íntegra) con su esplicacion y crítica bajo la forma de notas*. Volumes I–II, Buenos Aires: Impr. de Pablo E. Coni, 1881.

Semmes 1883 — Thomas J. Semmes; *The Civil Law as Transplanted in Louisiana: A paper read before the American Bar Association at Saratoga Springs, N.Y., August 10th, 1882*. Philadelphia: Harris & Sons, 1883.

Sempere y Guarinos 1805 — Juan Sempere y Guarinos; *Historia de los vínculos y mayorazgos*. Madrid: Imprenta de Sancha, 1805.

Semprún y Gurrea (de) 1933 — José M. de Semprún y Gurrea; *Sentido Funcional del Derecho de Propiedad como caso concreto del que corresponde a todo derecho. Con un ensayo de representación matemática.* Madrid: Editorial Revista de Derecho Privado, 1933.

Seoane 1861 — Juan Antonio Seoane; *Jurisprudencia Civil vigente Española y Estranjera, según las sentencias del Tribunal Supremo desde el establecimiento de su jurisprudencia en 1838 hasta la fecha*. Madrid: Bailly-Bailliere, 1861.

Seoane 1981 — María Isabel Seoane, *La Enseñanza del Derecho en la Argentina: Desde sus Orígenes hasta la Primera Década del Siglo XX*. Buenos Aires: Editorial Perrot, 1981.

Shoked 2011 — Nadav Shoked; 'The Reinvention of Ownership: The Embrace of Residential Zoning and the Modern Populist Reading of Property'. *Yale Journal on Regulation 28*, 2011, pp. 91–149.

Shuey 1941 — John M. Shuey; 'Civil Codes-Control of the French Text of the Code of 1825'. *Louisiana Law Review 3*, 1941, pp. 452–454.

Shugg 1939 — Roger W. Shugg; *Origins of Class Struggle in Louisiana–A Social History of White Farmers and Laborers during Slavery and After 1840–1875*. Baton Rouge: Louisiana State University Press, 1939.

Siete Partidas 1587 — *Las siete partidas del sabio rey Don Alonſo el Nono, nueuamente Gloſadas, por el Licenciado Gregorio Lopez, del Conſejo Real de Indias de ſu Mageſtad. Con su Reportorio muy copioſo, aſsi del Teſto como de la Gloſſa*. Volumes I–IV, Valladolid: En caſa de Diego Fernandez de Cordoua, 1587.

Silva 1987 — Patricio Silva; *Estado, neoliberalismo y política agraria en Chile 1973–1981*. Dordrecht: Centrum voor Studie en Documentatie van Latijns Amerika, 1987.

Simpson 1998 — A[lfred] W[illiam] B[rian] Simpson; 'Land Ownership and Economic Freedom', in: Harry N. Scheiber (Ed.); *The State and Freedom of Contract*. Stanford: Stanford University Press, 1998, pp. 13–43.

Sindler 1956 — Allan P. Sindler; *Huey Long's Louisiana: State Politics, 1920–1952*. Baltimore: The Johns Hopkins Press, 1956.

Singer 1996 — Joseph William Singer; 'Property and Social Relations: From title to Entitlement', in: G[errit] E. van Maanen and A[ndré] J. van der Walt (Eds.); *Property Law on the*

Threshold of the 21st Century: Proceedings of an International Colloquium 'Property Law on the Threshold of the 21st Century', 28–30 August 1995, Maastricht. Antwerp: Maklu, 1996, pp. 69–90.

Slater 2009 — Victoria Slater; '"To Govern Is To Populate": Argentine Immigration Law and what it can suggest for the United States'. *Houston Journal of International Law 31*, 2009, pp. 693–731.

Slomp Aguiar 2011 — Anelize Slomp Aguiar; 'The Law Applicable to International Trade Transactions with Brazilian Parties: A Comparative Study of the Brazilian Law, the Cisg, and the American Law about Contract Formation'. *Law & Business Review of the Americas 17*, 2011, pp. 487–553.

Smith 1973 — T[homas] B[roun] Smith; 'Mixed Jurisdictions', in: Frederick H. Lawson (Ed.); *International Encyclopedia of Comparative Law. Volume VI: Property and Trust. Chapter II: Structural Variations in Property Law.* Tübingen: J.C.B. Mohr, 1973, pp. 115–136.

Smith 1996 — F. Todd Smith; 'Spanish Indian Policy in Louisiana: The Natchitoches District, 1763–1803', in: Gilbert C. Din (Ed.); *The Louisiana Purchase Bicentennial Series in Louisiana History: Volume II, The Spanish Presence in Louisiana 1763–1803,* Lafayette: Center for Louisiana Studies, 1996, pp. 284–295.

Solórzano Pereira (de) 1703 — Juan de Solórzano Pereira; *Politica indiana.* Antwerp: Henrico y Cornelio Verdussen, 1703.

Spillman 1919 — W[illiam] J. Spillman; 'The Agricultural Ladder'. *The American Economic Review 9:1 Supplement, Papers and Proceedings of the Thirty-First Annual Meeting of the American Economic Association*, 1919, pp. 170–179.

Stavenhagen 1970 — Rodolfo Stavenhagen; 'Introduction [to Part I]', in: Rodolfo Stavenhagen (Ed.); *Agrarian*

Problems and Peasant Movements in Latin America. Garden City: Anchor Books, 1970, pp. 3–10.

Stoetzer 1998 — O[tto] Carlos Stoetzer; *Karl Christian Friedrich Krause and His Influence in the Hispanic World.* Cologne: Böhlau Verlag, 1998.

Stolleis 2009 — Michael Stolleis; *La Historia del Derecho como Obra de Arte.* Translation by Ignacio Gutiérrez Gutiérrez, Granada: Comares, 2009.

Stone 1955 — Ferdinand Stone; 'A Primer on Codification'. *Tulane Law Review 29*, 1955, pp. 303–310.

Storni 1997 — Carlos Mario Storni; *Investigaciones sobre la historia del derecho rural argentino: Españoles, criollos, indios y gauderios en la llanura pampeana.* Buenos Aires: Instituto de Investigaciones de Historia del Derecho, 1997.

Storni 2000 — Carlos M[ario] Storni; 'Acerca de la regulación de la producción agropecuaria en el derecho indiano: Una mirada rioplatense sobre la política agraria de España en América'. *Revista de Historia del Derecho 28*, 2000, pp. 619–654.

Sunde and Skodvin 2010 — Jørn Øyrehagen Sunde and Knut Einar Skodvin; *Rendezvous of European Legal Cultures.* Bergen: Fagbokforlaget, 2010.

Sweet 1929 — William Warren Sweet; *A History of Latin America.* Revised edition, New York: Abingdon Press, 1929.

Tagle 2003 — Matilde Tagle; 'Sinsacate, tierra codiciada. Historia de una merced invalidada'. *Cuadernos de Historia 13*, 2003, pp. 177–186.

Tai 1974 — Hung-chao Tai; *Land Reform and Politics: A Comparative Analysis.* Berkeley: University of California Press, 1974.

Tanzi 1976 — Héctor José Tanzi; '*III* Congreso del Instituto internacional de Historia del Derecho Indiano. Actas y estudios (Instituto Nacional de Estudios Jurídicos). Madrid, 1973'. *Revista de Historia de América 81*, 1976, pp. 210–216.

Tanzi 1992 — Héctor José Tanzi; 'Los Estudios de Historia del Derecho en la Argentina'. *Revista de Historia de América 114*, 1992, pp. 165–169.

Tau Anzoátegui 1974 — Víctor Tau Anzoátegui; 'Los Juristas Argentinos de la Generación de 1910'. *Revista de Historia del Derecho 2*, 1974, pp. 225–283.

Tau Anzoátegui 1977a — Víctor Tau Anzoátegui; 'En Torno a la Mentalidad de Nuestros Juristas del Ochocientos'. *Revista de Historia del Derecho 5*, 1977, pp. 421–433.

Tau Anzoátegui 1977b — Víctor Tau Anzoátegui; *La Codificación en la Argentina (1810–1870): Mentalidad Social e Ideas Jurídicas*. Buenos Aires: Imprenta de la Universidad, 1977.

Tau Anzoátegui 1977c — Víctor Tau Anzoátegui; *Las Ideas Jurídicas en la Argentina (Siglos XIX–XX)*. Buenos Aires: Editorial Perrot, 1977.

Tau Anzoátegui 1987 — Víctor Tau Anzoátegui; 'Historia, derecho y sociedad. En torno a la concepción histórico-jurídica de Ricardo Levene'. *Investigaciones y Ensayos 35, separata*, 1987, pp. 87–120.

Tau Anzoátegui 1988 — Víctor Tau Anzoátegui; 'La Influencia Alemana en el Derecho Argentino: Un Programa para su Estudio Histórico'. *Jahrbuch für Geschichte Lateinamerikas 25*, 1988, pp. 607–634.

Tau Anzoátegui 1998 — Víctor Tau Anzoátegui; 'La 'Cultura del Código:' Un Debate Virtual entre Segovia y Sáez'. *Revista de Historia del Derecho 26*, 1998, pp. 539–564.

Tau Anzoátegui 2007 — Víctor Tau Anzoátegui; 'Peculiaridad del Pensamiento Jurídico Argentino', in: Víctor Tau Anzoátegui (Coord.); *Antología del Pensamiento Jurídico Argentino (1901–1945)*. Volume I, Buenos Aires: Instituto de Investigaciones de Historia del Derecho, 2007, pp. 11–35.

Tau Anzoátegui 2008 — Víctor Tau Anzoátegui; *La Codificación en la Argentina (1810–1870): Mentalidad Social e Ideas Jurídicas*. 2nd revised edition, Buenos

Aires: Librería Histórica—Emilio J. Perrot, 2008.

Tau Anzoátegui 2010 — Víctor Tau Anzoátegui; *El Futuro de la Historia Jurídica en las Aulas*. Córdoba: Advocatus, 2010.

Tau Anzoátegui 2011 — Víctor Tau Anzoátegui; 'La Jurisprudencia Civil en la Cultura Jurídica Argentina (s. XIX–XX)'. *Quaderni fiorentini 40*, 2011, pp. 53–110.

Texto Refundido del Código Civil 2015 — 'Fija Texto Refundido, Coordinado y Sistematizado del Código Civil'. Biblioteca del Congreso Nacional de Chile. http://www.leychile.cl/Navegar?idNorma=172986&idParte=8717776. Last visited on April 21, 2015.

Textos Constitucionales Chilenos 2015 — 'Textos Constitucionales Chilenos'. Fuentes Documentales y Bibliográficas para el Estudio de la Historia de Chile. http://www.historia.uchile.cl/CDA/fh_complex/0,1393,SCID%253D10717%2526ISID%253D417%2526JNID%253D12,00.html. Last visited on April 21, 2015.

Thalès 1933 — Jean-Jacques Thalès, *Histoire du droit haïtien*. Volume I, Port-au-Prince: s.n., 1933.

Thémis 1826a — 'Sur le nouveau Code civil de l'état de la Louisiane'. *Thémis ou bibliothèque du jurisconsulte 8*, 1826, pp. 62–82.

Thémis 1826b — 'Sur le Code civil de l'état de la Louisiane'. *Thémis ou bibliothèque du jurisconsulte 8*, 1826, pp. 187–208.

Thome 1971 — Joseph R. Thome; 'Expropriation in Chile Under the Frei Agrarian Reform'. *The American Journal of Comparative Law 19*, 1971, pp. 489–513.

Tomás y Valiente 1997a — Francisco Tomás y Valiente; 'El marco político de la desamortización en España', in: Francisco Tomás y Valiente; *Obras Completas*. Volume I, Madrid: Centro de Estudios Políticos y Constitucionales, 1997, pp. 547–634.

Tomás y Valiente 1997b — Francisco Tomás y Valiente; 'El proceso de desamortización de la tierra en España', in:

Francisco Tomás y Valiente; *Obras Completas*. Volume IV, Madrid: Centro de Estudios Políticos y Constitucionales, 1997, pp. 3381–3396.

Tomás y Valiente 1997c — Francisco Tomás y Valiente; 'Manual de Historia del Derecho Español', in: Francisco Tomás y Valiente; *Obras Completas*. Volume II, Madrid: Centro de Estudios Políticos y Constitucionales, 1997, pp. 916–1577.

Torre Revello 1965 — José Torre Revello; 'Bibliotecas en el Buenos Aires antiguo desde 1729 hasta la inauguración de la Biblioteca Pública en 1812'. *Revista de Historia de América 59*, 1965, pp. 1–148.

Torres Ramírez 1969 — Bibiano Torres Ramírez; *Alejandro O'Reilly en las Indias*. Sevilla: Escuela de Estudios Hispano-Americanos, 1969.

Trahan 2003 — J.R. Trahan; 'The Continuing Influence of le Droit Civil and el Derecho Civil in the Private Law of Louisiana'. *Louisiana Law Review 63*, 2003, pp. 1019–1066.

Troiano 2004 — Onofrio Troiano; 'Prefazione', in: Onofrio Troiano et al (Eds.); *Harmonisation involves history? : il diritto privato europeo al vaglio della comparazione e della storia: Foggia, 20–21 giugno 2003*. Milan: A. Giuffrè, 2004, pp. vii–xvii.

Tucker 1942 — John H. Tucker; 'Louisiana Civil Law Literature'. *Reports of the Louisiana State Bar Association for 1935–1941 34*, 1942, pp. 26–31.

Tunc 1955 — André Tunc; 'The Grand Outlines of the Code Napoleon'. *Tulane Law Review 29*, 1955, pp. 431–452.

Unpublished Draft Code 1890 — *Obras Completas de Don Andrés Bello: Proyecto Inédito de Código Civil*. Volume XIII, Santiago: Impreso por Pedro G. Ramírez, 1890.

Upton & Jennings 1838 — Wheelock S. Upton and Needler R. Jennings; *Civil Code of the State of Louisiana; with Annotations*. New Orleans: E. Johns & Co., 1838.

US Constitution 1789 — 'Constitution Annotated'. Library of Congress. https://www.congress.gov/constitution-annotated/. Last visited on April 21, 2015.

Valiente Noailles 1968 — Luis M. Valiente Noailles; *Comentarios a las reformas al código civil (Ley 17.711): Legislación, doctrina, jurisprudencia.* Buenos Aires: Ediciones Depalma, 1968.

Vance 1943 — John Thomas Vance; *The Background of Hispanic-American Law: Legal Sources and Juridical Literature of Spain.* New York: Central Book Company, 1943.

Vanderlinden 1967 — Jacques Vanderlinden; *Le concept de code en Europe occidentale du XIII au XIX siècle, Essais de définition.* Brussels: Editions de l'Institut de Sociologie Universite Libre, 1967.

van der Walt 2009 — A[ndré] J. van der Walt; *Property in the Margins.* Oxford and Portland: Hart Publishing, 2009.

van Erp 2002 — J.H.M. van Erp; 'A Comparative Analysis of Mortgage Law: Searching for Principles', in: María Elena Sánchez Jordán and Antonio Gambaro; *Land Law in Comparative Perspective.* The Hague, New York and London: Kluwer Law International, 2002, pp. 69–86.

van Erp 2003 — J.H.M. van Erp; 'Civil and Common Property Law: Caveat Comparator–The Value of Legal Historical-Comparative Analysis'. *European Review of Private Law 3–2003*, 2003, pp. 394–411.

van Erp 2008a — J.H.M. van Erp; 'Comparative Property Law', in: Mathias Reimann and Reinhard Zimmermann (Eds.); *The Oxford Handbook of Comparative Law.* Oxford: Oxford University Press, 2008, pp. 1043–1070.

van Erp 2008b — J.H.M. van Erp; 'Deconstruction and reconstruction of European property law: A research agenda', in: Eleanor Cashin Ritaine

(Ed.), *Legal Engineering and Comparative Law*. Zurich and Basel: Schultess, 2008, pp. 105–121.

van Erp 2013a — J.H.M. van Erp; 'From Euratom Property Law to European Union Property Law: A Concise Overview of the Development Towards a European Property Law', in: Luigi Moccia (Ed.); *The Making of European Private Law: Why, How, What, Who*. Munich: Sellier European Law Publishers, 2013, pp. 149–159.

van Erp 2013b — J.H.M. van Erp; 'The Functional Comparative Method in European Property Law–C. Godt Some Comments'. *European Property Law Journal* 2, 2013, pp. 90–94.

van Rhee & van der Meer 2011 — C.H. van Rhee and J.A.J.M. van der Meer; 'Teaching European Legal History at Maastricht University in the Netherlands', in: Kjell Å. Modéer and Per Nilsén (Eds.); *How to Teach European Comparative Legal History: Workshop at the Faculty of Law, Lund University, 19–20 August 2009*. Lund: Juristförlaget i Lund, 2011, pp. 143–155.

van Rhee & van Erp 2003 — C.H. van Rhee and J.H.M. van Erp; 'Introduction to the Special Issue on Property Law'. *European Review of Private Law 3–2003*, 2003, pp. 279–281.

Vas Mingo (del) 1985 — Marta Milagros del Vas Mingo; 'Las Ordenanzas de 1573, sus antecedentes y consecuencias'. *Revista Complutense de Historia de América 8*, 1985, pp. 83–101.

Vaughn 1992–1993 — Robert G. Vaughn; 'Proposals for Judicial Reform in Chile'. *Fordham International Law Journal 16*, 1992–1993, pp. 577–607.

Verfassung des Deutschen Reichs 1919 — 'Die Verfassung des Deutschen Reichs vom 11. August 1919'. *Reichsgesetzblatt 1919:152*, 1919, pp. 1383–1418.

Verkerk 2010 — Remme R. Verkerk; *Fact-Finding in Civil Litigation: A Comparative Perspective*. Antwerp [etc.]: Intersentia, 2010.

Vernengo 1977 — R[oberto] J. Vernengo; *La Interpretación Jurídica*. Mexico: Universidad Nacional Autónoma de México, 1977.

Vidaurrazaga (de) 1952 — Juan José de Vidaurrazaga; 'Offenses and Quasi-Offenses-Liability for Damages to Neighbor's Property-A Comparative Study of Articles 667 and 668 of the Louisiana Civil Code of 1870'. *Tulane Law Review 26*, 1952, pp. 524–528.

Villalobos R. 2002 — Sergio Villalobos R.; *Chile y Perú: la historia que nos une y nos separa, 1535–1883*. Santiago: Editorial Universitaria, 2002.

Villalobos R. 2004 — Sergio Villalobos R.; 'El Proceso de la Emancipación', in: Sergio Villalobos et al (Eds.); *Historia de Chile*. 24th edition, Santiago: Editorial Universitaria, 2004, pp. 327–402.

Villavaso 1999 — Stephen D. Villavaso; 'Planning Enabling Legislation in Louisiana: A Retrospective Analysis'. *Loyola Law Review 45*, 1999, pp. 655–667.

Vitar 1995 — Beatriz Vitar; 'Las fronteras "bárbaras" en los virreinatos de Nueva España y Perú'. *Revista de Indias 55:203*, 1995, pp. 33–66.

Wallach 1960 — Kate Wallach; *Research in Louisiana Law*. 2nd edition, Baton Rouge, Louisiana State University Press, 1960.

Walsh 2011 — Rachael Walsh; 'Private Property Rights in the Drafting of the Irish Constitution: A Communitarian Compromise'. *Dublin University Law Journal 33*, 2011, pp. 86–115.

Walton 1916 — F[rederick] P[arker] Walton; 'Civil Codes and their Revision. Some Suggestions for Revision of the Title "Of Ownership"'. *Southern Law Quarterly 1:2*, 1916, pp. 95–116.

Warriner 1969 — Doreen Warriner; *Land Reform in Principle and Practice*. Oxford: Clarendon Press, 1969.

Watson 1974 — Alan Watson; *Legal Transplants: An Approach to Comparative Law*. Edinburgh: Scottish Academic Press, 1974.

Watson 2006 — Blake A. Watson; 'John Marshall and Indian Land Rights: A Historical Rejoinder to the Claim of "Universal Recognition" of the Doctrine of Discovery'. *Seton Hall Law Review 36*, 2006, pp. 481–549.

Weber 1992 — David J. Weber; *The Spanish Frontier in North America.* New Haven: Yale University Press, 1992.

Welzel 1953 — Hans Welzel; 'Ahrens, Heinrich', in: *Neue Deutsche Biographie.* Volume 1, Berlin: Duncker & Humblot, 1953, pp. 113.

Wesel 2014 — Uwe Wesel; *Geschichte des Rechts: von den Frühformen bis zur Gegenwart.* 4th edition, Munich: C.H. Beck, 2014.

White 1839 — Joseph M. White; *A New Collection of Laws, Charters and Local Ordinances of the Governments of Great Britain, France and Spain, Relating to the Concessions of Land in Their Respective Colonies; Together with the Laws of Mexico and Texas on the Same Subject. To which is Prefixed Judge Johnson's Translation of Azo and Manuel's Institutes of the Civil Law of Spain.* Volumes I–II, Philadelphia: T. & J.W. Johnson, 1839.

Wigmore 1912 — John H. Wigmore; 'Editorial Preface to this Volume', in: John H. Wigmore et al (Eds.); *General Survey of Events Sources Persons and in Continental Legal History.* [Volume I The Continental Legal History Series], Boston: Little, Brown, and Co., 1912, pp. xxiii–xliv.

Wilkie 1974 — James W. Wilkie; *Measuring Land Reform. Supplement to the Statistical Abstract of Latin America with a special map and graph series on land reform by Richard W. Wilkie and John Marti.* Los Angeles: UCLA Latin American Center, [1974].

Williams 1947 — Tennessee Williams; *A streetcar named Desire.* New York: New Directions, 1947.

Williams 1983 — Robert A. Williams Jr.; 'The Medieval and Renaissance Origins of the Status of the

American Indian in Western Legal Thought'. *Southern California Law Review 57*, 1983, pp. 1–99.

Windell 1993 | Marie E. Windell; 'Can a Legislature Control a Constitutional Convention? The Constitution of 1913', in: Warren M. Billings and Edward F. Haas (Eds.); *In Search of Fundamental Law: Louisiana's Constitutions, 1812–1974*. Lafayette: Center for Louisiana Studies, 1993, pp. 110–123.

Yiannopoulos 1974 | A[thanasios] N. Yiannopoulos; 'Civil Responsibility in the Framework of Vicinage: Articles 667–69 and 2315 of the Civil Code'. *Tulane Law Review 48*, 1974. pp. 195–238.

Yiannopoulos 1977 | A[thanasios] N. Yiannopoulos; *Louisiana Civil Law System: Course book Part 1*. Baton Rouge: Claitor's Publishing Division, 1977.

Yiannopoulos 1988 | A[thanasios] N. Yiannopoulos; 'A Tale of Two Codes: The Code Napoleon and the Louisiana Civil Code', in: Robert B. Holtman (Ed.); *Napoleon and America*. Pensacola: Perdido Bay Press, 1988, pp. 195–218.

Yiannopoulos 1994 | A[thanasios] N. Yiannopoulos; 'Civil Liability for Abuse of Right: Something Old, Something New…'. *Louisiana Law Review 54*, 1994, pp. 1173–1197.

Yiannopoulos 1996 | A[thanasios] N. Yiannopoulos; 'Revision of the Law of Property; The Louisiana Experience', in: G[errit] E. van Maanen and A[ndré] J. van der Walt (Eds.); *Property Law on the Threshold of the 21st Century: Proceedings of an International Colloquium 'Property Law on the Threshold of the 21st Century', 28–30 August 1995, Maastricht*. Antwerp: Maklu, 1996, pp. 215–233.

Yiannopoulos 2001 | A[thanasios] N. Yiannopoulos; *Louisiana Civil Law Treatise: Property: The Law of Things—Real Rights—Real Actions*. 4th edition, Volume II, St. Paul: West Pub. Co., 2001.

Yiannopoulos 2004–2012 | A[thanasios] N. Yiannopoulos; *Predial Servitudes*. 4th edition, Volume IV Louisiana

Civil Law Treatise, St. Paul: West Pub. Co., 2004–2012.

Yiannopoulos 2008 A[thanasios] N. Yiannopoulos (Ed.); *2008 Compiled Edition of the Civil Codes of Louisiana*. Volume XVI West's Louisiana Statutes Annotated, St. Paul: Thomson West, 2008.

Zarrilli 1993 Adrián Gustavo Zarrilli; 'Un Cuestionamiento al Derecho de Propiedad. Estado, Plagas y Agricultura: El Caso de la Defensa Agrícola (1890–1930)'. *Revista de Historia del Derecho 21*, 1993, pp. 225–251.

Zavala 1935 Silvio Zavala; *Las Instituciones Jurídicas en la Conquista de América*. Madrid: Centro de Estudios Históricos, 1935.

Zavala 1992 Silvio Zavala; *La Encomienda Indiana*. 3rd revised edition, Mexico: Porrúa, 1992.

Zimmermann 2008 Reinhard Zimmermann; 'Comparative Law and the Europeanization of Private Law', in: Mathias Reimann and Reinhard Zimmermann (Eds.); *The Oxford Handbook of Comparative Law*. Oxford: Oxford University Press, 2008, pp. 539–578.

Zimmermann 2012 Reinhard Zimmermann; 'Mixed Legal Systems', in: Jürgen Basedow et al (Eds.); *Max Planck Encyclopedia of European Private Law*. Volume II, Oxford: Oxford University Press, 2012, pp. 1179–1182.

Zoomers & van der Haar 2000 Annelies Zoomers and Gamma van der Haar; 'Introduction: regulating land tenure under neo-liberalism', in: Annelies Zoomers and Gemma van der Haar (Eds.); *Current Land Policy in Latin America: Regulating Land Tenure under Neo-liberalism*. Amsterdam: Royal Tropical Institute, 2000, pp. 17–26.

Zorraquín Becú 1954 Ricardo Zorraquín Becú; *Marcelino Ugarte 1822–1872: Un jurista en la época de la organización nacional*. Buenos Aires: Universidad de Buenos Aires, 1954.

Zorraquín Becú 1966 Ricardo Zorraquín Becú; *Historia del Derecho Argentino*. Volume I, Buenos Aires: Editorial Perrot, 1966.

Zorraquín Becú 1976 Ricardo Zorraquín Becú; 'La recepción de los derechos extranjeros en la Argentina durante el siglo XIX'. *Revista de Historia del Derecho* 4, 1976, pp. 325–359.

Zweigert & Kötz 1984 Konrad Zweigert and Hein Kötz; *Einführung in die Rechtsvergleichung auf dem Gebiete des Privatrechts*. 2nd edition, Volume I, Tübingen: Mohr, 1984.

Index of Names

www.ingramcontent.com/pod-product-compliance
Lightning Source LLC
LaVergne TN
LVHW010542300926
849162LV00002B/207